The British Imperial Army
in the Middle East

War, Culture and Society

Series Editor: Stephen McVeigh, Associate Professor, Swansea University, UK

Editorial Board:

Paul Preston *LSE, UK*
Joanna Bourke *Birkbeck, University of London, UK*
Debra Kelly *University of Westminster, UK*
Patricia Rae *Queen's University, Ontario, Canada*
James J. Weingartner *Southern Illinois University, USA (Emeritus)*
Kurt Piehler *Florida State University, USA*
Ian Scott *University of Manchester, UK*

War, Culture and Society is a multi- and interdisciplinary series which encourages the parallel and complementary military historical and socio-cultural investigation of 20th and 21st century war and conflict.

Published:

The Testimonies of Indian Soldiers and the Two World Wars, Gajendra Singh (2014)

Forthcoming:

South Africa's 'Border War', Gary Baines (2014)
Cultural Responses to Occupation in Japan, Adam Broinowski (2014)
9/11 and the American Western, Stephen McVeigh (2014)
Filming the End of the Holocaust, John Michalczyk (2014)
Jewish Volunteers, the International Brigades and the Spanish Civil War, Gerben Zaagsma (2014)
Military Law, the State, and Citizenship in the Modern Age, Gerard Oram (2014)
The Japanese Comfort Women and Sexual Slavery During the China and Pacific Wars, Caroline Norma (2015)
The Lost Cause of the Confederacy and American Civil War Memory, David J. Anderson (2016)

The British Imperial Army in the Middle East

Morale and Military Identity in the Sinai and Palestine Campaigns, 1916–18

James E. Kitchen

Bloomsbury Academic
An imprint of Bloomsbury Publishing Plc

B L O O M S B U R Y
LONDON • NEW DELHI • NEW YORK • SYDNEY

Bloomsbury Academic
An imprint of Bloomsbury Publishing Plc

50 Bedford Square	1385 Broadway
London	New York
WC1B 3DP	NY 10018
UK	USA

www.bloomsbury.com

**BLOOMSBURY and the Diana logo are trademarks of
Bloomsbury Publishing Plc**

First published 2014
Paperback edition first published 2015

© James Kitchen, 2014

James Kitchen has asserted his right under the Copyright, Designs and Patents Act, 1988, to be identified as Author of this work.

All rights reserved. No part of this publication may be reproduced or transmitted in any form or by any means, electronic or mechanical, including photocopying, recording, or any information storage or retrieval system, without prior permission in writing from the publishers.

No responsibility for loss caused to any individual or organization acting on or refraining from action as a result of the material in this publication can be accepted by Bloomsbury or the author.

British Library Cataloguing-in-Publication Data
A catalogue record for this book is available from the British Library.

ISBN: HB: 978-1-4725-0527-9
PB: 978-1-4742-4785-6
ePDF: 978-1-4725-1131-7
ePUB: 978-1-4725-0928-4

Library of Congress Cataloging-in-Publication Data
A catalog record for this book is available from the Library of Congress.

Series: War, Culture and Society

Typeset by Newgen Knowledge Works (P) Ltd., Chennai, India
Printed and bound in Great Britain

Contents

List of Illustrations		vi
List of Figures		vii
List of Maps		viii
Acknowledgements		ix
List of Abbreviations		xi
Maps		xii
Introduction		1
1	The Nature of War in Sinai and Palestine	25
2	A Twentieth-Century Crusade?	61
3	Command, Control and Morale	101
4	Citizen Soldiers at War	123
5	The Anzac Legend, Mateship and Morale	151
6	The Indian Army Fighting for Empire	183
Conclusion		215
Notes		221
Bibliography		269
Index		295

List of Illustrations

I.1	Henry Lamb, 'Irish Troops in the Judaean Hills Surprised by a Turkish Bombardment', 1919	3
I.2	Unveiling of the Australian and New Zealand Mounted Division Memorial at Port Said, 23 November 1932	4
2.1	Bernard Partridge, 'The Last Crusade', *Punch*, 19 December 1917	68
2.2	Bernard Partridge, 'The Return from the Crusade', *Punch*, 17 September 1919	69
2.3	W. Humberrary, 'History Repeated after Eight Centuries', *The Northampton Independent*, 21 April 1917	71
2.4	2/15th London Regiment Christmas Card, 1918	93
2.5	54th Division Christmas Card, 1917	94
2.6	54th Division Christmas Card, 1917	95
2.7	54th Division Christmas Card, 1918	96
4.1	54th Division Christmas Card, 1917	127
4.2	Programme for 54th Division Concert Party, 'The Rose of Gaza', August 1917	131
4.3	1/4th Norfolk Regiment Christmas Card	137
4.4	54th Division Christmas Card, 1918	141
4.5	Model of the El Arish Redoubt used for training the 54th Division prior to Third Gaza	144
4.6	Cigarette card featuring the 54th Division badge	147
5.1	5th Australian Light Horse Regiment Christmas Card, 1918	162

List of Figures

1.1	54th Division Infantry Brigade Combat Deaths, 1917–18	47
1.2	161st Infantry Brigade Combat Deaths, 1917–18	47
1.3	162nd Infantry Brigade Combat Deaths, 1917–18	48
1.4	163rd Infantry Brigade Combat Deaths, 1917–18	48
1.5	New Zealand Mounted Rifles Brigade Combat Deaths, 1916–18	50
1.6	162nd Infantry Brigade Casualty Rates, 1916–18	54
1.7	1st Australian Light Horse Regiment Casualty Rates, 1917–18	54
1.8	3rd Australian Light Horse Regiment Casualty Rates, 1916–18	55
1.9	Malaria Hospital Admissions in the EEF, 1917–18	57

List of Maps

1 Northern Sinai Peninsula, August 1916　　　　　　　　　　xii
2 Palestine, 1916–18　　　　　　　　　　　　　　　　　　　xiii

Acknowledgements

This book has been many years in the making and along the way I have accumulated many debts. First and foremost, I owe the greatest thanks to my doctoral supervisor at the University of Oxford, Adrian Gregory, and to my college advisor at Balliol, Martin Conway; over several years of both undergraduate and postgraduate study I have benefited enormously from their wisdom, wit and support. I have also been fortunate to receive help and encouragement from a number of academics during the course of my studies, most notably Lesley Abrams, Joanna Bourke, John Darwin, Ashley Jackson, Rob Johnson, Pierre Purseigle, Lyndal Roper, Simon Skinner and Hew Strachan. I am indebted to Terry Kinloch, Christopher Pugsley, and Peter Stanley for giving me advice on carrying out research in Australia and New Zealand. Special thanks are due to Alisa Miller, Harry Munt, and Sam Wilson for their tireless assistance in reading drafts and helping to challenge and refine the ideas in this book. In addition, I wish to thank my friends at Oxford who have been particularly patient when listening to my ramblings on the EEF and the First World War: Jonathan Fennell, Michael Finch, Stuart Hallifax, Laura Rowe and Andy Syk. I am also most grateful to Rhodri Mogford, my editor at Bloomsbury, and Stephen McVeigh, editor of the 'War, Culture and Society' series, for the enthusiasm with which they have supported this book and the patience they have shown during its production. The usual caveat applies that I alone am responsible for any errors.

My former comrades at King's College London and the Royal Air Force College provided much encouragement and support to this project, and helped to broaden my outlook on the study of war. At University College Dublin I was very fortunate to be part of a friendly and stimulating research community. Among my former colleagues in Dublin I owe particular thanks to Robert Gerwarth and William Mulligan for supporting and helping to clarify my research over the past few years. Furthermore, I wish to thank all of the scholars who made the Centre for War Studies, and the European Research Council Project which I was lucky enough to be part of, such an interesting and exciting academic community: Tomas Balkelis, Suzanne d'Arcy, Julia Eichenberg, Christina Griessler, Mark Jones, Matthew Lewis, Stephan Malinowski, James Matthews, John Paul Newman and Gajendra Singh.

The research for this book would not have been possible without the financial assistance provided by Balliol College, the Frank Denning Memorial Charity, which contributed towards my research trip in Australia and New Zealand, and the European Research Council.

The research for this study was greatly assisted by the staff of various libraries and archives. In Britain, I would like to thank staff at the Bedfordshire Record Office in Bedford, the Bodleian Library at Oxford University, the British Library, the Essex Regiment Museum in Chelmsford, the Hampshire Regiment Museum in Winchester, the Imperial War Museum in London, the Liddell Hart Centre for Military Archives at King's College London, the Museum of Army Chaplaincy at Amport House, the National Archives in Kew, the National Army Museum in Chelsea, the Norfolk Regiment Museum in Norwich and the Suffolk Record Office in Bury St Edmunds. In Ireland, I extend my thanks to the librarians of University College Dublin and Trinity College Dublin. In particular, I would also like to thank the staff of the Australian War Memorial in Canberra, and, in New Zealand, the staff of the Alexander Turnbull Library in Wellington and the National Army Museum in Waiouru for their assistance during my Antipodean research trip.

I would like to thank the following organizations for permission to quote from particular collections of sources and to reproduce images from their archives: the Alexander Turnbull Library at the National Library of New Zealand, the Australian War Memorial, the Essex Regiment Museum in Chelmsford, the Imperial War Museum, the Kippenberger Military Archive at the National Army Museum in Waiouru, the Trustees of the Liddell Hart Centre for Military Archives at King's College London, Punch Ltd, the Royal Hampshire Regiment Trust and the Suffolk Record Office in Bury St Edmunds. I am extremely grateful to individual copyright holders who have granted me permission to quote from the papers of their relatives: Lord Allenby, Kathryn E. W. Blunt, Jane Selby Brown, Dinny de Celis, C. Everard, Richard Chauvel, Robert A. Hinde, M. D. Knott, D. B. Macgregor, Margery McCredie, Anne Oliver, P. J. Price and Enid Smith-Wood. Every effort has been made to contact copyright holders where applicable and any omissions will be corrected in future editions.

All quotations have been left, in terms of spelling, punctuation, and grammar, as they are found in the original sources, with any additional information added for clarity in square brackets. Transliterated Arabic place names are given as they were used during the campaign by EEF soldiers, who had no standard approach to spelling them.

My deepest thanks are extended to those friends who have encouraged me in my studies at Oxford, and without whose support undergraduate and postgraduate life, as well as the tribulations of an academic career, would have been much less fulfilling and enjoyable: James Arnold, Anthony Flynn, Lucie Foulston, Sarah Gowrie, James and Valerie Hume, Briony Lea, Hannah Kaneb, Andrew Mantilas and Michael Panagopulos. Finally, and most importantly, my thanks go to my family. Without the love, assistance, encouragement, and patience of my parents, aunt, grandparents, and Rosie, this book would never have been written.

List of Abbreviations

ADMS	Assistant Director Medical Services
AIF	Australian Imperial Force
ALH	Australian Light Horse
AMR	Auckland Mounted Rifles
ANZMD	Australian and New Zealand Mounted Division
ATL	Alexander Turnbull Library
AWM	Australian War Memorial
BEF	British Expeditionary Force
CID	Committee of Imperial Defence
CIGS	Chief of the Imperial General Staff
CMR	Canterbury Mounted Rifles
DMC	Desert Mounted Corps
EEF	Egyptian Expeditionary Force
ERM	Essex Regiment Museum
GHQ	General Headquarters
GOC	General Officer Commanding
GSO1	General Staff Officer, Grade One
HRM	Hampshire Regiment Museum
IOR	India Office Records
IWM	Imperial War Museum
KMA	Kippenberger Military Archives
LHCMA	Liddell Hart Centre for Military Archives
MACA	Museum of Army Chaplaincy Archives
NCO	Non-Commissioned Officer
NRM	Norfolk Regiment Museum
NZMR	New Zealand Mounted Rifles
RAF	Royal Air Force
RFA	Royal Field Artillery
RFC	Royal Flying Corps
SRO	Suffolk Record Office
TF	Territorial Force
TNA	The National Archives
WMR	Wellington Mounted Rifles
YMCA	Young Men's Christian Association

Maps

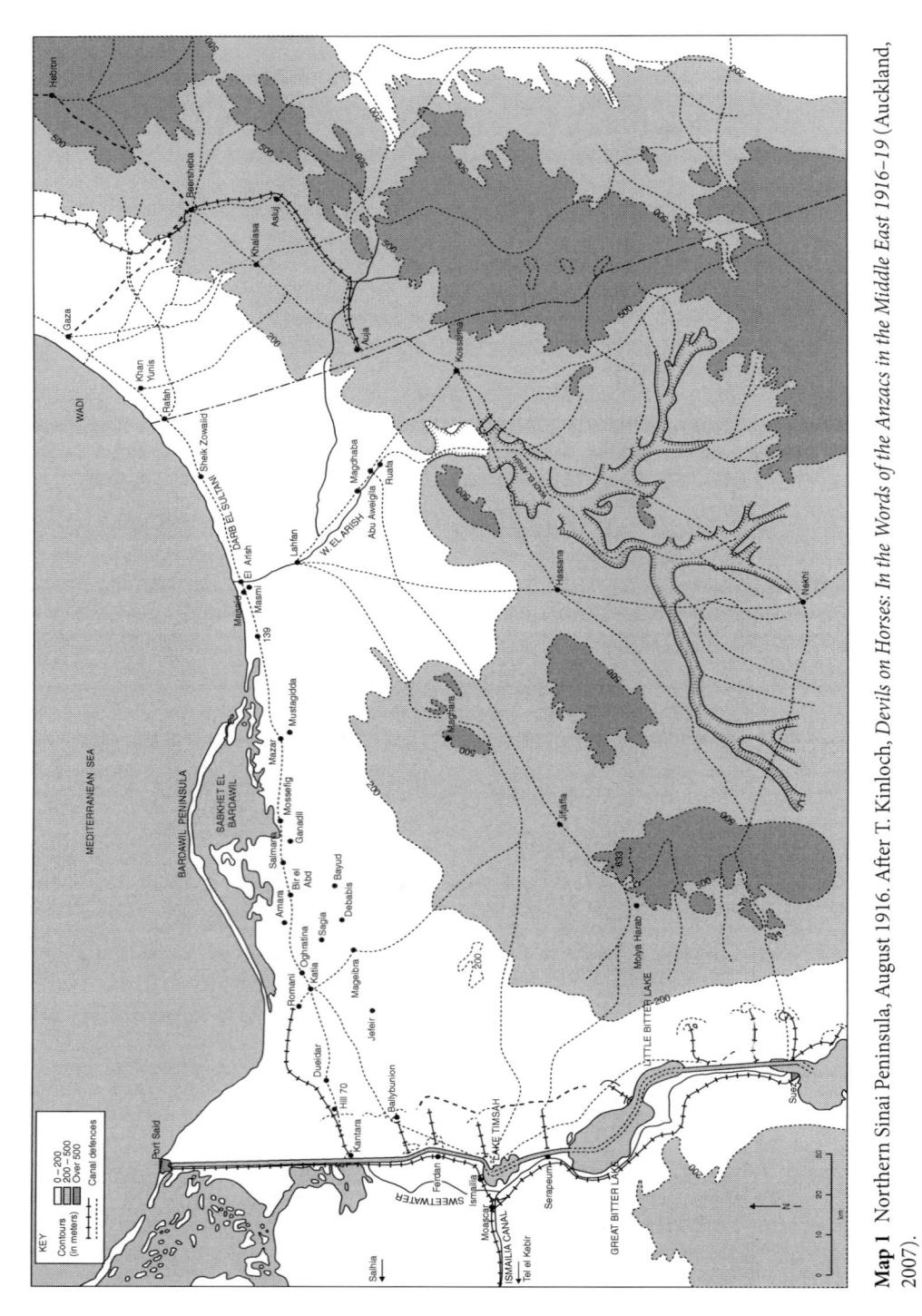

Map 1 Northern Sinai Peninsula, August 1916. After T. Kinloch, *Devils on Horses: In the Words of the Anzacs in the Middle East 1916–19* (Auckland, 2007).

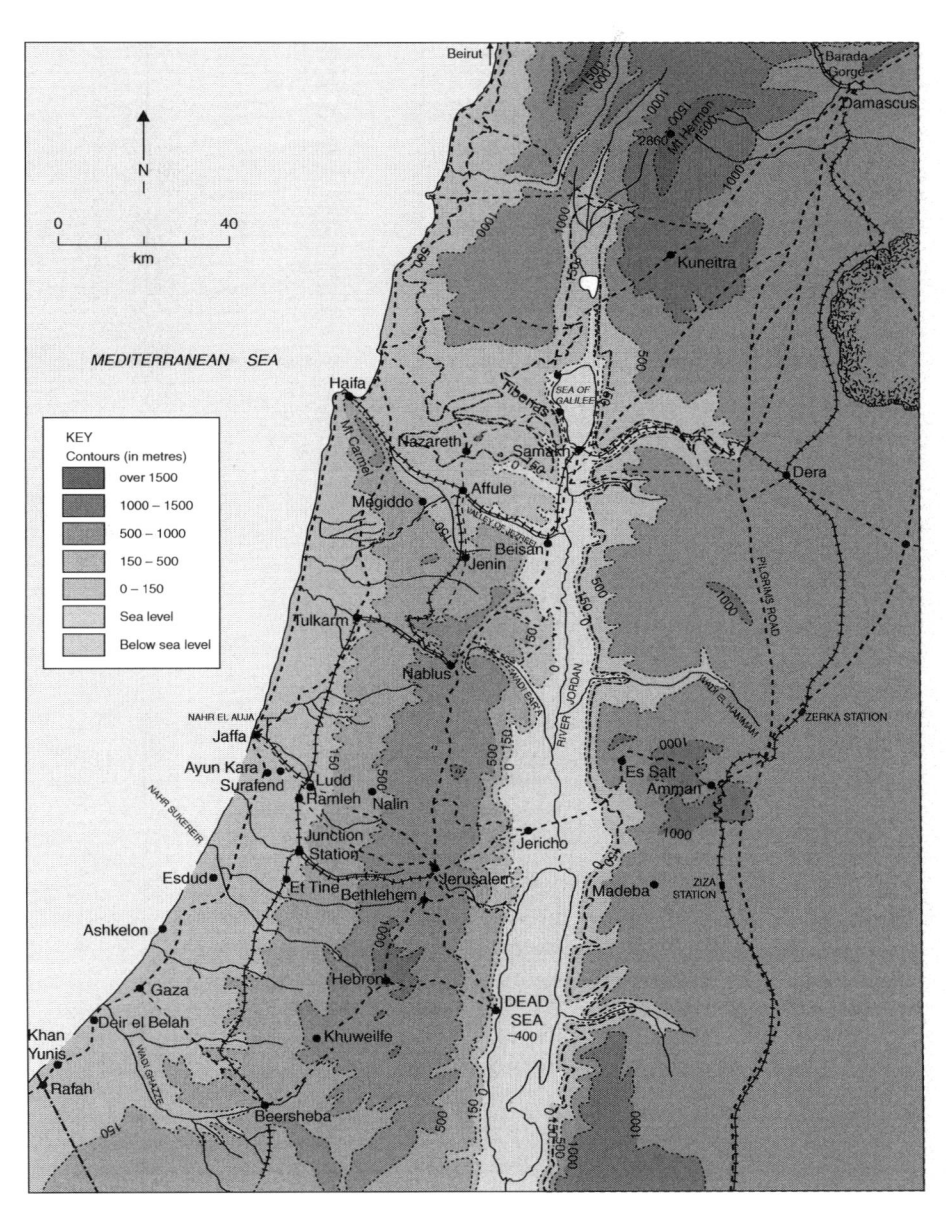

Map 2 Palestine, 1916–18. After T. Kinloch, *Devils on Horses: In the Words of the Anzacs in the Middle East 1916–19* (Auckland, 2007).

Introduction

I am afraid to forget. I fear that we human creatures do not forget cleanly, as the animals presumably do. What protrudes and does not fit in our pasts rises to haunt us and make us spiritually unwell in the present. The discontinuities in contemporary life are cutting us off from our roots and threatening us with the dread evil of nihilism in the twentieth century. We may become refugees in an inner sense unless we remember to some purpose. Surely the menace of new and more frightful wars is not entirely unrelated to our failure to understand those recently fought. If we could gain only a modicum of greater wisdom concerning what manner of men we are, what effect might it not have on future events?[1]

This powerful call to remember the horrors of modern war was written by J. Glenn Gray in the late 1950s as he struggled to come to terms intellectually with the complex set of experiences he took away from the European battlefields of 1944–5. As an intelligence officer dealing with the aftermath of operations in the immediate rear of the advancing US Army, Gray witnessed at first hand the chaos and dislocation that war brought to the peoples of Italy, France and Germany. His fear of forgetting was motivated, in part, by a desire to ensure that the nadirs of human civilization were not neglected in private and collective memory, and that when events and experiences were recalled they were used for a valuable purpose. The heightening tensions of the Cold War as he set down his combat memories imbued his memoirs with a strong sense of purpose. In many respects Gray was writing for the warriors of future generations; his concern was not simply with forgetting or remembering war, but crucially with attempting to understand it.

Despite the warnings of innumerable veterans not to forget the experiences of modern wars, many of the conflicts of the twentieth century, or aspects of the larger all-consuming 'total' wars, have been forgotten. Famously the men of General William Slim's 14th Army struggling through the jungles of Burma described themselves as a 'forgotten army'. They saw their campaign as being on the fringes of the British war effort in 1941–5 and, more importantly, on the fringes of the collective consciousness of an increasingly war-weary civilian population back home in Britain. This rhetoric of forgotten warriors has also been deployed in interpretations of those areas of the First World War fought beyond the Western Front. David Woodward's significant study of the Middle Eastern campaign was entitled *Forgotten Soldiers of the First World*

War, situating its account within a discourse of newly revealed aspects of a much-studied conflict. In many respects the forgetting of the sideshow theatres of the First and Second World Wars has a tinge of inevitability about it. These were invariably campaigns fought far from the eyes of the home population often for diffuse imperial goals, and which ultimately had little bearing on the overall outcome of either conflict. They were campaigns that were difficult to reconcile with the overarching narrative of worthwhile sacrifice in the struggle against German militarism or totalitarianism.

The interwar years saw numerous attempts made by the British state, society, and individuals to ensure that the sideshow theatres of the First World War, such as that in the Middle East, were not forgotten. The most prominent of which was the integration of all the theatres of war into the commemorative framework of the Imperial War Graves Commission.[2] The myriad cemeteries scattered around the globe conformed in large part to a common design that emphasized the equality in death of those interred within them. Shared features such as the stone of remembrance and Reginald Blomfield's cross of sacrifice reinforced the extent to which those who fought and died for the British Empire's war effort were taking part in a unified and universal cause.

There were, though, some attempts made to tailor individual cemeteries to better reflect their localities. The Jerusalem cemetery was sited prominently on Mount Scopus overlooking the city, a powerful reminder of British military success in Palestine during the war and imperial control under the post-war mandate. It contained architectural elements which alluded to a campaign fought in the Holy Land. The chapel was constructed with a domed roof, reminiscent of local Arabic architecture, and above its entrance was placed a bronze sculpture by Gilbert Baynes portraying St George slaying the dragon. These subtle references were overwhelmed by the drive to locate the cemetery's mode of remembrance within commemoration of an explicitly imperial British war effort. The diversity of the British imperial forces that fought in Palestine was continuously emphasized throughout the site. Opposite the main gate a lookout balcony incorporated the Australian memorial, and within the chapel itself extensive mosaics constituted the New Zealand memorial. The Jerusalem cemetery thus strove to make prominent the British imperial sacrifice in the war against the Ottoman Empire. It was a site of memory that encompassed multiple interpretations of the campaigns in Sinai and Palestine; these military operations were emphasized as part crusade, part struggle for imperial defence and expansion, and part moment of sacrifice.

The official memory of the First World War at the metropolitan heart of the British Empire also made space to commemorate the battles and losses of the Middle Eastern front. Under the aegis of the British War Memorial Committee, created in early 1918, a scheme was developed to build a Hall of Remembrance which would contain paintings depicting all aspects of the war, from the home front to the battlefield, alongside the wars at sea and in the air.[3] At the heart of the project would be a series of monumental battle paintings based on the dimensions of Paolo Uccello's fifteenth-century 'Battle of San Remano', and which were very much envisaged within a tradition of Renaissance models of art, celebrating heroism and sacrifice. Although the scheme never came to fruition due to lack of funding, the collection of art works ultimately came to reside in the Imperial War Museum. Visitors today can see hanging alongside evocative works such as Paul Nash's 'We are Making a New World' and John Singer Sargent's 'Gassed',

Henry Lamb's contribution representing the Palestinian front: 'Irish Troops in the Judaean Hills Surprised by a Turkish Bombardment' (see Illustration I.1). The painting was completed in 1919 after Lamb was demobilized from the army, having served as the medical officer of the 5th Royal Inniskilling Fusiliers in 10th (Irish) Division during operations in Macedonia and Palestine, his service earning him the Military Cross. It is an evocative depiction of modern combat, with an Irish encampment under bombardment from Turkish artillery in the early evening. Clouds of smoke from the exploding shells drift across the picture creating an almost ethereal atmosphere, which is shattered by the depiction of a casualty being evacuated by stretcher bearers while other soldiers run in terror to seek what shelter they can find in the barren landscape. The work brings into stark relief the vulnerability of soldiers to artillery, the weapon system that did most to define the nature and visual memory of modern warfare. In many respects Lamb also challenges what would later become the common tropes of the popular memory of the Middle Eastern war. He produced a painting that contained no burning desert sands, no triumphant charging soldiers mounted on horses or camels, and resolutely avoided the personalization of the campaign around the figure of T. E. Lawrence. Instead, this was the Palestine campaign as Lamb remembered it: dirty, deadly and disconcerting for the individual combatant.

Illustration I.1 Henry Lamb, 'Irish Troops in the Judaean Hills Surprised by a Turkish Bombardment', 1919 (IWM, ART 2746).

A very different memory of the war in the Middle East was emphasized in the memorial dedicated to the men of the Australian and New Zealand Mounted Division designed by Web Gilbert and Bertram Mackennal (see Illustration I.2). This sculpture was paid for by the men of the division, supplemented by money from the Australian government and was placed at Port Said, the entrance to the Suez Canal.[4] When unveiled in 1932, the former Australian Prime Minister William Hughes told the assembled dignitaries that it encapsulated a story comparable to that of the *Odyssey*. This sentiment of revelling in masculine heroism was not shared by the Egyptian population, and in 1956 during anti-British rioting the sculpture was destroyed beyond repair. For Egyptians it was a symbol of British imperial intervention and the subjugation of their

Illustration I.2 Unveiling of the Australian and New Zealand Mounted Division Memorial at Port Said, 23 November 1932 (AWM, A02755).

nation. The monument's depiction of an Australian Light Horseman reaching down to help a New Zealand Mounted Rifleman, as the latter's horse is shot from under him in the heat of battle, made clear the bonds that were at the heart of the Anzac relationship. It was evident that the New Zealander was the junior partner, being helped in battle, and metaphorically to nationhood, by his neighbour from across the Tasman Sea. Gilbert and Mackennal, however, created a sculpture that in many respects spoke less of the grand imperial narratives of the war or of Antipodean brotherhood, and much more of the bonds of comradeship arising from shared service and sacrifice on the battlefield. The sculpture poses a series of unresolved questions to a modern viewer: why were these Australian and New Zealand soldiers fighting for empire; what did they believe they were fighting for; and how did the bonds of mateship that it mythologizes actually play out in reality? Gilbert and Mackennal skilfully created an image that captured a brief moment of action in battle but also delved into the complexities of the soldiers' experience within that moment. In this sense, the memorial highlights many of the problems that have provoked, and continue to stimulate, considerable academic and public discourse around the topics of morale and combat motivation in relation to the experiences of soldiers in battle during the wars of the twentieth century.

As J. Glenn Gray forcefully asserted, understanding the soldier's experience of war, to which morale is central, provides a useful path to answering difficult questions on the nature of modern warfare. Delving into issues of personal combat motivation and the morale of military formations allows historians to address, in part, the impact upon individuals and societies of the mass violence and destruction that came to define the conflicts of the first half of the twentieth century. Morale, however, remains one of the most nebulous of terms within military history, despite undoubtedly holding a significant place in determining the operations of armies and the outcomes of their battles. Much recent analysis of warfare has attempted to rearticulate the individual's experience of battle, based on detailed and methodical research into the vagaries of combat and the motivations of soldiers. The 'new' military history that has emerged since the late 1960s has made these issues a prominent part of its analytical approach, keeping battle at the heart of its discussion.[5] This historical school has drawn off arguments and techniques first pioneered in sociological studies of combatants that appeared in the immediate aftermath of the Second World War. The work of S. L. A. Marshall, Edward Shils and Morris Janowitz, and Samuel Stouffer in particular has provided the bedrock upon which subsequent historians have attempted to reconstruct the soldier's experience in various modern conflicts. The study of the First World War has been a notable beneficiary of these debates, with a vibrant historiography developing around the questions of how men endured the hardships of military service and how they were motivated, or cajoled, into fighting.

Much of this work has been focused almost exclusively on the Western Front, to the detriment of those theatres that made the war a global struggle.[6] The campaigns fought by the British Empire in the Middle East sit within this neglected arena; there is a historiographical lacuna with respect to the issues of combat and morale in the deserts and hills of Sinai and Palestine. In so far as motivational factors have been analysed in this theatre, they have been seen largely as a function of the leadership skills of senior commanders. The aim of this book is to address morale in the British imperial army that fought in Egypt and Palestine, known as the Egyptian Expeditionary Force (EEF). It highlights how the men's resilience and combat performance was rooted in robust training mechanisms which inculcated a professional military identity among the force's soldiers. This was an identity which held up the pre-war regular British Army as the exemplar of combat performance.

Any discussion of morale needs first to focus on the intricacy of the term. It can be defined at its simplest as 'a mental attitude, in relation to happiness and confidence'.[7] This captures the dual nature of the term; morale concerns both how soldiers endure war (their happiness) and how they cope with the specific task of combat (where their confidence is put to the test). As the American sociologist Samuel Stouffer outlined in the late 1940s, this division could be pushed even further, as the question of how soldiers sustained themselves in battle was itself fundamentally distinct from that of 'why men fight'.[8] Much of the historiography of morale has examined why men enlisted, went through training, endured brutal army discipline, and suffered the physical and mental hardships of military service. Relatively little seeks to address this distinct issue of what drove men to get up out of their positions and to run towards the enemy's defences through rifle, machine gun and artillery fire that brought almost certain death.

At its heart battle was, and remains, a terrifying environment for the individual soldier. It is an arena of constant and extreme danger, and one which places the combatant into a state of sensory overload. The smells, sights, and sounds of battle, particularly during the industrialized conflicts of the first half of the twentieth century, were shocking and intense. Importantly, battle was an experience in which violent death and severe injury were defining and prominent elements, marking it out as distinct from normal, everyday civilian life. More pertinently, though, for the individual soldiers involved they were both on the receiving end of extreme violence but were also the practitioners of it. What really made battle a unique experience for combatants was the fact that it was a moment during which they were allowed by the state, even expected, to kill, thus breaking the ultimate social taboo.

The risk of death or injury, the expectation and realization of having to kill, and the sensory extremes of battle cumulatively contributed to the immense psychological strain it placed on the soldiers involved. This manifested itself through the overriding emotional response to combat experienced by soldiers: fear.[9] Given the danger involved in battle this was only a natural response; very few soldiers willingly chose to risk their lives. In order for armies to function, however, the bulk of the soldiers they deployed to the battlefield had to be persuaded, encouraged, cajoled or coerced into actions that risked death and injury. Morale acts as a suitably mutable concept to capture this motivational process in all its complexity. It is in essence a short-hand for the willingness of individuals and groups to overcome their personal and collective fears and fulfil the demands of the military institution of which they form a part. This requires soldiers to both psychologically override the fears associated with death and injury, but also to engage with the fears related to an individual's failure to live up to the expectations of their comrades, military institution, society and state. A soldier's fears were thus only a subtle degree removed from his personal, social and institutional sense of duty.

This book seeks to engage with the problems of morale among the soldiers who served in the Sinai and Palestine theatres of the First World War. It examines how they overcame their fears, and the willingness with which they took part in battle and responded to the demands of military authority. This is both a question of how men and armies coped with combat, but also of how morale affected military outcomes in this theatre, as the EEF's campaigns ultimately helped the British Empire to destroy the Ottoman Empire in the Levant, which would serve to reshape the political map of the Middle East. This study of morale involves unpicking both how individuals coped with combat but also how the formations the British Army deployed to the region, and the institution itself, prepared and organized soldiers for battle, as well as the manner in which the troops' welfare needs before, during and after conflict were addressed. Morale, endurance, combat performance, and the construction of military identities are thus interlinked concepts, which together provide the analytical frame to this study.

It was John Keegan's magisterial work, *The Face of Battle*, that drew the attention of military historians and public historical discourse to the problems concerning the motivations of troops in combat. He argued for the position of the individual soldier, which had become lost within the battle narratives that dominated much military historical writing.[10] His criticisms also focused on the fascination of many works with technological ephemera and military institutions, pointing to the numerous popular accounts that revelled in the calibres of weapons, or studies that failed to connect the military machine to the people who serve within it. Military history for Keegan was about battle; it is not through what armies *are* that they influence the lives of nations and individuals, but through what they *do*. The 'battle piece' that he criticizes has a long history, having first been developed by ancient authors such as Homer, and ultimately becoming a staple of literature, as seen in William Makepeace Thackeray's and Victor Hugo's depictions of Waterloo. It is often misused by historians who describe combat within a series of narrative presumptions, with many depictions of battle dominated by simplified and uniform descriptions of human behaviour, stratified characterizations, and a lack of attention to the dead and wounded. Fears of creating dry operational narratives have often led authors to produce accounts of battle that are simply knockabout affairs described in terms of endless clichés.

The problems inherent in describing battle, particularly its confusing, chaotic, and ever-changing aspects, have been compounded by the desire of many military historians to label the events they recount as 'decisive' and therefore worthy of study. Very few battles on their own actually decide anything conclusively, yet the notion of a decisive battle has persisted since Edward Creasy published *The Fifteen Decisive Battles of the World* in 1851.[11] Here Creasy examined engagements that he believed were of great significance for determining the course of world history, beginning with Marathon and terminating at Waterloo. Much popular military history has adopted this technique of claiming undue prominence for certain battles, as it helps to create dramatic, clear-cut, simplified events, for both author and reader. The failure to place battles within their political, social, and cultural context, causing the individual to disappear from sight, is in part a direct result of this desire to focus only on the decisive nature of battles. In this way, the rhetoric of the battle narrative has come to exercise a dictatorship over the minds of many historians.

Long before Keegan first addressed the issue of the soldier in battle, the ancient Greek author and general Xenophon was developing a theoretical critique of morale. In his account of the 10,000 Greek soldiers abandoned after the battle of Cunaxa in Persia in 401 BC, he demonstrated that issues of command and motivation could and should be studied, improved upon and deliberately practised by future commanders. Not all ancient societies reflected Xenophon's devout belief in leadership as the key determinant of battlefield success. The Theban Sacred Band relied instead on developing intimate homosexual bonds between its warriors to ensure the sustained coherency of its forces in the field; men would fight and die to protect their lovers. Similarly, the Roman Army's organization rested on its basic living and messing unit of ten men, the *contubernium*. The intention was to build robust bonds between soldiers who lived with each other day after day, tightening group loyalties when they were needed most, on the battlefield.[12]

Such ancient models retained their prominence for those military theorists who began to examine battle, and soldiers' experiences within it, in a systematic fashion in the wake of the Napoleonic Wars. In the 1830s Captain William Siborne was commissioned by the British Army to construct a terrain model of the battle of Waterloo.[13] He took the task extremely seriously, living in a farmhouse near the battlefield for eight months, and sending a circular letter to surviving officers asking for operational and tactical details. After 14 years he published a 2-volume study, contradicting the view that the commander could control events across the whole battlefield. Siborne's painstaking work demonstrated that some coherency could be brought to the interpretation of a battle through the rigorous accumulation of information from participants and the study of the locality.

In the late 1860s Colonel Charles-Jean-Jacques-Joseph Ardant du Picq, a veteran of the French Army's campaigns in the Crimea, Syria, and Algeria, began a more comprehensive study of nineteenth-century battle.[14] He sent a questionnaire to his fellow officers asking them what had occurred when their men entered into close combat with the enemy. Although only a few replies were received, these provided an insight into the experiences of units on the battlefields of the Second Empire. Ardant du Picq's analysis of these replies, combined with his work on ancient battles such as Cannae and Pharsalus, was set out in *Etudes sur le combat*, published posthumously in 1880. Here he emphasized the role of moral forces in combat, noting that 'success in battle is a matter of morale. In all matters which pertain to an army, organization, discipline and tactics, the human heart in the supreme moment of battle is the basic factor'.[15] Ardant du Picq came to the conclusion that troops did not run away due to the physical shock of being attacked. The side that fled did so because its nerve had faltered; self-preservation and fear thus dominated the modern battlefield. This was a situation only made worse with the advent of new weapon systems, most notably the magazine-loaded rifle and quick firing artillery, which led to soldiers becoming ever more dispersed during combat. For Ardant du Picq combat motivation was an issue that focused on the individual soldier and his conscience; men fought out of the fear of not fighting and being punished, or of fighting badly, resulting in death and defeat.

Although *Etudes sur le combat* combined ideas on morale derived from antiquity with a systematized analysis of battle, its conclusions were ignored when it first appeared, and were only considered in detail after the second edition appeared in 1903. The emphasis on moral forces then chimed with the ideas of those French Army officers, such as Colonel de Grandmaison, who in the decade prior to the First World War advocated the offensive at all costs as the solution to the fire-swept battlefield. In many respects, Ardant du Picq's analysis demonstrates many of the issues that would come to the fore in twentieth-century studies of morale and combat.

The mass industrialized slaughter of the First World War, and the surprising endurance of many of the citizen armies that were involved, as well as the numerous cases of personal mental breakdown, prompted a number of commentators to consider the issue of morale. In 1917 the American psychologist Charles Bird produced a detailed study of the transition faced by a new recruit, moving from a civilian to a military existence and ultimately to the horrors of the battlefield. Bird highlighted a number of the characteristic components of military morale; training, robust discipline, the value of the small combat unit, and the role of officers are all discussed as factors that contribute to the combatant's ability to engage the enemy in battle. Following the First World War, a Cambridge-based psychologist, Frederic Bartlett, produced a more expansive study of the factors that influenced the psychological strength of the soldier. The work was based on a series of military psychology lectures that had been given at Cambridge in the six years following the war. Much of his analysis focused on the role of group identity in helping to motivate men in combat, although he also drew out the specific characteristics that defined effective leadership.[16]

The Second World War prompted a much more detailed examination of the morale of soldiers in battle. Lord Moran's classic study, *The Anatomy of Courage*, drew on the diaries he had kept while serving as a medical officer on the Western Front in 1914–18 and the lectures he had given to Bomber Command crews during the Second World War. Moran believed that every individual had a certain stock of courage, which would be depleted by constant exposure to battle; each soldier thus had his breaking point. In addition, he highlighted the need for efficient selection processes during recruiting to weed out those of a sensitive, emotional or unstable type. Moran's study became one of the seminal British attempts to understand the stresses involved in fighting on the modern battlefield, with his ideas reinforced by subsequent British studies of military personnel.[17]

The most influential analyses of the combat soldier were, though, carried out by American researchers, and appeared after the Second World War. The key work was that of S. L. A. Marshall, a member of the American Army's fledgling historical section. Marshall's *Men Against Fire*, published in 1947, argued that the suppression of fear was the task of every soldier in the firing line and an army should therefore try to create strong links between its soldiers, developing small groups of friends each centred on a natural fighter who would reinforce each other's morale. His most startling discovery was that only 15–25 per cent of soldiers actually fired their weapon during combat. Although Marshall claimed to have based his research on interviews with approximately 400 rifle companies in both the Pacific and European theatres, his findings have been subject to considerable criticism, and it is unlikely that *Men Against Fire* was based on the wide sample he claimed. Moreover, the foundations of his analysis rested on the notion that a soldier's primary function in combat was simply to fire his weapon, failing to recognize that at times it was not always necessary, appropriate or possible to do so. He also ignored the relationship of geography to the battlefield and the extent to which it could influence the flow of combat.[18] Despite these shortcomings Marshall's writings had a significant impact within the American military establishment throughout the first two decades of the Cold War. His ideas on improved training for soldiers, intended in part to improve the weight of fire that could be brought to bear at a tactical level, shaped the way the US Army prepared men for war.

The prominence of Marshall's ideas was aided by the support given to his conclusions by the work of Edward Shils and Morris Janowitz, who focused on the *Wehrmacht* during the Second World War and used a series of interviews with captured German soldiers. The authors attempted to develop a theory as to why Germany's armed forces had managed to keep fighting effectively almost to the close of hostilities, despite their imminent defeat becoming increasingly evident. Although accepting some degree of ideological motivation among a hard core of dedicated Nazis, it was to primary group theory that Shils and Janowitz turned in order to explain this rugged endurance. The *Wehrmacht* soldier was portrayed as reliant upon the psychological bonds with his comrades in his squad or section to prevent mental disintegration during combat. This corroborated many of the findings of Marshall, suggesting that the primary group concept was an idea that cut across national and cultural boundaries. Ultimately all modern armies trained their soldiers to fight as members of small groups of warriors. The soldiers sampled by Shils and Janowitz were not, however, representative of the *Wehrmacht* as a whole. They only examined men captured in the European theatre who had fought against the Western Allies, neglecting the struggle on the Eastern Front against the Soviets. This produced a skewed picture of the German soldier's combat motivation. As Omer Bartov has suggested, a considerable section of the *Wehrmacht* was influenced by Nazi ideology, in particular through loyalty to the image of the Führer and a belief in the need to crush the Bolshevik threat. The Nazification of the army's junior officers and the widespread use of propaganda, alongside the influence of political officers, meant that such motivations transferred down to the rank and file. It was this which principally explained the remarkable endurance of the *Wehrmacht* and contributed to the barbarization of warfare on the Eastern Front.[19]

Nevertheless, the work of Shils and Janowitz fitted into the general pattern of studies of combat soldiers emerging after the Second World War. In 1949 Samuel Stouffer and his research team produced a mammoth study entitled *The American Soldier*.[20] Like its predecessors, it was largely based on answers to questionnaires given to men serving in American divisions in the European and Pacific theatres. The aim was to examine the whole experience of serving in the American Army, from enlistment through to battle. Due to the vast range of the source material, Stouffer produced a number of conclusions as to what motivated men in combat. National war aims, the role of leadership and the impact of religious values all seemed to play a part for some combatants. Above all, though, it was again the soldier's integration into a small group of his peers that rested at the heart of Stouffer's conclusions. In a modernist twist he allied this factor to the individual soldier's deeply internalized code of 'being a man'.

Despite the vast scope of Stouffer's work its conclusions, encompassing a multiplicity of factors, lacked the analytical punch of Shils and Janowitz or the sensationalist claims of Marshall. Stouffer's grand scale and sweeping approach produced too many generalizations about combat motivation, leaving the work as one which can be used to reinforce virtually any take on soldiers' morale. It was the unifying idea of the primary group, present in all three studies, that was to have the greatest legacy.

By the time of the Korean War the ideas relating to primary group theory were defining the US Army's approach to the tactical aspects of warfare and the way in which it prepared its men to fight. The influence of Marshall, Shils and Janowitz, and Stouffer within the military sphere and upon the methodologies used by scholars of morale was considerable. Analyses of soldiers in battle from the early 1950s onwards have principally developed this triumvirate's basic ideas. The Korean War saw the characters of the 'hero' and the 'dud' emerge within the squad to complicate the picture of group dynamics. These figures served to set the upper and lower bounds of activity considered as acceptable by one's comrades. Studies of combat motivation in the Vietnam War began to suggest that the American Army's reliance on primary group theory was proving highly problematic. Concerns were raised about the ability of soldiers to fight complex counter-insurgency campaigns which often lacked the ideological clarity of earlier 'total' wars, raising fears that these men might not adapt well to the battlefields of the future. It appeared that the American Army had lost the ability to motivate its soldiers, a problem that rested in part on the detachment of military operations from widespread political goals. The apparent illegitimacy of the war in Vietnam meant that few men cared about the success of the operations they were taking part in, but were instead preoccupied with their personal survival. Problems were worsened by the rotation of troops through the theatre, meaning that as soon as a stock of combat experience was built up within a unit it was lost, as new drafts arrived and veterans returned home. These factors gave rise to 'FIGMO (fuck it, got my orders) alienation' among soldiers in Vietnam.[21]

The solution appeared to be to ensure that soldiers understood the political legitimacy of the war they were fighting. As a corollary to this argument, it was suggested that the army had to be reintegrated into the fabric of American civil society. Military problems were only exacerbated by the army's absolutist notion of its separation from the civilian sphere.[22] Not all analysts saw the solution in this manner. Colonel W. L. Hauser argued that, as the problem was a military one, it had to be fixed within the army. He suggested developing more extensive training regimes, creating a unit rotation system, enhancing unit distinctiveness, improving officer appraisal and extending command tenures as means to enhance cohesion. Hauser pushed this argument even further suggesting a number of controversial solutions, including the idea that officers should be given lifetime commissions to promote professionalism. This would be matched by the creation of a regimental system modelled on that in the British Army and combined with a reintroduction of conscription, to foster a military identity among citizen soldiers. These criticisms of the prominence of primary group theory which emerged in the 1980s and 1990s provoked considerable debate, elements of which have influenced the growing historiography of combat in the First and Second World Wars.

While the abstract analysis of morale which defines the studies discussed above runs the risk of missing key constituents of the soldier's experience, many popular accounts of battle simply regurgitate the evidence of those who have taken part, recounting stories at length with little interpretation save for assertions of how the testimonies speak for themselves.[23] More rigorous academic works of social and cultural history that address combat are also problematic, elevating the individual soldier and his motivations over and above the events in which they acted. This is an approach typified by Joanna Bourke's *An Intimate History of Killing*, which eschews any examination of war at a strategic, operational or tactical level.[24] Combat motivation and the drive to kill is thus examined in an abstract sense, separate from the battles in which it supposedly played such a critical role. Concentrating so minutely on the individual soldier does not allow an examination of the wide range of factors identified by the likes of Stouffer as influencing the willingness of men to fight. The experience of battle is separated out from the events of the war, breaking the link between the two phenomena. Such analyses suggest a universality of experience between soldiers in divergent conflicts; killing in the trenches of the Somme was similar to killing in the jungles of Vietnam. This fails to address the specific grand strategic concerns that produced particular wars and the operational decisions that determined where, when and how certain battle would be fought, as well as ignoring the extent to which such issues impacted on the motivational frameworks of the men at the front line.

Morale-centric studies which focus on the universality of the combat experience also tend to gloss over the specificities of national approaches to warfare. Much of the work of Marshall and Stouffer reveals in great detail how armies fight, but only from the perspective of the American military. The importance of primary group theory is the clearest indication of this problem, as it reflects the prominence of the squad as the basic organizational unit of the US Army. Such assessments of morale may produce different results if focused on the British Army's historic regimental system. Unique elements of national military systems, cultures, and traditions, as well as tactical doctrines and training routines, need to be borne in mind when analysing the experiences of soldiers at war. It is in many respects unwise to isolate individual soldiers from the particular national army in which they served or from the conflict taking place around them, as this denies the complexities of the military experience. The vibrant historiography of combat motivation focused on the First World War reveals the extent to which nationally aware studies of armies can yield fascinating conclusions.

This is most evident in examinations of the 1914–18 experiences of French soldiers. The fabled *poilu* had no interest in the overall conduct of the war; instead he concerned himself with surviving at a local level. The vibrant trench press mirrored this interest by reporting on the minutiae of everyday army life. It was through these stories that the soldiers were able to retain their dignity among the horror and frequent personal humiliation of the war.[25] The descriptions of battle and the generally morbid tone of the majority of trench publications acted as a form of exorcism. These themes ran in parallel to a constant concern for home, even though the combatants were often critical of the lack of recognition they felt they were receiving from the French public. Soldiers expressed a constant desire to see their suffering witnessed by those on the home front. The trench press thus reflected the considerable gap that had developed between the horrific reality of the front line and the more romanticized and heroic image of the front prevalent at home. Resentment for the rear was not an absolute and was frequently mixed with a degree of fascination. The *poilu* was not driven to stay at the front, therefore, by a simple patriotism, although he did not doubt France's ability to defeat Germany. In the work of Stéphane Audoin-Rouzeau, patriotism as an analytical term is remoulded to reflect a much more subtle analysis of 'national feeling' among the men of the French Army. This was an off-shoot of pre-war republican patriotism, inculcated in every soldier since primary school. It was focused on the defence of territory by the everyday experience of the war. Land could not be lost, as it had been rendered precious by those Frenchmen who had given their lives defending it. The French Republic's demands of its citizen-soldiers were thus viewed as legitimate. 'National feeling' did not motivate soldiers in isolation, but was inextricably linked to a combatant's relationship to his comrades; ideology and the primary group reinforced each other.

The work on soldiers of the French Army indicates that the theoretical critique of morale, as raised by Marshall and others, operates within a framework of alternative, non-military factors. These elements of legitimate demand theory are not as universal as the primary group theories expounded after the Second World War, but instead relate to the responses of individuals and societies to specific conflicts. British Army unit newspapers from 1914–18 demonstrate that the complexities of morale found among *poilus* were also prevalent among Tommies. For British soldiers entertainments were of critical value, particularly when enjoying rest periods away from the line.[26] Sports fixtures, especially football matches, and concert parties were held on a regular basis and were found on all fronts of the war. These institutions of civilian Britain allowed the men to express briefly their peacetime identity, as well as providing a chance to mock the military authorities that controlled their daily lives. The dominance of civilian points of reference during military service proved vital in the post-war period, helping many men to assimilate smoothly back into everyday civil society. The British soldier's view of the conflict extended far beyond that of his immediate military situation and encompassed a wide frame of civilian reference.

At a micro-analytical level, British Army battalions, particularly those of the Territorial Force (TF) and Kitchener's New Armies, demonstrated many of the characteristics of civilian identity which sustained men across the British Expeditionary Force (BEF). Helen McCartney's examinations of two TF battalions of the King's (Liverpool) Regiment highlights the paramount importance of local county and regional identities within this mix.[27] The image of the county was reinforced through their service in the 55th (West Lancashire) Division, which adopted the rose of Lancaster as its divisional badge in 1916, playing off local cultural affiliations. The identification with home extended beyond the county to the city of Liverpool itself, with trenches and dugouts named after streets or famous buildings. An officers' billet was, for example, called the 'Angel', after Liverpool's most expensive hotel; the names represented an extension of existing social norms as well as creating a familiar landscape reflecting memories of home. Letters and photographs sent back by soldiers to local newspapers further illustrate the links to home prevalent among these Liverpool battalions. The men wanted to keep their friends, neighbours, and workmates, as well as their families, informed about their exploits in the war. Across the wire of no-man's-land a similarly prominent regional identity was found among Bavarian soldiers, who stressed their rural backgrounds.[28] These men did not go to war in 1914 out of any love for the Kaiser, but instead in response to calls from Ludwig III head of the local Wittelsbach monarchy. These strong regional identities were not always beneficial to promoting army cohesion. The men of Bavaria fostered a deep hatred of Prussia during their military service, blaming the Prussians for the 1916–17 problems of food supply on the home front, a hatred that contributed to army breakdown in late 1918. Such regionally based studies of First World War combatants enhance the picture presented in army-wide accounts, drawing out intricacies of morale that are too often neglected.

Much of the work analysing soldiers' experiences of war rests on a detailed analysis of surviving diaries, memoirs and letter collections. Regular letter writing and reading allowed men to escape mentally from the horrors of combat in the trenches, and provided a powerful psychological link back home to a more peaceful pre-war existence.[29] The distant worlds of the soldier and the civilian did not exist in isolation from one another. Michael Roper's psychoanalytical study of the correspondence of British soldiers highlights the figure of the mother as critical to sustaining troops, either through the physical support of food parcels or the psychological reinforcement provided by letter writing.[30] This emphasis on the link to home life confirms the importance of a strong civilian identity among First World War soldiers. It does, however, only highlight the extent to which these civilian factors helped troops endure the war. Such studies often ignore the world of combat and fail to locate the experiences of individual soldiers within a wider institutional and cultural context. Civilian identity and maternal care only goes part of the way to explain why men chose to fight on the battlefield.

Once soldiers had enlisted or been called to the colours, they were part of a military institution which controlled every aspect of their daily lives. The ultimate function of armies was battle, and it was for this end that men were trained, equipped, organized and disciplined. The complexity of military structures and cultures, which varied from nation to nation, clearly impacted on how men were motivated to take part in combat. The variation of troops within the British Army alone, from their task-oriented roles as infantrymen or artillerymen, to whether they were regular, TF, New Army, or conscript soldiers, determined particular elements of how they coped with the war. A unit's military identity, its regimental *esprit de corps*, could be a key component in sustaining its personnel in battle, as it provided the men with a strong communal bond to their comrades around them and set the minimum standards for soldierly conduct. This was often strongest among regular soldiers, who had been integrated deeply into their regiment's traditions and culture over many years of service.[31] The regimental system could at times, however, act as a barrier to combat effectiveness. Loyalty to a particular regiment produced an insular attitude among some officers and men, which hampered the creation of a strong tactical doctrine and the development of all arms cooperation on the battlefield.[32] These difficulties were manifest in the mass European warfare of the First and Second World Wars. In contrast, during the 'small wars' of empire the emphasis on a robust, professional military identity focused on the regiment allowed British soldiers to cope with the hardships of extended campaigns in harsh climates and inhospitable terrain. The regimental family was the focus for the army's cohesion in the imperial campaigns that dominated much of its nineteenth- and twentieth-century history.

Newly formed Kitchener battalions had little chance to look back to the historic traditions of the regiment for moral sustenance. For example, the 22nd Royal Fusiliers, formed in autumn 1914, did display a certain degree of *esprit de corps*, but this did not act as the primary motivational factor for its men in the line.[33] Instead its commanding officer developed an open and relaxed disciplinary system that allowed for close, personal relationships to build up between officers and men. At the same time officers who did not fit into this egalitarian atmosphere were either ostracized or removed, as they were seen as inefficient. Junior leadership at regimental level in the British Army during the First World War could do much to determine the endurance of soldiers and their performance in battle.[34] Officers acted as examples to their men of how they should behave in battle, and, more importantly, fostered a paternal bond with the men they led in their platoons and companies. This concern for the welfare of the other ranks was instilled during officer training, and suggests continuity between the prewar regular army and that made up of Territorials, volunteers and conscripts during 1914–18.

Alternatively, effective junior leadership in some circumstances could exacerbate military collapse, seen most prominently in the German Army's 'ordered surrender' in the closing stages of the war.[35] The Germans had failed to maintain an adequate cadre of officers by 1917–18, with increasingly junior commanders leading ever larger formations. Those officers left at the front were war weary and reluctant to fight; perceiving no alternative they therefore chose to lead their men into captivity. When compared to the German Army's experience it becomes clear that the particular nature of officer-man relations in the BEF played a crucial part in sustaining the army in the field. By drawing on a comparison of two armies, it is possible to examine those elements of the First World War combat experience that did cross over the front lines, and maybe point towards some elements of universal coping mechanisms used by soldiers facing the shared horrors of modern war. A fatalistic attitude among British and German combatants has been identified by Alexander Watson as a central element of personal psychological strategies which attempted to comprehend the industrialized slaughter of the Western Front. Such a focus draws together the theoretical concepts of morale studies developed since Marshall and places them within a robust comparative framework, recognizing the importance of national differences.

In contrast to such studies of the Western Front, the war in the Middle East has largely been neglected by historians focusing on the experiences of combat soldiers. Only David Woodward's *Forgotten Soldiers of the First World War* attempts to integrate the men who served in the Middle East into the wider narrative framework of the campaign. This approach is not without its difficulties, as the resulting narrative of operations, although highly readable, essentially replicates the official history, written by Lieutenant-General George MacMunn and Cyril Falls and published in two volumes in 1928 and 1930.[36] The major questions relating to the campaigns in Sinai and Palestine, and the morale and combat experiences of the men who took part in them, remain unanswered. Resurrecting the 'lost voices' of soldiers in the Middle East during the First World War is difficult, particularly when relying upon private paper collections drawn exclusively from British archives. The British imperial army, known as the EEF, that fought its way through Sinai and Palestine was a multinational and multi-ethnic force drawn from across the empire, and any consideration of its soldiers' experiences needs to bear this in mind.

The experiences of the soldiers of the Ottoman Empire have been even worse served by historians. Erik Zürcher's deconstruction of the Turkish soldier's motivations has begun a tentative process of examining Ottoman Army combat motivation in the era of the First World War. Through the medium of the 'Yemen Songs' he brings evidence of discontent among Anatolian soldiers, scattered around the empire's considerable territorial holdings, to the fore. Ottoman soldiers viewed their particular military operations as part of an imperial discourse, relating their parochial concerns to wider factors influencing their battlefield motivation. Scholars of the Ottoman Army face considerable difficulties in reconstructing the experiences of its combatants. The low literacy rate of the empire's population meant that few personal accounts of the First World War were written, and thus little documentary record has been left for historians to examine. Studies tend to consider only the experiences of a literate minority, usually officers, with little attention paid to the masses who filled the ranks. Geoffrey Lewis's account of the career of Falih Rifki, who served as Cemal Pasha's private secretary in Palestine in 1914–17, is one such example of this trend. Moreover, much of the Ottoman soldier's experience is considered in light of the political upheavals that followed the Young Turk Revolution in 1908 and the collapse of the empire in the wake of the First World War.[37] Consequently, it is hard to separate out the Ottoman soldier from the nationalist discourse surrounding the birth of modern Turkey in the early twentieth century.

The very nature of the EEF's wartime achievements has in many respects militated against the detailed study of the combat experiences of its soldiers. The story of its war has been one told through decisive victories and grand sweeping advances; this is not a world within which the little men of history seemingly played much of a role. Britain's war with the Ottoman Empire began on 5 November 1914, following the bombardment of Russian Black Sea ports by the Turks' newly acquired German warships.[38] The focus of British policy was to secure the Suez Canal, the main arterial route of the empire, which allowed men and material vital to the war effort to flow to the metropole. Concern over the internal security of Egypt, which still had an ambiguous relationship to its former Ottoman suzerain despite over 30 years of British rule, led first to the introduction of martial law and then to the declaration of a British protectorate before the end of 1914. It was not until early February 1915 that the Ottoman Army crossed Sinai in an impressive logistical operation and attempted to attack the Canal. The assault failed and Turkish forces were easily beaten back by the British and Indian defenders. For the rest of 1915 the war remained remote from Egypt, with the country acting as an important staging post supporting the extensive and ultimately forlorn operations at Gallipoli. It was to Egypt that these forces were evacuated in the closing stages of the campaign, with over 100,000 troops in the country by December.

In January 1916 General Archibald Murray took command of the forces in Egypt, and it was from these units that the EEF was formed. British forces were gradually pushed out into the western fringes of Sinai throughout the first half of 1916, with the aim of preventing any future Turkish operations from severing the Canal. When the next Ottoman attack came, on 4 August, it ran into stiff opposition at Romani from British infantry and Australian and New Zealand mounted soldiers. An extended period of pursuit followed with the EEF cautiously pushing out across the northern edge of Sinai, with its mounted forces leading the way. The EEF inflicted significant local defeats on the Turkish garrisons defending the posts at Magdhaba on 23 December 1916 and at Rafah on 9 January 1917. As British forces crossed Sinai and became established in southern Palestine opposite Gaza it became clear that the initial war of imperial defence, intended to secure the Suez Canal, was gradually metamorphosing into one of imperial offence, aiming to defeat and clear Ottoman forces from their Levantine empire.

On 26 March 1917 the EEF made an abortive attempt to seize Gaza in a *coup de main*, with the army's mounted wing enveloping the town from the north and east. Poor command, confusion on the battlefield and stout Turkish resistance resulted in the EEF being beaten back to its initial positions despite breaching the defences in numerous places.[39] First Gaza cost the EEF nearly 4,000 casualties. Despite this failure Murray pushed his forces into a second battle on 19 April, which saw a frontal infantry assault on the town's reinforced defences end in disaster. The casualty figure was this time much greater, with nearly 6,500 EEF dead, wounded and missing. Two costly defeats in a row served to undermine Murray's command and by late June he had been replaced as EEF Commander-in-Chief by General Edmund Allenby. Despite his battlefield failures, Murray had succeeded in developing a robust and extensive logistics network across Sinai. A water pipeline from Egypt, wire-netting road, and railway line allowed reinforcements to be brought up to the front line and, crucially, to be sustained in an extended trench network stretching from the Mediterranean coast inland towards Beersheba.

A summer of hard training and rebuilding of combat efficiency in the EEF produced startling results at the third battle of Gaza, which opened on 31 October with the seizure of the Turkish left flank at Beersheba by the Desert Mounted Corps (DMC). By 7 November the EEF's infantry, now organized into two corps (XX and XXI commanded by Lieutenant-Generals Philip Chetwode and Edward Bulfin respectively), had worn down the Turkish defenders and collapsed the defences around Gaza. This allowed for the DMC to drive the Ottoman Army northwards towards Jaffa. The EEF was by the end of the month able to wheel right into the Judaean hills and begin the process of advancing on Jerusalem, which eventually fell on 9 December. Subsequent Turkish counter-attacks running into January 1918 were repulsed, bringing to a close one of the most spectacular and significant operations in the Middle Eastern theatre during the First World War. In the space of a little over two months of operations the EEF had switched from a static war to one of rapid movement, driving back Turkish forces in a series of successful tactical engagements. More importantly, EEF operations possessed considerable and sustained tempo, which produced an unrelenting pressure upon their Turkish opponents. Arguably the battles beginning with Third Gaza in late 1917 played the pivotal role in wearing down the ability of the Ottoman Army to fight to defend Palestine.

Spring 1918 saw Allenby attempting to destroy Turkish positions in the Jordan Valley and around Amman. Initial moves into the malaria-ridden valley proved successful, but two attempts to drive across the Jordan and into the mountains of Moab in late March and then in late April and early May ended in failure.[40] Poor weather, vulnerable supply lines, unreliable local allies and an inability to judge the resilience of Turkish forces conspired to draw Australian and New Zealand mounted troops into costly defeats. 1918 also witnessed the transformation of Allenby's army. Mounting manpower pressures on the Western Front, exacerbated by the German's spring offensive, resulted in large numbers of British troops being transferred to the BEF. These men were replaced by Indian soldiers, many of whom were fresh recruits with little training and no combat experience. Over the course of the summer these units were gradually integrated into the formations of the EEF, learning to work alongside those British battalions that remained. Thorough training, meticulous planning, and the accumulation of a significant material advantage, particularly in artillery, meant that when Allenby launched his final offensive on 19 September across the Plain of Sharon the opposing Turkish forces crumbled.[41] Within a week the DMC had swept through the chaotic rear of the retreating Ottoman Army to capture Nazareth, Haifa and the towns around Lake Tiberias. By 1 October Australian Light Horsemen at the head of the advance were passing through Damascus. The EEF's campaign only drew to a close at the end of October with the DMC having captured Aleppo in northern Syria. Megiddo and the pursuit that followed resulted in the capture of over 75,000 prisoners for the loss of only 5,066 casualties in the EEF. Although it did not precipitate Turkey's exit from the war, which was in its immediate sense a product of the collapse of Bulgaria and the severing of the Turkish lifeline to the Central Powers, Allenby's final offensive had sealed the fate of the Ottoman Empire in Palestine and Syria. This set the stage for the tortuous, and often no less bloody, interwar history of squabbles between imperial and mandatory powers on the one hand and nascent Arab and Zionist nationalists on the other for control of the region.

The campaigns in Egypt and Palestine are frequently portrayed as a sideshow, worthy of only a few pages of comment, in general histories of the 1914–18 conflict.[42] This view reflected the debate over the theatre's relevance during the war itself and in the post-1918 period. The clash of opinions was encapsulated in the struggles of the 'Easterner' and 'Westerner' factions within the British political and military elite, nominally represented by the Prime Minister David Lloyd George and General Henry Wilson (Chief of the Imperial General Staff (CIGS), February 1918–February 1922) on the one hand and General William Robertson (CIGS, December 1915–February 1918) and Field Marshal Douglas Haig (BEF commander, December 1915–December 1918) on the other. Winston Churchill's *The World Crisis* did much to foster this overly simplified and bifurcated image of British grand strategy. His support for the Gallipoli campaign led him to advocate other non-Western Front options which held out the possibility of ending the war rapidly. Palestine proved to be one of the most appealing. In describing Allenby's actions Churchill suggested that 'no praise is too high for these brilliant and frugal operations, which will long serve as a model in theatres of war in which manoeuvre is possible'.[43] He argued that if the Palestine campaign had been fully supported from the beginning it could have produced similar results much earlier in the war, and at a much lower cost in manpower than was the case by November 1918.[44] Robin Prior has demonstrated that *The World Crisis*, although attempting some historical objectivity, was mainly concerned with exonerating Churchill's own war record. Descriptions of British grand strategy in terms of 'Easterners' and 'Westerners' are too simplistic, ignoring many of the variations in attitude adopted by senior politicians and generals across the course of the war.[45] Crucially, the defeat of the Turkish armies in Palestine did not in itself bring down the Ottoman regime as Churchill and Lloyd George argued. As the official history made clear, it was the success of the Allies on the Western Front and the pressure this placed on Germany that weakened the Young Turk regime in Constantinople. This came after three years of protracted and bloody fighting against Russia in the Caucasus which, more than any other front, served to drain Ottoman manpower reserves. Allied victories in Macedonia and the capitulation of Bulgaria sealed the Ottoman Empire's fate, cutting its precious rail link to Germany. The relative unimportance of the EEF's operations in the wider analysis of the war's outcome explains the need of subsequent historians to focus on the grand strategic debates that seemingly gave it relevance to policymakers at the time.

A political analysis of the Middle Eastern front has developed from a desire to locate the First World War as one of the many causes of the troubles that have plagued the Middle East in the twentieth century. As a result, some historians create a direct teleology from the British invasion of Palestine, through the Balfour declaration and defeat of the Turks, to the establishment of Israel and the subsequent Arab conflicts. This focus can be seen in David Fromkin's *A Peace to End All Peace*, which borrows its title from Colonel (later Field Marshal) Archibald Wavell's dismissive comments on the Versailles conference.[46] The EEF's campaign was simply a backdrop against which could be painted the imperial political machinations of Lloyd George, Mark Sykes and François Georges Picot. This political focus of the historiography, derived from the difficulties in reconciling the campaign's military value, has paid little attention to the details of combat or the experiences of the soldiers who endured it.

The only individuals within the historiography of the Middle Eastern campaign to be given attention are the generals and politicians, as it was they who made, altered and implemented the policies that came to have such dramatic effects after the war. These figures have gained added notoriety as a result of the inherent romanticism of the campaign. This was a war where itinerant adventurers could float around Arabia and determine the course of whole nations and societies through a few bold acts. Foremost among them was T. E. Lawrence, a man who came to represent the heroic warrior that the First World War's industrial slaughter had supposedly eviscerated on the bloody fields of France and Flanders. His actions were also highlighted as an example of the changing nature of warfare, with the noted interwar military historian Basil Liddell Hart praising Lawrence's ability to hold Turkish reinforcements down on the Hejaz railway using only a few Arab irregulars.[47] More importantly, the figure of Lawrence helps to add a touch of mysticism and glamour to those studies trying to deal succinctly with the whole of the conflict. Lawrence's exploits also tapped into a fascination with the murky history of Britain's intelligence war in the Middle East, and the subsequent role of many intelligence figures in shaping the post-war imperial landscape of the region. As Yigal Sheffy has elucidated, many accounts of espionage operations have relied on a narrow collection of published sources, with little systematic work done in the archives. Moreover, the obsession with the intelligence war and the stoking of Arab nationalism through the revolt of Hussein, Sherif of Mecca, has done little to place this campaign into a wider context. The Arab revolt ultimately contributed little of military value to the overall course of the campaign in the Middle East against the Ottoman Empire.[48] In many respects the arguments over the political aspects of the revolt, and the integration of Hussein's sons, Feisal and Abdullah, into the post-war mandatory rule of Britain in Iraq and Transjordan, has given the event far greater historiographical prominence than it deserves.

Much of Lawrence's fame after the First World War was thanks to the activities of the American journalist Lowell Thomas, whose picture show 'With Allenby in Palestine and Lawrence in Arabia' began in London in August 1919. By 1922 Allenby had been dropped from the title as Lawrence's notoriety sold enough seats on its own. Thomas's subsequent book recalling Lawrence's picaresque adventures became the first entry in the hagiographical canon surrounding his life and exploits. The biographies by Liddell Hart and Robert Graves only served to enhance the image of a 'man of mystery', a leader of irregular warriors who inspired romantic devotion. The aura surrounding his character has been cemented in the popular imagination by later theatrical and cinematic incarnations. Of these the most notable have been Terence Rattigan's *Ross* (1960) and David Lean's *Lawrence of Arabia* (1962). Lawrence himself served to best publicize his exploits through his own writings, notably the *Seven Pillars of Wisdom*, which first appeared in 1935. As Charles Cruttwell illustrated in the 1930s, Lawrence was unique: 'no other figure carried so mysterious a glamour of romance, enhanced as much by his aloofness and wilfulness as by the superb prose in which he has recounted his story.'[49]

The historiography of the Middle Eastern theatre has thus been analysed through grand strategic, political, and imperial lenses, with a dash of heroic romanticism added along the way. The individual soldier that Keegan sought to bring to prominence is largely absent. The official history, for instance, only briefly touches upon the men of the EEF when they provide examples of tactical ingenuity or supreme courage, such as in the case of the Victoria Cross winner Lance-Corporal John Christie.[50] The intention of this book is to use the experiences of EEF soldiers in the Sinai and Palestine campaigns of 1916–18 to test a number of the historiographical assumptions made about the war in the Middle East and the creation and maintenance of morale in the British Army of the First World War. A central element in the analysis is a consideration of the multinational and multi-ethnic nature of the EEF. As Hew Strachan has argued, First World War historians, particularly those of an Anglophone background, need to consider the conflict within a comparative framework.[51] Too little attention is paid to the varying responses and commitment to the war from the constituent parts of the European empires that were involved. The EEF offers an opportunity to look at the war effort of the British Empire in a wider sense: it was the archetypal imperial army. By 1918, the EEF contained soldiers drawn from Britain, India, Australia, New Zealand, and the Caribbean, as well as troops from Britain's allies France and Italy. A unit recruited from Rarotongan boat people in the Pacific was even used to land supplies on the Palestinian coast. Furthermore, the British infantry and yeomanry contingents within the EEF represented the whole of the Union. Over the course of the campaign six divisions served in the theatre composed mainly of English soldiers and by the end of 1917 the force also contained 52nd (Lowland Scottish), 53rd (Welsh) and 10th (Irish) Divisions. The Egypt and Palestine campaigns thus involved men drawn from across George V's empire who cannot be aggregated simply into a common 'British' military experience.

Chapter 1 considers how this British imperial army coped with the rigours of combat in the Middle East. Not only did the EEF's soldiers endure harsh terrain, oppressive climate, and extensive problems of disease, they also had to face the brutal realities of modern, industrialized warfare. Tanks, gas, artillery, and aircraft all played a prominent role in combat in Sinai and Palestine, and in consequence the war on the Middle Eastern front bore a great resemblance to that fought on the fields of France and Flanders. Chapter 2 concentrates on one of the most frequently made assumptions about the Middle Eastern theatre: that soldiers were motivated to fight their Ottoman opponents by configuring the campaign as a crusade against Islam. An examination of the contemporary letters and diaries of British, Australian and New Zealand soldiers reveals that this assumption is erroneous. A religious fringe within the army did perceive the campaign in such terms, but they were only a minority. Instead most soldiers' interest was focused on the Islamic world that they encountered in the Middle East, demonstrating that instead of crusading rhetoric a strong 'vernacular orientalism' was present in early twentieth-century British culture. The construction of the campaign as a crusade was largely a product of the need for politicians to demonstrate to the British public that operations in Sinai and Palestine were relevant to the wider course of the First World War; an approach that interwar memoirists and novelists also adopted in order to boost their sales.

General Allenby's impact on the morale of the British imperial army in Egypt and Palestine has determined much of the course of the scholarly discussion of the EEF's campaign over the past 20 years. The existing historical interpretation, suggests that Allenby played a key role in reinvigorating the army's morale in 1917. The hagiography and historiography surrounding his period of command, however, needs to be reconsidered in a much more critical light. Chapter 3 adopts such an assessment of the army's supposed 'morale crisis' in 1917 arguing that the EEF remained combat effective. Instead of a crisis among the rank and file, it was the army's command and control system that had fallen to pieces under the strain of operations. Allenby's contribution was to import Western Front techniques of battle management and to professionalize the approach to command across the force.

In order to cover the wide range of units that served in the EEF during the First World War, this book uses three divisional case studies to examine in greater detail the battlefield experiences of the soldiers. Chapter 4 focuses on the British TF infantrymen who made up a large proportion of the army in the Middle East during the crucial battles of 1916–17. These soldiers made frequent recourse back to their civilian pasts as a means of enduring the war. In combat the Territorial battalions and divisions fostered a strong *esprit de corps* in order to motivate their men. This utilized the malleable nature of historic regimental identities within the British Army to allow soldiers to take part in shaping their units' traditions. Such a method of achieving combat motivation replicated the approach used by the regular British Army during its nineteenth- and twentieth-century imperial campaigns. Chapter 5 focuses on the Australian Light Horsemen and New Zealand Mounted Riflemen who comprised the EEF's mobile fighting arm. Anzac historiography has often emphasized the unique fighting characteristics of the Antipodean soldier, but with little reference to the wider military organizations the men served in. These mounted troops, in a parallel to British Territorials, interpreted the war in terms of their civilian backgrounds. Moreover, their combat effectiveness was enhanced by their perception of themselves as the elite of the imperial forces in the Middle East. The small unit fighting formations of the Australians and New Zealanders were in many respects well suited to the military challenges of war in the Sinai Desert and Judean hills, suggesting that the myth of Anzac mateship, reflecting many of the elements of post-1945 American primary group theory, had some validity in the Middle Eastern campaigns. Chapter 6 explores the process of Indianization that took place in 1918. Traditionally seen as a response to the German spring offensives on the Western Front, it was in fact an organized process arising from much longer-term manpower difficulties. The policy's impact on the army in Palestine is considered through an examination of the Indianization of 10th (Irish) Division. Training, particularly through patrols and raids, proved critical to inculcating the army's overall professional military identity into the newly arrived Indian units, ultimately producing the EEF's stunning success in September 1918 at the battle of Megiddo.

The EEF's campaigns in Sinai and Palestine provide an interesting opportunity to consider the recent cultural turn in military studies. This has taken many forms, with Santanu Das's groundbreaking critique of First World War literature bringing the material world of combatants to the forefront of discussion. For soldiers in the front line in France and Flanders, often up to their necks in glutinous mud and operating in an environment of ceaseless noise and restricted vision, the war was frequently experienced through the medium of touch. Along similar lines, Joanna Bourke has suggested that the study of morale needs to be reinterpreted in terms of soldiers' emotional and psychological landscapes. Fear dominated the battlefields of the twentieth century, and it was in dealing with such intense emotions that soldiers often faced mental collapse in battle.[52] More significant, in some respects, has been the burgeoning study in the first decade of the twenty-first century of the truly global nature of the two world wars. Much of this cultural reappraisal of military affairs has been driven by the complex campaigns in Afghanistan and Iraq since 2001, although the analysis often rests on essentialized, and at times basically crude, interpretations of Western and Eastern forms of warfare.[53] The impact of this cultural shift can be seen in the American Army's reliance on anthropological experts to try to develop a better understanding of the opponents it has faced in counter-insurgency operations in both countries, often with limited success.

The fighting of 1914–18 drew in people and societies from around the world, despite its military focus on the battlefields of North-West Europe.[54] A war which involved the British, French, Austro-Hungarian, German, Ottoman and Russian Empires possessed a seemingly inevitable logic of globalization; all would need to mobilize their subject populations, both physically and ideologically, and material resources in order to sustain their military efforts for four years of 'total' war. Although the EEF was organized and operated as a British Army formation, its constituent parts were drawn from around the British Empire. These soldiers were thus subject to a range of competing military identities and cultures that were not simply defined by their position in one of two power blocs. Warfare in Sinai and Palestine in the First World War was a complex business; the armies that fought there reflected this complexity, as did the combat motivations of their soldiers.[55]

1

The Nature of War in Sinai and Palestine

On 8 November 1917, during the EEF's swift advance northwards from the Gaza-Beersheba line, troopers of the 1/1st Warwickshire Yeomanry and 1/1st Worcester Yeomanry carried out one of the defining combat actions of the war in Palestine. The Warwickshire's commander, Lieutenant-Colonel Gray-Cheape, was ordered by Major-General John Shea, commanding 60th (London) Division, to charge a force of Turkish infantry and artillery located on a ridge near the village of Huj. One squadron was directed against the Turks' 75mm battery and another against the Turkish infantry. The charge swept the Turks from the ridge and cleared the way for an attack on the flank of a Turkish column retreating from Gaza. This was the first time that the sword had been used in the Palestinian theatre, with impressive results. The spectacle of the event led the military historian Cyril Falls, writing in the official account of the Middle Eastern campaign, to comment that 'the charge itself must ever remain a monument to the resolution and to that spirit of self-sacrifice which is the only beauty redeeming ugly war'.[1] The pace and excitement of the charge was captured in a painting by the noted battle artist Lady Elizabeth Butler in 1918. In her autobiography, Butler compared the action favourably with that of the Light Brigade on 25 October 1854, stating that the 'charge outshone the old Balaclava one we love to remember, and which differed from the Crimean exploit in that we not only captured all the enemy guns, but *held* them'.[2] As with the militarily insignificant charge of the Light Brigade, which often dominates popular perceptions of the battle of Balaclava and the Crimean War, so the action at Huj has overshadowed the discussion of the EEF's pursuit of the Turks northwards into the Judaean hills in late 1917. Butler based her painting on the eyewitness account of Colonel the Honourable Richard Preston and originally wanted bombastically to entitle it 'Jerusalem Delivered'. The affair at Huj, with Butler's help, has developed as one of the defining events of the EEF's campaign. It embodied all of the dashing, romantic and heroic elements that seemed to characterize war in the Middle East; these features appeared to set the EEF's experiences in the First World War apart from the mud, trenches and horror of the Western Front.[3]

This interpretation of the war in the Middle East is highly problematic. It demonstrates an overemphasis on the experiences of the mounted troops of the EEF, at the expense of examining the role played by the army's infantry. This was a point noted by a number of senior EEF officers who commented upon drafts of the official history being prepared in the 1920s. Lieutenant-General Edward Bulfin, commander of XXI Corps from June 1917 until the end of the war, felt that the cavalry dominated Falls's narrative. He stated that 'if the poor old Infantry had not cleared the ground and so made it possible to start in safety, they [the cavalry] never could have brought off their splendid effort, had the XXIst muddled their job – well, amen'.[4] Colonel Anderson, of 52nd (Lowland) Division, echoed this analysis, believing that his formation's hard fighting at the third battle of Gaza and in the Judaean hills was completely overshadowed by the exploits of the mounted troops.

The concentration on the mobile nature of the EEF's operations was fuelled by the contrast between the substantial advances made in the Middle East with the hundreds of yards bitterly won on the Western Front. The use of mounted troops and manoeuvre in Sinai and Palestine appeared to provide a solution to the attritional, static warfare brought about by strategic immobility in France and Flanders. This contrast, however, cannot be sustained. As Alan Kramer and Hew Strachan have demonstrated, the period of highest battle deaths on the Western Front was the opening months of the war in 1914, when armies were not ensconced behind defensive earthworks.[5] Similarly, the open warfare in the Middle East saw very high casualty rates in particular units. Huj itself demonstrates the bloodiness of mounted operations, particularly when carried out without supporting artillery or machine gun fire. Despite his ebullience even Falls had to acknowledge the dreadful cost of the action, which saw 70 of the 162 men involved becoming casualties, with both of the squadron commanders killed, along with the loss of over 100 horses. The fact that EEF soldiers were able to advance vast distances did not mean that their combat experience was benign.

Describing battle is a notoriously complicated and difficult task, clouded by the paucity of detailed information on combat in letter, diary and memoir collections. In some cases soldiers chose to omit references to the brutality of the front-line experience from their correspondence for fear of causing distress to loved ones at home.[6] Alternatively, such details may have revealed important military information that would have been removed by the censor. More importantly, the strains and activity of front-line life meant that descriptions of combat were written some time after the events occurred with many of the details fading in the minds of the participants. For some men suppressing the memories of combat was the only way of coping with them, and thus their personal writings tended to focus on the comradeship of their immediate military unit and the mundane aspects of army life. Even the official chronicler of the New Zealand Mounted Rifles' (NZMR) exploits, Arthur Briscoe Moore, found it difficult trying to compile his work only two years after the end of the war. He noted that:

> Modern battle, with the importance of concealment so necessary in every phase, is uninspiring to watch, as so little is visible to the eye. The spectacular incidents such as a bayonet charge usually occur at night or in the indistinct half light of dawn. The features which impress themselves most strongly on one's senses are the noises, the horrible sights, and the smells.[7]

As a result of the abstruse nature of combat much of the historiography of the experience of war in 1914–18 has had battle excised from it. In the case of Bavarian soldiers on the Western Front, Benjamin Ziemann argues that everyday life in the trenches was little removed from their former rural civilian existence. Both periods saw extreme exertion and danger interspersed with relative calm and relaxation. Similarly, John Bourne has argued that the working-class soldiers who formed the bulk of the British Army in 1914–18 were able to cope with the hardships of military life because it replicated the dirt, danger and boring repetition of the industrial work place with which they were familiar.[8] This approach ignores the central role that combat played in defining the lives of men sent to the front. Soldiers' training was geared towards preparing them for battle as the defining part of their military identity. It was this experience of combat that specifically set military life apart from civilian society; to ignore it creates a lacuna in our collective understanding of the First World War.

A number of attempts have been made to integrate battle into wider narratives on the soldier's experience in the twentieth century. Both John Ellis and Denis Winter, in accounts of life in the Western Front trenches, provide some insight into the reality of fighting a modern, industrial war. Winter, however, includes a caveat to his analysis, stating that 'battle was thus an experience which only those involved could understand, a madness and a terror and an elation, which qualified men for the world's most exclusive club'.[9] Given the considerable amount of large-scale warfare between nation states fielding mass conscript armies in the twentieth century, and the profusion of insurgencies and civil wars, it is possible to question the validity of this assertion on the exclusivity of soldiering. One of the most erudite discussions of combat is that in Stéphane Audoin-Rouzeau's work on French soldiers at war on the Western Front. His use of trench newspapers allows the soldiers' personal descriptions of bloody infantry attacks to come to the fore. It is, however, in studies of the Second World War that the experiences of the combatants have often best been captured. In his description of the battles fought on the islands of the South Pacific, Eric Bergerud clearly illustrates the brutality and horror of combat. In a more succinct manner, Stephen Bungay's study of the battle of El Alamein in 1942 addresses the peculiarities of the 8th Army's war in Egypt's Western Desert. These two works come closest to capturing the visceral nature of the soldier's experience of twentieth-century warfare. It is possible, however, to overstate the extent to which war takes on a universal nature. Niall Barr's attempt to compare the desert warfare experiences of the EEF in 1916–18 and the 8th Army in 1941–3 only briefly touches on those elements that made each campaign unique.[10] Although hardships faced by men in the desert were common to both wars, each conflict threw up specific problems that had to be overcome.

The war against the environment

Before EEF soldiers could engage the Turks in battle, they first had to learn how to fight in the terrain and climate of Egypt and Palestine. For some soldiers this 'war against the land' became an all-consuming part of their existence, dominating their daily routine and ability to fight.[11] For the army as a whole the landscape of the Middle East shaped the operations that it undertook. War in the desert of Sinai was very different from that in the hills of Judaea; strategic, operational and tactical approaches had to be adapted accordingly. The EEF went through two distinct phases in its struggle with nature: the first involved the crossing of Sinai and fighting in southern Palestine; the second encompassed combat in the Judaean hills, Jordan Valley and on the coastal plains of central Palestine.

The most prominent difficulty in the deserts of Sinai and southern Palestine was the oppressive heat. In May 1916, temperatures averaged 110°F (44°C) in tents and 120°F (49°C) at the outpost defences along the Suez Canal. The diaries of a number of combatants note that on many days temperatures rose to even higher levels. Quartermaster Sergeant G. E. Lee, of the 1/5th Suffolks, found that 130°F (54°C) was common in his tent in summer 1916. During sandstorms the problem became even more acute, with temperatures reaching 160°F (69°C).[12] Such heat made it impossible for men to carry out their duties during the daytime. In the 1/4th Northamptonshires, Sergeant W. Barron noted that 'between nine o'clock in the morning and four in the afternoon it was almost too hot to breathe and we used to strip naked and lay in the tent, trying to keep cool, but even then we simply poured out sweat, and our skin blistered'.[13] Battalions thus constructed their daily routine around the extreme heat of the desert. Defence work would be carried out early in the morning, with the men either eating or resting during the peak midday temperatures. Training would not resume again until the early evening and the night would be devoted to improving defensive works. It was left to the medical services of the EEF to ensure that troops were capable of taking part in operations in the desert. The Assistant Director Medical Services (ADMS) of 54th Division issued a series of guidelines which stressed the need to build up gradually the men's tolerance of the Sinai. He stressed that marches should only be carried out between 6 p.m. and 7 a.m. and that the men were to do so in shirt-sleeves without packs or greatcoats. In addition, men were to be warned not to rest with their backs to the sun, to smoke as little as possible, and to avoid eating tinned meat, which excited the thirst. All of this activity was expected to be carried out on a water allowance of two gallons a day; due to logistical difficulties the supply was rarely maintained at this level. By August 1916 the ADMS was having to develop innovative solutions to tackle the problems of heat exhaustion. In a letter to the Quartermaster General of 54th Division he suggested that luxuries such as doughnuts and ice cream could be provided for the men to alleviate their thirst.[14]

Despite these precautions the climate of Sinai gradually took its toll on the combat effectiveness of the EEF's soldiers. In May 1916, the 1/6th Essex experienced a prolonged heat wave while on outpost duty. Private R. J. France, a stretcher-bearer in the battalion, noted in his diary that 30 men went mad with thirst and overpowered the guard placed on the post's water tanks on the night of 16 May. The next day 60 cases of sunstroke were treated at the regimental aid post and France estimated that nearly 40 per cent of the battalion was incapable of engaging in its duties.[15] Conditions were often far worse for mounted troops who ventured out into the Sinai Desert away from the EEF's medical and support apparatus. A reconnaissance by the 6th Australian Light

Horse (ALH) Regiment to Bir Bayud had to be called off as the heat became unbearable. Four officers and 32 men were evacuated to hospital suffering from sunstroke, and nearly all the regiment's 500 horses were unfit for duty, taking 3 days to recover. The unrelenting high temperatures found in Sinai and southern Palestine therefore acted to severely curtail the EEF's ability to conduct operations.

Heat was not the only factor that undermined the endurance of soldiers. Sand proved a constant irritation to the men of the EEF and references to it abound in letters, diaries and memoirs. As Lieutenant-Colonel T. Gibbons, commanding the 1/5th Essex, noted after the war:

> The sand of the Sinai peninsula is surely the finest in the world. It gets into everything, one's hair, eyes and ears were full of it. So was the food. It got in between the layers of the soles of one's boots, gradually forming a lump inside as hard as stone. It stopped every watch in camp. It was constantly on the move in the daytime, blown along by a wind which got up just before the sun and went down with it.[16]

It was the effect sand had on the men's food that caused the greatest annoyance. Private Albert Surry, of the 1/7th Essex, recalled that his battalion's camp was inundated regularly by sand drifts and as a result 'eating was made the reverse from pleasure'.[17] An additional problem was the glare produced by the sun on the sand, which placed a considerable strain on soldiers' eyes. Only a small number of men were lucky enough to be issued with goggles.[18] The unvarying colour of the desert created a landscape that dulled the senses of many soldiers. One unit's history noted that Sinai 'exuded monotony, [and] it engendered loneliness'.[19] In such surroundings it became difficult to maintain the morale of the EEF's troops. For the majority Sinai was a dull wilderness where there was not even any combat to break up the tediousness of army life. From a military point of view the desert sand proved an even greater problem. Not only did it get into the clothing and food of soldiers but it also damaged their rifles, clogging the main springs and causing misfires. As a result 1/4th Essex continually pestered their brigade to issue them with rifle covers in 1916.[20]

The notorious khamsin, a hot desert wind that blew across Sinai whipping up sandstorms, made desert life even more unbearable.[21] Being hit by one of these storms was 'like a hot blast from an oven', with visibility reduced to a few yards while the particles of sand stung the men's skin. The intensity and surreal nature of enduring a khamsin was captured in the memoirs of Sergeant Tom Crase, serving in the 3rd ALH Regiment:

> The wind was searing hot even at night time and must have been at least 100 M.P.H. The desert gravel was lit up with electricity, and when the airborn gravel hit the ground there were sparks flying everywhere. There were electric flares about 4″ long on the end of our horses ears, our horses were tethered to the horse lines with light metal chains and all these chains were ablaze with electricity. If we held up our hands each finger tip had a 2″ electric flare on its end. In all the place was lit up like a large city.[22]

Sandstorms could cause considerable damage to the EEF's equipment and logistical train. At Sidi Bishr camp in Egypt 500 tents were flattened during a khamsin in January 1916. These events left the EEF's soldiers in no doubt that nature still ruled the Sinai Peninsula.

The desert of Sinai did not lend itself to the military engineering projects attempted by the EEF along the Suez Canal. The decision to move the defences from a line along the Canal out into the desert in late 1915 meant that considerable construction work had to be undertaken by units stationed at each post. Soldiers found trench digging was 'especially tedious' as the soft sand continually fell back into the area being excavated. As Quartermaster Sergeant Lee elucidated, trenches required to be 7 feet deep and 2 feet wide would have to be dug to a depth of 25 feet in order to take account of the sand collapsing back in. Timber shuttering was then used to revet the edge of the trench to keep it stable. It would take a party of 30 men 5 hours to dig only 2 yards of trench. Such work would then be rendered useless once a strong wind blew the sand back in.[23] Labour duties on the Canal defences seemed doubly pointless by mid-1916; the Turks were far away and any defensive work was soon obliterated by the desert. Such conditions placed considerable strain on the endurance of the EEF's soldiers.

Coupled with the sand and heat of the desert was the irritation caused by the wildlife in Sinai and southern Palestine. The desert was not an entirely barren wilderness and a number of creatures flourished in the region.[24] While serving on the Canal defences Quartermaster Sergeant Lee recorded in his diary seeing foxes, cobras, sand snakes, locusts, eagles, vultures, desert hares, desert mice, chameleons and scarab beetles. In general, encounters with most of these animals added some excitement to the mundane routine of military life. It was the legions of flies that made the men's existence miserable. Flies plagued all armies that fought in Sinai, as soldiers brought with them their rubbish and soon left dead bodies upon which the insects flourished. Lieutenant Bertram Delpratt, serving in the 5th ALH Regiment, explained in a letter to his sister that the flies made it almost impossible to eat any food, the problem being as bad as he had experienced at Gallipoli. Flies were such a ubiquitous feature of life in the desert that Lieutenant H. G. Mansfield, of the 1/6th Essex, wrote a poem about them, included in a collection of his poetry published after the war. In his doggerel he recalled the annoyance that flies caused:

> When you're tired right out and full of thirst.
> That's when they come along:
> That's when this beastly tribe accurst
> Advantage take, and do their worst,
> Wronging you till you think you'll burst –
> Buzzing their hateful song.
>
> Tickling you till you tear your hair,
> This horrid little pest:
> Causing you both to grouse and glare,
> Lose your wool and almost swear,
> Kick the bucket and, go to – where?
> And *all* done with such zest.

They come around so full of glee,
All hungry, strong and well, –
Just so you're going to sleep may be
In the blessed shade of an olive tree,
While the barometer stands at one-twenty-three
About as hot as Hell.[25]

Attempts were made by the medical services to control the prevalence of flies around camps and outposts, but these largely proved fruitless. As Captain E. B. Hinde, a medical officer with 1/2nd East Anglian Field Ambulance attached to 54th Division, noted in his diary, poison was put down all over his camp, but it was almost impossible to exterminate the flies at a level that kept pace with the rate of breeding.[26]

Flies were just an irritation for the men of the EEF compared to the barren nature of the terrain in Sinai and southern Palestine. The lack of cover meant that a number of major offensives had to be launched against Turkish positions across open ground. Major-General Steuart Hare, commanding 54th Division, noted in his diary that the assault by his troops on 19 April 1917 at the second battle of Gaza crossed 'country without a scrap of cover'.[27] This fact was echoed by Major W. E. Wilson, second in command of the 1/5th Essex, who described the ground traversed by his battalion at the first battle of Gaza (26–27 March 1917) as resembling a billiard table.[28] The absence of water proved a significant impediment to the EEF's operations in this terrain. This forced EEF units, particularly mounted ones, to remain within close contact of water sources and restricted the army's freedom of movement. Lieutenant-General Philip Chetwode, commander of XX Corps from June 1917 to the end of the war, stressed this problem in his correspondence with Lieutenant-General George MacMunn, co-author of the first volume of the official history. Chetwode felt that the narrative had to emphasize how much operations were curtailed by the landscape and lack of water, otherwise students in future years would wonder why the seemingly beaten Turkish Army was often left alone by the EEF and not destroyed, as would have been the case in 'normal country'. He stated clearly that 'nearly every fight was a fight for water, and if you did not drive the enemy off the water you had to go back to where you started from and begin all over again'.[29] In the deserts of the Middle East military operations, rather than utilizing the terrain, were instead often dictated by it.

The advance northwards into Palestine following the defeat of the Turks at the third battle of Gaza (31 October–7 November 1917), introduced the men of the EEF to a more verdant landscape. Wild flowers were found on many of the hillsides, with Lieutenant-Colonel Gibbons describing the area around the Wadi Ballut as looking like a 'big rock garden'.[30] In addition, the coastal plain of Palestine was highly cultivated, with orchards and vineyards in abundance. All of this was in stark contrast to the barren sands of the desert where the EEF had spent the past 22 months. The heavy rains that struck in the winter of 1917–18 soon altered this seemingly idyllic setting. Corporal W. M. Town, of the 1/5th Essex, was stationed on a hill overlooking the Auja River north of Jaffa in December 1917. He recalled that 'it rained almost incessantly day and night' and that during the daytime 'we strove to get shelter beneath sodden blankets'.[31] At Yebna, Corporal Robert Chandler, of the Australian and New Zealand Mounted Division's (ANZMD) 1st Signal Squadron, recorded that 12 inches of rain fell in 10 days, which was equivalent to the region's average annual rainfall.[32] The 3rd ALH Regiment's camp near Bethlehem received so much rain in March 1918 that the horse lines were standing in a pool 3 inches deep. In some cases the rain was so bad that trenches began to collapse under the flow of water. One such incident led to the death of a member of the NZMR Machine Gun Squadron in December 1917.[33] The heavy rains turned the coastal plain of Palestine into a sea of mud, making it difficult for men, animals and vehicles to cross it. Corporal Town noted that during the march of 161st Brigade to Yazur the mud was knee-deep in many places, and that 'men constantly fell over and had to be hauled to their feet'.[34] Private Surry described the same march as leaving a memory of crossing 'oceans of mud on ploughed and sodden ground [that] remains a nightmare of misery'.[35] Such scenes echo the experiences of soldiers on the Western Front.

The Judaean hills also introduced troops to freezing temperatures not yet experienced in the Middle East. While at a rest camp near Bethlehem in February 1918, Lieutenant Stanley Prince, of the 3rd ALH Regiment, suffered from the coldest weather he had ever been through. He wrote to his mother that 'it was absolutely impossible to keep warm try as you liked by running along on foot for several hundreds of yards, but on mounting you felt twice as cold'.[36] Combat in these hills was particularly trying on the physical endurance of the EEF's soldiers. During the final advance at the battle of Megiddo, begun on 19 September 1918, the 1/4th Northamptonshires had to cross a series of ridges in order to close on the Turkish positions. By the end of the battle the battalion war diary noted that as a result of fighting in such rugged terrain 'the men were utterly exhausted and were physically incapable of proceeding further'.[37]

The Judaean hills were also a difficult location in which to build defences. The rocky ground did not lend itself to the construction of trenches and thus the EEF's infantry had to build sangars, similar to the defensive positions used on the North-West Frontier of India, to create a series of interlinked posts. As a poem by Lieutenant Mansfield noted, sangars provided only limited protection during Turkish bombardments. He captured the significant danger posed from rock splinters sent flying by exploding shells:

> And then, there ain't no place to 'op
> When the crumps they come along –
> No trenches deep where you can stop,
> No dug-outs stout and strong.
>
> Nothin' but bloomin' piles of stone
> Built up among the rocks;
> And nasty bits long ways are blown,
> And give some 'orrid knocks.[38]

Lieutenant W. F. Cook, the 1/6th Essex's transport officer, was so concerned by the manner in which rock fragments enhanced the danger of a Turkish bombardment that he felt 54th Division would not be able to hold its position at Mejdel Yaba in the Judaean foothills.[39] As with the Sinai Desert the terrain in Palestine had an impact upon the operations carried out by the EEF. In the case of the Judaean hills the rocky ground affected tactical decisions made at divisional level and below. The shortages of water found in the desert and southern Palestine, by contrast, shaped the strategic decisions made by the EEF's Commander-in-Chief and corps commanders.

The most difficult conditions were faced by those soldiers serving in the Jordan Valley in 1918. Its location, nearly 1,300 feet below sea level, meant that the valley and surrounding mountains experienced extremes of climate. Sergeant Crase's memoirs provide a succinct description of the conditions faced by the men of the 3rd ALH Regiment:

During the summer months the temperature is around 120°/125° Fahrenheit [49°/51°C] every day, never a breath of wind, just flat, dead calm. Also there is a heavy evaporation mist over the Dead Sea. The soil is a powdery grey semi-clay and when we were moving mounted, it churns up to a heavy type of powder. As there is no wind it hangs over you all day and you can scrape the dust off your face with your finger nails.[40]

The arduous climate in the valley was satirized in a poem by Major Archie Dick, also serving in the 3rd ALH, which he entitled 'Beauty Spots'. Although the intensity of the heat by the Jordan River was reminiscent of that found in Sinai, once men began the trek out of the valley back to Jerusalem they found that temperatures fell rapidly. In half an hour of marching the fall could be as much as 30°F (15°C). Corporal Edwin McKay, of the Auckland Mounted Rifles (AMR), recounted how, when making the trip in reverse, he would leave Jerusalem clad in a balaclava, scarf, and greatcoat and by the time he reached the valley floor he would be stripped down to his shirt. Combat in such conditions proved particularly strenuous. The ANZMD found that its combat performance at Amman during the first Transjordan Raid in March–April 1918 was blunted by the extreme weather encountered in the Mountains of Moab. A report by Major C. Bolingbroke, of the 5th ALH Regiment, blamed the raid's failure on the rain and cold encountered in the hills, which demoralized the men, who were equipped and clothed for the heat of the Jordan Valley. The wet weather also robbed them of their mobility on the narrow, sodden tracks found in the mountains.[41]

The landscape and the climate of Sinai and Palestine thus imposed considerable hardships on the men of the EEF and also served to restrict the operations that they could undertake. The soldier's first task on the Middle Eastern battlefield was to learn how to live and fight in the harsh and inhospitable terrain of the region. Acclimatization took a considerable amount of time and required much physical training. The EEF was fortunate that for the first seven months of 1916 combat operations in Sinai were relatively limited allowing newly arrived units and exhausted Gallipoli veterans to adjust. From the battle of Romani, fought in early August 1916, onwards the EEF's primary task would be engaging the Turks in battle.

The reality of combat

Combat lies at the heart of the EEF's wartime experiences in the Middle East.[42] It was an experience that many soldiers found hard to record in detail in their letters, diaries and memoirs; in many cases references are only brief, but provide a glimpse of the intensity, violence, and horror of battle in Sinai and Palestine. In his description of the 161st Brigade's advance on the Ali Muntar hill at First Gaza, on 26 March 1917, Corporal Town's memoirs go some way to capturing a sense of the rapid pace of an infantry attack:

> Men were gasping for breath, stumbling forward heavily under their loads, or giving a shriek and crumbling up into shapeless heaps – running forward with teeth clenched, and wheezing breath, stopping to undo a wounded fellow's equipment, or rolling over on their backs to get a sip of water from their bottles, if they were lucky enough to have any.[43]

The physical exertions involved in fighting coupled with the arid climate of the Middle East meant that many men found themselves suffering from debilitating thirst during periods of combat. Private Surry felt that the dreadful effect of such thirst on soldiers could only be understood by those who had seen battle at close quarters.[44] This difficulty was often exacerbated by the problems involved in getting water supplies up to the men at the firing line. During First Gaza the men of 1/10th Londons, providing covering fire from the Sheikh Abbas ridge, had to survive on only 1 bottle of water for 30 hours. The situation was even more acute for the ANZMD at Romani, where the 1st ALH Regiment's soldiers survived on their water bottles for 35 hours and the regiment's horses were not watered for 56 hours.[45]

It was often the sound of battle that was one of the most significant and enduring elements of combat for the participants. Following the defeat of a Turkish force at Romani on 4 August, the ANZMD was tasked with pursuing the enemy column as it fell back from the oases of western Sinai. During an engagement at Bir el Abd, Ion Idriess, a trooper in 5th ALH Regiment and a prolific post-war author, noted that 'the air was just one sizzling hiss – flying bullets at point-blank range possess an awful sound'.[46] As on the Western Front it seemed to the men of the EEF that machine guns dominated the battlefield. At Third Gaza, while advancing on Tel el Saba near Beersheba, Sergeant Crase's section came under sustained fire from the Turkish defenders. In his memoirs he recalled that 'their machine guns had their ranges to a T and bullets were spraying up the dust right along the line of advance, they were cracking like stockwhips around us, when you hear those whipcracks, you know they are mighty close to you'.[47] The intensity of action that machine gunners saw in battle in the Middle East can be seen by the amount of ammunition expended. The 163rd Machine Gun Company fired 16,000 rounds in only half an hour while supporting a raid on part of the Gaza defences in July 1917. Even in quiet periods on the line the company still fired 1,200 to 2,000 rounds a day, mainly at indirect, overhead targets, intended to harass Turkish soldiers in rear areas.[48] The fire of machine guns and rifles created a hellish scene on the battlefield. At the capture of the Turkish post at Rafah on 9 January 1917, the small arms fire of the NZMR was recorded as having 'made the Redoubt appear like a smoking furnace'.[49] Attacking through such intense fire produced very different reactions from soldiers. Trooper John Hull, of the AMR, succinctly captured the sensation in a letter to his brother describing his regiment's advance at Romani:

> Plenty of bullets came as we got into action especially after we dismounted and went forward on foot. When one is going through a hail of bullets the sensation is like walking through a rain storm. You put your head down and go on. It was so awfully hot that noone could get more than a walk on.[50]

Combat could be so sustained and intense that troops found their equipment was often not up to the standard required. Private Surry, of the 1/7th Essex, having fallen back from Ali Muntar during First Gaza, found himself attached to the 2/4th Royal West Surrey Regiment, and became involved in a prolonged exchange of fire with the Turks that saw 'our rifles become so hot that it was with difficulty [that] we fired them'.[51]

On occasion battle in the Middle East could return to more primitive forms, with men engaged in hand-to-hand combat. At Second Gaza only a small number of men from the 1/5th Norfolks reached the Turkish trenches, of whom 2 officers and 14 other ranks were left behind when the rest of the battalion was forced to withdraw. This group became engaged in a continuous firefight with the Turks, using two Lewis guns to keep them off. Once the ammunition for these had run out the Turks charged the position and a bloody bayonet fight ensued. Of the original 16 defenders only 8 made it back to the British lines.[52] Trooper Idriess's description of 5th ALH Regiment's fighting among the cactus hedges on the outskirts of Gaza on 26 March illuminates what close quarter combat felt like to those involved:

> It was just berserk slaughter. A man sprang at the closest Turk and thrust and sprang aside and thrust again and again – some men howled as they rushed, others cursed to the shivery feeling of steel on steel – the grunting breaths, the gritting teeth and the staring eyes of the lunging Turk, the sobbing scream as a bayonet ripped home. The Turkish battalion simply melted away: it was all over in minutes.[53]

Hand-to-hand combat was, however, rare during the EEF's campaigns; bayonet wounds accounted for only 0.5 per cent of wounds during the First World War. Nevertheless, preparation for close combat remained a key element in troops' training. As Paul Hodges has argued, this produced a fetishization of the bayonet in the British Army, which shaped its approach to combat. Given its infrequency in battle it is possible to question the propensity with which accounts of bayonet fighting occur in soldiers' memoirs. To a certain extent this is a reflection of a received image of the masculine warrior, which veterans felt their personal accounts had to conform to.[54]

Major engagements, such as Romani, the three battles of Gaza, the Transjordan Raids, and Megiddo, were not the only occasions on which EEF soldiers went through intense combat. At the level of the company or battalion minor actions could take on particular significance, either due to losses suffered or resistance posed by the opponent. For the

1/4th Northamptonshires one of their bloodiest and most fraught battles occurred at the village of Wilhelma, south of the Auja River on 27 November 1917, after the Turks had retreated from the Gaza-Beersheba line. The battalion's positions were assaulted twice in the afternoon by a Turkish force estimated to be between 2,000 and 3,000 men strong. In order to avoid falling back the Northamptonshire's commander, Lieutenant-Colonel J. G. Brown, ordered two platoons to launch attacks on the flanks of the Turks, which eventually caused the much larger Turkish force to withdraw. The engagement cost the battalion 20 men killed and another 73 wounded.[55] Both of the two Victoria Crosses won by men of the 54th Division in Palestine were awarded for small-scale patrol actions fought in the Judaean foothills along the Jerusalem-Jaffa line. The first was attained by Lance-Corporal John Christie, of the 1/11th Londons, for single-handedly bombing a Turkish communication trench on Bald Hill on 27 December 1917, allowing the battalion's position to be consolidated. This was followed by the bravery of Private Samuel Needham, of the 1/5th Bedfordshires, at Kufr Qasim on the night of 10–11 September 1918. The patrol that he was part of was attacked by a large body of Turks and was quickly overwhelmed. Needham chose to fight on and by maintaining a rapid fire on the Turkish force he allowed his patrol time to retreat with their wounded.[56] Such small unit actions could often be harrowing for those taking part, as they felt isolated from the support of larger formations.

The overriding experience of combat, whether in major battles or patrol actions, was a pervasive sense of confusion among the participants. The disorientation involved in battle was often more prevalent in actions that saw EEF men advancing from their own positions onto the largely unknown defences of the Turks. This was particularly the case at Third Gaza where 54th Division attacked along the coastal side of the town and then attempted to turn eastwards into the Turkish positions. This led to seven days of intermittent combat as the division attempted to build up enough manpower and artillery support to finally rush the defences. The confusion of the final assault, made on 7 November 1917, was recorded in the diary of Sapper E. C. Thompson, serving with the division's Royal Engineer field company:

> The shrapnel barrage commences and then over go the Bedfords and Londons shouting like mad. We follow with our wire. We cannot see where we are going for smoke from bursting shells and the noise of the barrage and machine guns is deafening. On we go until we see the Bedfords digging in, then on through them over the ridge and in with our pickets and out with the wire. Nobody notices in the excitement that Abdul is not answering our fire and it is not until we are consolidated that we realise that Abdul has cleared out and has sold us a pup.[57]

Such confusion could have a significant impact upon the ability of military formations to conduct coherent operations. In the initial assault made by 54th Division on 1 November, the battalions of 163rd Brigade became disorientated in the smoke and dust produced by the British barrage. The 1/8th Hampshires' attack split in two directions under intense Turkish machine gun, artillery and mortar fire. As a consequence of this, two companies of the 1/4th Norfolks followed the 1/8th Hampshires and also lost direction. Some semblance of order was only restored once the battalion commanders reached the front line among the captured Turkish trenches. Despite the EEF's growing combat effectiveness and improved training in 1917, the events at Third Gaza demonstrate that tactical difficulties could still arise from the uncertain and unpredictable nature of the modern battlefield.[58]

For the individual soldier fear was often a constant part of the battle experience. Most of the men in the EEF were Territorial, volunteer, or conscript soldiers and were unlikely to have had prior experience of combat before they saw service in the First World War. The violence, horror and danger that they encountered in battle were not comparable to any aspects of their pre-war civilian lives. For Trooper Beet Algar, of the Wellington Mounted Rifles (WMR), it was during the attack on Rafah that he first realized how terrifying battle could be. On this occasion the absence of any cover as his regiment rushed towards the Turkish trenches left him with a deep sense of vulnerability in the face of the machine gun and rifle fire directed at his unit. For many soldiers it was not death from bullets or shells that caused the greatest worry but the risk of being severely wounded. Private Surry discussed the dangers of battle with his comrades in the 1/7th Essex who unanimously agreed that dying quickly would be a blessing compared to a lingering death from wounds under the hot sun of Palestine.[59] In some cases the exhaustion of continuous combat could exacerbate the men's fears. Corporal Town, of the 1/5th Essex, recalled that after 48 hours of marching and fighting at First Gaza, the 'nerves [of his company's soldiers] were badly frayed' and one officer 'seemed at the end of his tether'.[60] On occasion some soldiers were driven to the limits of what they could physically and mentally endure. In August 1917, Lieutenant Webb, serving with 271st Brigade Royal Field Artillery (RFA) attached to 54th Division, attempted to shoot himself. Captain V. H. Bailey, a staff officer with 270th Brigade RFA, was able to intervene and prevented the suicide.[61]

In a minority of cases soldiers thrived on the experience of combat. Finding excitement in battle was one means of psychologically coping with the extreme experiences that had to be endured.[62] Trooper Idriess recalled such a sensation while riding up to the Katia oasis shortly after the British garrison had been destroyed by a Turkish attack in April 1916. He wrote that 'it always comes just when I am going into action – a curious exciting thrill, tinged with a deadly coldness'.[63] It was more often the case that men simply chose to think about anything but combat when engaged in battle. Trooper Algar stated that as he went into action at Magdhaba, a small Turkish post to which the garrison of El Arish had retreated in December 1916, he had no fear at all. This was a result of the fact that he was fixated on acquiring Turkish Army souvenirs from any dead or captured Turks he came across; in particular he wanted a belt buckle which depicted a crescent moon and star. Suppressing fear, either through distracting oneself or revelling in the thrill of combat, was thus a form of mental coping strategy that allowed soldiers to live with the brutal realities of war in the Middle East.[64]

The continuous presence of death around the battlefield remained the principal horror of war for most soldiers. Major F. S. Hammond, of the 1/11th Londons, noted in his diary when going over the Turkish trenches after Third Gaza that the area 'was just appalling both to the eyes and the nose, and the dead Turks everywhere were just ghastly'.[65] From his battalion's position in the trenches opposite Gaza, Lieutenant-Colonel Gibbons could observe the area over which 54th Division had advanced on

19 April 1917, during the disastrous Second Gaza assault. He recounted that the dead of the Northamptonshire and Norfolk battalions 'lay very thick on the slopes, as if they had been washed up on a shelving beach by a high tide and left there by the ebb'.[66] In battle, however, the sensory detachment illustrated by Gibbons was not possible as the sights and smells of death were much closer. Private Surry stated that during 161st Brigade's attack on Ali Muntar he and another soldier were met by a gruesome sight on entering the enemy's trenches. The two of them had to 'climb over whole rows of bodies piled two and three feet high', and he reported that 'it was simply awful and the stench was simply chronic'.[67] Due to the heat of Sinai and Palestine the horrific effects of death were often accentuated. Decomposition occurred rapidly, with bodies becoming bloated in the sun and turning black after only 2 hours. Captain Bailey recalled the vile nature of the task facing those men detailed to clear the dead from the battlefield after Third Gaza. He observed a group of soldiers removing a dead Turk on a piece of netting, but due to the rate of decomposition the body simply dripped through the wire.[68]

It is clear from the accounts examined here that some letters sent home to friends and relatives provided lurid portrayals of battle. As Helen MacCartney and Martha Hanna, have demonstrated the bonds between the home front and the front line were very strong. This correspondence allowed civilians to gain a clear picture of the reality of the First World War combat. Notions of front-line soldiers hiding the realities of war from their loved ones are often overemphasized, with many men choosing to paint an accurate picture of their lives at the front.[69] Lieutenant J. H. Jewson, of the 1/4th Norfolks, provided such realistic descriptions of the brutality he witnessed at Second Gaza that he felt he had to write to apologize for upsetting his father.[70] Warfare in the Middle East could be as intense, savage, and horrific as any engagements that took place in France or Flanders, and this experience needs to be considered as central to any account of the EEF's wartime service.

Technological warfare comes to the Middle East

Many aspects of the campaign in Sinai and Palestine were characteristic of modern industrialized warfare; the Middle Eastern theatre can, therefore, be seen as emblematic of twentieth-century conflict, in much the same way as the Western Front.[71] As in France and Flanders some of the EEF's war was spent in trenches. Between Second and Third Gaza, the EEF was confined to a trench line opposite the town while the army's manpower and equipment strengths were brought up to the levels required to break through the Turkish defences. In contrast to the Western Front this trench network had an open right flank, resting on the desert. The scarcity of water in the region meant that it was very difficult for attacks to be launched over it. On this part of the line the EEF's mounted troops were vital, providing security along the unprotected flank. The distance between the Turkish and British lines varied greatly along the Gaza front. Opposite the town the lines were only 400 yards apart, but in the east of the position the distance increased to 2,500 yards. The size of the gap and the general inactivity of the Turkish Army meant that the EEF's soldiers often did not have to take the same front-line precautions as the men of the BEF. During an inspection of the 1/5th Bedfordshires' trenches on 20 June 1916 the battalion's adjutant was able to keep his head and shoulders above the parapet for 15 minutes without being sniped. Similarly, the Reverend E. C. Mortimer, attached to 1/4th Essex, recalled that he would walk back from the front line to the regimental dressing station along the parapet. Such lax trench discipline was to cause a worryingly high casualty rate in those EEF units sent to the Western Front in mid-1918.[72]

Nevertheless, much of the routine and organization of trench life was shared between the European and Middle Eastern theatres.[73] Divisions were rotated between the line and the rear for rest periods, to allow them to cope with the strains of combat. When divisions were in the line they would move brigades and battalions through front sectors and reserve areas. It does not appear, however, that there is any evidence of a 'live and let live' system in the Middle East, as was evident in some quiet sectors on the Western Front. This was a result of the relatively limited nature of combat along the Gaza-Beersheba position, in comparison to that in France and Flanders. There was thus little need for a systematic means of restricting the intensity of fighting. In order to ensure that there was a continuity of action at the front, battalion commanders were ordered to keep detailed trench diaries containing information on alterations made to the defences, the trench routine, patrolling and action by the Turks. These were passed on to new units taking over the battalion's position. However, not every formation fulfilled this role to the best of their abilities. The 1/5th Norfolks' war diary was keen to note that the trenches they took over from the 1/4th King's Own Scottish Borderers in June 1917 were in 'a dilapidated state, communication trenches very poor and practically non-existent'. In contrast, some areas saw particularly sophisticated defences built. 54th Division issued a memorandum to its battalions in late April 1917 instructing them to construct dummy trenches and machine gun posts. These were intended to mislead the Turks, who would hopefully waste their ammunition on attempting to destroy them.[74] Construction work dominated much of the time spent at the front. While holding the line, a battalion would normally keep 25 per cent of its strength in the trenches as a day garrison, with the remaining men working in shifts to improve the defences. During the first 17 days of May 1917 the 1st ALH Regiment built 1,015 yards of fire trench, 865 yards of communication trench, 3,000 yards of wire entanglements and 31 machine gun emplacements. As Lieutenant-Colonel Gibbons noted, this labour activity was often resented by his men in the 1/5th Essex as it dominated their supposed rest periods out of the front line. Consequently, moving out of the trenches elicited little elation from the men of the battalion.[75]

As on the Western Front in 1914–15 the shift to trench warfare opposite Gaza was a product of the strategic immobility caused by the increased destructiveness of modern weapons. Of all the weapon systems deployed on the battlefields of the First World War it was artillery that caused the greatest number of casualties.[76] The prominent role that artillery units played in the battles fought in France and Flanders was mirrored in the Middle East. The engagements fought in Sinai in 1916 involved relatively small amounts of shelling, with an emphasis instead placed on the role of mounted troops. Once the Turks had retreated behind their defences at Gaza, the EEF's senior commanders decided to deploy their artillery en masse to act as a force multiplier. At Second Gaza the shelling of the Turkish trenches dwarfed any previous battle in the region. For example, 54th Division's artillery fired over 8,500 shells during the 5 days of action, including nearly 5,600 shells on 19 April alone. As Lieutenant-Colonel Clive Garsia, the former General Staff Officer, Grade One (GSO1), of 54th Division, elucidated in his analysis of the battle, the EEF's barrage was nonetheless insufficient to deal with the strength of defences encountered.[77] The weaknesses of the EEF's artillery preparations were, however, known to Murray before he chose to attack. The commander of the Eastern Force's artillery units, Major-General S. C. U. Smith, protested against the use of a 2-hour barrage. He later wrote that:

> This bombardment was the most futile thing possible resulting, as I had stated, only in warning the enemy of the point of attack and in gross waste of ammunition. The fire trenches were the object of the bombardment and to think that any intelligent enemy will hold his front line trenches in strength when there is no threat of an infantry attack was ridiculous – considering the distance apart of the opposing forces.[78]

Similar concerns were also expressed prior to Second Gaza by divisional artillery commanders. Brigadier-General H. G. Sandilands, Commander, Royal Artillery, of 54th Division, disputed the order to carry out a 2-hour barrage with Major-General Hare, the divisional commander. He argued that he did not have sufficient reserves of shells and due to the distance involved he could not guarantee that the Turkish redoubts would be hit.[79] Nevertheless the division attacked and suffered severe casualties in the ensuing fighting.

Following Second Gaza and the stagnation of the front the EEF began to develop a larger and more sophisticated artillery arm. Allenby's organizational reforms in July 1917 saw the creation of a mounted corps and two infantry corps; in the latter case both corps were given heavy artillery groups. These changes ensured that the growing professionalization of the British Army's approach to warfare on the Western Front was exported to the Middle East.[80] Over the course of the summer divisional artillery units began to experiment with techniques then in use in the BEF, such as flash spotting for counter-battery work. At Third Gaza the artillery took a central role in the planning and execution of the battle. The preliminary bombardment began on 27 October, increasing in intensity on 29 October when Royal Navy warships provided additional firepower. The artillery plan of XXI Corps, which was tasked with assaulting Gaza, was carefully devised and involved each battery being given 1,000-yard squares in which they could engage targets at certain times of day. The six-day bombardment was also used to ensure that the registration of targets was accurate for the final assault.[81] The resulting bombardment was the largest outside of the European theatre in the First World War, with the density of fire rivalling that of the preliminary bombardment for the battle of the Somme in 1916. For example, 54th Division's artillery alone fired over 46,000 shells from 27 October to 1 November. After the initial assault it then expended another 64,000 rounds over 6 days of fighting.[82] At the front line this artillery support proved particularly useful for battalions that became bogged down in the Gaza defences. A report by 163rd Brigade noted that as a result of the continuous British shelling of the enemy they received little interference from Turkish snipers. In some cases, however, the barrage appeared to be erratic, with rounds falling among advanced British infantry units. This may have been the result of battalions becoming caught up in the excitement of battle and advancing too far at too rapid a pace. In general the intensity of the artillery fire and its precision acted as a fillip to the confidence of the attacking infantry.[83]

Coming under Turkish artillery fire was an experience that EEF men dreaded. The barrages put down by Turkish guns were rarely as intense as those fired by the British, particularly in engagements after Third Gaza. Nevertheless, enemy shelling could at times match the sophistication of that done by the EEF. While fighting at Ras el Nagb the war diary of the Canterbury Mounted Rifles (CMR) noted that 'a noticeable feature was the extreme accuracy of the Turkish artillery and the rapidity with which they changed from one target to another'.[84] A similar experience was undergone by the 1/11th Londons, who were shelled for 2 hours on 3 November, while occupying poorly constructed slip trenches captured from the Turks to the west of Gaza. Major Hammond stated that the bombardment 'nearly drove the men mad'.[85] In the 1/5th Suffolks Captain H. C. Wolton felt that being fired upon by high explosive shells was a veritable hell. He also highlighted the sense of helplessness that soldiers in fixed positions experienced when they came under artillery fire:

> Being shelled is a peculiar sensation. I think it is much more trying when one is passively sitting down in a dugout making no attempt to hit back. One is then comparatively safe. But when one is advancing the sensation is different and you do not notice it so much as there are so many other things to occupy your mind. Curiously enough you are then in greater danger.[86]

While being shelled in the trenches opposite Gaza the infantrymen of the EEF could do little to hit back at their tormentors. Coming into close proximity with artillery fire had a particularly telling effect on the nerves of some soldiers. During the shelling of Captain Bailey's artillery brigade headquarters a shell fell within a few feet of his position, knocking him to the ground. He noted that the event had 'rather shaken me up', so much so that he spent the next day collecting fragments of the shell as a memento of the event. Sustained periods of shelling could lead to mental breakdown among soldiers. The 1/4th Essex endured 7 days of artillery fire beginning at Second Gaza, and during this period 20 men were evacuated with shell shock. This far exceeded the physical injuries inflicted, with only two men killed and three wounded.[87] Artillery fire came to be a constant and much resented part of the combat experiences of the men of the EEF.

Artillery was not the only element of twentieth-century industrial warfare that made an appearance in the Middle East. The EEF turned to gas to increase its striking power as it pushed against the Gaza defences.[88] In late 1916, Murray asked the War Cabinet for permission to deploy gas against the Turks. Initial reluctance in Whitehall gave way as significant evidence came to light regarding the mistreatment of British prisoners of war in Turkey and the atrocities committed in Armenia. The decision to use gas was thus as much a response to the barbarous manner in which the Ottoman state was choosing to conduct its war, as the tactical obstacles faced by the EEF on the battlefield. This was different to the justification used on the Western Front in 1915, which required the enemy to use gas first, thus legitimizing its retaliatory deployment by the British. A stockpile of gas shells was built up and made ready for use at Second Gaza. Murray was insistent that they should only be used on fully manned Turkish redoubts where they could achieve a considerable effect on the defenders' morale. The fear was that if they were deployed too soon and ineffectually the Turks would pay little attention to them.

Concerns about the use of gas were not only prevalent in the higher echelons of the EEF; a number of the rank and file were reluctant to see it deployed. Sergeant Harold Judge, of the CMR, recorded in his diary that there were numerous rumours going round the regiment in early April that gas shells would be fired in the coming offensive. He hoped the EEF's generals would not use them 'as the Turks have never used it on us and have always played fair so far anyway, but am sorry to say that as the struggle gets more intense the methods get more doubtful'.[89] Ultimately any advantage offered by gas was squandered, with the gas shells intermixed into the general 2-hour bombardment. Only 240 gas shells were allocated for firing onto each Turkish redoubt, and these were used up within the first 30 minutes.[90] Much of the gas had therefore dissipated by the time the infantry were ready to launch their assault and the Turkish defences remained fully armed and operational.

Despite this failure Allenby chose to continue with Murray's policy of deploying these new weapons on the Palestinian battlefield. Gas shells were used at Third Gaza, this time in much larger quantities. The 4.5 inch howitzer battery attached to 54th Division fired 2,400 gas shells alone during the 6-day preliminary bombardment.[91] In this case the shelling was used to reinforce the Turks' mistaken perception that Gaza was to be the main point of the EEF's attack. Although not a decisive weapon on the battlefield, gas could fulfil a crucial role as a force multiplier causing panic and confusion in the enemy's rear areas and artillery positions. The EEF feared, ultimately erroneously, that once they had used gas the Germans would provide the Turks with the capability to respond in a similar manner. Gas schools were set up to train soldiers to cope with gas attacks. The men were given lectures on the history of the weapon and were then passed through a gas chamber for 10 minutes to test their protective helmets. Battle drills were also carried out while wearing gas masks, including live firing practices. Trooper David Currin, serving with the New Zealand Mounted Field Ambulance attached to the ANZMD, recorded in his diary that after half an hour the glass in his gas mask became blurry and he could no longer fire his rifle.[92] Gas may not have killed many soldiers but it could, along with the preventative measures its use necessitated, easily disorientate men in battle. The tactical difficulties that resulted from the use of gas and the parlous state of the Turkish Army by September 1918 militated against its further use at Megiddo. Nevertheless, the EEF had stockpiled nearly 100,000 gas shells for deployment in the final offensive, which were slowly destroyed after the First World War. Sufficient quantities still remained in the region in the 1920s for the British to consider using gas to quell Arab unrest in Palestine.

Second and Third Gaza also saw tanks deployed in support of the EEF's infantry assaults. In both cases they were obsolescent versions which were no longer of any use on the Western Front. Although the tank would later come to exercise an important role on the twentieth-century battlefield, the early variants that joined the EEF were little more than slow-moving pillboxes. They were not a panacea to the problems of mobility in the First World War; this role in the Middle East remained the preserve of mounted troops. Tanks were first used at Second Gaza to support the attack of 54th Division. Only one tank managed to cross no-man's-land intact and reach the Turkish defences, where it proved of brief help to the men of the 1/5th Norfolks and 1/8th Hampshires, providing fire support for a successful infantry attack on a Turkish redoubt.[93] This position was later known as 'tank redoubt' as the burnt-out carcass of the vehicle remained a prominent feature on the battlefield. At Third Gaza it was again 54th Division that fought alongside the tanks, with six of them this time taking to the field. Again they failed to achieve much of military value during the division's assault on 1 November. They were, however, useful for bringing up large quantities of equipment under fire to assist Royal Engineers' units. In addition, a report on the battle by the staff of 54th Division noted that tanks had a particularly stimulating effect on the morale of the infantry waiting to advance.[94]

That said, during battle tanks could prove to be more of a hindrance than a benefit to divisional commanders. In the advance onto the Sheikh Abbas ridge on 17 April 1917, as part of the run up to Second Gaza, two tanks preceded the 1/5th Suffolks. Both vehicles lost their way almost from the beginning of the operation, and the infantry followed their lead, causing much confusion. Such were the concerns about troops doing the same at Third Gaza that the 1/4th Norfolks issued specific instructions that their men should not follow tanks blindly around the battlefield and should instead concentrate on their allotted objectives. It noted that 'too much trust should not be placed in tanks, which should be regarded merely as auxiliary to the infantry attack'.[95] Their poor performance at Third Gaza led to tanks never being used again in the theatre. Brigadier-General T. Ward, commanding 163rd Brigade during the battle, wrote a scathing report on the tanks' activities. He was particularly critical of their lack of mobility, pointing to the difficulty they encountered crossing sandy ground and the Turkish trenches. In addition, he felt that their shock value was limited as they created significant amounts of noise during their deployment to the jumping-off point prior to the commencement of the battle. More importantly he was concerned by the fact that as soon as a tank appeared it drew all of the fire from nearby Turkish guns, making life difficult for any infantry in the area.[96] The tank thus had an inauspicious start to its career as a weapon of war in the desert. This stands in stark contrast to the role of armour in the desert of North Africa in 1940–3, a campaign very much defined by sweeping tank advances.

Throughout the war in Sinai and Palestine aircraft played an important role in the conduct of operations.[97] Their use grew significantly over the course of the campaign and they performed a range of roles. In contrast, much popular literature, notably Biggles's foray in the Middle East, portrays aircraft as merely an adjunct to espionage operations, ferrying spies around the region.[98] Aircraft were first dispatched to Egypt in November 1914, and by the early months of 1915 the Royal Flying Corps (RFC) was carrying out regular reconnaissance flights over Sinai. The Royal Naval Air Service's seaplanes enhanced the EEF's intelligence gathering capabilities, collecting information on the Turkish Army's lines of communication in Palestine. By 1916 the EEF's aircraft had taken on an offensive role, often raiding enemy airfields in retaliation for air strikes on the Canal defences by the German Air Service. Despite a quantitative superiority the lacklustre performance of the RFC's aircraft meant that from mid-1916 German pilots were able to operate with impunity. German aircraft, although small in number, could fly higher and faster than their British opponents, and were better armed. Only with the arrival of Bristol fighters in the autumn of 1917 did the RFC's equipment begin to outclass that of the Germans. This allowed the RFC, now organized as the Palestine Brigade under Major-General Geoffrey Salmond, to establish local air superiority over the front line at Gaza, greatly aiding the operations of the EEF.

Throughout 1918 the air space over Palestine came to be dominated by the Royal Air Force (RAF), as new fighter aircraft, such as the S.E. 5a, supplemented its strength. German pilots now found it almost impossible to take to the air. In one week in June 1918 German aircraft had crossed the British lines 100 times, by the last week of August this had been reduced to 18 flights, and over the next 3 weeks only 4 flights were made. During Megiddo and the advance that followed, the RAF carried out a wide range of interdiction operations, launching air strikes against the nodal points of the Turkish communication network and destroying fleeing Turkish columns. Although a powerful addition to Allenby's offensive armoury by September 1918, the RAF's most important role was that of aerial reconnaissance. From 1917 onwards it had greatly improved its intelligence gathering capabilities, particularly with regards to aerial photography. This allowed the EEF to develop highly accurate maps of Turkish front-line positions, greatly improving the accuracy of its artillery.[99] From Third Gaza onwards the Palestine Brigade was able to provide 50 interpretations of a photograph for the EEF's 3 corps within 5 hours of it being taken. During 1918, with its control of the air, the RAF was able to report in detail on Turkish dispositions, while denying this intelligence to the enemy.

For most soldiers the exploits of the EEF's pilots were observed at a distance and seemed remote from their activities. Corporal W. H. Bland, of the 1/5th Norfolks, noted in his diary on 15 August 1917 that he had observed a fight between a Taube and one of the RFC's scout aircraft. The action was 'very exciting whilst it lasted'.[100] Despite revelling in the spectacle of such combat it was obvious that the RFC's pilots were at a distinct disadvantage until autumn 1917. Captain Hinde described a brief encounter between a British reconnaissance aircraft and a German fighter. From the beginning the combat appeared to be one-sided as 'the German was much higher and much faster and had him entirely at his mercy'.[101] The impressive abilities of the enemy's aeroplanes left some EEF soldiers with a begrudging admiration. Having witnessed an indecisive dogfight in August 1917 Lieutenant-Colonel F. H. Wollaston recalled that 'the way they [the Germans] go for our machines like a hawk is really a splendid but a sickening sight'.[102] Even the EEF's ground-based anti-aircraft defences proved ineffective at dealing with the threat from the air. On one occasion a German aeroplane carried out a series of loops to demonstrate to the gunners that their fire was proving useless. In 1916 this ineffectiveness was largely the product of a lack of dedicated anti-aircraft artillery, with mountain gun batteries being used as substitutes in some areas.[103] The brutal realities of aerial combat were on occasion brought home to the EEF's soldiers when aircraft crashed near to the front line. Private France, of the 1/6th Essex, recorded a gruesome description of a dead pilot whose aeroplane had crashed in flames in May 1918: 'fellow was properly smashed up, too. Bullet through right cheek, smashed arms and legs, broken back. Proper hard lines. Only a youngster too.'[104] Despite the dangers some EEF officers chose to transfer to the RFC, particularly during 1916 and early 1917, as it offered an apparently more exciting role for the individual in modern war. Second Lieutenant G. B. Buxton, serving in 54th Division, left his position as aide-de-camp to Major-General Hare in January 1917 and began training with the RFC at Abbassia, in Egypt. In a letter to his aunt he set out his reasons for transferring:

> They [the RFC] were awfully short of men, and I decided I could no longer stay in my soft job but go out and risk things with the others. Many fair finer fellows have done so, and therefore I was not going to cling to my safe cotton wool joy ride of a job – when they were in need of men to do the valiant.[105]

By the summer he had been sent to an RFC squadron on the Western Front, where he was killed on 28 July 1917. Although often observed as a distant spectacle that enthralled the troops, aerial combat could be as brutal and bloody as fighting in the front ranks of the infantry.

The offensive power of aircraft was on occasion brought home to the men of the EEF when they were bombed by the German Air Service. In a raid by a single aeroplane that dropped 8 bombs on the 1st ALH Brigade's camp early on 1 June 1916, 8 men were killed and 22 wounded. In addition 36 horses were killed and 9 were wounded. The bombing also caused the remaining horses to stampede, with 123 running off into the desert. Lieutenant S. R. Macfarlane, of the 1st ALH Regiment, was not entirely perturbed by the effect of the raid, noting in his diary that 'some amusement was caused when we were getting a scatter on, some of the new hands were taking cover under shrubs etc. and others were scratching holes in the sand as fast as they could with their hands'.[106] The physical effects of aerial bombs on the human body were often horrific. In a letter to his wife Major Ernest Hudson, a staff officer with the 1st ALH Brigade, recorded after a raid that 'one officer in his tent 2 from me had his scalp blown off and his brains all over the top of his tent'.[107]

It was the psychological effect of being bombed that had the greatest impact upon EEF soldiers, many of whom felt impotent in the face of aerial weapons. Recalling a raid in June 1916 in which a German aeroplane had flown repeatedly over his position without dropping any bombs, Captain Arthur Rhodes, serving on the NZMR's staff, noted that 'it was really a terrible 10 minutes one feels such a fool and can do nothing'.[108] Only two months later he was again bombed while moving the brigade's headquarters to Bir el Abd. In his diary he explained the way in which soldiers simply had to endure air raids:

> Being bombed from an aeroplane is the most awful thing that can happen. The Gen and I lay down on the ground and we heard this bomb coming an awful row. I could have sworn that it was going to get us. 15 yds quite close enough. A second one came and landed 9 yards from us but did not burst if it had there would have been no more Arthur.[109]

The powerlessness of infantry and mounted troops when facing aircraft enhanced the physical effects of bombing. Crucially, aerial attacks were able to reach troops in previously safe rear echelon positions. This extension of the battle space beyond the front line, greatly enhancing the sense of vulnerability for a soldier, underlines air power's impact on morale.

It was the RAF that put air power to its greatest use in the Middle East, during the September 1918 advance. As the Turkish Army fled from the Plain of Sharon through the Judaean hills, a series of air strikes was launched on the roads carrying Turkish columns. For 6 hours on the morning of 21 September the RAF bombed the Wadi Fara, with flights of 6 aircraft arriving at intervals of half an hour. Nearly 10 tons of bombs were dropped and over 56,000 machine gun rounds fired into the wadi, from which the Turkish troops had little ability to escape. The next day 100 guns, 55 motor lorries, 4 motor cars, 912 wagons, and 20 water carts and field kitchens were found abandoned in the wadi. William Thomas Massey, an official correspondent with the EEF, described the scene as 'one of the most remarkable sights which a soldier has ever gazed upon' and noted that 'in no section of Napoleon's retreat from Moscow would there have been a more terrible picture of hopeless and irretrievable defeat'.[110] The official history of the 1914–18 air war described the attacks as having 'degenerated into a slaughter which made pilots sick who took part'.[111] By September 1918 the aircraft had come of age as a key weapon within the arsenal of any commander, able to wreak havoc on the battlefield. In particular, the open terrain of Egypt and Palestine made it difficult for troops to hide from aerial observation and attack, increasing the aeroplane's psychological potency.[112]

The use of innovative weapon systems in Palestine, such as gas, tanks, and aircraft, as well as the dominance of artillery, demonstrates the extent to which war in the Middle East resembled that on the Western Front. Despite the historiographical obsession with the EEF's mounted troops, it was the creation of a professional ethos in the force, based around all arms cooperation which saw aircraft and artillery fully integrated with the army's infantry and mounted units, that allowed the British to sweep the Turks out of Palestine in 1917–18.[113] Although in strategic ambition the EEF's war was very much a nineteenth-century imperial campaign, the manner in which it was fought demonstrated all of the elements of twentieth-century industrialized warfare.

The intensity of combat

Combat in the Middle East was at times very intense, as demonstrated by the testimony in the many collections of personal papers from the combatants involved. The experiences of battle, though, were clearly not a regular feature of soldiers' lives, and instead represent a series of momentary exposures to the horrors of modern warfare. The variation in the intensity of fighting in 1917–18 can be demonstrated by analysing the combat deaths within an individual infantry division, in this case 54th Division, the only division to remain with the EEF throughout its three years of campaigning (see Figures 1.1, 1.2, 1.3 and 1.4). The division's losses in 1916 ran at a very low level,

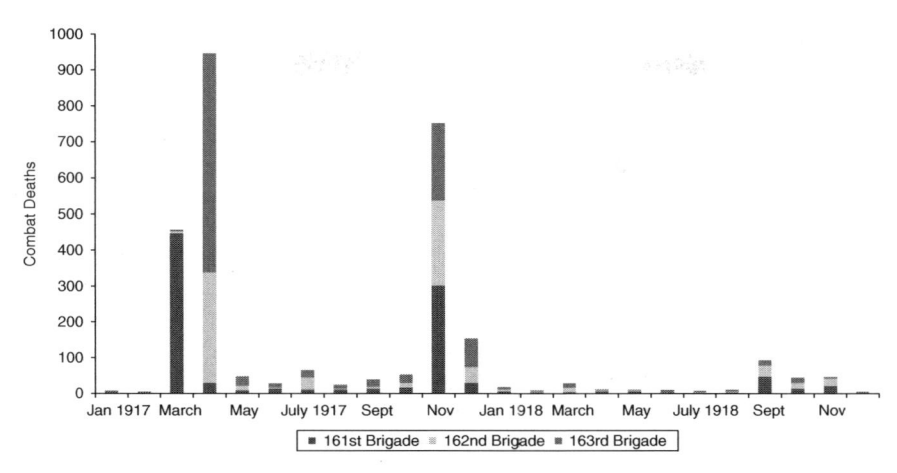

Figure 1.1 54th Division Infantry Brigade Combat Deaths, 1917–18.
Source: War Office, *Soldiers Died in the Great War 1914–1919* (London, 1920).

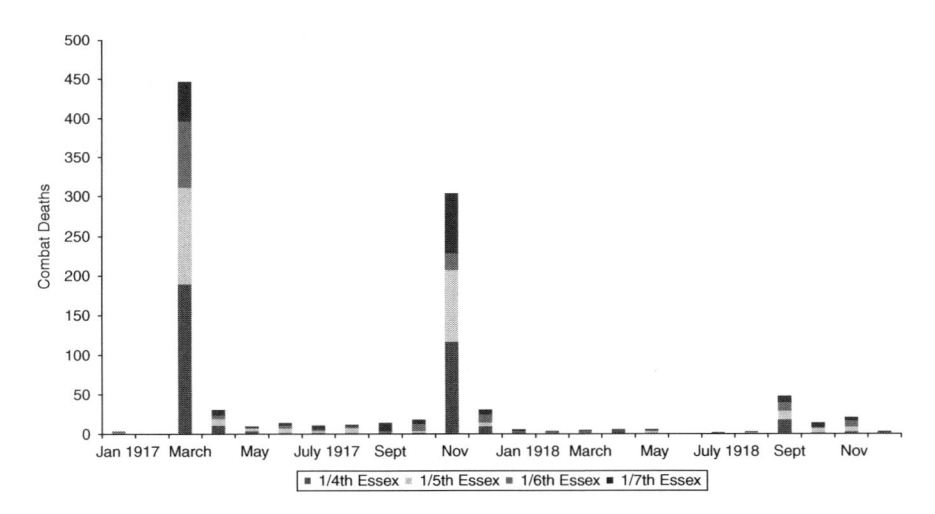

Figure 1.2 161st Infantry Brigade Combat Deaths, 1917–18.
Source: War Office, *Soldiers Died in the Great War 1914–1919* (London, 1920).

with most being the result of illness. This is hardly surprising considering that the period spent in Sinai was devoted to training and improving defensive posts.[114] The distance from the nearest Turkish forces and the lack of an assault on the Canal made 1916 an anomalous year in the division's combat history. The death rates for 1917 and 1918 reveal the considerable difference in the military experience that would occur once the division entered Palestine. It is clear that the temporal intensity of combat

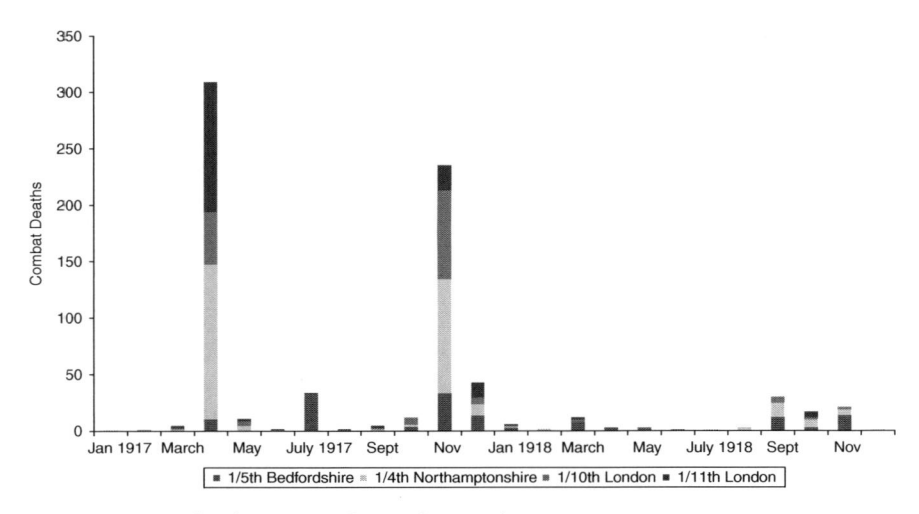

Figure 1.3 162nd Infantry Brigade Combat Deaths, 1917–18.
Source: War Office, *Soldiers Died in the Great War 1914–1919* (London, 1920).

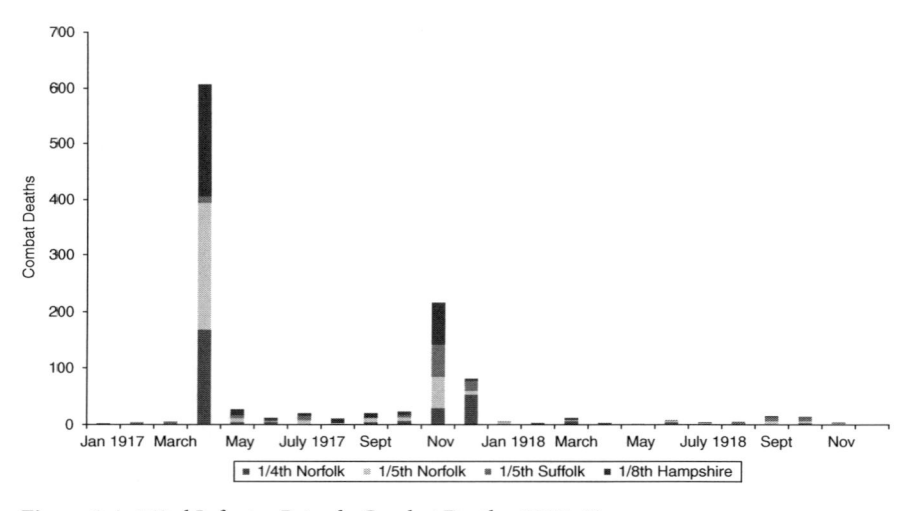

Figure 1.4 163rd Infantry Brigade Combat Deaths, 1917–18.
Source: War Office, *Soldiers Died in the Great War 1914–1919* (London, 1920).

varied significantly between the brigades of the division and even more so between its battalions.

54th Division went through a series of extremes of combat activity. The peaks in combat deaths correspond to the formation's involvement in the major battles of the Palestinian campaign, at Gaza in March, April, and November 1917, and at Megiddo in

September 1918. The differences extend beyond divisional level to that of the brigades and even individual battalions. For the 161st Brigade it was First Gaza that saw them suffer their greatest losses, whereas for the 162nd and 163rd Brigades it was the débâcle at Second Gaza that cut down their strength. Major-General Hare estimated the casualties of the 161st Brigade at nearly 1,400 on 26 and 27 March 1917, with the 162nd and 163rd Brigades suffering a combined loss of 2,870 on 19 April. This division alone had suffered 44 per cent of the EEF's casualties at Second Gaza, leaving it with a rifle strength of only 6,000.[115] In a report to the EEF's Chief of the General Staff after the battle, Lieutenant-General Chetwode, having taken over as commander of Eastern Force from Lieutenant-General Charles Dobell, confirmed the severe damage done to 54th Division, whose strength was now the lowest of the four infantry divisions available to him. Even by the end of May 1917 the division had only rebuilt its strength to just over 7,800 officers and men.[116]

In contrast to these brief periods of intense combat, the front-line experience of the 54th Division's men was relatively subdued. In August, September and October 1917 161st Brigade suffered a total of 43 casualties while stationed in the trenches opposite Gaza. This stands in stark contrast to the 1,137 officers and men killed, wounded or missing during the fighting in November. Similarly, February to May 1918 saw another period of inactivity as the EEF dealt with the reorganization problems imposed by Indianization, and the Turkish Army refrained from an offensive in Palestine as it struggled to maintain its manpower reserves. Across this 4-month period a total of only 64 casualties were incurred.[117] For individual battalions, however, relatively quiet months could be shattered by brief periods of vicious combat. 163rd Brigade suffered 242 casualties in December 1917, the bulk of which were accounted for by 124 men lost in the 1/4th Norfolks.[118] The majority of these losses were sustained in only one morning of fighting by the battalion for control of Zeifizfiyeh Hill.

The casualties for 54th Division only reveal part of the picture of the combat experiences of the EEF. An examination of the combat deaths for the NZMR for 1916–18, which can be taken as indicative of those for the ANZMD in general, reveals a very different temporal pattern for the intensity of battle (see Figure 1.5). In contrast to the infantry, the EEF's mounted wing was engaged in significant actions from summer 1916 onwards. Engagements such as those fought at Romani, Magdhaba and Rafah were particularly intense for the small number of mounted troops involved. At Romani the 1st ALH Brigade suffered 133 casualties and at Rafah it lost 129 officers and men. The losses of this one brigade accounted for 25 per cent of the EEF's casualties at Romani.[119] Importantly it is also evident that the NZMR was engaged with greater frequency in battle across the EEF's campaigns than was the infantry of 54th Division. Whereas each brigade of 54th Division only suffered heavy losses at two of the three Gaza battles, the NZMR had a large number of combat deaths on at least four occasions. In 1918 the two Transjordan Raids saw the EEF's mounted units heavily engaged while its infantry divisions were largely involved in static defensive operations.[120] The first Transjordan Raid, lasting from 23 March until 2 April, witnessed very heavy casualties in the ANZMD: 724 officers and men were reported killed, wounded or missing after the operation.[121] The use of mounted troops to pursue the retreating Turkish forces in 1916–18 also meant that these regiments were engaged in combat for longer periods

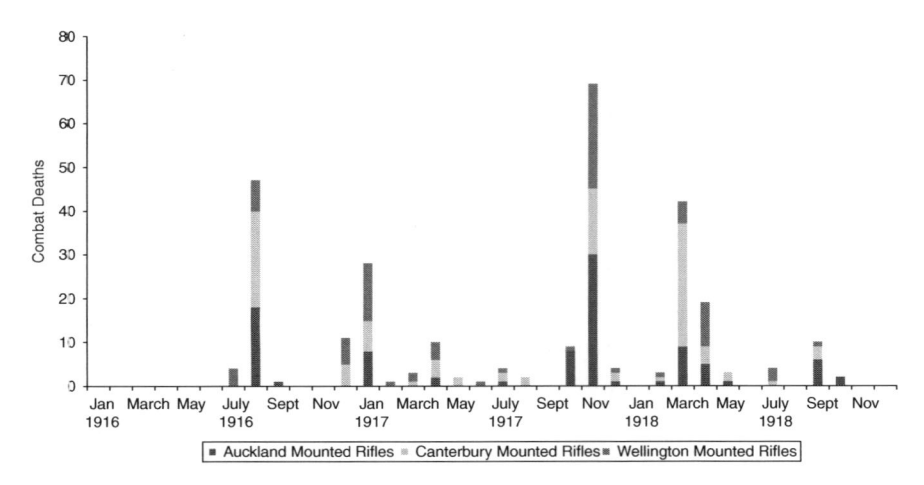

Figure 1.5 New Zealand Mounted Rifles Brigade Combat Deaths, 1916–18.

Sources: C. G. Nicol, *The Story of Two Campaigns: Official War History of the Auckland Mounted Rifles Regiment, 1914–1919* (Auckland, 1921); C. G. Powles, *The History of the Canterbury Mounted Rifles 1914–1919* (Auckland, 1928); A. H. Wilkie, *The Official War History of the Wellington Mounted Rifles Regiment 1914–1919* (Auckland, 1924).

than infantry battalions. This can be seen clearly in ANZMD's losses during Third Gaza and the subsequent advance to the Auja River. In the fighting at Beersheba and in the Judaean foothills to the north between 31 October and 6 November 1917, the division suffered 340 casualties. By 7 December the division's losses had risen to 854 soldiers. Thus 60 per cent of those men killed or wounded between 31 October and 7 December were lost during the pursuit northwards from 7 November onwards.[122] For one of the EEF's battles there was a correlation in the relative casualties suffered by mounted and infantry units. At Megiddo, in September 1918, 54th Division experienced 535 casualties and ANZMD suffered only 139 casualties.[123] In both cases this battle represented the least intensive period of major operations for the units involved.

In total the EEF's losses in Egypt and Palestine were relatively limited. Across the course of its campaigns 54,311 officers and men became battle casualties in Sinai and Palestine. In comparison to the 2.7 million casualties suffered on the Western Front, the EEF's losses appear to be relatively meagre.[124] This is reinforced by an examination of the EEF's reserves during the Third Battle of Gaza and subsequent pursuit. Between 27 October and 31 December 1917, 21,559 officers and men became casualties in the heavy fighting. Over the same period the EEF was able to move up 26,643 officers and men as reinforcements.[125] This continuous period of fighting did not push Allenby's manpower resources to the limit. If combat losses within the EEF's divisions are broken down it is, however, evident that in certain engagements the numbers of men being lost were equivalent to some of the bloodiest battles of the war. These casualties could thus have a significant impact on the morale and cohesion of individual units.

At First Gaza the losses of 54th Division fell primarily on 161st Brigade, which was attached to 53rd (Welsh) Division for the assault on the town, while the other two brigades provided fire support from nearby ridges. The losses in individual battalions were very high, with a reasonable amount of variation between them. The 1/5th, 1/6th, and 1/7th Essex lost 330, 345, and 228 men respectively, but these figures were significantly lower than those of 1/4th Essex at 483 casualties. The devastating impact of this one battle on these battalions can be seen by the fact that 1/4th Essex when paraded a day after the battle could only muster 12 officers and 357 other ranks.[126] The battalion had lost 56 per cent of its strength in only 2 days of combat. The losses at battalion level in 54th Division during Second Gaza were even more horrific. On 19 April the 163rd Brigade lost 61 officers and 1,767 other ranks, including two battalion commanders and every company commander in the 1/5th Norfolks and 1/8th Hampshires.[127] The 1/4th and 1/5th Norfolks suffered particularly badly, with the former losing 471 men and the latter 659. The experience of the 1/8th Hampshires is illustrative of the scale of these devastating losses. The battalion had advanced with a strength of 777 officers and men, but by the end of the day it had experienced 568 casualties; this was a loss rate of 73 per cent. For the 1/5th Suffolks, however, the experience of the second attack on Gaza was very different. The battalion only took to the field in the afternoon in support of the remainder of the 163rd Brigade, and as a consequence was fortunate to see only 4 men killed and 83 wounded. At the close of the battle Major-General Hare noted in his diary that the 1/5th Norfolk, 1/8th Hampshire, and 1/4th Northamptonshire Battalions had been 'almost wiped out', and that the 1/4th Norfolk, and 1/10th and 1/11th London Battalions had 'suffered severely'.[128] A similarly devastating level of combat losses can be seen in the casualties suffered by 163rd Brigade at Third Gaza later in 1917. During this seven-day engagement the 1/4th and 1/5th Norfolk, and 1/5th Suffolk Battalions were lucky to lose only 120, 187 and 158 men respectively. The 1/8th Hampshires by comparison suffered 215 combat casualties along with 27 men evacuated sick to hospital. These losses were significant as the battalion had gone into battle with only 630 officers and men, thus 38 per cent of its strength had been lost. In only eight months on the front line the 1/8th Hampshires had seen their battalion's strength destroyed in two separate engagements.[129]

Combat casualties tended to fall primarily on members of a battalion's rifle companies. Men serving in a battalion's headquarters staff and its logistical arm often managed to avoid the brutality of infantry attacks. From Third Gaza onwards units were also required to keep a cadre of officers and men in the rear from which the battalion could be rebuilt if its manpower was destroyed in battle. The losses at company level and lower thus accentuated the intensity of combat evident from battalion and brigade casualties. It was not only major battles that saw large numbers of men killed and wounded, small-scale engagements could be equally bloody. In the action at Kufr Qasim that won Private Needham the Victoria Cross, his patrol of 50 men suffered 25 casualties in a very short, but brutal engagement with the Turks.[130] At Third Gaza, 'D' Company of the 1/5th Suffolks attacked on 1 November with 163 officers and men, and came out of the battle 7 days later having suffered 50 casualties. This gave the company a loss rate of 30 per cent, similar to that of the 8th Hampshires in the same engagement.[131] In some cases the casualty rates in companies reached destructive proportions. Private Surry noted that his company of 1/7th Essex had gone into action on 26 March 200 men strong, but left the battle the next day with only 43 soldiers;

79 per cent of the company had been lost.[132] In his memoirs of his service with the 1/10th Londons, Major Frederick Clarke stated that he had been fortunate to avoid leading his company into battle at Third Gaza as he was invalided back to Egypt with malaria. He recorded that his company had attacked with 150 officers and men, and ended the battle with no officers and only 27 other ranks in the unit. This represented a horrific loss rate of 82 per cent.[133]

It is clear from these cases that the battles of the EEF's campaigns in Sinai and Palestine could be just as bloody as those fought on the Western Front during the First World War. On 1 July 1916, the BEF's VIII Corps, attacking at the Somme around Beaumont Hamel with 29 battalions, suffered an average battalion casualty rate of 66 per cent. In some units of VIII Corps the losses were much higher, with 11th Hampshires incurring over 80 per cent casualties.[134] The losses of their regimental brothers in the 8th Battalion at Second Gaza were almost at the same level, demonstrating that 19 April 1917 can be seen as the EEF's 'first day of the Somme'.

The loss rates in EEF battalions and companies were often worse than those suffered by units during Second World War engagements. As Jonathan Fennell has demonstrated, the 8th Army's campaign in North Africa in 1941–2 was a particularly bloody period of combat activity for the British Army.[135] For example, 51st (Highland) Division's infantry battalions suffered 40 per cent casualties at El Alamein and in the 7th Black Watch this rose to 50 per cent across its 4 rifle companies, with 'B' Company losing as much as 66 per cent of its strength. In the South-West Pacific theatre loss rates were often heavily skewed by the high levels of sickness. The casualties that resulted from combat were, though, comparable with those experienced by the EEF 25 years earlier. At the battle of Isurava on the Kokoda Track, in August 1942, the Australian Imperial Force's (AIF) 2/14th Battalion emerged after 2 days of fighting with a strength of only 230 men, half its initial complement.[136] Battles such as Second and Third Gaza thus saw casualty rates similar to those at El Alamein and Kokoda, two of the most intense and bloody battles fought by British and Commonwealth troops in the Second World War, demonstrating the ferocity of combat in Palestine in 1917. More surprisingly, the EEF's engagements also bear comparison with those of the *Wehrmacht* on the Eastern Front in the Second World War. Ultimate casualty rates for EEF units never reached the terrifying levels seen across the whole of the war in Russia, where, for example, the *Grossdeutschland* Regiment lost three times its initial manpower strength between June 1942 and May 1945. Although combat was not sustained in Egypt and Palestine for such extended periods as on the Eastern Front, it could be just as intense during particular battles. The encirclement of the Demyansk pocket in February 1942, saw a total of 41,212 men lost out of the 96,000 German soldiers involved; a casualty rate of 43 per cent, comparable to some EEF engagements.[137] Warfare in the twentieth century was horrific for the men at the sharp end, whether in Palestine, North Africa, New Guinea or Russia.

The EEF's battles were often brutal and bloody at the level of the company or battalion, reflecting the intensity of combat for infantrymen in the First and Second World Wars. In such circumstances it was impossible for the primary group, which has lain at the heart of much of the discussion of morale in the twentieth century, to survive. During 1917, many brigades, battalions and companies of the EEF were reduced to a small cadre of battle veterans and were reconstructed with large numbers of new drafts. These men would have to be integrated into their new units before they could bond with the men around them, a process which required time and training. Primary group loyalties were simply not robust enough to endure the rigours of modern, industrial combat.[138]

The greater enemy: Disease

From the perspective of the EEF's senior commanders the losses from combat across the army were not as significant when compared to the ever-present threat posed by sickness.[139] The army was fortunate to possess an extensive medical support infrastructure in its Egyptian base, developed during 1915 to cope with the large influx of casualties evacuated from Gallipoli. Static warfare in 1916 along the Canal defences allowed the EEF to refine its medical services and sanitary arrangements, resulting in a very low sick rate, which continued into early 1917. Even after the exertions of the first two battles of Gaza 54th Division only suffered a sickness rate of 0.2 per cent of its strength each day. By May 1917 the EEF's occupation of a line beyond its railhead in the inhospitable country of southern Palestine was beginning to take its toll. Sick rates across the EEF rose rapidly, with a 2.76 per cent rate recorded in 54th Division and 3.33 per cent in the Imperial Mounted Division.[140] Lieutenant-General Chetwode, then in temporary command of the forces on the Gaza front, was greatly concerned by the wastage due to illness, with septic sores and diarrhoea being the main problems. He also felt that the variations between divisions demonstrated a lack of personal care for the health, cleanliness, and living conditions of soldiers by some company officers, medical officers and divisional commanders.[141] Sickness rates remained around this level into 1918, and by the summer around 3,500 to 4,000 men across the EEF were sick each week. In contrast, from the end of the second Transjordan Raid in early May until Megiddo, the number of men wounded in combat each week never exceeded 400.[142] Within the EEF some units did manage to control their levels of illness more effectively than others. 163rd Brigade saw its sick rate vary between 1.08 per cent and 1.54 per cent in June 1918. The war diary of 1/5th Suffolks proudly stated that their rate of 1.5 per cent in August was one of the lowest in the whole army.[143]

Over the course of the campaign in Sinai and Palestine soldiers were far more likely to suffer from severe illnesses that warranted their evacuation to hospital, than they were to be wounded or killed in battle. As can be seen from the casualty rates of the 162nd Brigade, and 1st and 3rd ALH Regiments, the sick rate of individual units in the EEF was only rarely exceeded by the number of combat casualties (see Figures 1.6, 1.7 and 1.8). This was also true for the EEF as a whole, with the ratio of battle to non-battle casualties standing at 1:9.78 for the three years of campaigning. In total there were 503,828 non-battle casualties in the Egypt and Palestine theatres, dwarfing the 54,311 men killed and wounded in combat. This difference becomes even more evident when the admissions to EEF hospitals during 1916–18 are examined. In 1916 only 1,608 men went to hospital after being wounded in combat, but 136,110 were admitted due to disease and injury. This trend continued for the rest of the war, with the ratio for 1917

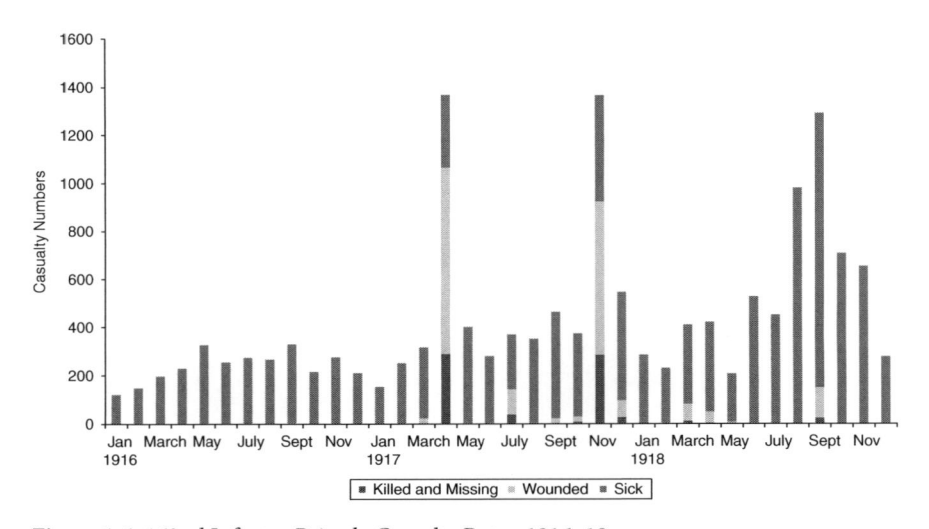

Figure 1.6 162nd Infantry Brigade Casualty Rates, 1916–18.
Source: TNA, WO95/4652, War Diary of 162nd Infantry Brigade Headquarters, Casualty Returns, 1916–18.

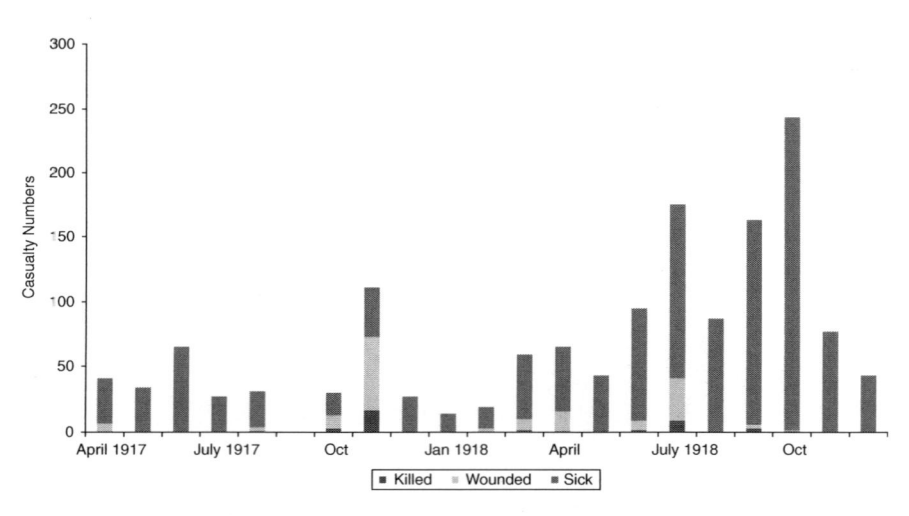

Figure 1.7 1st Australian Light Horse Regiment Casualty Rates, 1917–18.
Note: There is no data available for September 1917.
Source: AWM, AWM4 10/6, War Diary of 1st Australian Light Horse Regiment, Casualty Returns, 1916–18.

standing at 29,342 wounded to 138,821 sick and injured, while in 1918 the contrast was even more startling with 9,168 wounded compared to 221,034 sick and injured.[144] The levels of admissions to hospital for men sick and injured thus vastly exceeded those wounded in action in each of the three years of campaigning.

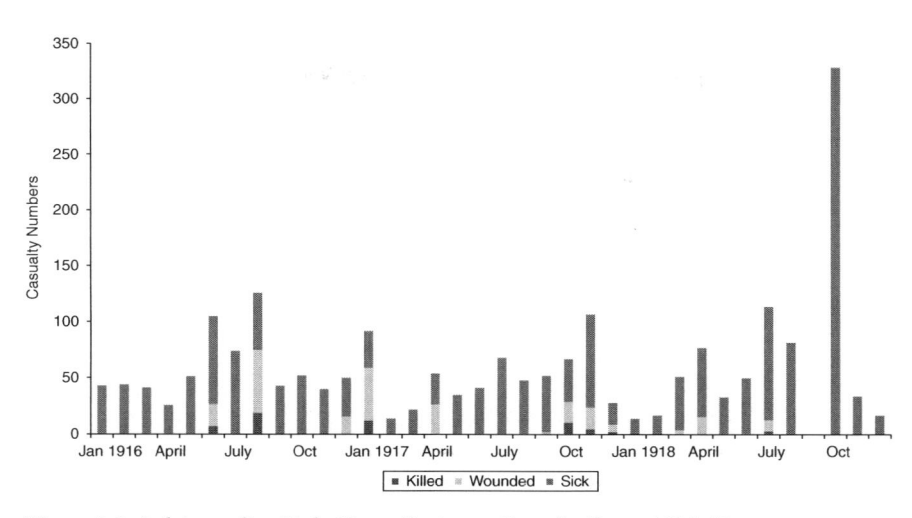

Figure 1.8 3rd Australian Light Horse Regiment Casualty Rates, 1916–18.
Note: There is no data available for September 1918.
Source: AWM, AWM4 10/8, War Diary of 3rd Australian Light Horse Regiment, Casualty Returns, 1916–18.

As with the other sideshow theatres of the First World War, such as Salonica, Mesopotamia, and, most notably, East Africa, sickness posed the primary threat to the manpower resources, and thus the operational effectiveness, of the EEF. In this sense the war in Egypt and Palestine bore greater resemblance to the imperial conflicts of the nineteenth century, where combat losses were far lower than those incurred due to illness and disease. Medical care for troops invalided to hospital in the Middle East was generally of a high standard, with only a small proportion of those hospitalized sick dying. This stands in stark contrast to the situation just over a decade earlier in South Africa, where two thirds of the nearly 20,000 British dead were due to sickness.[145]

The majority of the EEF's sickness cases were the result of septic sores, sandfly fever or malaria. The climate of Palestine combined with the fact that most soldiers lived in a world shrouded in dirt and dust meant that even slight abrasions could turn septic. 1/5th Bedfordshires found it useful for each company headquarters to keep a bottle of iodine in order to treat minor cuts received while building the defences opposite Gaza. In the 1/10th Londons septic sores and boils accounted for the majority of the 70 men who paraded sick each day during late June 1918.[146] This problem was much greater when troops were stationed for long periods in the trenches opposite Gaza, a particularly unsanitary position. The only effective treatment for septic sores proved to be the evacuation of soldiers from southern Palestine back to base areas in Egypt. Here they could have fresh dressings applied regularly, and be provided with fresh fruit and vegetables.[147] Epidemics of sandfly fever could cause even higher loss rates. As a result of one such outbreak in August 1918, the 1/5th Bedfordshires saw 82 men admitted to hospital in only 3 days, while the 1/10th Londons lost 234 men across the month.[148] Septic sores and sandfly fever meant that the sanitation of camps in Sinai and Palestine became a constant concern for the EEF's medical staff. During the early phases of the campaign in Sinai, sanitary procedures were improvised by individual units. Some camps used local contractors to dispose of their waste, while others employed sweepers brought over from India. The introduction of incineration for rubbish and excreta, an unpleasant task handled mainly by the men of the Egyptian Labour Corps, greatly improved the sanitary situation. Mobile disinfection units, modelled on ones first used in Serbia during 1915, were established and deployed at the front, allowing the kit of 60,000 men a month to be thoroughly cleaned.[149] Despite the considerable organizational efforts and man hours put into sanitary precautions, the EEF never managed to eradicate the threat posed by the unsanitary living conditions on the front line, merely to contain it.

Malaria posed an even greater problem, with the potential to debilitate large proportions of the EEF's manpower.[150] Units located near to the Auja River or in the Jordan Valley were particularly at risk, as these areas proved fertile breeding grounds for the anopheles mosquitoes that spread the disease. Private Surry described the enervating effects of being infected:

> There are few things more soul destroying or frustrating than the surreptitious bite of a malignant mosquito for when it takes effect you feel like nothing else on earth with your aches and pains, unable to sit down and enjoy the simple things, even food is an anathema, with painful clearness you accept the need to creep away to some hole, your bivvy or dugout, lie down hoping for sleep and perhaps, eventually, fall into a fitful sleep of uneasy dreams and possibly a little delirium.[151]

In order to try to lessen the effects of malaria the EEF devoted a considerable amount of time and effort to sanitary measures designed to prevent the mosquitoes breeding around the Auja and Jordan Rivers. Units, while resting away from the front, were employed canalizing streams, clearing reeds from river banks and oiling stagnant pools. Quinine was also issued to soldiers as a prophylactic measure, but was found to be ineffective by the ANZMD. Attempts to reduce the incidence of malaria were not helped by the reluctance of some soldiers to engage in basic sanitary defences. An inspection of the Mellahah and Aujah wadis in the Jordan Valley by the ADMS of the ANZMD, found that mosquito net discipline among the soldiers camped there was poor. The commanding officer of one regiment told the ADMS that the extreme heat of the valley made his men reluctant to sleep under nets. A non-commissioned officer (NCO) also informed him that some men wanted to come down with malaria so that they could be invalided out of the valley.[152] A key element in the EEF's anti-malarial campaign was the rapid detection and diagnosis of malaria cases in order to provide the infected soldiers with appropriate treatment. During March and April 1918 medical staff were trained and then deployed to malaria diagnosis stations, of which two were attached to each corps.[153] Over the course of summer 1918 these units helped to improve the responsiveness of the EEF's medical infrastructure to the problems faced by units deployed in the malarial valleys of Palestine.

The EEF's medical difficulties reached a nadir in September and October 1918, following the offensive at Megiddo and the rapid advance into Syria. In mid-September over 5,500 officers and men were sick, and numbers only grew as soldiers advanced across the Turkish lines.[154] The medical services had managed to control disease in the areas behind the British front; the Turkish Army, due to its logistical overstretch, had made no attempt to do so in its rear or front-line areas. As a consequence sickness was rife in many Turkish units, greatly reducing their available manpower. The EEF's troops were warned about the prevalence of disease in the areas they were about to enter. General instructions issued two days before the Megiddo offensive stressed that men were not to sleep in caves or native houses as they were likely to be infected with relapsing fever, typhus and sandfly fever.[155]

Despite these precautions little could be done to prevent damage to the health of the EEF's troops. Malaria was common in the rear areas of the Turkish Army in Palestine and Syria, and as a consequence of the EEF's rapid advance northwards towards Damascus and then on to Aleppo it had to traverse these malarial areas. As is demonstrated in Figure 1.9, the number of men admitted to hospital with malaria from the whole EEF, grew significantly in October and November 1918, following a slight fall in September.[156] The sickness rates in individual formations and battalions give an even starker indication of the damage done by illness in the last stages of the war in the Middle East. In September 1918, the 162nd Brigade's number of sick reached 1,139 soldiers, having been 977 in August, and only 450 in July (see Figure 1.6). A similar toll was taken on the strength of 1st and 3rd ALH Regiments as they advanced towards Amman (see Figures 1.7 and 1.8). The greatest difficulties were encountered by the DMC as it advanced deeper into Palestine and Syria, finally reaching Aleppo. After the fall of Damascus its hospital admission rate rose from 2.85 per cent to 5.51 per cent. For the week ending 12 October the DMC admitted 3,109 soldiers to hospital. Over October and November, 479 men of the corps died in hospital, while only a quarter of that number died in battle. As a result of these crippling losses Allenby and

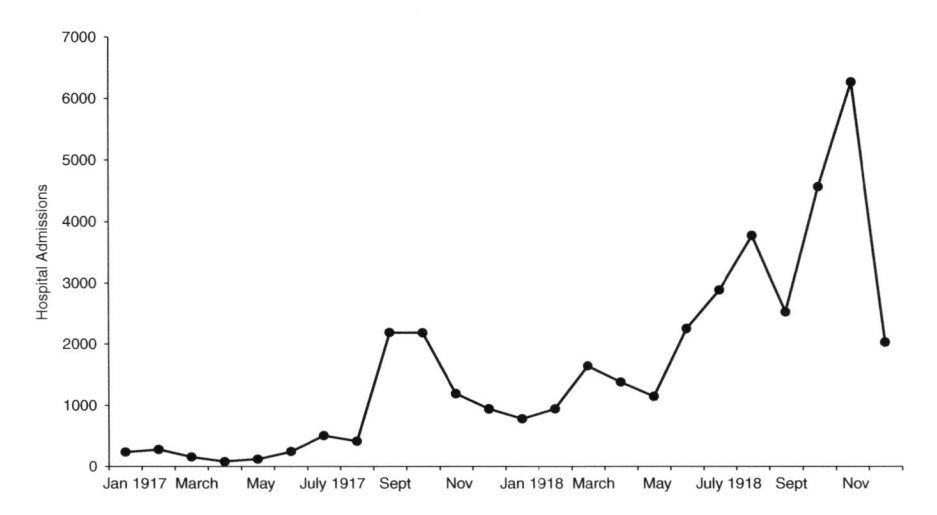

Figure 1.9 Malaria Hospital Admissions in the EEF, 1917–18.

Source: W. G. Macpherson, W. H. Horrocks and W. W. O. Beveridge (eds), *Medical Services: Hygiene of the War* (London, 1923), II, 215.

Lieutenant-General Henry Chauvel, commander of the DMC, found it difficult to push troops up beyond Damascus. 5th Cavalry Division was the only formation capable of mustering sufficient strength for this advance.

The sick rate had thus begun to affect the ability of the EEF to conduct operations. The enormity of the problem is evident in a comparison of the combat casualties and the admissions of sick troops to casualty clearing stations between 19 September and 31 October. In this period 5,506 men were killed, wounded, or missing, while 47,828 were taken ill; combat casualties made up only 10 per cent of the total losses.[157] The impact of malaria and other diseases was accentuated by the influenza pandemic that swept all combatant nations in the closing months of the First World War. At regimental level the effects of influenza could be devastating; in the 1/4th Essex influenza caused 190 admissions to hospital in October. In the 3rd ALH Regiment matters were even worse, with 218 cases occurring in only nine days.[158] As a result of influenza the 1/10th Londons, stationed at Beirut, were left with just 18 officers and 252 other ranks to carry out duties. Illness destroyed the EEF's ability to wage war in October 1918, and it was therefore fortuitous that the Ottoman Empire sued for peace at the end of the month.

An additional burden for the EEF's medical services was having to cope with a high incidence of venereal disease in the army.[159] The problem was greatest in 1915–16 while large numbers of soldiers, in particular those from the Dominions, were training in Egypt close to the temptations found in the brothel quarters of Cairo and Alexandria. Over the course of 1916 there were 14,153 admissions to hospital for venereal disease in Egypt, equating to a rate of 75.31 cases per 1,000 men on the ration strength of the EEF. No other cause of illness came close to this level of admissions; diarrhoea, which caused 5,889 cases, and dysentery, which resulted in 5,597 admissions, were dwarfed by the venereal figures. The incidence of venereal disease fell dramatically in 1917, with only 5,242 hospital admissions recorded, a rate of just 28.10 per 1,000 men. As most combatant units were stationed in the southern Palestinian wilderness, which was devoid of female company for the troops, most of these cases occurred in rear echelon formations. In comparison diarrhoea and dysentery had become a much more serious issue, leading to a total of 18,458 cases. Moreover, malaria had now emerged as a significant threat to the health of the EEF's personnel, with it leading to 8,480 men being admitted to hospital in 1917. By 1918 venereal disease was again on the increase among the EEF's soldiers, who were now stationed among the villages and temptations of Palestine. The problem was so acute that during July 1918 there were 40 officers and 1,399 men being treated in Alexandria for venereal disease. Troops visiting Jerusalem and Bethlehem in July 1918 produced 313 cases alone, the majority of which occurred not among combat formations but in the EEF's support structure, such as units of the Royal Engineers, Army Service Corps, Ordnance Corps and Royal Army Medical Corps.[160] Over the course of 1918 the EEF recorded 11,656 hospital admissions for venereal disease, a rate of 50.44 cases per 1,000 men. As in 1917, malaria and dysentery remained the principal concerns, producing 30,241 and 14,487 cases respectively. Nevertheless, the doubling of the rate of venereal disease infections caused alarm among sections of the EEF's higher command, as it exacerbated the rapidly rising rates of wastage due to illness and disease.

In order to get to grips with the venereal problem lectures were instigated for soldiers on the dangers of contact with the indigenous female population. 3rd ALH Regiment were informed of these risks by their brigade commander, Brigadier-General Charles Cox, who, in an avuncular manner, also pointed out the necessity of preventative treatment at the prophylactic tank for those men who succumbed to temptation.[161] In January 1918 Lieutenant-Colonel Garner, the EEF's Principal Medical Officer for Jerusalem, suggested a scheme for the city similar to the Contagious Diseases Act. The EEF's Director Medical Services, however, was not keen on such stringent measures being employed, as men could simply be kept away from brothels by placing Palestinian towns and villages out of bounds. In addition, he was deeply concerned that such measures would be seen by the British public as a form of licensed prostitution. He noted wryly that 'Syphilis is not spread by the professional prostitute so much as by the clandestine amateur prostitute, and consequently the locking up of the professional prostitute would have little effect on the incidence of Venereal'.[162] The medical services found it difficult to cope with the fact that some soldiers viewed acquiring venereal disease, despite the immoral and dishonourable connotations, as a means of escaping the horrors and tedium of military life.

A modern military campaign?

War in the Middle East in 1916–18 poses a series of questions about the modernity of the First World War and of particular theatres of operations away from the much studied Western Front. The EEF's campaigns in Sinai and Palestine encompassed the brutality, violence and horror that are often viewed as emblematic of the First World War in France and Flanders. For the men of the EEF their war contained all the elements of modern, industrialized slaughter, which in particular was the product of the central role of artillery on the battlefield. This was a war in which the individual's role in battle had become subsumed within mass firepower solutions to tactical and operational challenges. In some units combat casualties in these industrialized engagements reached the levels attained in the most unrelenting struggles of the BEF. For the soldiers of 54th Division, who suffered horrific losses at Second Gaza, particularly at infantry battalion and company level, the romanticized depiction of the Palestine campaign presented by Elizabeth Butler would have been unrecognizable. Industrialized slaughter remained one of the lasting memories of the war for these men, as it did for many Western Front veterans.

This inflection of modernity in the Middle Eastern theatre was challenged by other aspects of the EEF's war. For much of the campaign in Sinai and Palestine the soldiers involved were busy struggling not against the Turks but against the inhospitable climate and forbidding terrain of the region. The war with nature reflected the defining experience of many of the British Army's imperial campaigns in the nineteenth century. This becomes even more evident when examining the impact of illness and disease on the EEF. Throughout 1916–18 high sickness rates tore away at the army's manpower reserves. The medical tools of a modern army could only serve to stem the impact of this problem, and in late 1918 the EEF was effectively rendered useless by the combined effects of battle exhaustion, unsanitary Turkish positions, influenza and malaria. War in the Middle East displayed many aspects and utilized many of the tools of a twentieth-century military campaign, but in the end it was the traditional enemy of armies throughout history – disease – that emerged victorious.

From the perspective of the EEF's morale and combat motivation, the severe loss rates, produced both by intense combat and the high level of illness, served to undermine the coherence of the primary group. This had a corresponding impact on the way that the men of the EEF chose to cope with the hardships of war and stresses of battle; alternative solutions to bolster endurance and morale had to be found. For a small number of men solace was sought not in the camaraderie of the section or platoon, but in the chimerical notion of the campaign as a religiously endorsed crusade, which would free the Holy Land from the oppressive Turk.

2

A Twentieth-Century Crusade?

Over the past century the EEF's campaign in the Middle East has become shrouded in myth. The exploits of daring cavalry charges over the desert sands, such as that at Beersheba in October 1917, have only been matched by the quixotic adventures of British political and intelligence agents. These romantic tales come to the forefront of the narrative in descriptions of the EEF's operations in late 1917, which ultimately led to the capture of Jerusalem from the Turks. It has often been asserted that the British success fulfilled a traditional Arabic prophecy that the city would be freed from Ottoman occupation when the prophet brought the waters of the Nile to Palestine. By early 1917 the EEF had engineered a water pipeline across the Sinai Desert to sustain its troops opposite Gaza, and by coincidence Allenby's name sounded out in Arabic, *al-Nebi*, meant prophet. These pieces of portentous historical symbolism were matched by the fact that the city fell to the British on 9 December, which in 1917 marked the Jewish festival of Hanukkah, the celebration of Judas Maccabeus' liberation of Jerusalem from the Seleucids in 165 BC.[1] Stories such as these provided the EEF's Middle Eastern campaigns with a romantic tinge all too absent from the mechanized slaughter that dominated the war on the Western Front.

This romanticism was reinforced by the association of the campaign with one of the First World War's most enigmatic heroes: T. E. Lawrence. After his death in 1935, Lawrence was memorialized in terms which emphasized the historical allusions that had seemingly permeated his Arabian exploits. Eric Kennington's effigy of Lawrence in St Martin's church in Wareham, Dorset, has the recumbent figure resting his feet upon a piece of Hittite sculpture while beside his head lie three unlabelled books. The sculpture refers to Lawrence's pre-war archaeological activities at Carchemish and the books to those that he carried with him while serving in Arabia: the *Morte d'Arthur*, *The Oxford Book of English Verse* and *The Greek Anthology*. In addition, Kennington produced an effigy which in its design was reminiscent of a fourteenth-century knight's tomb. Lawrence of Arabia was thus portrayed as a crusading warrior and was integrated into the romantic tradition prominent in early twentieth-century British culture. With his acute sense of history, Lawrence had himself helped to construct this mythical background to his military career, recording the possibly apocryphal story that one of his ancestors, Sir Robert Lawrence, had served in the Third Crusade.[2]

These allusions to the religious and historical context of the Middle Eastern campaign are not confined to the hagiography that has arisen around Lawrence. The official history of the campaign, produced in two volumes in 1928 and 1930, contained many of these rhetorical flourishes. Cyril Falls's military narrative of the surrender of Jerusalem, for example, is interspersed with references to Judas Maccabeus. When it came to describing the climactic battle of Megiddo, Falls could not resist the opportunity to launch into a lengthy discussion of the myriad armies that had fought over the same ground, providing examples going back to Pharaoh Thotmes III's defeat of King Kadesh in the mid-fifteenth century BC. The massed use of cavalry by Allenby allowed these historical references to be carried even further; the 4th Cavalry Division's advance on 19 September 1918 seemed to demonstrate to Falls that 'warfare had recovered in this spectacle the pageantry whereof long-range weapons had robbed it'.[3] It was not just Falls who succumbed to the allure of romanticism. Lieutenant-General George MacMunn, co-author of the official history's first volume, was also prone to similar literary distractions, despite the fact that his narrative style rarely moved beyond the prosaic. He referred to the route taken by the EEF across Sinai in 1916 as following the 'way of the Philistines' and noted that when they reached the Palestinian border the army had left the land of wilderness, but had yet to enter the promised land. These historical and biblical references were, however, not intended simply to enliven the narrative. Falls's masterful concluding chapter to the second volume pointed to the historical and religious landscape of Palestine as having had a fundamental impact on the morale and fighting capabilities of the men of the EEF. An opinion that he boldly asserted was reinforced by the 'testimony of officers of all grades of seniority'.[4] No attempt was made to see if these opinions were corroborated by the other ranks that had served in the EEF.

Nevertheless, this assertion has become a sacrosanct tenet of attempts to comprehend combat motivation in the armies that fought in the Middle East during the First World War. For many historians the EEF's campaign can best be understood as a 'holy war' fought in a landscape that abounded with innumerable references to the Bible and the crusades. As a consequence, general accounts of the war tend to dismiss the Middle Eastern front as nothing more than a sideshow until the dramatic capture of Jerusalem. This achievement, alongside the city's historical and religious resonances, appeared to give the EEF's war a wider relevance, allowing A. J. P. Taylor to reverently describe Allenby as the city's 'first Christian master since the crusades'.[5] Even works of narrative military history that specifically focus on the military operations of the Egyptian and Palestinian fronts are bedevilled by the need to place themselves in an expected historical context, as demonstrated by Anthony Bruce's compact account entitled *The Last Crusade* (2002). David Woodward's detailed and scholarly assessment of the military experiences of British soldiers in the Middle East at times fits a similar pattern. He states that 'the idea of a crusade [. . .] resonated with many of his [Allenby's] men', implying that the biblical relevance of the landscape acted as an important fillip to their morale.[6] John Grainger has taken this concept a stage further by erroneously asserting that nearly all of the EEF's troops were at least nominally Christian and familiar with the biblical importance of Palestine. This leads him to the conclusion that 'to invade Palestine and wrest it from the grip of the Muslim Turk was to many of the British troops no more than a Christian duty'.[7] Moreover, he notes that many contemporary accounts refer to the campaign as a crusade and thus it should be viewed as a holy war. Even works of a more academic focus have on occasion succumbed to an overly reductionist interpretation of EEF soldiers' attitudes towards combat in the Holy Land. Matthew Hughes's definitive examination of Allenby's command states that religious references were clear in much of the correspondence of those involved. Similarly, Michael Snape asserts that a neo-crusading ethos was to the fore during the campaigns against the Turks. His argument is, however, a product of an examination of only a narrow range of sources. The views of two Roman Catholic officers, one of whom had been a monk at Downside Abbey before enlisting as an army chaplain, are taken by Snape as representative of the whole EEF.[8]

Some attempts have been made to reconsider the role of crusading and religious ideas among the men of the EEF, approaches driven largely by cultural rather than military historians. Elizabeth Siberry's study of crusading rhetoric in the nineteenth and twentieth centuries places the Palestine campaign into a wider frame of cultural reference. She eventually comes to a similar conclusion to Falls, noting that crusading imagery was prevalent in many of the first-hand accounts, with frequent parallels being drawn to the Third Crusade and the actions in particular of Richard the Lionheart. The majority of her sources, however, consist of post-war published accounts of the campaign, rather than unpublished letter collections, diaries or memoirs.[9] In contrast, Eitan Bar-Yosef's examination of how the Holy Land was constructed and viewed in English culture in the nineteenth century makes extensive use of a range of unpublished sources held at the Imperial War Museum. He notes that crusading rhetoric was very much 'socially and culturally confined' to British officers. The rank and file of the EEF instead reverted to using a biblical vernacular culture derived from hymns, Sunday school classes, sermons, and the family Bible, in order to comprehend the war in Palestine. This approach ultimately undermined the crusading image as constructed by the officer class, which appeared overly imperialistic. The rank and file chose to focus on their homes in England as their primary motivating factor. For this reason Bar-Yosef labels the men of the EEF as 'homesick crusaders'.[10] His interpretation is the first to consider fully the ideological roots of much of the writing on crusading connected with the Palestine campaign. This analysis is still too accepting of the role religious traditions played in British society, particularly that of working-class men, without considering the limits of biblical vernacular culture in the early twentieth century. Importantly, it is also limited by the fact that Bar-Yosef focuses exclusively on the experiences of British soldiers in late 1917 around the time of the capture of Jerusalem. This leaves a regional and temporal penumbra over the experiences of the EEF. In addition, Dominion troops, who made up a large part of the EEF's fighting arm, are ignored. This chapter will take a broader approach to the cultural context of the EEF's war, considering how its imperial soldiers viewed the campaign against the Ottoman Empire from its inception in 1916, through the battles of 1917–18 and into the post-war period.

The post-war construction of a crusading army

The rhetoric of the Bible and the crusades was present in much of the interwar writing on the Palestine campaign. Allenby's death in May 1936 allowed the British press to deploy a range of historical allusions that they thought fitting to describe the general's wartime exploits. *The Times* published a brief series of anecdotes about Allenby by Colonel Ronald Storrs, former military governor of Jerusalem, which were entitled 'Lord Allenby: "The Last of the Paladins"'. A few days later *The Times* published a message of condolence from Colonel Franz von Kress von Kressenstein, former commander of the Turkish 8th Army, stating that Allenby was one of Britain's greatest generals. Kressenstein announced that Allenby 'was a chivalrous soldier, at whose bier his former opponent lowers his sword in veneration and admiration'. Attempts in the late 1930s to create a suitable memorial for Allenby, who had resisted the idea of a grandiose statue being erected in his memory, saw Alfred Duff Cooper, then Secretary of State for War, advocating the construction of a soldiers' club. Despite the utilitarian nature of such a memorial, Duff Cooper felt that this was 'a worthy monument to the memory of the last of the Crusaders'.[11] It was not only Allenby who was described with reference to the crusades, but also the rank and file veterans of the EEF. An account of a battlefield pilgrimage to Egypt and Palestine in the late 1920s made by Trevor Allen deployed much of the same ornate language. Allen referred to his former comrades sailing with him as 'new Crusaders in the Holy Land', men who had stood on the same ground as Richard the Lionheart. More importantly, the dead that the EEF had left behind in the Middle East were recalled in explicitly Christian terms. Allen believed their sacrifice had created 'another and diver[s] Via Dolorosa with rough-hewn crosses marking the Calvaries'.[12] The physical, financial, and emotional difficulties involved with such a trip to the Middle East by the relatives and comrades of dead servicemen came to the fore in the description given of the EEF cemetery on Mount Scopus, overlooking Jerusalem. It was portrayed as a place that gave meaning to the pilgrimages made by relatives to the city's other sacred sites, notably the Holy Sepulchre and Mount of Olives. The massed soldiers' graves tied together contemporary and historic sacrifices made in the Holy Land.

The explosion of war literature in the 1920s and 1930s, a large proportion of which dealt with the Egypt and Palestine campaigns, did not just dwell on the glorified memories of the dead. Numerous personal accounts sought to place the military careers and exploits of the authors into a wider frame of historic reference. The most absurd expression of this was the work of Major Vivian Gilbert, in his memoir *The Romance of the Last Crusade* (1923). The book begins with a short fictional chapter in which a first-year Oxford undergraduate, Brian Gurnay, sits in the garden of Ivythorpe Manor in the summer of 1914, reading a novel on the crusades. The chapter contains an excerpt from this novel, describing Richard I refusing to look down on Jerusalem while the 'valiant knight' with him, Sir Brian de Gurnay, looks forward to a future last crusade that would 'wrest the Holy Places from the Infidel'.[13] This leads the contemporary Brian Gurnay, who is clearly supposed to stand as a cipher for Gilbert, to look up to the sky and exclaim that he too would like to take part in a worthwhile crusade. This expostulation is followed by the trite dramatic device of Gurnay's mother appearing to inform him of the outbreak of the Great War. The book then shifts to Gilbert, who in 1914 was an actor on the New York stage, records his return to Britain, his subsequent enlistment in the London Regiment and service with 60th Division in France, Salonica and Palestine. A similar desire to place one's Middle Eastern service into a crusading context is evident in the memoir of the war artist Donald Maxwell. In 1918 he was commissioned by the Admiralty to produce illustrations of the Palestine campaign for the Imperial War Museum. Despite the fact that he arrived after the armistice with Turkey, agreed on 30 October 1918, and thus failed to directly experience combat, he entitled his work *The Last Crusade* (1920). In it he makes it clear that he is looking back to medieval literary models in order to construct his narrative. At one point Maxwell has an imaginary interlocutor questioning him about why he has failed to mention any of the details of the military campaign, instead choosing to dwell on the local landscape. Maxwell replies to his questioner, and presumably to the similarly exasperated reader, that chronicles of the crusades would also have begun with 'long, rambling and discursive writing' and that 'no crusader who was worth his salt ever got to the Holy Land without taking an enormous time about it'.[14] This helps to draw the readers' attention away from the fact that the vast majority of the illustrations in the book were drawn from Maxwell's imagination. Both Gilbert and Maxwell were attempting to use the crusading context to give their often rather banal or imagined accounts of military life a degree of romantic resonance with the wider reading public.

This was an approach taken not only by personal narratives of the campaign, but in many of the mundane regimental and battalion histories that appeared in the interwar period, often written by former members of the units concerned. J. W. Burrows's history of the Essex Regiment stated that when the 161st Brigade, which was entirely composed of Essex TF battalions, entered Palestine the men felt like the Israelites of old gazing upon a land of promise after their desert wanderings. An account of 'B' Battery of 271st Brigade RFA went even further, directly referring to Bible passages in order to prove that the historical context being set out was accurate. The account of the 1/5th Essex's service in the Middle East contained considerable detail on the lands through which the battalion had passed. An entire chapter was devoted to describing the various armies and personalities that had crossed Sinai before the EEF, ranging from Pharaoh Necho to Napoleon. These allusions to the historic milieu often involved nothing more than perfunctory references to crusading in the region. The 1/5th Bedfordshires' history thus described the battalion as fighting 'the last Great Crusade into the Holy Land'.[15] Similarly, the Essex Regiment's historian stated that by early 1918 the 161st Brigade was serving on the ground where Richard the Lionheart and his men-at-arms had fought Saladin. Such grandiloquent accounts were not confined to British unit histories, but also occurred in those of Australian and New Zealand mounted regiments. The historians of the 5th ALH Regiment described receiving the unexpected news of Jerusalem's fall in December 1917. This was followed by the unambiguous statement that 'after four centuries of conquest the Holy City of Christendom was at last rid of the Turks'.[16] Similarly, the AMR's troopers were described in a uniquely antipodean phrase as 'dinkum crusaders'. The raft of historical and biblical references that peppered many unit histories fulfilled two distinct purposes. Allenby made clear in the preface to the history of the 1/5th Suffolks that the names of Gallipoli, Gaza, and Jerusalem were able to 'stir the blood', and that 'the campaigns that centre on them have an interest that is magnetic'.[17] The historical context, therefore, lent an appealing air of romance to the military exploits of the EEF's units, which helped to attract readers to what were often very humdrum texts. Secondly, these works were often intended for a limited audience, mainly the men who had served in the respective regiments and battalions in the Middle East as well as their interested relatives. Lieutenant-Colonel T. Gibbons, commander of the 1/5th Essex, noted in the preface to the work he wrote on his own battalion, that he wished he had known more about the region he had been fighting in. The account would fill in the gaps from the battalion's service and allow its former soldiers to learn about the historic significance of their battles and marches. The use of crusading and religious imagery therefore had both a literary and didactic function to fulfil.

During the interwar period it became almost a necessity to refer to the crusades in works on the EEF. A large number of personal narratives and unit histories alluded to the phenomenon in their titles, but then carried on with their formulaic military historical accounts: Arthur Briscoe Moore's work on the NZMR was subtitled *The Story of New Zealand's Crusaders*. The published exploits of a South African artillery battery was similarly entitled *Khaki Crusaders* (1919) and given a dramatic cover depicting a crusading knight incongruously offering his blessing on a modern artillery piece and its crew. Works of fiction based on the Palestine campaign, many of which were written in the bombastic style of George Henty and aimed principally at adolescent boys, also turned to crusading rhetoric to help entice in their readers. The prolific author Lieutenant-Colonel Frederick Brereton wrote a tale of two British agents trying to undermine the Turkish Army defending Gaza in 1917 entitled *With Allenby in Palestine: A Story of the Latest Crusade* (1920). In a corresponding vein Joseph Bowes produced *The Aussie Crusaders* (1920), the last of his trilogy of works on the Anzacs in the Middle East, that was set around the events of the Light Horsemen's charge at Beersheba. It was presented inside a cover portraying the archetypal Australian warrior, wielding a sword as he charges down his Turkish opponent.[18] This was a depiction that drew more on artistic fantasy than fact, as Light Horse units were not equipped with swords in 1917. The Australian Mounted Division was only given swords in mid-1918 and the ANZMD never carried swords in battle. Part of the fame of the Light Horse charge at Beersheba on 31 October 1917 derived from the very fact that the men attacked using their bayonets as an improvised *arme blanche*; a tale that the adolescent audience for Bowes's work would undoubtedly have been aware of.

It is unsurprising given the potential commercial benefits of referring to the crusades that another notable ripping yarn about the First World War, Lloyd George's war memoirs, got in on the act. During his discussion of the replacement of Murray as commander of the EEF, Lloyd George described the interview he had with Allenby before he was sent out to Egypt. He stated that it was on this occasion that he gave the general a copy of George Adam Smith's *The Historical Geography of the Holy Land* (1894). Lloyd George felt that this would be a better guide to fighting in Palestine than 'any survey to be found in the pigeon holes of the War Office'.[19] By 1917 Smith's work was very famous and had been produced in a number of editions, and it is unlikely that Allenby would have been unaware of it. This possibly apocryphal anecdote on the meeting between the Prime Minister and Allenby does, though, illustrate the power that the crusading metaphor had come to exercise by the mid-1930s. It seems that even Lloyd George felt his memoirs had to pander to the idea that the Palestine campaign could only be understood as a modern crusade firmly rooted in historical allusions, albeit one in which he played a decisive guiding role.

The wartime construction of a crusading army

The notion of the Palestine campaign as a crusade was not just the post-war construct of regimental historians, memoirists and novelists in search of sales. It had its origins in how the EEF's operations were perceived by, and presented to, the British public during the First World War. In its account of Allenby's entry into Jerusalem on 11 December 1917, *The Times* made it clear that the holy city had been liberated from oppressive Turkish rule. Moreover, William Thomas Massey's article was keen to demonstrate how the EEF had avoided damaging the city during the operations to secure its capture, unlike all of its previous conquerors. He noted that 'it is to the glory of British Arms that this most venerated place on earth should come through the ordeal of battle unharmed by the disturbance of even a particle of its ancient dust'.[20] Allenby was recorded as receiving a joyous and spontaneous welcome from the city's inhabitants. Importantly, Massey stressed the fact that the general had entered the city on foot, through the Jaffa Gate, in direct contrast to the visit of Kaiser Wilhelm II in 1898. On that occasion a large gap had been made in the city wall allowing the Kaiser to ride in on his horse, dressed in the radiant white uniform of a field marshal. *The Times* was not going to miss the opportunity of portraying one of the grandest moments of Britain's war in 1917 without the requisite pomp that it deserved.

Nor for that matter was the satirical magazine *Punch*, which commissioned its chief cartoonist, Bernard Partridge, to create a suitable image for the occasion. The result was a depiction of Richard I looking down on Jerusalem, with the caption 'My Dream Comes True' (see Illustration 2.1), printed in December 1917. Partridge's work alluded to Edward Gibbon's claim that on being unable to capture the city in 1191 Richard had declared that 'those who are unwilling to rescue, are unworthy to view, the sepulchre of Christ!'[21] This was the same tale with which Major Gilbert began his account of his Palestinian service, and clearly would have had some resonance among the predominantly middle-class readership of *Punch*. Partridge followed this up with a second bombastic cartoon in September 1919 which showed Allenby dressed as a knight returning home from the crusades and being welcomed by a grateful Britannia (see Illustration 2.2). Any doubts that *Punch* readers may have had about the crusading nature of the EEF's operations were now definitively rendered obsolete.

It was Lloyd George who was, in part, responsible for this casting of the Palestine campaign as part of a historic Middle Eastern holy war. In his summing up of the war during 1917 to the House of Commons he drew particular attention to the unique characteristics of Allenby's victory. The fall of Jerusalem, alongside that of Baghdad earlier in the year, had enhanced Britain's prestige in the world. He described Palestine

THE LAST CRUSADE.

Cœur-de-Lion (*looking down on the Holy City*). "MY DREAM COMES TRUE!"

Illustration 2.1 Bernard Partridge, 'The Last Crusade', *Punch*, 19 December 1917 (reproduced with permission of Punch Ltd).

as a 'famed land' that 'thrills with sacred memories', and noted that 'Beersheba, Hebron, Bethany, Bethlehem, the Mount of Olives are all names engraved on the heart of the world'.[22] It is unsurprising that for Lloyd George, well versed in chapel life and rhetoric, the EEF's success conjured up such romantic biblical images. This was not a spontaneous outpouring of joy at Allenby's success, but a carefully constructed assessment reflecting wider imperial concerns. The War Cabinet had decided on 21 November 1917 to control very carefully how the story of Jerusalem's capture would be reported. No announcement of the city's fall was to be made until the British government had had the opportunity to give assurances that its holy sites would be protected. The War Cabinet was aware of the enormous potential propaganda value

THE RETURN FROM THE CRUSADE.
FIELD-MARSHAL ALLENBY. "'SINGING FROM PALESTINE HITHER I COME;
LADY-LOVE, LADY-LOVE, WELCOME ME HOME.'"
BRITANNIA. "I DO INDEED—WITH ALL MY HEART!"

Illustration 2.2 Bernard Partridge, 'The Return from the Crusade', *Punch*, 17 September 1919 (reproduced with permission of Punch Ltd).

attached to the liberation of the holy city. This was particularly evident to Lloyd George as Jerusalem's fall seemed to vindicate his support for non-Western Front operations in opposition to the stance of the CIGS, General William Robertson.

The government, therefore, chose to assiduously promote around the world the success it had achieved in Palestine. Allenby's entry into Jerusalem was filmed and the War Office Cinematograph Committee produced a newsreel, released in February 1918. The feature proved very popular wherever it was shown in Britain and subsequently exported overseas with appropriate intertitles inserted, even including classical Hebrew for the Grand Rabbi at Salonica. As Matthew Hughes has noted, the short-term propaganda impact of Jerusalem's fall may have been limited in North America as a result of the media's focus on the explosion of a munitions ship in Halifax harbour on 6 December 1917 killing over 1,900 people, although this had a more limited impact in Britain. It is clear that the British government intended to milk Allenby's success for all that it was worth and kept promoting it well into 1918. Eight other films were produced on the campaign with titles that alluded explicitly to the perceived crusading context, including 'The New Crusaders – With the British Forces in Palestine' and 'With the Crusaders in the Holy Land – Allenby the Conqueror'.[23] In part, the dissemination of these newsreels was aimed at counteracting the loss of positive publicity in the United States due to the Halifax explosion.

It was not only noted publications, politicians and government propaganda that referred to the Middle Eastern campaign in terms of its crusading and religious elements. At a parochial level in Britain, community organizations and the regional press drew on similar rhetoric to portray the actions of local men and units in terms of a wider discourse on the aims of the war. *The Northampton Independent*, for example, produced a cartoon in April 1917, in a somewhat more simplistic style than those of Partridge, which depicted a British soldier shaking hands with a crusader in the Holy Land (see Illustration 2.3). The cartoon was headed 'History Repeated after Eight Centuries' and was followed by a brief article explaining the details of the medieval reference. The paper pointed to the fact that the 1/4th Northamptonshires were currently serving in Palestine and were on the same ground that the crusader Simon de Senlis, the first Earl of Northampton, had fought over 821 years before. It was described as 'a romantic coincidence' that the battalion, whose commander worshipped at the church constructed by returning crusaders in Northampton, should be 'marching over the same hallowed ground, fighting against the same enemy, and for the same object as did the Crusaders of old'.[24] In Norwich similar sentiments were expressed during a May 1917 memorial service for Major W. H. Jewson and Captain S. D. Page of the 1/4th Norfolks, killed at Second Gaza. The Reverend Albert Lowe, of the Prince's Street Congregational Church, stated that the regiment was fighting 'against the Turk with a view to ridding the Holy Land of his corrupting presence'.[25] The rhetoric of the crusades was thus prevalent among a number of communities whose local units were serving with the EEF in Palestine. It is also notable that both of these examples predate Allenby's entry into Jerusalem by over half a year. At this stage of the campaign the EEF had suffered two devastating defeats at Gaza and seemed highly unlikely of ever achieving the glorious crusading goals being set for it at home.

By mid-1918 the EEF was in a much stronger position, having driven the Turks from southern Palestine and now occupying a line from Jaffa through Jerusalem and down to the Dead Sea. This allowed British troops to be given leave in the holy city, providing article writers at *The Times* with an opportunity to again reinforce the religious connotations of the EEF's campaign. It was noted that in April 1918 the British Army had been able to celebrate Easter in a location where English soldiers had never before prayed at Easter. Moreover, the Christians of the city were now protected by the 'victorious sword of St. George'.[26] *The Times* also drew out the crusading context that surrounded those British soldiers who visited and prayed in the churches of Jerusalem. Thus in the Church of the Holy Sepulchre troops could see the tomb of the Anglo-Norman knight Sir Philip Daubigny, drawing a direct link to the historic

Illustration 2.3 W. Humberrary, 'History Repeated after Eight Centuries', *The Northampton Independent*, 21 April 1917.

military service of English warriors in the Middle East. In addition, the paper stressed the reverence that British soldiers showed to the Christian heritage of the city, with men kissing the stone that covered Christ's traditional tomb in the Holy Sepulchre.

It is unsurprising that, with the prevalence of such rhetoric by 1918, the General Secretary of the Palestine Exploration Fund, Ernest Masterman, saw this as a good opportunity to produce a book on Jerusalem's liberation, and *The Deliverance of Jerusalem* appeared before the war's end. The bulk of the work was concerned with the history of the city, but three chapters were devoted to describing the contemporary war with Turkey and the course it had taken in Palestine. Masterman's account of the EEF's advance was, like many of the works that would follow it, liberally seasoned with references to the region's biblical past. The route taken during the advance on Jerusalem was thus noted to be the same as that used by Antiochus III, who had defeated Judas Maccabeus, and which was later used by Richard I.[27] By the end of the First World War it was evident that audiences were expected to view the EEF's campaigns through a particular rhetorical framework. These operations were portrayed as a crusade, fought to liberate the Holy Land from oppressive Turkish rule, and as such had to be described with frequent reference to the biblical and historic context.

The wartime quest for moderation

This wartime emphasis on the Palestine campaign as a crusade ran counter to the manner in which the British government wished to portray the EEF's operations. The official aim was to provide a balanced view of Britain's activities in the Middle East at both a cultural and a religious level. It was for this reason that an article in *The Evening Standard* on 8 November 1917 was brought to the attention of Colonel John Buchan heading a department of information at the Foreign Office. The extract suggested that Allenby's recent capture of Gaza offered up a range of possibilities as Jerusalem could now be directly threatened. This would allow it to be liberated from the thousand-year rule of the 'infidels' and would mean 'that for the first time the flag of a Christian nation will float over its walls'.[28] This controversial and potentially inflammatory piece of journalism led the Press Bureau to produce a D-Notice on 15 November, reminding the press of how they should approach the British Army's Middle Eastern operations. The notice stated that:

> The attention of the Press is again drawn to the undesirability of publishing any article paragraph or picture suggesting that military operations against Turkey are in any sense a Holy War, a modern Crusade, or have anything whatever to do with religious questions. The British Empire is said to contain a hundred million Muhammadan subjects of the King and it is obviously mischievous to suggest that our quarrel with Turkey is one between Christianity and Islam.[29]

In light of much of the reporting in 1917 and 1918, it is clear that this proclamation from the Press Bureau was widely ignored. It nevertheless indicates the government's aim of avoiding the serious implications for the British Empire that may have resulted from any religious strife provoked by incendiary reporting of the Palestine campaign.[30] More importantly, by mid-1918 the majority of the EEF's fighting formations were composed of Indian units, a large proportion of whom were recruited from the subcontinent's Muslim population and were fighting their co-religionists. Portraying Allenby's campaign as a crusade, with Christian set against Muslim, thus had the potential to undermine the loyalty of a large proportion of his soldiers and of harming the army's morale.

Despite the failure of much of the British press to stick to the terms of the D-Notice, it is clear that the ethos of producing a balanced and non-provocative view of the Palestine campaign began to pervade a number of government departments by late 1917. In November, Wellington House, the government's propaganda arm, noted that care was being taken to label any photographs of the EEF as taken 'in Palestine', rather than 'in the Holy Land'.[31] Similarly, the Foreign Office turned down the idea of producing a Jerusalem medal in December 1917, as it could be perceived as endorsing the idea of the campaign as a modern crusade. The prohibitions of the D-Notice had a great effect on the desire of Mark Sykes, then acting as a liaison between the EEF and Foreign Office, for articles to be written about the Palestine campaign, which could then be passed on to promote the theatre in the press. In a request to Reginald Wingate, High Commissioner for Egypt, he asked for three different pieces: the first was to deal with the situation at the Church of the Holy Sepulchre and in Bethlehem, the second was to be an account of the Mosque of Omar (also known as the Dome of the Rock), and the third was for a description of the condition of the Jewish colonies.[32] The aim was to provide the press with information that covered the beneficial implications of nascent British rule in Palestine for all of the region's three major religions.

The article that Sykes eventually received from Colonel Storrs, however, did not meet these high expectations. Sykes objected to the 'highbrow line' that Storrs had taken and instead wanted a 'popular reading for English church and chapel folk; for New York Irish; Orthodox Balkan peasants and Mujihs; French and Italian Catholics; and Jews throughout world; Indian and Algerian Moslems'. He wanted articles that would 'rivet British on to Holy Land Bible and New Testament' as well as 'jam Catholics on Holy places, sepulchre, via Dolorosa, and Bethlehem'.[33] Bar-Yosef has argued that Sykes realized that a secular narrative of the Palestine campaign would fail to excite the British public, and instead the reports had to describe the region in the biblical vernacular tradition with which they were familiar. This interpretation neglects the fact that Sykes stressed the need for articles which also appealed to Orthodox Christians, Jews, and Muslims. He wanted the latter group to be rallied by descriptions of the Muslims' absolute control of the Mosque of Omar. Sykes was happy to have press reports laden with biblical rhetoric, so long as they were complemented by ones that appealed to Jewish and Islamic sentiments, which were increasingly viewed as vital to the conduct of Britain's imperial war effort.

The desire to avoid antagonizing non-Christian opinion around the world, and particularly in the British Empire, came to the fore in relation to discussions over Allenby's formal entry into Jerusalem on 11 December 1917. Lloyd George set down a strict set of criteria that Allenby had to follow during the ceremony which included placing a political officer in charge of the city's Christian holy sites and establishing a protective military cordon around the Islamic ones. In accordance with tradition, the historic custodians of the Wakf at the gate of the Holy Sepulchre were also to be maintained. It was decided that Allenby would make his entrance on foot, to stand in deliberate contrast to the Kaiser's bombastic entry on horseback in 1898. General Robertson noted in a telegram to Allenby that when the Kaiser had ridden into Jerusalem a saying went round that 'a better man than he walked' and consequently the 'advantage of contrast in conduct will be obvious'.[34] The War Cabinet insisted that no flags should be flown during his entry, 'in view of the unique character of the city and of the many difficult political and diplomatic questions that were raised in connection with it'.[35] The ceremony was designed to be the opposite of a triumphal occupation. Great effort was made to ensure that troops from all of the various nationalities serving with the EEF were represented in the occasion. Thus Allenby walked in accompanied by a few members of his staff, the commanders of the French and Italian detachments, the head of the Picot mission, and the military attachés of France, Italy and the United States. The guards that received him at the Jaffa Gate consisted of men from England, Wales,

Scotland, Ireland, Australia, New Zealand, India, France and Italy. A key element in the entry was the issuing of a proclamation which set out that the city was under martial law. Crucially, it also stated that 'every sacred building, monument, holy spot, shrine, traditional site, endowment, pious bequest or customary place of prayer, of whatever form of the three religions, will be monitored and protected according to the existing customs and beliefs of those to whose faiths they are sacred'.[36] The proclamation was issued in English, Arabic, Hebrew, French, Italian, Greek and Russian to ensure its wide circulation among the various communities of the local population. The aim was to show that the British would not be Jerusalem's Christian conquerors, but would continue and attempt to improve upon the Ottoman's ecumenical rule of the holy city preventing interfaith and inter-denominational strife.

Lord Curzon and Mark Sykes were responsible for the tone of the proclamation, which was primarily a response to Foreign Office concerns about Muslim opinion around the world and particularly in India. It was made clear at a War Cabinet meeting in mid-November 1917 that the Mosque of Omar was one of the three most sacred sites in Islam, after the Kaaba of Mecca and the Home of the Prophet in Medina. By issuing such a proclamation and successfully protecting the holy sites of Jerusalem, the British gained a significant propaganda victory that resounded to their benefit. Reginald Wingate pushed the propaganda value of the city's liberation and occupation by British imperial forces, arguing that it should be widely reported in India that troops of the Indian Army were being used to guard the sacred sites of Islam. Allenby felt that such stringent protections were necessary, as otherwise souvenir hunters would have soon pulled the Wailing Wall and Temple site to pieces. He was also aware of the need to placate not only the wider Islamic world but also local Muslim opinion; the risk of a Palestinian uprising in the rear of the EEF was a serious concern. The dangers of any unrest, which could threaten the EEF's vital logistical infrastructure, were clear to Allenby who was utilizing Prince Feisal's Northern Arab Army to cause just such difficulties along the Turks' lines of communication.

The concerns over the protection of Islamic sites predated Allenby's seizure of Jerusalem in December 1917. In May, Murray had reprimanded Lieutenant-General Philip Chetwode, then commander of Eastern Force, for the destruction of the mosque in Gaza. He stated that clear orders had been given that it could only be shelled with the express permission of the Commander-in-Chief.[37] Chetwode was, however, unrepentant, arguing that as the Turks were making extensive use of the mosque's minaret for artillery observation the protection of the lives of his men had to be his paramount concern. This demonstrates that at times a desire to protect the religious fabric of Palestine could run into conflict with military imperatives. It also illustrates the fact that the EEF's commanders were well aware of the problems that could ensue if they were seen to wantonly attack Islamic holy sites or places of worship, a concern which Allenby would have inherited long before the War Cabinet stressed it to him.

The EEF's care towards the sacred infrastructure of Palestine ensured the quiescence of the local population. By January 1918 Allenby was able to inform the War Office's Director of Military Intelligence that Muslim opinion in the region was improving, although at times it was non-committal. He noted that 'it is remarked that measures taken to protect Moslem sacred places caused universal satisfaction'.[38] More importantly, the reporting in India of Allenby's entry into Jerusalem and proclamation was stated by the Viceroy to have had the 'sedative effect on Moslem feeling' that Curzon desired. It is also of note that the Indianized EEF, which emerged in mid-1918, experienced relatively few disciplinary problems and only a limited number of desertions. Indian Muslim soldiers appeared to have accepted the official line that they were not taking part in a modern crusade and remained loyal to the British Empire.

The army's religious fringe

In order to examine the impact of the crusading and religious rhetoric that surrounded the campaign it is necessary to engage with the personal attitudes of the EEF's officers and men, and the manner in which they interpreted their war in the Middle East. Any such discussion inevitably touches on the nebulous question of the extent of religious belief and practice in early twentieth-century Britain. It is possible to see this period as demonstrating a steady decline in Christian worship, with only 2.75 million practising Anglicans, 2.5 million Catholics, and nearly 2 million members of the Free Churches, out of a total population of 36 million at the outbreak of the First World War. In London there was a considerable fall in the number of people regularly attending church, from 30 per cent of the metropolitan population in 1851 to only 22 per cent by 1903. In some rural areas the fall was proportionately even larger, with Oxfordshire seeing a shift from 45 per cent attendance in 1851 to 25 per cent in 1913.[39] Much of this change was related to falling numbers of middle-class worshippers, who had played a critical role in the religious revival of the first half of the nineteenth century. Although working-class districts saw a smaller reduction in attendance rates these were generally much lower to begin with. As S. J. D. Green has argued, this decline in regular church attendance had a significant impact on the ability of the churches to disseminate their Christian teachings widely throughout society. If people stopped going to church then it was likely that they would stop believing, or at the very least their beliefs would lose doctrinal rigidity. To a certain extent the shift in Sunday worship can be viewed as a product of the rapid growth of the leisure industry in the late nineteenth and early twentieth centuries. The Churches were struggling to maintain their popularity in the face of competition from more materialist sources for the time of the British population. This decline arguably represented a 'crisis of faith' in Britain by the outbreak of the First World War.[40]

On the other hand, as Adrian Gregory has elucidated, 'reports of the death of God in Edwardian Britain are much exaggerated'.[41] The problem of the 'Godless masses' sparked a significant evangelical movement in Britain during the nineteenth and early twentieth centuries, which had achieved considerable success in the fields of education and church building by 1914. Sunday school teaching proved very popular, with attendance rates of around 50 per cent of all children under 15 years of age between 1880 and 1914. The majority of day schools provided some form of religious education and a large number were attached to a specific denomination. Criticism of declining national church attendance rates also fails to take account of strong and distinct regional and denominational variations, such as the importance of

Wesleyanism in Yorkshire and Lancashire, or Presbyterianism in Scotland. Although Sunday worship was not as healthy as it could have been, other church-based practices proved resilient. Nearly 80 per cent of marriages took place in church and 75 per cent of the population received baptisms. It is also inaccurate to portray urbanization as the sole force acting to undermine working-class beliefs. As Sarah Williams has made clear in her study of the London borough of Southwark, many church-based rituals were intermingled with urban folk religion. This practice helped to ensure that large numbers of workers were still taking part in some form of religious worship, such as the match-night services associated with the prevention of bad luck. The creation of the University Missions, such as Toynbee Hall, in many of Britain's towns and cities suggests that the Churches were adapting to the changing patterns of working-class belief. Moreover, the commemorative processes and sites of remembrance that sprung up after the First World War demonstrated the prevalence and resilience of religious belief and practice in British society. As Catherine Moriarty has noted, the vast bulk of war memorials contain some form of Christian iconography, and a number are located within a Christian setting.[42]

Reflecting the analysis that the early twentieth century still saw widespread Christian belief in Britain, Callum Brown's work demonstrates that the process of secularization needs to be handled with much greater care. He locates the rapid fall in church attendance in the 1960s, showing that even in 1957, 72 per cent of all marriages were still taking place in church, only falling to 60 per cent by 1970, a trend of decline that continued through to the end of the century.[43] Brown argues that the problems of religiosity in the 1960s were caused by the loss of female members of the Churches. Piety had increasingly been conceived since the late nineteenth century as an overwhelmingly feminine trait which challenged masculinity and had already driven a large proportion of the male population away from the Churches. This had a direct impact on the extent of religious belief among male combatants serving in the First World War. The levels of church attendance in 1914, although showing a slight rise on those of the late nineteenth century, still demonstrate the limited extent of religious practice in Britain. The Church of England received 2.2 million Easter communicants that year, representing 9.2 per cent of the adult population. Even taking into account the other denominations, it is hard to argue that more than 20–30 per cent of Britons in 1914 were attending one of the key ceremonies of the sacred calendar. This leaves an unanswered question as to what the other 70 per cent of the population were doing; it is clear that they, and in this case predominantly working-class men, were not taking part in regular religious worship.

The lack of male participation in, and understanding of, Christianity was an issue that deeply concerned contemporary churchmen. This led to the production of *The Army and Religion* survey, which attempted to comprehend the problems that the Churches faced by 1918. It was based on 300 questionnaires sent out to British and Dominion soldiers, from generals through to privates, and including chaplains. The responses were studied by a committee in 1917–18 convened by Edward Talbot, the Bishop of Winchester, and the Reverend David Cairns, Professor of Dogmatics and Apologetics at Aberdeen University. The report found that a number of soldiers did turn to religion in times of need, with praying before combat a common practice.

It was felt that 'at the front the impact of danger awakens the religious consciousness even of the most unlikely men'. This success for the Churches was tempered by a deep concern among respondents as to whether soldiers actually understood even the basic tenets of Christianity. The report made it clear that there was considerable ignorance on this front. One of the respondents was quoted as stating that 'the whole deeper side of the Church's teaching about Jesus Christ seems to have little or no hold upon them, except of the loosest kind'. The overall conclusion of the survey was summed up by the aphorism that 'the soldier has got religion, I am not so sure that he has got Christianity'.[44]

As *The Army and Religion* survey made clear, the faith of British combatants was a complex matter, one that can rarely be conceptually organized so as to fit neatly into the analytical theories of historians wishing to illustrate religious decline or revival during the First World War. It is evident from soldiers' personal accounts that, as Rich Schweitzer has noted, religious responses to the war are best understood in terms of a spectrum of belief, varying from individuals of devout faith through to ardent atheists. Crucially, individual soldiers did not occupy a fixed position on this spectrum, and could therefore move freely along it altering their attitudes in relation to their experiences of the war and thinking on religion. Furthermore, attempts to categorize religious faith at the front line in terms of conventional Christianity, particularly that of the Church of England, face similar interpretative obstacles. Although criticism of conventional religious worship could be prominent among British soldiers, men often indulged in a diffuse and loosely defined form of spirituality. Edward Madigan's superlative study of Church of England chaplains makes clear that fatalism, superstition and an idealism of archetypal military traits often competed for the spiritual attention of combatants.[45] At the front line, and particularly under the strains of battle, the religion of the British soldier, like that of the peacetime society from which he came, could not be easily pinpointed. In many respects it appears that early twentieth-century Britain was defined by a vague cultural Christianity that produced unconscious Christians in the trenches of the First World War.

Within this often forthright historiographical debate on wartime religiosity little attention is paid to the multiplicity of attitudes and experiences of the men who served in the Middle East with the EEF. In particular, there is a need to engage with the accounts of those soldiers who did express strong religious beliefs while fighting the Ottoman Empire, in contrast to the lamentable findings of *The Army and Religion* survey in relation to the BEF. These men may have represented a religious fringe to the EEF that was able to see the Holy Land through the lens of a biblical vernacular culture, and who may, therefore, have been open to considering their military service as a form of crusade.

Both of the commanders of the EEF demonstrated a clear understanding of the religious significance of the land they were fighting in. An American pilgrim who met Allenby during a tour of Palestine in 1918–19 was greatly impressed by the general's interest in the Old Testament and Smith's *The Historical Geography of the Holy Land*. Allenby's biblical knowledge was evident in his letters home to his wife. In one he recalled a visit to Kuryet el Enab in the Judaean hills, which he noted was a sacred well at which Jesus had met two men on the way to Emmaus.[46] In letters to his mother

Allenby revealed an even greater degree of biblical understanding. He described a ride that he had taken to the site of Abu Shushe, and noted that it was 'built by King Horam, in Joshua's time; and was a Canaanite stronghold, till Pharaoh killed them off and gave the place as a dowry to Solomon with his daughter'. Included with this quotation was a reference to the Book of Kings from which he had drawn the information. Allenby went further than just peppering his letters with references to engaging biblical anecdotes. He drew out military parallels between campaigns in the Bible and those of the EEF. He stated in correspondence to his mother that: 'I have been reading Isaiah; and have been following the campaigns of Joshua. I have fought over much of this country. In Makkidah, where he hanged the five kings of the Amorites, to us Magra; where my Bucks Yeomanry rode a fine charge in the middle of November.'[47] It is important to consider the audience that Allenby was writing for in this correspondence. Both his mother and his wife clearly had a strong interest in the historic and religious associations of his Middle Eastern service. Such descriptions may also have served to fill out the contents of letters that could reveal little of the detail of military operations or potentially harrowing descriptions of the effects of modern war. It is interesting to note that biblical references are found in these personal letters and very rarely in his military correspondence, suggesting that any avowed curiosity he had for Christianity was a private matter and not part of Allenby's carefully cultivated military image. In addition, a considerable proportion of his letters were dominated by references to the wild flowers and bird life of Palestine.[48] In many respects Allenby saw himself as more of a naturalist than a crusader.

Murray demonstrated a similar interest in religion, frequently attending church parades when in Egypt and holy communion at the General Headquarters (GHQ) recreation tent. This led one chaplain, serving with the 24th Royal Welch Fusiliers, to exclaim that Murray was 'a true Christian man'.[49] Reverend Price echoed this sentiment after dining with Murray in April 1916, although his conclusion was based on the fact that the general took a keen interest in reducing the rates of venereal disease within the EEF. It was not only the Commanders-in-Chief who exhibited a degree of Christian belief. Major-General Steuart Hare, commanding 54th Division, made a point of regularly attending church and was described by his aide-de-camp as 'very Christian in his ideas'.[50] Public expressions of faith could, though, take on more theatrical qualities for some officers. Lieutenant-Colonel Charles Mackesy, commanding the AMR, was reputed to have taken his hat off as the regiment crossed the border into Palestine and thanked God for allowing him to see the Holy Land. Such effusive displays of public Christianity reveal little about those officers' private beliefs. Some commanders felt that the outward observance of Christian rituals and ceremony was what was expected of officers of their rank and status. For example, on the Western Front, Lieutenant-General Ivor Maxse, one of the few avowed atheist generals, frequently attended church parades as he considered it a good encouragement to the morale of his men.[51] Moreover, from the mid-nineteenth century onwards Christianity had assumed a prominent place in the identity and cultural routine of the regular army. This was seen clearly in the growth of the chaplains' department and the role of regular worship in the army's imperial stations, as well as the crusades against the soldiers' moral laxities in respect of sex and drink. Senior officers were very much a product of this tradition and, irrespective of their personal beliefs, may have indulged in elements of Christianity for its perceived impact on morale and fostering of communal military identities.

References to locations in Palestine in terms of their biblical significance were not restricted to the correspondence of Allenby. A number of officers and men across the EEF alluded to a variety of locations with religious significance. Captain V. H. Bailey, an artillery officer in 54th Division, noted in his diary that when he advanced over the Wadi el Arish its biblical name was 'the River of Egypt'. Similarly, on seeing the orchards and olive groves at Ras Deiran, Lieutenant James Greatorex, an officer in the 1st ALH Machine Gun Squadron, recorded that he was in a land 'flowing with milk and honey'.[52] Some soldiers made trips to visit particularly renowned biblical sites in Egypt and Palestine. Second Lieutenant S. Blagg, of 53rd Division, visited Rebekah's well at Romani and then went to see a sycamore tree that was alleged to be at least 2,000 years old and which had sheltered the Holy family. It was often the case that soldiers described the local inhabitants of the Middle East as resembling illustrations in their Bibles. Private F. V. Blunt, of 60th Division, was struck by this when he observed Palestinian women filling their bottles at a well. In these cases the Bible was helping to provide familiar points of cultural reference for EEF soldiers serving in an alien land.

The value of Christian faith could go further for some men and act as a psychologically protective force during combat. Lance-Corporal William Hickman, of the 1/8th Hampshires, believed that the dangers of war brought him closer to God. He recalled offering up silent prayers, as a result of which he claimed that he would 'feel stronger and steadier and more able to stand the strain that is put on your nerves'.[53] The pressures of combat and the presence of a landscape that could be readily interpreted in Christian terms led some men to become more deeply involved with religion. Corporal Charles Livingstone, of the 6th ALH Regiment, was so taken by the fact that his unit was camping near to the spot where Jesus was baptized in the Jordan that he decided to follow this spiritual example. After much persuasion he managed to convince a monk from the monastery on the Mount of Temptation to baptize him. It was not just British and Anzac troops who were affected by the sacred soil they found themselves fighting on. In the 39th (Reserve) Mountain Battery three of its Indian NCOs asked one of their British officers to give them a short lecture on Palestine. Only one of the three had been educated in a mission school and the officer was surprised to find his Muslim NCOs to be well acquainted with much of the region's biblical history.

There was a considerable amount of interest across the EEF in uncovering the Christian heritage of the battleground. This may reflect the use of a biblical vernacular culture, imbibed at school, home, and in Sunday schools, as a means of giving meaning and relevance to a theatre of operations seemingly removed from the main course of the war. These examples, however, only demonstrate the barest of understanding of this Christian tradition, with religious references simply used to illustrate particular events or places related in letters, diaries or memoirs. A small religious fringe within the EEF did demonstrate a strong and detailed engagement with the Christian significance of their military service in the Middle East. Private Albert Surry, of the 1/7th Essex, represents one such example. He felt that the need for prayer and quiet communion was much stronger while he was stationed in the solitude of the Sinai Desert than when he was among the comforts of home. The spirituality of Sinai was self-evident, leading Surry to note that 'privation and hardships on the desert bring one nearer to one's maker'. When he witnessed a moonlit rainbow on Christmas Eve 1917 Surry found it one of the most inspiring moments of his life; it was of course an event laden with religious symbolism. He described it as stretching from Bethlehem through to Nazareth and that it sanctified 'the Glory of Goodness in God through Jesus'.[54]

These fervent Christian beliefs were mirrored in the letters written home by Second Lieutenant G. B. Buxton, of the 1/5th Norfolks. Both his parents had been missionaries in Japan and this led him to follow their evangelical example while serving in the EEF. This began before he even reached Egypt, as he handed out copies of the New Testament to the men on his troop ship. Once serving with his battalion he held weekly prayer meetings and Bible reading sessions, which served to build bonds between the unit's fellow Christians and enhance his proselytizing efforts on behalf of the Church. Buxton took as his military and Christian model the figure of General Gordon, who he had read about while recovering from German measles in a military hospital. He claimed that it was the most thrilling book he had ever read and left him with the desire to emulate his new hero, a man who was 'fearless to the last degree, a real Christian', and as a result undoubtedly 'England's finest General'.[55]

This proselytizing ethos was demonstrated to an even greater degree by Trooper Alec McNeur, of the NZMR Machine Gun Squadron. McNeur held prayer meetings and Bible classes each week for the squadron as well as taking two Sunday services in October 1917. His fame as a preacher was such that the CMR's Major Whithorn, who were without a chaplain, asked him to take their church parades. By March 1918, McNeur was still preaching at Sunday services for his squadron. He referred to his religious mission in a letter to his brother, stating that 'I feel that I have done right coming in the ranks as those I come in personal contact with at work are just the ones I have been able to help the most'.[56] His concern for religious matters was such that he even engaged in discussions in his correspondence about the denominational difficulties he faced. On one occasion he apologized for writing on Catholic notepaper headed with an engraving of the College of St Joseph in Jaffa. He also absented himself from a Bible class regularly attended by New Zealand brethren, whose conscientious objections clashed with his more bellicose Christian stance. The war remained a divisive topic among Christians reflecting the fact that the Churches did not have a settled view on their relationship to the national and imperial military effort.

The examples provided by Surry, Buxton and McNeur represent the only strong cases of individuals who were fully engaged with a biblical vernacular tradition in the EEF out of the over 80 unpublished personal paper collections of EEF soldiers covered in this study. Although this in itself is only a miniscule fraction of the correspondence and personal narratives produced by soldiers in the Middle East during the First World War, it nevertheless demonstrates that such ardent beliefs constituted only a Christian fringe outside of the mainstream avenues of weak and diffuse sacred thought found across the EEF.

There was one occasion during the course of the Palestine campaign when official sanction was given to the expression of such strong Christian beliefs. This was the Roman Catholic Soldiers' Congress, held in Jerusalem on 15 August 1918.[57] The event took the form of a pilgrimage made by 1,500 Catholic soldiers coinciding with the Feast of Our Lady's Assumption. It was the brainchild of Major-General W. G. B. Western, the EEF's Deputy Adjutant General, and Father Felix Couturier, assistant to the EEF's Principal Chaplain. The event proved popular among the Catholic soldiers of the EEF, with the Catholic chaplain at Mustapha Camp near to Alexandria only allowed to choose 16 men from 250 applicants. The pilgrimage took the form of a parade that visited the Church of the Holy Sepulchre and the Via Dolorosa, where a chaplain explained each stage of the cross to the men. It culminated with a service at St Stephen's basilica, during which the Franciscan Custos of the Holy Land gave the Benediction of the Blessed Sacrament and the Papal Blessing, the latter having been granted by telegram from Rome.[58] The congress represented a strong expression of religious belief that would suggest a potent Christian ethos among a sizeable proportion of the EEF. The pilgrimage, however, actually underlines the limits of these beliefs. Although attended by 1,500 men it represented only a small proportion of the EEF's strength, which had risen to 306,274 men by September 1918.[59] The fact that men had to be drawn from across the EEF, including units in Egypt, demonstrates that the take-up among the army's front-line battalions and regiments in Palestine was relatively low. This was the result of the Indianization of the 10th (Irish) Division in mid-1918, a division which had contained a sizeable Catholic presence. It is also unclear how those soldiers who took part in the pilgrimage viewed the event. Many of those who attended may have seen it simply as an opportunity for a break from military duties, rather than as a deeply spiritual experience.

Not to be outdone by Rome, the Church of England also attempted to influence the ideological approach of the EEF during the course of the Palestine campaign. In July 1917, Randall Davidson, Archbishop of Canterbury, wrote to Rennie MacInnes, the Anglican Bishop in Jerusalem who was at that stage in Egypt, regarding the Church's attitude to a potential Allied seizure of Jerusalem. Davidson made it clear that he wanted a Christian presence during any triumphal entry into the city, believing that Britain, as a Christian power, should send formal greetings to Jerusalem's Christian religious chiefs. MacInnes was chosen by Davidson to act as his representative on this occasion and was to be provided with letters of introduction. In light of the numerous restrictions placed on Allenby by the government to ensure that his entry would not offend Muslim opinion, it is unsurprising to find that in October he rejected MacInnes's entreaties to be allowed to accompany him as an honorary chaplain.[60] The rebuttal referred directly to the fact that MacInnes's presence would anger the ecclesiastics of Britain's allies, who may well have had a better claim to taking part in such a ceremony.

MacInnes's religious ethos placed him at odds with the desire of the high command of the EEF to avoid controversy in the Middle East. In May 1917, he had written to Wingate, High Commissioner for Egypt, to make the highly dubious suggestion that on conquering Palestine the British administration should take over all buildings that had once been churches and were now used as mosques. He enunciated his belief that the British government was often too eager to placate Muslim opinion, and that this could be damaging, as 'the measure designed by the Western mind to show magnanity and tolerance, is regarded by the Eastern as a sign of weakness and fear'.[61] In a counter-intuitive argument he suggested that the Muslim population would expect Britain to seize such buildings, and the conqueror's image would ultimately be weakened if they were left in the hands of those who had desecrated them. The British administration in Egypt took rapid steps to dissuade MacInnes from taking his idea any further. It was suggested that the matter would have to be approved by the Archbishop of Canterbury first and then a commission set up to look into the exact situation on the ground in any Ottoman territory acquired by Britain. Wingate felt that any future military administration would attempt to alter the administrative *status quo* as little as possible in occupied areas. He argued that a statement of this fact would 'prove the most effective check to proposals of an impolitic nature made by ecclesiastics of various denominations'.[62] In order to finally close off avenues for argument, a staff captain from the EEF was appointed to make a feasibility study into MacInnes's scheme. The report found that the suggestion had been natural enough for a bishop to make, but did not take any account of the military or political situation in Palestine. It pointed out that the Orthodox and Catholic Churches, with their historic presence in the region, would have much more to gain than the Church of England from such a proposal. The report's author felt the objections were obvious and unanswerable, stating that 'Bishop MacInnes appears to regard our invasion of Palestine somewhat in the light of a Crusade, the success of which should place Christianity in a predominant position over Islam and other Confessions'.[63] MacInnes was an example of an individual whose strong Christian faith led him to see the war with Turkey as a religiously endorsed struggle. In part this was simply a product of his Episcopal position in the Middle East. When consecrated in this post in 1914 he was told that 'the Bishop in Jerusalem must be a missionary'; in 1917 MacInnes appeared to be pressing just such an evangelizing agenda.[64] It is unsurprising to find that his consecration was carried out by the Bishop of London, Arthur Winnington-Ingram, who rose to national fame during the First World War for his controversial, patriotic and bellicose rhetoric that saw the destruction of the Kaiser's Germany in the terms of a holy war.

MacInnes's approach to the Middle East was replicated in some of the comments evinced by EEF soldiers. In a relatively limited number of cases explicit references were made to the campaign as a crusade. The most public espousal of this idea was contained in Major-General Hare's Order of the Day issued to 54th Division after Third Gaza in November 1917. He praised his division's combat success, stating that:

> This gateway between Egypt and the Holy Land is one of the historic battlegrounds of the world, and the 54th Division has shown fighting qualities worthy of this scene of countless battles between Assyrians and Egyptians, Israelites and Philistines, Saracens and Crusaders.[65]

In some cases these crusading references were brought out by the specific local historic geography of the areas that units were operating in. Major Fredrick Clarke, serving in 1/10th Londons, noted that the crusader castle at Ras el Ain was reported by a number of the East Anglian men in 54th Division to be haunted by armoured knights.[66] Similarly, when the CMR was stationed at Tel el Jemme Sergeant Harold Judge recorded in his diary that the hills were artificial defences built by the crusaders. It was not only medieval military architecture that sparked the men's interest. The Reverend E. C. Mortimer, a chaplain with 54th Division, visited the Church of St George at Ludd, and while there contemplated the similarities between the legend of the saintly warrior and the Greek myth of Perseus and Andromeda. It is to be expected that chaplains and other members of the EEF's religious fringe would be most likely to see crusading allusions in the world around them. As he approached Jerusalem the Reverend W. A. Jones, attached to the 24th Royal Welch Fusiliers, took care to note in his diary that he was looking down on the city from Neby Samwil, where Richard I had supposedly gazed upon the holy sites with great reverence. After visiting Jerusalem in December 1918 Private Surry wrote a 13-page letter to his parents going into great detail about the sacred locations he had visited, proclaiming that: 'I little thought that I should ever stand in the Holy Sepulchre itself and now after thirty months of one might say, crusading, that privilege has been mine.'[67] Even Allenby was capable of being entranced by the historic ambience of Palestine. He wrote to his wife in late November 1917 that the EEF was fighting its way up north 'by the road taken by Richard Coeur de Lion; and we have reached about the point at which he turned back'.[68]

In some cases the event or location that caused a soldier to hark back to the medieval past did not always fit such a logical pattern. While studying on an officer cadet course in Cairo, Second Lieutenant S. Blagg, of 1/4th Royal Sussex, quizzed his dentist about his origins discovering that he was Syrian but had Greek ancestors. This led Blagg to write home to his mother that the discussions had apparently 'brought the Crusades nearer to me than ever before to know that the Greeks were there too; doubtless running the canteens and robbing from the troops'.[69] These references from a small cross section of the EEF demonstrate that the use of crusading imagery was not confined to the officer elite as argued by Bar-Yosef. In many respects the evidence from the EEF runs counter to traditional interpretations of the high cultural role of chivalric ideology in the First World War. Much of this analysis is, though, overly concerned with a select group of literary luminaries, among whom John Masefield's use of the *Chanson de Roland* in his account of Gallipoli and Rupert Brooke's rhetorical flourishes stand out.[70] A wider focus across the army that served in Egypt and Palestine reveals that all ranks were capable of indulging in romantic notions of a medieval crusading past.

The army's religious infrastructure: Chaplains and the YMCA

Much of the basic knowledge of the historic and biblical landscape of Palestine was provided for the men of the EEF by the chaplains who served alongside them. Services were often used to pass on local information that was thought to be of interest. At a service for a company of the 1/5th Bedfordshires on Zweifi Hill, the chaplain talked about the miracles of St Peter which had occurred at Ludd and Jaffa, both of which were in sight of the troops' position.[71] Trooper Ion Idriess, serving in the 5th ALH Regiment, felt that his unit's chaplain had become obsessed with the region's historical ruins, constantly giving lectures about them. As a result a number of the men of the regiment turned to amateur archaeology to fill their spare time. Not all of these attempts at providing information for the men proved popular. Reverend McNeile wrote a pamphlet entitled 'In the Footsteps of the Lord in Palestine', but it failed to appeal to the EEF's soldiers and remained largely unknown. These spasmodic attempts at passing on biblical information were aided by the fact that the Army Chaplaincy Department formed an integral part of the EEF's organizational structure. This meant that soldiers were in almost constant contact with chaplains. These spiritual representatives were a ubiquitous part of military service in the British Army of the First World War, and played an important role in aiding the maintenance of morale and motivating men for combat.[72]

The EEF's Chaplaincy Department was based in Alexandria from April 1916 and its structure was modelled on that of the BEF.[73] A Principal Chaplain was placed in charge of all the chaplains of all denominations, a post filled by Arthur Hordern until June 1918 when he was replaced by E. R. Day. Both men had considerable experience of ministering to soldiers, having served in the Boer War. In addition, a Senior Chaplain organized each denomination, corps, division and area. Hordern was faced with considerable obstacles in his attempts to create an efficient organization, the greatest of which related to the total number of chaplains allocated by the War Office. The EEF's chaplains were viewed as a pool that could be milked to provide reserves for the Sudan, East Africa, and Mesopotamia, often leaving Hordern with too few men to minister to all of the troops in Egypt and Palestine.

In addition, the War Office failed to take account of many of the denominational intricacies found in the EEF's subordinate formations. In December 1916, Hordern was instructed to increase the number of chaplains in 53rd (Welsh) Division to nine nonconformists, four Church of England and four Roman Catholics. This, however, ignored the fact that in the division there were 11,606 Church of England men, 3,544 nonconformists and only 675 Catholics. The four Anglican priests would thus be left with an enormous number of men to care for. The War Office may have been out of touch on this matter with the situation on the ground, but it would have seemed logical to expect a Welsh division to contain a large proportion of nonconformist soldiers. The TF nature of the division, possibly resulting in it containing more middle-class soldiers, may have affected this denominational balance. In addition, casualties sustained at Gallipoli in 1915, which were replaced by English recruits, would have weakened the original regional identity of the division. Ultimately, this difficulty was circumvented by making use of the reserve force of chaplains that Hordern had at his disposal. The resolution of such difficulties demonstrates the adaptability of the EEF's Chaplains' Department. When Day came to take over command in 1918 he found the organization he inherited to be excellent and in much better health than that of his previous appointment with 3rd Army on the Western Front. The department's extensive ministration duties were aided by the voluntary preaching carried out by a number of visiting ecclesiastics. The Bishop of Buckingham, for example, arrived in February 1917 and held services and confirmations among the men stationed in Egypt. Over the course of 1917 the Bishop in Jerusalem spent much time with the troops, carrying out 1,798 confirmations of officers and men.

This organizational success was mirrored at the front, where chaplains were expected to take an active role in boosting the morale of the units they were attached to. Hordern noted in mid-1917 that all of the generals he had interviewed spoke very highly of the chaplains they had served with. Major-General John Shea, commander of 60th Division, in a lecture to the Staff College in 1923, defined chaplains in terms of three categories: those left behind at the hospitals; those who stayed at dressing stations; and those who went into battle with the men. As he noted 'a clergyman who has been in battle with the men has a most remarkable influence over them and is a very effective means of raising their morale'.[74] He was correct to identify the fact that chaplains who risked their lives with the troops in the front line were given greater respect by their fellow officers and the rank and file. Lieutenant H. L. Milsom, of the 1/5th Somerset Light Infantry, recalled the padre attached to his battalion as 'a splendid man and very popular with the officers and men, always well up to the fore when he thought his duty demanded it, no matter how thick the bullets were falling, indeed there were times when I was much concerned as to his safety, but he was absolutely fearless'.[75] The prevalence of chaplains in the front line during the First World War can be illustrated simply by the fact that 166 were killed in combat across all fronts.

The risks run by some padres meant that Senior Chaplains often tried to prohibit their men from going further forward than field ambulances. This was an understandable approach given the difficulties the department faced in getting enough manpower of the correct denominational balance to minister to the EEF. The Reverend Mortimer, attached to the 1/10th Londons, thus found himself restricted to a field ambulance in November 1917, to which he 'objected hotly'.[76] The commander of 162nd Brigade, Brigadier-General A. Mudge, did not feel that a chaplain's place was in the rear, and ordered Mortimer to move up with the battalion.

At the front a chaplain's role was not exclusively to provide spiritual sustenance to the men; often he would find himself acting as a general factotum. The Reverend Young, attached to the 1/1st Middlesex Yeomanry, was remembered by Sydney Hatton for his ability to scrounge desperately needed stores for the men. On one occasion he managed to find boots for Hatton's section having unlaced good pairs from the dead, and on another he helped move ammunition boxes up to the front line. Similarly, Mortimer found that his role involved organizing various entertainments for the men. He set up a series of sports matches and prepared a concert party, which even included a professional drawing-room entertainer who had toured Egypt before the war.[77] The evidence from the EEF reinforces the assessment made in Edward Madigan's recent study of Church of England chaplains on the Western Front. Chaplains who grasped the need to undertake temporal duties to aid the welfare of their units, and who shared the hardships of the front line, came to be viewed as indispensable props to morale.

Although the EEF chaplains were respected for their temporal activities, these did little to influence the religious beliefs of the men. In terms of their spiritual role, the chaplains were often far from successful. The Reverend Jones found that the turnout at his services for units of 231st Brigade was often very low. At Easter 1917 only 70 men of the 24th Royal Welch Fusiliers attended Holy Communion, at the 10th King's Shropshire Light Infantry the figure fell to 60, and at the brigade headquarters his congregation diminished to just 40. It is illustrative of the generally low rates of turnout for such services, which reflected the low levels of church attendance before the war particularly among working-class male communities, that Jones felt the wartime figures were most encouraging. The solution of making soldiers attend compulsory church parades did not always ensure that chaplains had a receptive audience. Trooper Robert Chandler, of the ANZMD's 1st Signal Squadron, considered such parades 'just so much wasted time'.[78] In part this was a product of the fact that such occasions ate into what soldiers considered to be their well-earned rest periods. Matters were not helped by the fact that some unit commanders also saw church parades as a chance to engage in the finer details of army discipline. Jones felt it was absolutely absurd that Colonel McNeile had ordered the troops of the 24th Royal Welch Fusiliers to wear full kit and carry their rifles to a service while training in Egypt in January 1917. In the 1/1st Middlesex Yeomanry compulsory church parades became so reviled that the men began holding ballots among themselves to see who would have to attend. The enterprising regimental chaplain persuaded the commanding officer to abolish compulsory parades and instead held voluntary services, which he also moved to the cool of the evening. This boosted attendance and as a result 'removed from the restraint of spit and polish the men sang the old hymns with gusto'.[79]

It was not only the eccentricities of the military attitude towards church parades that stood in the way of services reaching a wide and receptive audience. The exigencies of combat often meant that services could not be held or that congregations were very much reduced. In November 1917 the Reverend Mortimer arrived at the 1/4th Northamptonshires, stationed on the defences at the village of Wilhelma close to Jaffa. He asked the battalion commander, Lieutenant-Colonel J. G. Brown, if he could hold a service, and was met with the sardonic reply: 'I'm awfully sorry, Padre, but the fact is we're just going to have a battle and all the men are busy. Have a drink.'[80] Reverend Jones also found it difficult to arrange services in May 1917, as the 74th Division's commander was reluctant to allow large groups of men to gather together. These assemblages would have been far too tempting targets for Turkish artillery and aircraft. Some units, however, simply had an institutional intolerance for the work of chaplains, who they viewed as interfering with their well-developed weekly routines. On a number of occasions ministering to rear echelon troops in Egypt, Reverend Mortimer found himself waiting for congregations to turn up while a commanding officer struggled to remember if the service had been placed among the orders of the day. He lamented that 'I never became quite inured to the habit of arriving with cassock and surplice and supply of hymn-books, and a carefully prepared sermon to find myself offered a lounge-chair and a long drink and a perfunctory apology for the impossibility of holding a service that morning'.[81] The obstructions placed in the way of chaplains often meant that they had relatively few opportunities to guide the men they were supposed to be ministering to in even relatively simple theological matters.

In a minority of cases, some soldiers evinced a strong dislike for the chaplains they came into contact with in the Middle East. Captain H. C. Wolton, of the 1/5th Suffolks, wrote home to his mother that the arrival of ten priests at his camp in Egypt caused much anger among the men.[82] A more vitriolic and continual disdain for religious representatives is evident in the diary of Captain E. B. Hinde, who served in the 1/2nd East Anglian Field Ambulance attached to 54th Division. He felt that the allocation of three chaplains to his unit was a ridiculous over-provision, which created much disgruntlement among the officers. He asserted that the chaplains 'seem to have nothing to do, and it is rather irritating to have 3 men "loafing" in the Mess all day, wanting all the advantages of the Mess, but not very eager to share in the work of maintaining it'.[83] For Hinde it was the dogmatic beliefs of these clergymen that most rankled. On one occasion he clashed with a Church of Ireland padre over a game of bridge due to the latter's strong defence of Ulster. Hinde declared that the chaplain was a 'narrow-minded bigot' who became a 'raving lunatic' whenever matters pertaining to Ireland were discussed. In September 1917 the field ambulance received a new padre, a Reverend Tooth, whom Hinde dismissed as a narrow Socialist and a missionary. His worst fears were realized when he argued with Tooth over pacifism, a position that Hinde found most indefensible and hypocritical for an army chaplain to adopt. Hinde clearly felt that chaplains should hold a closely circumscribed set of opinions that fitted the generally conservative ethos of the army's officer corps, rather than attempting to promote more novel social or political points of view.

It is of note that much of the criticism of chaplains came from their fellow officers and not the other ranks. Often this criticism concerned the ability of chaplains to fit into the military routine of a unit, where they risked disrupting well-established patterns of service. Alternatively, some of this disdain was aimed at the moral virtues evinced by some chaplains, an attitude Reverend Mortimer experienced when he was posted as chaplain to the Nasrieh Hospital. After his first dinner in the officers' mess he ordered a small whisky, which produced sighs of relief around the room. His predecessor had been a teetotaller and had forced the mess to adopt a universal prohibition on drink.[84] It seems that the strength and pertinence of a chaplain's spiritual message would soon be forgotten if it obstructed British officers' propensity to indulge in dipsomania.

In addition to these problems of resentment, chaplains often lacked any autonomy to minister to their congregations entirely as they wished, and thus to adapt their spiritual message to better appeal to the attitudes of the men in a particular unit. Retreats were held for chaplains in Jerusalem during 1918, at which Lieutenant-General Chetwode, then commanding XX Corps, would come to tea and address the padres on their role, from the point of view of a soldier. This would have given them a clear and specific military context within which they would be expected to operate. Local commanders at times would even take over control of the contents of services. At the 54th Division's thanksgiving service, held in December 1918, all of the hymns were chosen by Major-General Hare, the divisional commander. On 21 October 1917 Mortimer was asked to preach to the 4,000 men of 162nd Brigade, but found it almost impossible to give the 'God of Battles' speech that Brigadier-General Mudge was expecting. Instead a compromise was reached and he spoke on the joy of adventure and duty.[85] In such circumstances it is difficult to see how the chaplains of the EEF, although in regular contact with the men, could have passed on to them anything more than a perfunctory understanding of the Bible and the historic Christian context of the Palestinian battlefield.

Chaplains were not the only source of organized religion that soldiers encountered in the Middle East. The Young Men's Christian Association (YMCA) provided an important welfare network throughout Egypt and Palestine, which soldiers could easily access. This replicated the situation on the Western Front, where the organization set up over 1,500 centres during the course of the war. These huts provided troops with canteens, sporting facilities, and reading and writing materials, as well as staging lectures, concert parties and cinema shows. In the Middle East there were 56 centres in operation by the end of 1917, a year which had seen a great deal of adaptation to the EEF's move across Sinai and into southern Palestine. Its work was not just confined to British soldiers, as a range of social activities were carried out among the Indian troops who came to dominate the EEF in mid-1918. The scale of its welfare work was vast, particularly in Egypt where troops were often given leave. The Soldiers' Recreation Club at the Ezbekiah Gardens in Cairo sold over 400 loaves of bread a day and 60,000 cakes a week in 1916. The Anzac Hostel in Cairo offered men 700 beds, cheap food, a library and regular concerts. The YMCA's activities earned much praise from the soldiers of the EEF, one of whom noted that its canteens came even further forward than some army chaplains. Allenby offered effusive commendation in his preface to the published history of the YMCA's activities in Egypt. He asserted that 'throughout the campaign, its workers have followed closely the fighting line; and their labours have done much to keep up the moral, mental, and physical efficiency of my troops'.[86]

The YMCA had a strong patriotic ethos and an avowedly inter-denominational nature. As a result it proved very popular with liberal-minded Free Church clergymen who could not reconcile themselves to taking chaplains' commissions. The YMCA in Egypt did much to promote its open-minded approach to Christianity among the men of the EEF. In 1916 a campaign was held at its 35 centres which aimed 'to give the men the message of hope and cheer, the message of a fight for character, and to give the men an opportunity of making a stand which is after all the best way to bring victory to Christ'. Thousands of men were alleged to have signed a War Roll, which was a declaration of allegiance to Christ. At a more prosaic level YMCA centres, such as that of the Alexandria Central Branch, held weekly Bible classes and Sunday evening services. As part of its emphasis on a non-denominational approach to Christianity the YMCA's Anzac Hostel in Cairo produced a guide to the city which listed all of the local church services. The YMCA did have the opportunity to preach a particular interpretation of the religious history of Palestine as it provided guides for a limited number of men touring the religious sites of Jerusalem. The avowed aim of these tours was 'to endeavour to help them [EEF soldiers] catch something of the inspiration that ought to be felt by every Christian who follows in the steps of the Master'.[87]

The impact of the YMCA's spiritual activities was, however, limited. Its non-denominational ethos, although attractive to some, meant that from the point of view of many EEF soldiers it lacked ideological clarity. A YMCA representative with a mounted brigade in Palestine complained about the traditional YMCA song service. He felt 'perfectly certain that owing to its lack of the forms of worship and reverence it fails to attract any but men of a certain type of nonconformity'.[88] More scathingly he proclaimed that the form of service was nothing more than 'playing to the gallery'; the YMCA's ecumenical strength was also its greatest weakness. The lack of a clearly defined religious direction meant that the YMCA was associated by most troops, whether Christian or not, primarily with the provision of cakes, tea and writing materials. Its activities failed to excite any religious enthusiasm among the rank and file of the EEF, although it did act as a vital prop to combatant morale.

Anti-religious and anti-crusading rhetoric

In contrast to the biblical references that peppered some accounts of service in the Middle East it was often the case that soldiers wrote of their dislike for all things sacred. Such an anti-religious streak suggests that a number of EEF men would not have seen their service as part of a holy war. This attitude was partly a reflection of the disappointment felt when they finally reached Jerusalem. For Private C. T. Shaw, serving on the 60th Division's medical staff, the city struck him as 'the dirtiest and most miserable place I have ever set eyes on'.[89] This was a sentiment echoed by Major-General Hare, who felt that the city's appearance was spoilt by the fact that it had become overrun with modern buildings, churches, convents and hospitals. For one soldier Jerusalem seemed to be no better than an English provincial town. The men of the EEF had built up grandiose images of the city, a product of any religious education they had received particularly at Sunday school, which could not be sustained by the reality. Moreover, closer inspection led to further disappointment as the local sanitation system was seen to be inadequate, leaving the famed city a dirty and stench-filled place. Many men made little allowance for Jerusalem's seemingly non-European aspects, expecting to find the heart of Christianity to be a modern, developed urban centre. Some soldiers turned to the biblical vernacular tradition in order to offer satirical comment on the scene they encountered. Captain A. MacGregor noted that his artillery battery sang the hymn 'Jerusalem the Golden with milk and honey blessed' as a result of their experiences. He informed his family that this 'was a joke because those who have been there state that for stenches of filth it knocks an Indian Bazaar hollow'.[90]

This disdain for the sacred sites of Palestine was exacerbated by contact with the Eastern Churches. For the vast bulk of the EEF's soldiers, brought up in a somewhat austere Protestant culture, the aesthetics of the churches they visited proved a considerable shock. Complaints were made about the fact that as soon as a biblically important location had been identified it was immediately obliterated by a modern chapel adorned with lamps, images, pious inscriptions and rich wall hangings. It was noted by one soldier that 'to the ordinary Anglican, who is neither a pilgrim nor an iconoclast, there is something repugnant about the way in which the Holy Places have been treated by their guardians'. The taint of commercialism was felt to be ever-present at many of these locations. One soldier was appalled that at the Church of the Holy Sepulchre the guardian 'complacently exacts "bakshish" from the pilgrim, as if he were the proprietor of a peepshow'.[91]

It was this most sacred of sites that often caused the greatest dismay among EEF soldiers who visited it. Trooper Chandler described the building as being of the 'usual gaudy Eastern type'. This fact was picked up on by Second Lieutenant G. W. Gotto who, in a letter to his parents, felt that he could not 'even attempt to describe to you the ghastly tawdriness of the place', adding that 'it looks more like a shop with a display of Xmas tree decorations'.[92] Lieutenant W. F. Cook, the 1/6th Essex's transport officer, produced a similar description of the interior being covered with tinsel balls. It was his belief that he was simply unable to view the church as the local 'people of primitive ideas' did, noting that 'what was cheap and nasty to us was probably holy to them'.[93] Much of this disgust stemmed from the deeply ingrained Protestant cultural tradition of iconophobia. Plain, simply decorated holy sites were not an integral part of Eastern Christianity, of which most EEF soldiers had little or no exposure until they arrived in Palestine. It is unsurprising then that Chandler was appalled at the sight of a statue of the Virgin Mary in the Church of the Holy Sepulchre bedecked with jewels and rings. This was in his opinion sacrilegious and he wrote home to his family that 'the whole thing is a travesty from start to finish.'[94] Local Christian traditions, imagery, and architecture, rather than acting as a reassuring bulwark to the men's experience of the Middle East grounding them in a familiar biblical framework, only served to highlight the alien nature of their surroundings.

The constant disputes between the Eastern Churches did little to endear them to the men of the EEF, who expected to find Palestine a place of Christian harmony not discord. Visits to sacred sites reinforced the internal problems that Christianity faced in the region. After seeing the Church of the Holy Sepulchre Captain Wolton noted that at first glance the division of the building between various denominations seemed like an act of Christian unity. He soon discovered that this was not the case, as each of the local denominations vied for the attention of pilgrims: 'what annoys one at Jerusalem is the fact that the wretched people assure you that about 20 of the main incidents of the New Testament took place in an area of about 40 square yards:- i.e. just in their particular part of the church.'[95] The same problem of internal Christian conflict was to be found in Bethlehem's Church of the Nativity. Here Captain R. Dening, serving on the 4th Cavalry Division's staff, lamented that 'where our Lord is reported to have been born a British guard [is] there to keep the peace, between Greeks, RCs and Armenians – it's sad that Christians fight in such places – and formerly had to be kept in order by a Muh[amme]d[an] guard.'[96] The eccentricities of the Eastern Churches thus served to undermine the latent faith of many EEF soldiers. Christianity as practised in Palestine did not live up to the model that many men had constructed in their heads, derived from a received view of English Protestantism.

These anti-religious sentiments could also be expressed as explicit criticism of the crusading notion among EEF soldiers. For many the war that they were fighting against the Turks in 1916–18 did not seem to fit the bombastic rhetoric of holy war. In the conclusion to his narrative of the EEF's campaign, published in 1919, Major Henry Lock, of the Dorsetshire Regiment, launched a stinging attack on such portentous notions:

> Will our campaign be passed down to history as 'The Last Crusade'? Presumably not. Throughout the campaign there was little or no religious animosity, except that the Turk extended no quarter to the Hindoo. To speak of this as a campaign of The Cross against The Crescent is untrue. The Turkish high command was controlled by Germans, so-called Christians. The British soldier fought with no less zest than when opposed to Turks. At the final battle, the Moslems, serving in our armies, by far outnumbered the Christians.[97]

The military reality of the war in Egypt and Palestine was far removed from any notion of a crusade. As Lock makes clear the battle of Megiddo saw Christian, European soldiers in the minority, and would be better viewed as a clash between two imperial powers using troops drawn from throughout their empires. It was not only at the operational level of the EEF's campaign that the holy war notion seemed to be inappropriate. The brutal fighting that took place in November and early December 1917 to drive the Turks back from Gaza and eventually to secure Jerusalem did not suggest to the troops involved that they were on a crusade. Major Lord Hampton, commanding 'D' Squadron of the 1/1st Worcester Hussars Yeomanry, recalled that on 9 December 1917 his unit was taking up new positions in the line in appalling weather conditions, and as such 'even the news of the surrender of Jerusalem failed to lift us entirely out of our misery'.[98] As a result of the bitter combat he had witnessed, Gunner T. G. Edgerton, of 60th Division's artillery, found it hard to describe his battery as 'Christian soldiers', and was adamant that 'the spirit of the Crusaders was conspicuous by its absence'.[99]

The EEF's soldiers were aware, however, that back in Britain their exploits might well have the tinge of a holy war about them. Lieutenant Milsom recalled seeing a cartoon by Louis Raemaekers that depicted British soldiers kneeling bareheaded, seemingly at prayer, before Jerusalem, which was being pointed out to them by an officer using his sword. This did not fit the scene in his battalion, the 1/5th Somerset Light Infantry, when it approached Jerusalem: 'the general thought seemed rather to be "So that is the --- place is it?" The truth is that we were all dead tired, foot-sore, and very "fed-up-and-far-from-home-sort-of-feeling"'.[100]

This sentiment of exasperation at how the EEF's campaign was being misinterpreted was to the fore in Cecil Sommers's published account of his Middle Eastern service, based on his diary. In the preface, nominally addressed to his daughter, he attempted to debunk such myths. He stated that if his daughter took an overly sentimental approach and tried to recall her father dressed as Richard I in shining armour, emblazoned with a red cross, then she would fail. It was made clear that the reminiscences of some of his comrades could also not be trusted, as the temporal distance from the events they were involved in would lead to an enchanted view being created that did not resemble the grim reality. Sommers took time to attack other books on the campaign that he expected would soon be written about it. His argument sagaciously noted that 'the atmosphere in which heroes move is so much more enthralling – and profitable – than the stale tobacco of the ordinary man'.[101]

It was this desire to recall the prosaic elements of the EEF's campaign that motivated Sydney Hatton in 1930 to produce an account of his wartime exploits. He stated in the preface to his work that he was writing deliberately against those war books such as *All Quiet on the Western Front* which he felt were too narrow in their portrayal of the conflict. Instead his aim was to produce a human account as he felt it would have been told 'over a pipe of baccy and a pint of beer'. Hatton's argument was that the high diction used by many war authors in fact distorted the historical record, stating that:

> The soldiers we knew and fought with were neither hysterical nor given to introspective analysis. According to several morbid modern war books, the appearance of a 'Jordan boil' on the nape of the neck would demand a soliloquy – 'This deep yellow canker gnawing away my flesh, my own flesh, flesh that is me – this pool of pus, three millions of virulent micro-cocci eating away down to my

very bones – perhaps even to my soul', whereas what the British Tommy actually said was, 'Gawd, I've got another beauty'.[102]

It is clear that both Hatton and Sommers represent a reaction against the way the EEF's campaign was being remembered in interwar Britain. For them this was not a glorious crusade, but a dirty, brutal and uncomfortable war in which spiritual solace seemed a long way off.

Orientalist tourists

If the men of the EEF were not crusaders, influenced by a strong Christian tradition, it is possible to see them as indulging in the rhetoric of vernacular orientalism to interpret their service in the Middle East. In this case vernacular orientalism represents a common or popular cultural interpretation of the Orient, as a counter-point to the learned or high cultural depiction that has dominated much academic discourse since the late 1970s. A number of EEF soldiers' accounts expressed a detailed and continual interest in an essentialized version of the Orient which stressed its exoticism, mystery and otherness from Europe. The troops' first experience of this world was in Egypt, where they encountered the remains of its ancient civilization. Trooper Chandler's first few days in the country were spent visiting the tourist hot spots around Cairo. Inevitably he made his way to the pyramids, about which he stated 'one cannot explain the sensation one experiences when looking at these world wonders for the first time'.[103] Captain Hinde expressed similar sentiments when he travelled to Sabharah, a village south of Cairo, littered with ancient treasures including a step pyramid, tombs and a mausoleum for sacred bulls. Later in 1916 he followed this up with a ten-day excursion down the Nile to visit Luxor and Karnak. The temple at Edfou stunned Hinde, in particular its intricate reliefs and architecture. It was not just the physical remains of Egypt's past that attracted attention but also the country's living inhabitants. The troops of the 1/5th Essex were amazed by the Zikr dance put on for them by 20 men of the Egyptian Labour Corps, in which they chanted incantations and swayed from side to side. At the end of 20 minutes only 6 of the men were left standing and were deemed to be the holiest of the company.

This fascination with the Orient was not confined to the region's ancient past or its current inhabitants' intriguing cultural traditions. For many EEF troops it was the Islamic culture and heritage of Egypt and Palestine that proved of greatest interest. Captain Wolton and his brother, both serving in the 1/5th Suffolks, were so taken by the history of the Arab peoples after visiting the Cairo Museum that they purchased Qu'rans in a nearby bazaar.[104] The notebook kept during his service by Quartermaster Sergeant G. E. Lee of the same battalion, illustrates a similar interest. Among the general travelogue, he included a description of a holy rock he had seen, which Muslim women visited to ensure that they were 'fruitful'. This was hardly one of Egypt's foremost tourist attractions and must have been specifically sought out by Lee.

It was the many mosques that formed the spiritual landscape of the Middle East, which created the most interest across the EEF. Among these it was the Mosque of

Omar in Jerusalem that received the highest praise. Sergeant Roy McCormack, of the AMR, visited the city in April 1918 and recorded that the Mosque of Omar was 'a wonderful place of worship, having a tremendous big dome, no end of bronze work and colouring and writings'.[105] John Lockhart was more effusive in his acclamation, stating that it was 'the noblest building in Jerusalem, and after the Taj Mahal, probably the finest Mohammedan work in the world'.[106] Similar comments were made by Second Lieutenant Gotto, in a letter to his parents, which highlighted the 'wonderful mosaic work in the Dome' and the rugs that covered the floor, which he stated 'would have rejoiced your hearts'.[107] It was noted by one New Zealand Mounted Rifleman that the mosque's 'artistic grandeur' stood in direct contrast to the 'comparative tawdriness of the Christian Church built over the Calvary'.[108] The EEF's soldiers thus had far greater commendations to bestow on the Islamic architecture of Palestine than they did on its Christian buildings. This is an attitude that would seem to demonstrate the presence of a strong vernacular orientalism in British and Dominion culture.

A number of EEF units went further than simply observing the Islamic culture of the Middle East, and began to use it to represent and interpret their experiences for a wider audience. This can be seen most clearly in some of the Christmas cards that were produced by divisions or battalions for soldiers to send home to their friends and families. 2/15th London Regiment's 1918 card, a very elaborate production containing three separate illustrations and a map, depicted a British soldier standing in front of a Palestinian village (see Illustration 2.4). The image made no references to the Christian heritage of the region. Similarly, one of 54th Division's 1917 Christmas cards showed a bucolic Middle Eastern coastal scene, in the centre of which was the Islamic shrine at Sheikh Ajlin, near Gaza (see Illustration 2.5). The imagery could be

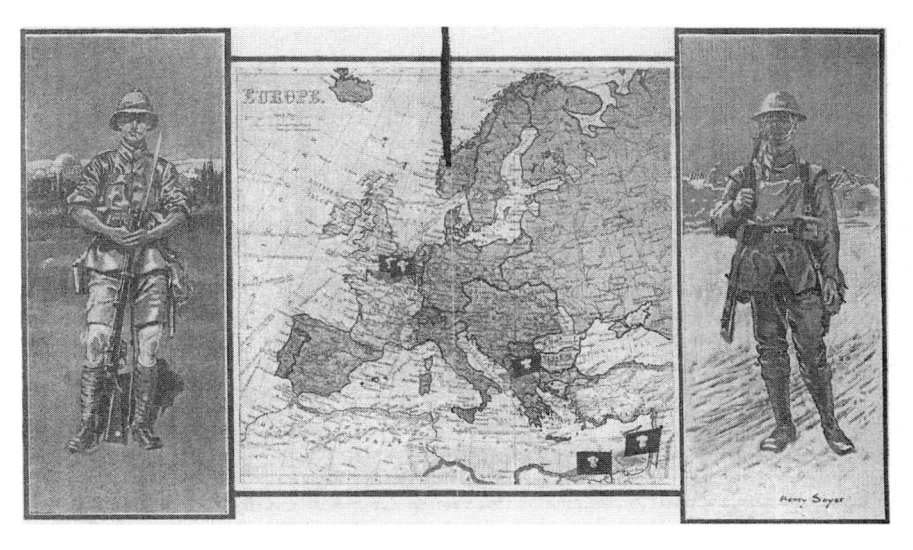

Illustration 2.4 2/15th London Regiment Christmas Card, 1918 (IWM, 94/5/1, Blunt Papers).

Illustration 2.5 54th Division Christmas Card, 1917 (IWM, 85/4/1, Wink Papers).

even more explicit in its use of Islamic points of reference. The cover of another of 54th Division's 1917 cards (see Illustration 2.6) and the inside of the one produced in 1918 (see Illustration 2.7) both contained well-executed sketches of mosques. For those relations back in Britain who received these cards the inference intended could not be clearer. These were not soldiers fighting a crusade in the Holy Land, but serving in a region steeped in the culture of Islam. For more Christian-minded soldiers, the Russian Hospice in Jerusalem produced a commemorative Christmas card in 1917 as a souvenir of the British occupation of the holy city.[109] It contained the traditional imagery of the nativity story, although with the addition of a macabre depiction of the massacre of the innocents. This was, however, a product of a religious institution in Palestine and cannot be seen as indicative of how EEF soldiers chose to represent their experiences.

This absorption of the Middle East's Islamic elements demonstrates that rather than seeing British and Dominion soldiers as crusaders it would be apposite to portray them as the region's first mass tourists. Indeed some EEF men recognized this themselves. Driver J. Evans, serving in the ANZMD's train, wrote of his service in Palestine in a letter home to his mother that he 'would not miss this for anything – in one way it is a huge tourist trip, we see something fresh and interesting every day'.[110] Lance-Corporal Hickman even went so far as to describe his travels between Gallipoli, Mudros and Egypt as like being on a Cook's Tour. Major Bailey, serving on the staff of 53rd Brigade RFA attached to the 3rd (Lahore) Division by the war's end, did not just imagine his

Illustration 2.6 54th Division Christmas Card, 1917 (IWM, 02/16/1, Hinde Papers).

service in such a way, he actually set out to use his time in Egypt for a holiday. As the archetypal British tourist he went to the Cairo Express Agency to organize his travel to Luxor and Assouan, where he was met by prearranged guides. The desire to explore the exotic landscape of Egypt and Palestine was not only pursued for the personal satisfaction of tourist soldiers. It also provided them with considerable amounts of information with which they could fill letters home. Captain MacGregor, of the 39th (Reserve) Mountain Battery, lamented in one of his missives that: 'I have not succeeded in seeing anymore places of particular historical interest so I am just a bit short of "copy".'[111] In Egypt and Palestine, where combat was often confined to clearly delineated short periods and men spent much of their time on mundane military tasks, the proximity to an abundant historical landscape allowed soldiers to write letters that

A STREET IN JAFFA

Illustration 2.7 54th Division Christmas Card, 1918 (NRM, Box 11, 1/4th and 1/5th Norfolk Regiment Papers).

would be found of interest by their friends and relatives, thus stimulating a regular correspondence.

Moreover, these periods of tourist activity provided crucial breaks away from the intense military operations at the front line which were mentally and physically wearing. These periods not only enabled soldiers to rebuild their endurance, but also allowed them to recover a sense of normality in the midst of the chaos of war. Tourist visits to Cairo or Jerusalem represented brief forays into a somewhat circumscribed civilian existence, but one in which the rigours of military life could be largely forgotten. By allowing men to return to their past civilian identities for brief periods, leave trips and tourist activities reinforced important psychological coping mechanisms for individual combatants. The indulgence in tourism in the Middle East thus, in part, helped to reinforce the resilient morale of the EEF.[112]

It was for this reason that commanders at various levels of the army's hierarchy aided their soldiers in exploiting to the full the tourist process. They recognized the voracious appetite of the men for information on the Middle East. Lectures on the history of Egypt and Palestine thus became a regular part of many units' routines. The ANZMD, for example, were given addresses on the mythology of ancient Egypt and Napoleon's Middle Eastern campaigns.[113] Local information was of critical importance to help the men enjoy their leave fully. The YMCA Anzac Hostel guide to Cairo contained a section which detailed routes to see the city's main sites in only six days, thus reducing the cost to visiting soldiers. The pamphlet contained 13 pages of descriptions of places of interest, such as the bazaars, citadel and mosque of Sultan Hassan.[114] The hope was that these guides would facilitate the men's sightseeing. The YMCA and military authorities were also very keen to keep visiting soldiers out of the Wazza, Cairo's notorious red light district; breeding an interest in local history and culture, rather than sex, was one means of achieving this.[115]

From 1918 information on the history of the region was provided in the EEF's educational newspaper, the *Palestine News*. Charles Pirie-Gordon, the editor, asked Mark Sykes to obtain permission to reproduce sections from various noted works on the Middle East, including the *Latin Kingdom of Jerusalem*, the *Itinerarium Regis Ricardi*, the *Caliph's Last Heritage*, *Baedecker's Palestine* and a work on Saladin.[116] However, it was the pamphlets written by Victor Trumper, a retired Royal Naval officer and honorary secretary of the Palestine Exploration Fund in Port Said, that had the greatest impact on the historical mindset of the EEF's soldiers. From late 1917 through to 1919 he produced four short guides to Palestine, one of which covered the south of the country, two the centre and the last the north. The first pamphlet appeared in November 1917 just as the EEF began to advance northwards through Gaza and on to Jerusalem. In the preface Trumper stated that the work had been written so 'that the troops in Palestine might get a more general idea as to the sites of ancient localities in the places where they are'.[117] The guides were largely based on Smith's *The Historical Geography of the Holy Land* and the works of the Palestine Exploration Fund. Each pamphlet followed the same pattern containing descriptions of various locations based on their ancient, biblical or medieval heritage, and arranged under the current names for those sites. Only in the first work, on southern Palestine, did Trumper include two narrative passages relating ancient Egypt and Judea's relations and then Napoleon's expedition to Syria in 1799. This was one of the rare occasions on which Trumper told soldiers anything of the region's history since the crusades. The third pamphlet, finishing his analysis of central Palestine north of Jerusalem, was published in October 1918, and it was thus the first two works that would have been extensively read by soldiers during the course of the campaign. In total the four pamphlets sold over 20,000 copies, which must make them some of the most widely distributed educational documents among the men of the EEF. They proved so popular that the Nile Mission Press brought out a single volume in 1921, which ran to 124 pages, containing all of the information from the 4 pamphlets. Trumper expected the book to be read by Bible students and future tourists to Palestine. The soldiers of the EEF were thus the trailblazers for individuals travelling to the region in the interwar period.

The emphasis on tourism, much of it focused on the Middle East's Islamic heritage, and the clear existence of a vernacular orientalism among the letters, diaries, memoirs, and souvenirs of men who served in Egypt and Palestine in the First World War eradicates the notion that they were engaged in a crusade. It also serves to undermine the farrago of ideas brought to prominence in Edward Said's *Orientalism* (1978), which have exercised considerable influence on postcolonial studies ever since.[118] Said's work has been subject to detailed criticism since its first publication, yet its academic prominence is far from diminished. One of the most erudite deconstructions of *Orientalism* has been made by Robert Irwin, highlighting numerous errors of fact and interpretation in Said's argument. In particular, Irwin demonstrates effectively that a reliance on British and French sources, along with the exclusion of the vast body of German nineteenth-century orientalist scholarship, led Said to construct an essentialized image of Western imperialism, whose interactions with the oriental world are often described in terms of crude abstractions. In many respects this resulted in an interpretation as skewed from reality as the orientalist scholarship that Said denounced. This derived not just from his selective discussion of national sources, but more crucially from his over-reliance on the high literature of nineteenth- and twentieth-century Britain and France. Said's *Orientalism* has little time for mass popular culture and as a result the voices of the vast bulk of European society have been ignored.[119]

The First World War represented the largest period of contact between the Orient and Occident since the crusades. Interpreting this period simply through the lens of Lawrence and a handful of orientalist scholars, as Said does, is far too restrictive an approach. Tens of thousands of British and Dominion soldiers, predominantly drawn from the working class who would have had little opportunity to visit the Middle East before 1914, were now exposed to its culture and heritage en masse.[120] In such circumstances it is striking that the way in which soldiers chose to view this world demonstrated that they had imbibed a vernacular orientalist tradition. This was an idiom of cultural interaction that would persist into the British mandate period, often defining the relations between British civil and military officials and the Palestinian population. Its most prominent expression was seen in the adoption of a colonial regionalism for the architectural style of the High Commissioner's residence outside Jerusalem.[121] Crucially, the experiences of EEF soldiers suggest that it is necessary to move beyond an overly intellectual or high cultural interpretation of orientalism, and instead discuss its vernacular iteration, which represented simply an expression of interest in the history and culture of the non-Western world, rather than an attempt to dominate it.

It is evident that the post-war reconstruction of the campaign as a crusade was in opposition to the experiences and attitudes of the majority of soldiers who served in Egypt and Palestine. Only the EEF's religious fringe would have recognized the discourse in the British press that surrounded Allenby's death. This approach, however, was the product of the British home front's construction of the campaign in 1917–18. As Adrian Gregory has argued with relation to the Church of England in the First World War, it was Winnington-Ingram's bellicose rhetoric which appealed to popular patriotic sentiment.[122] The emphasis on moderation that Sykes, Curzon and Allenby wished to pursue did not fit the public's prevailing interpretation of the EEF's war. Lloyd George's bombastic and self-serving announcements on the EEF's campaigns, particularly the fall of Jerusalem, were much more closely tied into the public's mood. This perception of British soldiers crusading against the Ottoman Empire helped to give the Middle Eastern war a degree of relevance to Britain's overall war effort, which an otherwise expansionist imperial campaign may have lacked. It was this legacy that is succinctly captured in the romanticized cartoons of Bernard Partridge in *Punch*, and which persisted into the interwar period.

Not only did such notions help make the battles fought in Sinai and Palestine less remote from the sacrifices of the Western Front, they also served to make military operations in a sideshow theatre marketable during the literary boom of the 1920s and 1930s. Many a dry narrative was enlivened by references to Lawrence, crusading and the Holy Land. In contrast, the EEF soldiers' view of the campaign during the war itself was best expressed in the imagery of Alfred Leete's famous 'See the World' recruiting poster produced in 1919. In a bold image Leete portrayed two Scottish soldiers striding through a Middle Eastern bazaar, soaking up the local atmosphere; this was soldiering reinterpreted simply as glorified tourism. If the troops that served in the EEF were not motivated by crusading and religious rhetoric then other elements must have played a prominent role in the creation and maintenance of the army's morale, and it is to these that we now turn.

3

Command, Control and Morale

The imposing figure of Field Marshal Viscount Allenby of Megiddo and Felixstowe dominates discussions of the EEF's wartime experiences in Sinai and Palestine. In direct contrast to the generals on the Western Front he is portrayed as an individual who was able to return warfare to its natural state of manoeuvre. The rapid advances of the EEF, notably at Third Gaza and Megiddo, involved Allenby using his cavalry to great effect, enveloping Turkish armies and forcing the surrender of large numbers of men. All this was achieved without the slaughter characteristic of battles in France and Flanders. Allenby, although a cavalry general by training and experience, is not portrayed in the historiography as an archaic remnant of the nineteenth century; he is a general at home with artillery, tanks and air power. His use of deception schemes before each major operation, most notably the 'haversack ruse' in 1917 and the construction of dummy horse lines in 1918, reinforces the image of him as a thinking general.

Critically, Allenby is also credited with reinvigorating the EEF in the summer of 1917 when the army faced a morale collapse. Particular emphasis is placed on his decision to move the army's GHQ from Cairo to Khan Yunis, only a few miles behind the British trenches opposite Gaza. This demonstrated to the troops that their commander and his staff would now face the same hardships as them. Allenby was also famed for his tours of front-line units. This personal contact with their Commander-in-Chief, a man noted for his bullish and driving style of leadership, underpins much of the discussion of EEF combat motivation. There is, however, a need to separate out the command and leadership roles that Allenby undertook. This rests on a re-examination of the EEF's morale in 1917 and the impact that his predecessor as commander of the EEF, General Archibald Murray, had on his troops.

Allenby in the words of his contemporaries

The portrait of Allenby as a beloved leader of the EEF was first propagated in the immediate post-war period. William Thomas Massey, an official correspondent with the EEF for a number of London newspapers, produced two accounts of the British Army's exploits in the Middle East which appeared in 1919 and 1920. In *How Jerusalem was Won* he described how Allenby's proven track record as a general, both in open and trench warfare, helped to build the men's confidence in their new commander. Allenby's Stakhanovist work ethic also had an impact: 'his own vigour infected the whole command, and within a short while of arriving at the front the efficiency of the Army was considerably increased.'[1] Massey noted that as a result of Allenby's constant tours of the front line no one knew the roads of Palestine better than his driver. In the follow-up volume the EEF's war record was continued into 1918 culminating at Megiddo. Allenby was given full credit for the success of the campaign, an opinion that Massey made explicit for the reader by entitling the work *Allenby's Final Triumph*. He erroneously suggested that the Ottoman collapse was entirely precipitated by the EEF's actions and that this was one of the principal causes of the destruction of the Central Powers' war effort.[2] The thesis of the work appeared to be nothing less than that Allenby had single-handedly won the war.

This effusive praise from Massey, a journalist who had only observed Allenby from a distance, was reinforced by the influential accounts of those who had served alongside him. Unsurprisingly, T. E. Lawrence's sprawling tale of the Arab nationalist revolt and his role within it, the *Seven Pillars of Wisdom* (1935), had much to say about his former commander. He reiterated many of the key concepts surrounding Allenby's period of command, such as his central role in determining the course of Megiddo and his rebuilding of EEF morale in 1917.[3] The description of the first meeting between these two great wartime personalities, following the capture of Aqaba in July 1917, gives a clear indication of Lawrence's attitude towards his commander:

> It was a comic interview for Allenby was physically large and confident, and morally so great that the comprehension of our [the Arab Revolt's] littleness came slow to him. He sat in his chair looking at me – not straight, as his custom was, but sideways puzzled. He was newly from France, where for years he had been a tooth of the great machine grinding the enemy. He was full of Western ideas of gun power and weight – the worst training for our war – but, as a cavalryman, was already half persuaded to throw up the new school, in this different world of Asia, and accompany Dawnay and Chetwode along the worn road of manoeuvre and movement.[4]

Allenby, although slightly bemused at first by Lawrence, was ultimately swayed by his arguments and came round to supporting the Arab Revolt in full. The *Seven Pillars of Wisdom* created an artificially bifurcated image of the EEF's two commanders. Lawrence lavished praise on Allenby and his exploits, even absolving him of blame for the failure of the Transjordan Raids. In contrast, Murray did not emerge well from Lawrence's narrative. He was described as having 'a very nervous mind, fanciful and essentially competitive'; he saw the Arab Revolt as a threat to his campaign in Sinai, which would be drained of its resources.[5] Lawrence went so far as to state that 'the jealousy of Sir Archibald Murray might have wrecked the Sherif's rebellion at its start', and that it was only saved by the assistance rendered by Admiral Rosslyn Wemyss (commander of the Royal Navy's East Indies Station). Much was also made of Murray's detached style of command, which left him ignorant of the situation at the front. This was to have disastrous results at Second Gaza where, as Lawrence saw it, he sacrificed men's lives against strong Turkish defences simply to demonstrate to the War Cabinet that he was trying to prosecute an offensive campaign in southern Palestine.[6]

The portrayal of Murray and Allenby in the *Seven Pillars of Wisdom* did much to influence subsequent popular depictions of the two generals. David Lean's *Lawrence of Arabia* (1962) was heavily reliant on Lawrence's personal view of the war in the Middle East. Allenby, as portrayed by Jack Hawkins, is shown as a powerful leader, able to control the mercurial personality of Lawrence and to recognize the value of the Arab Revolt to his campaign. In contrast Murray, played by Donald Wolfit, is only encountered once, seated behind a desk in his Cairo GHQ, oblivious to the military needs of the Arabs.[7] Lawrence's depiction of these two generals was designed to drive on the narrative of his account of the Arab Revolt. The weak and vacillating Murray could thus be blamed for the early failures of the Arab cause, while its later successes, most notably the disputed entry into Damascus in October 1918, could be tied to the sweeping success of the EEF's final advance. Allenby gave Lawrence and the Arabs a wider military relevance, which helped to justify their nationalist cause. This helped to disguise the fact that the revolt had little impact on the outcome of the war in Sinai and Palestine or on the collapse of the Ottoman Empire, and that many of the Arabs' greatest battlefield triumphs were achieved on the back of EEF formations.[8]

Colonel Ronald Storrs in his voluminous memoirs continued the approach towards Allenby adopted by Lawrence. In late December 1917 he was appointed military governor of Jerusalem and was greatly impressed by the speed with which Allenby responded to his requests for assistance, particularly over the issue of food supplies. Storrs added a new aspect to the emerging description of Allenby. After a visit to the EEF's Advanced GHQ at Bir Salem in 1918, Storrs recalled that he was left 'wondering what sort of a General was this, who had gained a brilliant and decisive victory, who knew all there was to be known about birds, beasts, and fishes, who had read everything, and who quoted in full at dinner one of the less-known sonnets of Rupert Brooke'.[9] This was Allenby as a cultured warrior, an element of his character that would be reinforced in many biographies. Storrs's aim, however, was primarily to elevate the figure of Lawrence, who had died only two years before the publication of his memoirs and was a close personal friend. Allenby, only an incidental figure in the narrative, thus garnered much praise as a result of his support for the Arab Revolt, which tied him directly into the panegyric on Lawrence. The First World War in the Middle East was being portrayed very much as a conflict where great men could still alter the course of history, in contrast to the anonymous slaughter of the Western Front where the individual had seemingly lost all agency.

A number of senior commanders and staff officers who served alongside Allenby in the EEF added their opinions on his career in their voluminous memoirs. Major-General George Barrow, formerly commander of 4th Cavalry Division, recollected how Allenby's energy and drive had spurred on brigade and regimental commanders in September 1918. As with Lawrence's and Storrs's accounts, Barrow concentrated on the general's personal characteristics. Barrow had known Allenby at Staff College and commented that even then he was an impressive figure, not for his military skills, but due to his striking personality. His popularity with his fellow officers was such that he was elected to the prestigious position of Master of the Drag Hounds, much to the chagrin of Douglas Haig.[10] Considering how much contact Barrow had with Allenby over the course of his military career it is striking how little space is given to recollections of such a key individual.[11] In part this reflected the temporal distance of Barrow from the events he had chosen to recount, with his memoirs not being published until 1942.

In contrast, Raymond Savage, a former officer on the EEF's General Staff, produced a biography of Allenby as early as 1925; a sycophantic account in which the great general could do no wrong. Its influence, however, has been considerable as it established the principal topos about Allenby's early command of the EEF. Savage asserts that in mid-1917 the army was in crisis, riven with 'an air of apathy', and that cases of desertion and absence without leave were prevalent, while drunkenness and petty crime were on the increase.[12] Within only one month of Allenby's arrival there had been a transformation, with a stiffening of purpose. As a result the incidence of crime fell and the EEF became an effective fighting force. This was Allenby as the invigorator of the EEF's morale; a general in touch with the needs of his men.

A similar point of view was voiced by Lieutenant-Colonel Richard Meinertzhagen, one of the EEF's forward intelligence officers. He was credited with thinking up and carrying out the famous 'haversack ruse' prior to Third Gaza. This involved passing false plans for the attack to the Turks, including a scheme for a direct assault on Gaza rather than the indirect one via Beersheba that was actually used. The deception supposedly misled the Turkish commanders as to British intentions prior to the battle, allowing for the successful turning of the Turkish line via its desert flank. Meinertzhagen, in one of his more esoteric moments, also claimed to have implemented a scheme to drop cigarettes laced with opium over the Turkish lines in order to disorientate the defenders of Gaza.[13] In his published diaries he asserted that Allenby awoke the EEF from its 'lethargic sleep under Murray' and was able to provide the drive that a number of senior officers lacked, most notably Lieutenant-General Philip Chetwode.[14] Meinertzhagen recorded his first meeting with Allenby to discuss intelligence matters in his diary:

> My word, he is a different man to Murray. His face is strong and almost boyish. His manner is brusque almost to rudeness, but I prefer it to the oil and butter of the society soldier. Allenby breathes success and the greatest pessimist cannot fail to have confidence in him.[15]

Meinertzhagen, however, raises a number of problems as a reliable witness to the war in Palestine. He was only attached to the EEF during the second half of 1917, having previously served in East Africa, and in January 1918 he was transferred to the War Office. Thus he only witnessed the first five months of Allenby's command, and saw nothing of his failures in the two Transjordan Raids.

A close textual analysis of the published diaries further undermines their value as a historical source. As J. N. Lockman has succinctly demonstrated for Meinertzhagen's *Middle East Diary 1917–1956* (1959), many of its entries on Lawrence were derived from biographies, most notably that of Richard Aldington. Critically, an examination of the manuscript copies of the diaries reveals that the entries on Lawrence were added in at a later date. There are, therefore, serious doubts about the validity of the account that Meinertzhagen produced. In an examination of the 'haversack ruse', contained in his *Army Diary, 1899–1926* (1960), Brian Garfield has found similar discrepancies, which demonstrate that much of the material was created after the Second World War and was intended to boost the prominence of Meinertzhagen's role in the affair.[16] In addition, his career as an internationally respected ornithologist has been destroyed by revelations concerning the faking and theft of a large proportion of the 20,000 specimens that he donated to the Natural History Museum. It is evident that 'Meinertzhagen was a congenital liar and fantasist'.[17] His references to Allenby are thus highly suspect and are fundamentally unreliable as evidence for the general's career as commander of the EEF.

Part of the reason erroneous accounts have risen to prominence is the fact that Allenby left no personal record of his career in which he could shape the post-war image of himself.[18] To a certain extent there was no need for him to intervene in this discourse, which portrayed him in a favourable light. Murray, by contrast, had every need to defend his reputation. His attempts to vindicate the decisions he had taken as commander of the EEF were hindered by the War Cabinet, which decided in August 1917 to prohibit the publication of his final despatch. A cut-down version of it, with which Murray was deeply unsatisfied, only appeared in the *London Gazette* on 20 November 1917, by which stage Allenby's crushing military victory over the Turks at Third Gaza had already stolen the limelight. His subsequent attempts to have it published in full after the war also ran into difficulty, largely due to the opposition of Lloyd George, as it was highly critical of the Prime Minister's wartime leadership. Only in 1920 was permission granted for its publication, and then only if it was prefaced with a copy of a War Office letter. This missive stressed that the changes in policy made in Whitehall concerning the Middle East, which Murray blamed for hampering his command, were the product of a wider consideration of the war effort of Britain and her allies.[19] The restrictions placed on Murray's account of his leadership of the EEF and the silence of Allenby over his period of command left a void that was filled by the memoirs of those who served alongside them.

Allenby according to historians

The works of historians on the EEF have only served to enhance the view of Allenby that emerges from this memoir literature. Cyril Falls, writing in the official history of the campaigns in Egypt and Palestine, concurred with the idea that Allenby's arrival had reinvigorated the EEF. He noted that the constant visits to the line made Allenby known to the rank and file, but that his greatest influence was on brigade and battalion commanders. Crucially, Allenby was able to martial a multinational force and to build confidence in his leadership. This in part stemmed from his decisions to withdraw troops from attacks that were not progressing, thus avoiding any unnecessary loss of life. In the official history's conclusion, Allenby was key to the moral sphere of the EEF.

Falls, though, was careful to illustrate the extent to which Allenby was reliant on the achievements of Murray. He noted that it was Murray who had made the logistical preparations that underpinned the invasion of Palestine. It was the successful completion of this 'engineer's war' which gave the EEF the ability to destroy the Turkish Army's combat capabilities in late 1917 and in 1918. Falls was keen to stress the advantages that were possessed by Allenby, most notably the EEF's superiority in manpower, artillery and aircraft during the second half of 1918. In addition, the army had developed a well-organized supply infrastructure since 1916 and was given significant support by the Royal Navy in the Mediterranean.[20] As Hew Strachan has emphasized, Falls was one of the foremost historians of the First World War. His precision and skill meant that he produced a coherent and balanced narrative of the EEF's campaigns. Objectivity, however, came at a price. In his comments on the second volume of the official history, Lieutenant-Colonel Clive Garsia, the former GSO1 of 54th Division, noted that it read like a bland German account of the Franco-Prussian War. The descriptions of failures were blamed on factors such as the weather, unexpected resistance by the enemy or the weariness of the troops. Little attempt was made to analyse and criticize poor orders or faulty leadership, and thus the work, in Garsia's opinion, lost its value for future students of military history.[21]

Falls's subsequent account of the Middle Eastern campaign in his study of the whole of the First World War again demonstrated his concern to produce a balanced point of view. He gives credit to both Murray and Allenby for their leadership of the EEF, but is hampered by the fact that a one-volume work did not provide enough space for detailed discussion of the key themes.[22] In 1964 he returned to the EEF with a monograph on the battle of Megiddo, which demonstrated his ability to examine with great care the course of the war beyond the Western Front. Some of the balance of the official history was lost in the drive to produce an exciting narrative of the battle. Great emphasis was placed on the mobile operations of the DMC, with only one chapter devoted to the infantry's role in breaking through the Turkish line.[23] By focusing on this one battle Falls produced an image of a campaign dominated by cavalry and manoeuvre. This did not reflect the entirety of the EEF's experience across over two and a half years of fighting, and presented a misleading interpretation of Allenby's role in the final victory.

Falls was not the first historian to turn his hand to discussing the EEF's war in scholarly detail, as at the same time as the first volume of the official history appeared Colonel Archibald Wavell was publishing his renowned *The Palestine Campaigns* (1928). Wavell had direct experience of the war in the Middle East, having served on the EEF's staff.[24] Three weeks after Allenby arrived in Egypt on 28 June 1917, Wavell was sent out to act as a liaison officer for the CIGS, William Robertson; this was a difficult role to fulfil requiring him to be loyal to two masters. In early 1918 Wavell was sent to the Allied Supreme War Council at Versailles to act as an expert on the Palestine campaign, a task that he found incredibly dull. By April he was back in the EEF, this time as the Brigadier-General, General Staff, of XX Corps, under Lieutenant-General Chetwode, serving until the end of the campaign. Although he got on well with Allenby, Wavell was not popular with all of the senior officers in the EEF. Major-General Steuart Hare, the commander of 54th Division, described him as 'a most objectionable type of swollen headed Staff Officer', and noted wryly that 'whatever his abilities may be he doesn't know much and I could find several GS[O]'s in the army who could give him a stroke a hole'.[25] Despite conflicting personalities in some cases, Wavell was to turn to his Middle Eastern experiences as the foundation for his interwar military writing career.

While on half-pay in 1925 Wavell was asked by Basil Liddell Hart to write an entry on the Palestine campaign for the *Encyclopaedia Britannica*, of which the latter was the military editor. Over the following two years Wavell wrote frequently in a number of periodicals, including *The Army Quarterly* and *The Times Literary Supplement*. He was then asked by Major-General Sir Charles Callwell, who was editing a series of books entitled 'Campaigns and their Lessons', to write a volume on the war in Palestine. It was the success of this work, *The Palestine Campaigns*, which laid the foundations of Wavell's reputation as a military author, although it only earned him £50. Nevertheless, it ran to several editions and became a textbook at the Royal Military Academy Sandhurst. The bulk of the book was a narrative of operations in Palestine, which set out in succinct fashion the shape of the campaign. Wavell used the final chapter to demonstrate what he felt were the key lessons from Palestine; it would be unsurprising if this was the only part of the book that most Sandhurst cadets chose to read.[26] He noted that above all else the war in Palestine was one of manoeuvre and movement, with Megiddo as a striking example of how cavalry could be used to best effect. The speed of the EEF's advance helped it to produce results on the battlefield and to minimize casualties. Only at the end of the chapter did he point to the importance of thorough training and deception measures in helping to achieve victory in Palestine.

This forthright analysis of the value of movement in the EEF's battles was deliberately intended to make a point about the state of the British Army in the late 1920s. The imposition of the Ten Year Rule in 1919 and the subsequent retrenchment in military spending had done much to curtail the effectiveness of the army.[27] At the heart of the debate about its future role in either a colonial war, or a seemingly unlikely continental conflict, was the discussion over mechanization. Wavell played a leading role in the gradual reforms in this direction during the interwar period. In November 1926 he was appointed GSO1 to 3rd Division on Salisbury Plain, which was chosen to carry out the trials of the Experimental Armoured Force in 1927–8. Wavell and the divisional commander, Major-General Jock Burnett-Stuart, created a series of training exercises to learn about the tactical handling of the force. In January 1929 the lessons from the two-year scheme were discussed at a Staff College conference, during which Wavell lectured on the power of armoured units to disrupt the rear echelons of traditional infantry-based formations. He stressed the need for mechanized units to make full use of their mobility, avoiding engagements except where they had no choice. In addition, he argued that future tank designs had to reflect this concern, with the respective values of mobility, firepower and armour expressed in the ratio of 3:2:1. Wavell's subsequent command of 6th Brigade from 1930 saw him again dealing with issues of mechanization, as the unit received a light tank battalion to test cooperation with infantry. At the same time, further writing helped to establish his reputation as one of the army's foremost thinkers on future conflict. Most notably his article 'The Army and the Prophets', published in *The Journal of the Royal United Service Institution* in 1930, endorsed many of the concepts put forward by Liddell Hart and J. F. C. Fuller regarding the future of warfare and the key roles that would be played by armour and air power. These ideas were also at the heart of Wavell's analysis in *The Palestine Campaigns*, where he specifically compared the cavalry's sweeping manoeuvres to those that mechanized units would be able to carry out in the future. He argued that an armoured force, if it had served in Palestine, would have possessed great advantages in firepower and protection, and would not have been reliant on local water supplies. He did, though, acknowledge that the need for fuel and repairs, coupled with the rugged terrain of the region, might have inhibited the movements of such a force.[28]

As valuable an account as it is of the EEF's operations in Palestine, Wavell's work has to be viewed in light of the climate in which it was written. His conclusions on the centrality of movement and manoeuvre were a product of his desire to stress these elements to the senior echelons of the British Army in the late 1920s and early 1930s. *The Palestine Campaigns* was thus a paean to the role of cavalry, which Wavell saw as a substitute for the mechanized formations of a future conflict. This view inevitably shaped the way that he analysed Allenby's leadership and command of the EEF.

Wavell returned to the subject of the EEF with the publication of his two-volume study of Allenby, which appeared in 1940 and 1943. Following Allenby's death in 1936 his widow had asked Wavell to write a biography, a task that he found difficult to accomplish due to the lack of private papers.[29] Matters were further complicated by the fact that Wavell was in command of a division and was sent in 1937 to command British forces dealing with Arab unrest in Palestine. The second volume was completed while he served in India, and dealt with Allenby's career after the First World War. The first volume not only presented an account of the Palestine campaign laden with praise but also sought to rehabilitate Allenby's career on the Western Front. Service in command of the BEF's initial cavalry forces in 1914 and then as commander of 3rd Army had seen him involved in a number of débâcles, most notoriously the battle of Arras in April–May 1917. The eventual lack of success in this operation and the heavy losses involved led directly to Allenby being given command of the EEF, a position that he at first saw as a demotion.[30] All of the key elements of any description of Allenby were present in Wavell's account, with references to the improvement of EEF morale in mid-1917, the strength of the general's personality and his emphasis on deception and manoeuvre. The work serves to demonstrate how great an impact Allenby had on Wavell's attitude to command, rather than his role in shaping the EEF. As a result the biography stresses the importance of character in the military, which was of greater value than intelligence, training or experience.[31] Although he had avoided the partisan failings of Savage's work, Wavell was still guilty of being too close to the subject that he analysed. Liddell Hart was not impressed by the book, feeling that it was a far too formal biography with only brief flashes of 'critical perspicacity' and that as a result the account of the EEF's operations appeared too reticent in its criticisms.[32]

Liddell Hart also turned his hand to writing about Allenby's exploits in the First World War. In *Reputations* (1928) he produced a chapter on Allenby which drew a strict contrast between his failures on the Western Front and his success in Palestine, arguing that the Mediterranean voyage in June 1917 was the turning point in his career.[33] Once in the Middle East he became one of the 'Great Captains' of military history, most notably through his success at Megiddo. Importantly, Allenby had possessed the necessary skills all along and it was only with the EEF, away from the siege warfare of the Western Front, that he was able to put them into practice. Liddell Hart returned to the EEF's operations in his history of the First World War. It was Megiddo that for him sealed Allenby's reputation as one of the superlative commanders of history. He went as far as to compare it to Caesar's victory at Ilerda, Scipio's near Utica, Cromwell's at Preston and Moltke's at Sedan. In short, it was 'one of the most quickly decisive campaigns and the most completely decisive battles in all history'.[34] His analysis of the battle stressed the role played by the EEF's cavalry and its aircraft, as well as the assistance provided by Lawrence and the Arabs. These elements had allowed Allenby to recapture those aspects of surprise and mobility that had been lacking on the Western Front.

Liddell Hart failed to understand the nature of modern industrialized warfare, believing that generals had to be heroic leaders in order to achieve victory, rather than astute managers of military bureaucracies. This was a reflection of his own wartime experience of command, which had been exclusively at company level. He thus concentrated on the personal characteristics of the great commander, and it was these aspects that he found in abundance in Allenby.[35]

The influential views of Wavell and Liddell Hart have dominated much of the historiography on the Palestine campaign. The arguments about Allenby's personality and influence on the EEF continue to dominate the biographies of him. In the case of Lawrence James's work the narrative fails to provide any interesting new details and is largely reliant on that laid down by Wavell. Similarly, Anthony Farrar-Hockley accepts Liddell Hart's assertion that there was a dividing line in Allenby's career, portraying him as stifled by the Western Front command system, but flourishing once in Palestine where he could take personal command of the direction of the campaign. More worryingly Savage's myopic account has gained credence and a number of its dubious assertions are to be found in other biographies that strive for objectivity, such as that of Brian Gardner.[36] He produced an almost verbatim copy of Savage's description of the morale problems in the EEF in mid-1917, even accepting his unreliable reference to widespread desertions. These problems are not confined to the biographical studies of Allenby, as a number of recent accounts of the campaign suffer from the same limited viewpoint. John Grainger's skilful analysis of the battles in 1917 clearly demonstrates the centrality of that year's operations to the EEF's destruction of the Turks' combat effectiveness, thereby shifting the emphasis away from Megiddo. Nevertheless, he still repeats the assertions about Allenby's impact on the morale of the troops in mid-1917. Paradoxically, this is after dismissing many of these accounts as describing an exaggerated revolution in the EEF, which had served only to produce a legend around the general.[37]

David Woodward provides a strong narrative account of the EEF's campaigns, capturing much of the succinct style that made Wavell's work so popular. When it comes to assessing Allenby's role, however, his argument begins to unravel. His emphasis on the personal nature of warfare in the Middle East, supposedly a recourse to the style found during the Napoleonic Wars, fails to address many of the elements of modern industrialized combat that found their way to the theatre. Later, Woodward begins to muddle his military comparisons when he asserts that Allenby's use of concentration, speed and surprise at Megiddo demonstrated a form of 'blitzkrieg warfare'.[38] He makes no attempt to analyse the validity of *Blitzkrieg* as a complex historiographical concept, particularly its actual applicability to Second World War battles in which firepower was as critical as manoeuvre. It is clear that Woodward has imbibed both Liddell Hart's and Wavell's interpretations of the campaign, mediated through the military historical lens of 1939–45. The majority of these works suffer from a failure to analyse the source material upon which they are based, accepting the opinions of some authors as gospel. They therefore serve to contribute further to the hagiography around Allenby that Massey established after the First World War.

A scholarly focus on the commands of Murray and Allenby has been achieved in the works of Jonathan Newell and Matthew Hughes. Both attempt to move away from the bifurcated analysis of the Palestine campaign, which has portrayed Murray as a 'bad thing' and Allenby as a 'good thing'. Newell has attempted to rehabilitate the career of Murray by focusing on his logistical achievements in supporting the EEF on the far eastern side of Sinai, thus providing a springboard for subsequent operations in Palestine. He argues that Murray's arrival in Egypt in January 1916 had a similar impact on the EEF as Allenby's did one and a half years later. Both men were faced with disorganized armies that needed strong leadership. Despite these successes Newell still has to engage with the fact that Murray was responsible for the two devastating defeats at Gaza in March and April 1917. He tries to rescue Murray's reputation by turning to the argument that the general made in his final despatch: the EEF and its commander were hamstrung by the capricious nature of the War Cabinet towards the Palestine campaign, which resulted in it being under-resourced. Importantly Newell has also identified and criticized the seemingly illogical published accounts on the Palestine operations and Allenby's role within them. Falls, Liddell Hart, and Wavell are identified as the key players in this discourse, although the focus is on Wavell's biography of Allenby rather than the much more influential operational account of 1928. Lawrence is highlighted as the main progenitor of the cultural interpretations of the campaign, given popular resonance in the cinema by Lean's *Lawrence of Arabia* and on the stage by Terence Rattigan's *Ross* (1960).[39]

Recognizing the failings of many biographies Matthew Hughes has attempted to place Allenby's role within an analysis of the grand strategic decisions that were being taken by the British in 1917–18. He reconsiders Allenby not just in light of his successes, as at Third Gaza and Megiddo, but also in terms of his failures in the two Transjordan Raids and the difficulties in dealing with the post-war peace settlement in the Middle East. This approach highlights Allenby's cautious attitude towards operations in Palestine and the extent to which he, like Murray, was distracted by the needs of his political masters in London. More importantly it also stresses the numerical and technological superiority of the EEF by 1918, and the comparative weakness of the Turks. Hughes, although recognizing the existence of a hagiography around Allenby, does not deny its validity. At the heart of his discussion rests the assumption that Allenby had an immense impact on the EEF when he arrived in mid-1917, which requires a denigration of Murray's tenure as commander and a stress on the morale problems in the army. Hughes asserts that the EEF was 'psychologically fragile' in June 1917 and that its 'morale had collapsed'.[40] Allenby managed to rebuild the force's combat effectiveness through visits to front-line units, which lifted morale and ameliorated the boredom and difficult conditions encountered serving in southern Palestine. As Hughes makes clear this argument stresses the immense impact that an individual could have on an army, running counter to the historiography of morale in the 1990s which had stressed the impersonal nature of the First World War. Consequently Allenby is compared by Hughes to two of the most striking commanders of the Second World War, who produced morale improvements in their armies: Field Marshals Bernard Montgomery and William Slim.[41] He stresses that Allenby's achievement was as much in terms of leadership as it was command, returning to the Liddell Hart model of the great general. Hughes does concede that, to a certain extent, Allenby was reliant on Lieutenant-General Chetwode and the remnants of Murray's staff for the detailed plan he adopted at Third Gaza. He simply provided the EEF with good leadership and the effective management of the existing command structure.

Within this narrative of great generals the voice of the ordinary soldier of the EEF has been lost. The discourse between Newell and Hughes does little to resolve this problem. Much of the interpretation of the careers of Murray and Allenby is reliant on the memoirs of a few select individuals, most notably Lawrence, Storrs, Barrow and Meinertzhagen. Aside from the problems over the validity of these sources, of which Meinertzhagen's diary represents the most extreme case, the use of memoir material itself raises problems. All of these accounts were written after the events they described, and were thus subject to the vagaries of memory. Some of these authors also made explicit and implicit attempts to reconstruct the history of the campaign in the Middle East to suit their interwar causes.[42] Occasionally oral history collections have been used to reinforce the ideas found in these memoirs. The testimony of veterans, while representing more than 'old men drooling about their youth', has to be used with care, and each case needs to be treated as possessing its own historiography. Memoirs, written accounts, and oral testimonies recorded after 1930 have also been subject to the influence of the key texts on the campaign, notably those of Falls, Liddell Hart and Wavell. Barrow even acknowledged the accuracy and thoroughness of Wavell's biography of Allenby when he came to write his memoirs.[43] The underlying assumptions of the historiography need to be examined in greater detail to reveal the intricate nature of the construction of morale within the EEF and the role of Allenby in that process.

Morale crisis in the Middle East

At the heart of the discourse on Allenby is the notion that he reinvigorated the EEF after his arrival in Egypt on 28 June 1917. This rests on the assumption that there was a morale crisis in the force after its two failed attempts to take Gaza, in March and April. In fact the EEF remained combat effective at the end of Second Gaza, holding a line south of the Turkish defences that stretched from the coast to Beersheba. The EEF did not flee the field of battle nor did it suffer mass surrenders. 54th Division, whose brigades had cumulatively experienced the heaviest casualties across the two battles, was far from being at full strength, but it was not at the point of collapse. Its commander, Major-General Hare, made no mention in his otherwise detailed diary of any problems with morale.[44] The influential notion, first raised by Savage, that the EEF was suffering from widespread desertions and men going absent without leave appears bizarre. The official correspondence between the staffs of the EEF's three corps and GHQ in mid-1917 makes no mention of such disciplinary problems, nor do the letters and diaries of men at the front.[45] If morale had been as bad as Hughes and others have asserted then there would have been a considerable number of letters and reports flowing between various commanders discussing remedies for the situation. Equally, if desertion was sapping the force's strength it is likely that references would have survived in the personal paper collections of EEF troops. Little attempt has been made to criticize the illogical nature of Savage's assertion on desertion. The EEF in mid-1917 was stationed in southern Palestine connected to its resource base in Egypt via a single railway line running between Kantara and Rafah. In such circumstances only the bravest or most foolhardy of soldiers would have chosen to risk being caught by the military police along the railway or would have undertaken the treacherous walk across the Sinai Desert. Even if such an exploit proved successful the obstacle of the Suez Canal would still have presented itself. The reason that the EEF suffered few desertions was due to the fact that desertion was almost impossible.

As has been argued by Jonathan Fennell with regard to the 8th Army in North Africa in 1941–2, it is difficult to statistically assess the morale of a particular army. It is, however, possible to get to grips with the 'outcomes or correlates of morale', such as desertion, surrender or sickness rates.[46] Figures for the first two categories are not available in the historical records of the EEF's higher command structures, but an assessment of sickness rates in a selection of units can be undertaken utilizing information from some of the more detailed war diaries. This gives us a snapshot of the fluctuations, on a monthly basis, of sickness rates which can be used to give some sense of alterations in EEF morale, particularly in relation to major engagements. A rising level of sickness has been viewed by both commanders and historians as indicating increased levels of dissatisfaction among troops.

It is striking that in previous studies such quantitative and comparative analysis has not been undertaken in order to inform the assertions on EEF morale in mid-1917.[47] Detailed monthly figures for admissions sick to hospital are available for the 162nd Brigade and the 1st and 3rd ALH Regiments. These give a picture of the illness levels at the cutting edge of the EEF's infantry and mounted combat arms. These figures clearly demonstrate that the first two Gaza battles had little impact on sickness levels in any of the three formations studied here. 162nd Brigade did see a small rise in the number of men evacuated sick to hospital in May over the level in April; this was, however, less than subsequent levels of sickness experienced under Allenby's command (see Figure 1.6). A similar pattern can be discerned in the 1st and 3rd ALH Regiments (see Figures 1.7 and 1.8). Notably, the sick rate of 162nd Brigade began to fall off in June, while the EEF was still under the command of Murray. It is much more likely that small movements in the level of sickness in the EEF were related to the incidence of disease at the front line rather than to any morale difficulties that were encountered. As argued in Chapter 1, the EEF's front-line positions opposite

Gaza were a particularly unsanitary place, with widespread minor ailments, such as septic sores, having a debilitating effect on some units. Such injuries would have been more common in the weeks after Second Gaza, when the EEF was engaged in constructing its defensive trench line, and this may explain the slight rise in sickness in May 1917. Even Allenby, after first visiting the front in July 1917, made no mention of the supposedly impending morale collapse. In a letter to his wife he noted that 'all the men and animals are looking well and in good condition and spirits'.[48] Moreover in his first report to Robertson after visiting the front, Allenby stated laconically 'I was pleased with what I saw'.[49] If there was a psychological malaise affecting the EEF then Allenby, despite his much famed trips to forward units and ability to commune with the ordinary soldier, could not detect it.

From a comparative perspective, the First World War provides historians with a number of clear-cut cases of morale collapse, which stand in stark contrast to the events in Palestine. The leave problems experienced in the French Army coupled with growing disdain for the manner in which the war was being fought produced significant mutinies in 1917. Although eventually contained, the outbreak caused concern for senior Allied commanders.[50] The collapse of the Italian Army at Caporetto in autumn 1917 demonstrated how dangerous morale problems could be if left unchecked. The resulting retreat led to German and Austro-Hungarian troops occupying a large swathe of north-eastern Italy and forced the French and British to send divisions to help. The examples of Russia and Bulgaria highlight the fact that an army's morale collapse, if severe enough, could ultimately bring an end to a nation's ability to resist.[51] Alexander Watson's analysis of the ordered surrender of German units in summer and autumn 1918 illustrates how even armies which had demonstrated some of the highest levels of efficiency and combat expertise in the war could also succumb to a loss of confidence.[52]

If the comparison is extended further, to the Second World War, it is evident that British formations also suffered severe morale difficulties. Notably, 8th Army experienced low levels of combat motivation in 1941-2. Operation Crusader in late 1941 saw 42 per cent of British casualties accounted for by surrenders. By July 1942 General Claude Auchinleck informed the Army Council that prisoners of war made up 88 per cent of the army's casualties. Such startlingly high surrender rates demonstrate that there was little desire among the 8th Army's men to resist the Axis forces facing them. Auchinleck and his subordinate commanders were so concerned by the level of desertions from the front line that they pressed the government to reintroduce the death penalty for 'desertion in the field', in order to help set clear boundaries for unacceptable military behaviour. A total collapse in morale was also evident in the British imperial forces operating in Malaya, which culminated in the ignominious surrender at Singapore in February 1942.[53] These examples demonstrate how morale could slump in the First and Second World Wars, and the impact this had upon combat effectiveness. By contrast, the EEF remained a fully functioning army whose morale never sank to the nadirs experienced at Caporetto and Singapore. Although the men's willingness to fight the Turks undoubtedly fluctuated in relation to combat successes and failures, there was no morale collapse in the EEF during the First World War.

Allenby as a leader

The psychological fragility of the men of the EEF has been overstated, but it is still necessary to examine the impact Allenby had on the force when he arrived as its new Commander-in-Chief in mid-1917. There is a clear divergence between the roles of a commander and a leader in an army. The commander's task is a managerial one, running a complex military bureaucracy. By contrast a leader is someone who inspires and motivates.[54] This was a difference recognized by the French military theorist Colonel Charles-Jean-Jacques-Joseph Ardant du Picq in the 1860s. In *Etudes sur le combat* (1880) he opined that:

> Mediocre troops like to be led by their shepherds. Reliable troops like to be directed, with their directors alongside of them or behind. With the former the general must be the leader on horseback; with the latter, the manager.[55]

Great leaders could play a critical role in reinvigorating dejected armies, as with Montgomery in North Africa in 1942.[56] In contrast, there was no morale collapse for Allenby to rectify in the EEF in summer 1917; what the army actually needed was effective, professional management.

Nevertheless, a number of senior officers believed that Allenby had made a real difference to the troops' confidence in the command structure. Major-General Edward Chaytor, commander of the ANZMD, noted that it was the fact that Allenby made an effort to show himself to the men that impressed them most.[57] This was a view shared by Lieutenant-General Chetwode, who stated in a letter to Falls that:

> He [Allenby] quite rightly left his headquarters entirely and was to be seen in his motor right up at the front and in situations where I think very few high commanders have ever been seen before, personally driving on tired men and horses at a time when his personal influence just meant the extra mile or two which closed the last hope of escape of the enemy.[58]

Being close to the action at the front line was an attribute appreciated by divisional and corps commanders who were also frequently near to combat. Lieutenant-General Henry Chauvel, commander of the DMC, recorded in a letter to his wife that Allenby was seen everywhere and that he was a 'most energetic commander' who explained what he wanted brusquely and forcefully.[59] It is unsurprising that Allenby appeared in the correspondence and recollections of other generals as they would have encountered him on a regular basis.

For the ordinary rankers of the EEF he was not such an omnipresent figure. Allenby is only referred to by 6 soldiers out of the 77 letter collections and diaries written in 1916–19 covered in this study. In contrast, Allenby is an ever-present figure in soldiers' memoirs, both published and unpublished, from the mid-1920s onwards. This reflects the prominence he came to assume in the main accounts of the campaign, such as those of Massey, Lawrence and Wavell. It is unsurprising that these later accounts also seem to involve encounters with Lawrence, the other great 'celebrity' of the Middle Eastern war. Those letters and diaries compiled during the First World War that do refer to Allenby nearly always do so only when he is seen personally by the author. Thus Private R. J. France, of the 1/6th Essex, recalled seeing the general as his battalion marched north into Palestine after Third Gaza. Similarly, Captain H. C. Wolton, of the 1/5th Suffolks, noted that he saw Allenby looking pleased with himself in late November 1917 while inspecting units moving up to the Jaffa line. At times Allenby did go beyond being merely a military figurehead, seen in the distance. Captain C. S. Wink recalled a visit by the general to his field ambulance in which he asked if the unit needed any assistance.[60]

Opinions on Allenby could, however, change very quickly depending on the circumstances in which he was encountered. On 4 July 1917 the CMR formed part of an advanced guard for a reconnaissance ride by Allenby and his staff. Sergeant Harold Judge recorded in his diary that he had heard good things about the new general who was 'shaking things up in Cairo already a lot of "backsheasch" officers have got shunted out'.[61] Four days later this newfound liking for his Commander-in-Chief turned to disdain when he learnt that the patrol he had been on to cover Allenby's reconnaissance ride was only a rehearsal for the real visit. He noted that the rehearsal had cost the life of one trooper and several men had been wounded. In most cases, though, Allenby was simply not commented upon by the men of the EEF. He was not a prominent part of their lives at the front. This reflects a common trend in writings from soldiers across the theatres of the First World War; correspondence and diaries from the Western Front rarely refer to Haig or other senior officers. The ordinary soldier's world view had little space for these members of the military elite. What is striking in the case of the EEF is the contrast with the post-war memoir literature, where Allenby looms large.

Allenby did not escape the censure of his men for any errors in command or leadership that he was believed to have committed. One of the most strident critics was Lieutenant-Colonel Garsia, a staff officer with 54th Division, who was the main progenitor of what came to be known as the 'Gaza School' concerning the EEF's operations at Third Gaza. Throughout the interwar period he pressed the argument that the bulk of the EEF should have attacked along the coast in November 1917, rather than at Beersheba. He believed that such a move would have allowed the DMC to break through and to have encircled the Turkish forces on the Gaza-Beersheba defence line. Essentially the scheme prefigured the attack at Megiddo a year later. This was an idea that Garsia had put up to XXI Corps, via Major-General Hare, in 1917, and which had been largely ignored. In letters to the authors of the official history he tried to insist on some recognition for this alternative scheme. His opinion had only been reinforced when he met Colonel Franz von Kress von Kressenstein, the senior German officer with the Turks until after Third Gaza, in Berlin in 1920. From this interview he gained the impression that the EEF had been very close to beating the Turks in November 1917. Garsia stated in a letter to Hare that 'I am satisfied in my own mind that an extra division on the left and then cavalry would have predated the Turkish débâcle by 11 months'.[62] In 1940 Garsia published his criticism of the EEF's command decisions at all three Gaza battles as *A Key to Victory*. Here he posited the idea of an automatic system of planning, which was a model that could be copied by staff officers. In a postscript dated 28 May 1940, he argued that the British Army still had much to learn about planning operations, as had been demonstrated by the fall of Norway.[63] Like

Liddell Hart, he saw military history as didactic and hoped that as crisis approached in Europe his ideas would be examined. Garsia's work represents the most considered and detailed attempt to get to grips with the failures of the EEF in all three Gaza battles. Allenby, although portrayed as much more competent than Murray, was still far from the perfect commander of legend.

Aside from his command decisions at Third Gaza, Allenby's methods, that were supposed to have built morale within the EEF, are also open to scrutiny. His snap inspections of units, coupled with his notoriously bad temper, left many officers wary of meeting him. Although treated with affection by most of the historiography, the infamous 'BBL' (Bloody Bull's Loose) signal that emanated from GHQ whenever Allenby left for an inspection tour of the front demonstrates the real concerns that existed among some staff officers. Allenby could be very aggressive and treated those who could not justify their opinions with disdain. While carrying out an inspection on the Western Front he had notoriously responded to a positive comment from an officer by shouting back 'I want none of your bloody approbation'.[64] Allenby often became obsessed with trivialities, such as matters of dress, while inspecting front-line units, rather than concentrating on more important tactical issues. In a possibly apocryphal story, he was alleged to have castigated a company commander whose troops were not abiding by the regulation that steel helmets and leather jerkins were to be worn at all times in the trenches. On this occasion the soldier who had broken the rules was in fact dead. In the Middle East he also famously threw piles of papers that he did not wish to read across his office. It is thus unsurprising to find that Major-General Hare was relieved when he discovered that he had missed a visit from Allenby in late November 1917. The Commander-in-Chief had apparently been upset when he found a group of horses near the divisional headquarters tied to trees.[65] Rather than helping to build morale Allenby's visits may actually have been counterproductive, causing trepidation among the officers of the EEF. The notoriety of these more abrasive aspects of his character lingered on after the war, given literary fame with the publication of C. S. Forester's *The General* in 1936, the year of Allenby's death. Although the fictional figure of Lieutenant-General Sir Herbert Curzon was an amalgam of various stereotypical military personality traits, Forester clearly drew on elements of Allenby's reputation, even including a corps commander in the novel who was referred to by his staff as 'the buffalo'.[66]

For the other ranks of the army, the parades that accompanied senior officers' tours of the front line were looked on with apprehension. Such events involved considerable cleaning of equipment, a particularly onerous task in mounted units. As one trooper in the 1st ALH Regiment noted, all the polishing of rusty bits and stirrup irons was often in vain as only a day later the sea air would discolour them. After all this hard work the subsequent comments of generals that the equipment was invariably not up to the standard required left many men disheartened. A number of soldiers saw such army 'bull' as a complete waste of their time when on active service. To a certain extent such activities were used to distract the men from the reality of combat in the Middle East. Cleaning of equipment gave troops a routine they could fall into once out of the line, reducing the amount of time spent dwelling on the casualties suffered by their unit. Nevertheless, such activity served to embitter some soldiers against the higher echelons of the EEF, who were seen as the instigators of such demands for cleanliness. Parades could produce even greater disenchantment when men were left waiting in the sun for hours as generals turned up late or failed to carry out inspections entirely.[67] Although he tried to make his presence felt in the EEF it is clear that Allenby could not have visited every unit on a regular basis. His tours, if beneficial, probably only served to boost morale for a limited time period and within a small collection of units.

The transfer of the EEF's GHQ from Cairo to Khan Yunis, south of Gaza, is often highlighted as demonstrating Allenby's connection with the concerns of his men. It clearly provided some symbolic significance, demonstrating that the senior commander would share the hardships of the men at the front. Allenby, though, was able to retain the services of Murray's excellent French chef despite this move closer to the front line.[68] Crucially, this change of location also had real practical value for Allenby's ability to command the EEF in battle. One of the key problems demonstrated by First Gaza was that Murray was powerless to act if he commanded from a distance. He had travelled across Sinai on his train, but could do little except observe the decisions taken by Lieutenant-General Chetwode, then commander of the Desert Column, and Lieutenant-General Charles Dobell, commander of Eastern Force. By locating his GHQ at Khan Yunis Allenby was able to direct the course of operations, enhancing the effectiveness of the EEF's command and control structure.[69]

Murray as a commander

In terms of his impact among the ordinary men of the EEF Murray is even more anonymous than Allenby in the correspondence and diaries. This does suggest a slight shift in perception of the Commander-in-Chief after June 1917. Nevertheless, it was not among the other ranks that Murray was castigated, but among the EEF's staff officers. Chetwode felt that Murray had treated Dobell very badly at Second Gaza, forcing him to take command even though Murray was only a few miles back in his train. Second Gaza, however, was a relatively straightforward operation for the EEF to carry out, only running into difficulties due to the strength of the Turkish defences and the limited abilities of the EEF's artillery. First Gaza proved more illustrative of Murray's inability to command an army in the field. Lieutenant-Colonel Garsia opined that Murray had created a 'bloated military secretariat' at GHQ rather than a General Staff capable of conducting operations.[70] This criticism was expanded upon by James Gammell, a former staff officer under Murray, in his correspondence with the former Brigadier-General, General Staff, of Eastern Force, Brigadier-General Guy Dawnay. In the letter Gammell listed three key failings of Murray's command:

(i) Was not the organization wrong? Was not advanced G.H.Q. a bit of a War Office sitting on the back of a commander in the field?
(ii) If the C.-in-C., was really going to take charge, was not Advanced G.H.Q. too far back? Should he not somehow or other have been able to see General Dobell personally on the ground?
(iii) The commander who has no reserves ceases to play any real part in the battle.[71]

Gammell noted that such opinions were effectively 'rank heresy' for a former officer at GHQ, but he felt that they should be passed on in some way to the authors of the official history. The criticisms of Chetwode, Garsia and Gammell all demonstrate that Murray was not able to command an army in the field. He had lost the faith of the EEF's middle-ranking commanders (corps and divisional level officers), effectively making his position untenable by mid-1917. Murray was better suited to being a desk general in Cairo, from where he could assess and remedy the EEF's logistical problems, a task he carried out effectively. He was not a battlefield commander, a point that had been proven by his poor performance in France in 1914 where he served as Chief of the General Staff in the BEF.[72] It is here that Newell's attempt to rehabilitate Murray falls down. He may have been an intelligent staff officer but he could not win battles; Allenby was a general who could bring victory in the field.

Victory in itself has often been viewed as a crucial component in building strong morale in an army. This is, however, rather a moot point, as all armies, if they are even to take to the field, must perceive themselves as having the potential to be successful. One of the principal roles of training systems found in military organizations is to create this confident attitude among soldiers, sailors or airmen. Those military personnel who lack such confidence are unlikely to view a particular cause as worthy of risking their lives for. An approach that focuses solely on the importance of commanders providing battlefield victories ignores cases of previously victorious armies suffering morale collapses, and armies that were clearly facing defeat fighting to the bitter end. The *Wehrmacht*, which fought itself to annihilation in 1944–5, provides a good case in point.[73] Morale is not simply an expression of battlefield victory, nor of a general's ability to provide such success.

The crucial problem of Murray's tenure as Commander-in-Chief of the EEF was his failure to create a modern, effective corps command structure. This meant that the EEF's technological superiority over the Turkish Army was not fully utilized in combat. First Gaza demonstrated the confusion that resulted from the ad hoc use of Eastern Force as a command headquarters for operations. The battle saw a lack of clarity as to who was in charge, with Dobell competing for authority with Chetwode and Murray. The result was a lack of drive early in the morning of 26 March that resulted in 53rd Division, with 161st Brigade attached, failing to push on quickly into the Turkish defences around Ali Muntar. These difficulties resurfaced at the close of the battle when the ANZMD was precipitately withdrawn from its position encircling Gaza, despite British infantry having entered the town. There was no single hand directing operations, and as a result individual formation and divisional commanders were left to interpret their imprecise orders as they wished. This produced confusion and a lack of coordination between units.

The absence of an adequate corps command structure stemmed from the manner in which the EEF had adapted to tackle the changing combat situation in 1916. Up until and including Romani the EEF's main task was to defend the Canal, a purpose for which a regionally based command system was ideally suited. From August 1916 onwards the EEF became a pursuit force, chasing the retreating Turks across the Sinai Peninsula. Within these operations command and control was left to the Desert Column. The two battles fought in this period, Magdhaba and Rafah, were only small-scale engagements, involving one mounted division with some supporting units. First Gaza was a battle on a much grander scale, involving two mounted divisions and three infantry divisions. Attempts to integrate this force into the command structures of Eastern Force and the Desert Column led to overstretch at the respective headquarters. Murray had relied on an ad hoc command and control system capable of undertaking *coups de main* and minor battles, very much similar to those fought on imperial campaigns. It was not capable of organizing an army for modern industrialized mass warfare. As a consequence it is possible to detect a collapse in confidence in Murray among senior commanders after First and Second Gaza. If there were morale problems in the army then they were not located at the front line, but among the overworked staff officers of Eastern Force and the Desert Column who could see that the EEF was incapable of conducting major combat operations.

Allenby as a commander

Faced with these problems in July 1917 it is unsurprising that Allenby concentrated his efforts on reforming the command and control structure of the EEF.[74] He organized it to mirror the forces he had used on the Western Front. This importation of organizational structures from the BEF represented the professionalization of the EEF by Allenby. His experiences in France and Flanders provided a mixed learning curve that could be transferred to his new command. Only at Arras in April 1917 had he been given control of a major offensive. The stunning success of the initial attack on 9 April, which saw the furthest advance by the BEF up to that point in the war, was overshadowed by the attritional struggle that followed, resulting in the highest daily casualty rates of any British Western Front battle. Nevertheless, over the course of his three years' service on the main European battlefields Allenby had got to grips with the requirements of a modern, industrialized war. He was acutely aware that detailed planning and a professional military staff were vital to achieving coherent and sustained operational success.

Allenby, therefore, deconstructed Murray's ad hoc system of command and created in its place two infantry corps, XX and XXI, commanded by Lieutenant-Generals Chetwode and Edward Bulfin respectively, and a cavalry corps, the DMC, under the command of Lieutenant-General Chauvel. As part of these reforms corps heavy artillery groups were created which enabled the EEF to make use of its rapidly increasing firepower. This allowed the army's qualitative and quantitative superiority in technology to be utilized fully on the battlefield. Summer 1917 saw the EEF adapting to its new organizational structure. As part of this process of reorganization Allenby removed lacklustre staff officers, such as Major-General A. L. Lynden-Bell, Murray's Chief of the General Staff, and brought in competent ones with proven track records on the Western Front, most notably Major-General Louis Bols in Lynden-Bell's role. EEF staff officers who had shown promise were quickly promoted into positions where they would be of use, as seen with Brigadier-General Dawnay who Allenby appointed as Bols's assistant.

Although still famed for his irascible temper which he also brought over from the Western Front, Allenby in Palestine was prepared to listen to the suggestions and operational schemes of his subordinate commanders. This can be seen most obviously in his adoption of Chetwode's appreciation of how to crack open the Gaza defences for the attack in October and November. A listening approach from Allenby appears to have been a direct response to his experience as commander of 3rd Army at Arras. Here he had dutifully carried out Haig's orders to continue the offensive after the initial successes, resulting in heavy losses. As a consequence three divisional commanders, who objected and felt Allenby was ignoring the situation on the ground, complained directly to Haig. This 'generals' mutiny' had tacit support from 3rd Army's corps commanders and led to Haig halting major operations for a week. By May Allenby had grasped the situation and also made the case to Haig that further attacks would achieve very little. As Matthew Hughes has demonstrated it was this, combined with the complaints of the divisional commanders, that led Haig to remove him from command of 3rd Army.[75] Allenby had thus learnt in the trying circumstances of the Western Front and at the cost of his BEF career the need to engage with and listen to the views of his subordinate commanders, many of whom had a better grasp of the tactical and operational challenges. His leadership of the EEF was marked by a greater willingness to absorb the learning of those he commanded. This was helped by the fact that two of his corps commanders, Chetwode and Chauvel, were among some of the best British imperial officers of the war; both were also veterans of the Sinai and Palestine theatres.

What Allenby created in Palestine during mid-1917 was a modern army that was capable of conducting all arms operations on a grand scale.[76] The reforms made the EEF capable of defeating the Turks in a series of attritional battles in the last months of 1917. These began at Third Gaza and culminated with the destruction of a Turkish counter-attack north of Jerusalem after Christmas. In 1918 the EEF again proved successful in battle, destroying the Turks at Megiddo with its newly Indianized formations. The efficient integration of these Indian Army units clearly demonstrated Allenby's skill as commander of the EEF.[77] As Edward Erickson has elucidated, the concentration on the EEF's numerical superiority at Megiddo and the use of cavalry neglects the fact that the army's infantry fought a skilful operation to crack open the Turkish defences. The EEF's performance on 19 September 1918 can be seen in direct and favourable comparison with that of 4th Army at Amiens in August 1918, a battle which resulted, as Erich Ludendorff saw it, in the notorious 'black day of the German Army'.[78] Allenby's troops, in particular the staffs at army, corps, and divisional levels, were more than capable of matching the operational sophistication being shown by the BEF on the Western Front. The EEF reflected the culmination of the British Army's 1914–18 'learning curve', demonstrating an ability to coordinate major engagements which ultimately drove the Turkish Army in Palestine and Syria towards destruction.

The relative impacts of Murray and Allenby on the EEF in 1916–18 raises a pertinent question about the importance of senior commanders in determining the outcomes of battles, campaigns and wars in the twentieth century.[79] As suggested by Ardant du Picq, by the late nineteenth century and certainly by the era of the First World War, the figure of the great general heroically leading his men into battle had been replaced by the general as a manager of a complex military bureaucracy. The distance between the commander and his men had become considerable, a concept exploited in much satire of the conflict, from *Oh! What a Lovely War* through to *Blackadder Goes Forth*. In such circumstances it seemed that men such as Haig, Falkenhayn or Ludendorff could exercise very little influence on the lives of the ordinary private soldier. The war in the Middle East, however, offers an alternative picture. In this theatre generals seemed to be able to provoke crises and amazing improvements in the EEF's morale. These fluctuations in soldiers' combat motivation, as this chapter has demonstrated, have been greatly overemphasized in much of the historiography. Instead the generalship of the EEF needs to be integrated much more closely into interpretations of Western Front command. Generals could be great commanders in 1914–18, with the emphasis on their professional management of an army and its staff. Equally, they could fail in this role, as Murray did in 1917. Here was a case of a general who was overwhelmed by the scale and pace of the modern military campaign that was unfolding in Palestine. In these circumstances an approach to operations derived from nineteenth-century imperial wars had its limitations; the EEF's British infantry discovered this to their cost twice in front of Gaza.

In comparison, Allenby's command reforms of the EEF demonstrate that he had got to grips with the problems of modern warfare. Crucially, there was no morale crisis for Allenby to rectify among the troops in Palestine. The combat effectiveness of the EEF's reliable infantry and mounted soldiers meant that the army was strong at a tactical level. Allenby's command and control improvements saw the operational level of warfare being treated with the seriousness it deserved. *Pace* Hughes's assertion that Allenby was a good leader and reliant on a strong pre-existing command structure; it is clear that in mid-1917 the reverse was true. The command structures he inherited from Murray were completely inadequate for the task of seizing Gaza and destroying the Turkish Army in southern Palestine. Allenby concentrated on creating a command and control system that would produce results on the battlefield. After nearly three years of fighting on the Western Front he knew how to organize and prepare an army for modern industrialized warfare. The fascination in the historiography and post-war memoirs with Allenby's personality has obscured the fact that it was actually his managerial skills that made him a general who could win battles. In North Africa in 1942, Britain's greatest desert general of the Second World War faced a morally broken 8th Army, in such circumstances he was required to *lead* it to victory at El Alamein; Allenby, on the other hand, *commanded* the EEF to victory at Megiddo.

4

Citizen Soldiers at War

The multifaceted nature of the EEF's organization adds to the complexities surrounding the nebulous subject of its soldiers' morale. The vast bulk of the infantry commanded by Murray and Allenby was drawn from the pre-war TF, Britain's so-called amateur or 'weekend' soldiers. Four of the divisions that faced the Turks at First Gaza in March 1917 were formed of Territorial soldiers. These troops continued to play a leading role until the German spring offensive of 1918 on the Western Front affected the Middle East, leading to the transfer of over 60,000 men to France.[1] Their replacement by Indian soldiers significantly altered the structure of the EEF, with most divisions replacing nine of their battalions with Indian units. The only infantry division to remain unaffected by this process was the 54th (East Anglia) Division. It provides a lens through which to analyse the specific problems faced by Territorial soldiers in the EEF during the challenging Sinai and Palestine campaigns of 1916–18.

54th Division's continuous service in the Middle Eastern theatre meant it passed through a wide range of combat experiences. These were tied together by the unity of battlefield opposition the division faced, only ever fighting against the Ottoman Army, from Gallipoli through to Palestine. In the latter, the division's troops suffered defeat twice at Gaza, but were also involved in the sweeping victory at Megiddo in September 1918. These battlefield exploits were tempered by the stagnation and boredom experienced guarding the Suez Canal during 1916, and in periods of trench warfare in southern Palestine. This variety in the division's service allows it to stand as a representative of the Territorial infantry who took part in the EEF's campaigns. Many of the studies of morale within the TF during the First World War have focused on the exploits of individual battalions and almost exclusively on the Western Front, failing to deal with the imperial aspects of the force's service.[2] The 54th Division thus provides a window through which to consider the peculiarities of the often overlooked military experiences of the Territorial soldier.

The Territorial Force at war in the Middle East

The TF was inaugurated in April 1908 amidst much fanfare provided by associations with Edward VII. This belied the difficult birth that the force had undergone as part of the army reforms enacted by Richard Haldane, the Liberal Secretary of State for War (1905–12). Haldane was faced with the difficulty of reconciling political retrenchment with the needs of national and imperial defence. As such the TF was an attempt to provide a degree of order to Britain's sprawling and disparate second-line army, which to contemporary observers had performed poorly in the South African War of 1899–1902. Haldane envisaged the TF as an alteration to the concept of a 'nation in arms', with units raised and administered locally but trained centrally. In essence this localization, embodied through the County Associations, was a continuation of the late nineteenth-century army reforms of Edward Cardwell and Hugh Childers (Secretaries of State for War in 1868–74 and 1880–2 respectively). The TF would embody the link between specific localities and the army, begun by the territorialization of regiments in 1881. These auxiliary elements of the British Army played a crucial role in bridging the gap between civilians and soldiers, the latter often portrayed as social pariahs.[3]

Haldane's proposals ran into significant opposition, mainly stemming from the colonels of existing militia units, who saw the TF as a threat to their sybaritic existence. The problems did not cease once the organization had come into existence. Recruitment was strong in the first six months, but then fell away sharply, with the TF's strength peaking in 1910 at 272,000 men. Many of its critics, among whom the most vehement were Lord Roberts and the National Service League, also pointed to the young age profile of the recruits, 98,000 of whom were under 20 years old. Furthermore, the level of training was often poor and the provision of equipment inadequate, with much of that provided being obsolescent. The greatest concern related to the TF's future role. Haldane had perceived it not just as a home defence force, but also as a second line behind the regular army's embryonic expeditionary force. The lack of an overseas obligation for Territorials meant that many of the TF's members could not actually serve in such a capacity. By 1913, out of a total strength of 251,000 men only 1,152 officers and 18,903 other ranks had taken the imperial service pledge, allowing them to fight overseas; this was barely 10 per cent of the force. These deficiencies led many in the regular army, both officers and other ranks, to treat the TF with disdain, a prejudice that carried over into the vastly expanded army of 1914–18. It is not, therefore, surprising to find regular officers who came to command Territorial units expressing concern for the lack of self-confidence among Territorial NCOs, or commenting that the men could not cope without their wives and mothers when away from them in barracks. The shared battlefield sacrifices of regulars, Territorials, volunteers and conscripts during the First World War altered many of these preconceptions.[4]

The wartime exploits of 54th Division in the Middle East served to counter many of the claims made against the military effectiveness of the TF. It was mobilized on 4 August 1914, under the command of Major-General F. S. Inglefield, and comprised twelve first-line Territorial infantry battalions drawn from seven different regiments, grouped into three brigades. 161st Brigade was formed exclusively from battalions of the Essex Regiment (1/4th, 1/5th, 1/6th and 1/7th) and 162nd Brigade included

1/5th Bedfordshires and the 1/4th Northamptonshires, alongside two battalions of the London Regiment (1/10th and 1/11th). The 163rd Brigade, initially comprised of battalions from the Norfolk and Suffolk regiments only (1/4th and 1/5th battalions in both cases), was altered in early 1915 when the 1/4th Suffolks left for France and were replaced by the 1/8th Hampshire Regiment. The presence of these Hampshire Territorials stretched the division's claim to represent an East Anglian military identity. When asked to serve overseas most of the soldiers in the division responded favourably, with the three quarters acceptance seen in the 1/5th Suffolks as representative of the general trend within TF battalions at the time. Until it embarked for Gallipoli in July 1915 the division was engaged in training to raise its military standards. The first battlefield test came in August 1915 at Suvla Bay, where it attacked across the Anafarta plain suffering severely at the hands of the more experienced Turkish soldiers. Captain Frederick Clarke, serving in the 1/10th Londons, saw it as a 'battle of lost opportunities and an outstanding example of how not to make an attack'.[5] The advance saw the loss of the commanding officer of the 1/5th Norfolks, as well as 16 of the battalion's officers and 250 other ranks; an inauspicious start to the division's campaign against the Ottoman Empire.[6] The subsequent vicious hill fighting took its toll, and the division was evacuated in early December. Combat losses were worsened due to the poaching of many battalions' best men prior to Gallipoli as drafts for units in France, and the generally insufficient training received for combat in such conditions. Sickness and disease were to claim most of the division's casualties at Gallipoli. The 1/8th Hampshires left the peninsula with just under 200 men, and the 1/5th Norfolks were so depleted that they could only muster 2 companies by December 1915. Similarly, the 1/5th Suffolks were evacuated with only 250 men in the battalion, of whom just 43 were classified as fit for duty on arrival at Mudros.[7] Gallipoli, for many of the division's soldiers, represented the nadir of the formation's wartime service.

The division moved to Egypt in order to recuperate and spent two months training at Mena camp near Cairo. The 161st Brigade was not given the chance to rebuild itself and instead spent its first months in Egypt guarding the railway line between the Mediterranean and the Western Desert from attacks by the Senussi. The experiences in Egypt stood in stark contrast to those at Gallipoli. From late March 1916 onwards, 54th Division was one of many units stationed in the extensive defences along the Suez Canal. The conditions found in the Sinai Desert made many of the soldiers' tasks extremely difficult, and the distance from the Turks meant that there was little action; this was simply a 'very laborious and tedious sojourn in the wilderness'.[8] 161st Brigade's machine gun company did, though, break up this monotony by participating in the clash with the Turks at Romani in August 1916.

A significant change in the higher echelons of the division occurred during this period, with Major-General Inglefield replaced by Major-General Steuart Hare; the poor performance of the division at Suvla Bay cost Inglefield his command. He was not popular among the men and many of the junior officers had developed a dislike for him even before they reached the peninsula. Hare was a competent commander, although no military genius, lacking the experience as a staff officer that Inglefield had gained in the South African War. His previous military exploits were at regimental level and limited to campaigns on the North-West frontier of India in the 1890s.[9] At

Gallipoli Hare had commanded the 86th Brigade, in 29th Division, but was wounded soon after landing at Cape Helles and saw little of the fighting.

Early 1917 witnessed the culmination of Murray's drives across the Sinai Desert, which had begun at Romani and ended at El Arish. The EEF's logistical support, with a railway and pipeline that stretched across Sinai to Rafah, provided the force with the opportunity to isolate and defeat the garrison at Gaza. 54th Division along with the EEF's other infantry divisions, crossed Sinai by the wire netting road, and concentrated at El Arish in late February. The division was in action again at First Gaza, over a year since Gallipoli. Two of its brigades saw little fighting in the battle and had few casualties. In contrast, 161st Brigade, attached to the 53rd Division, was heavily engaged on 26 and 27 March in the attacks on the Turks' defensive positions at Ali Muntar and Green Hill to the south of Gaza. The brigade suffered nearly 1,500 casualties, the majority resulting from having to cross one and a half miles of open countryside swept by machine gun fire before it could attempt to assault its objectives.[10] Following this débâcle, the division received little rest and was once again advancing on the Gaza defences along the Beersheba road on 19 April. On this occasion the 162nd and 163rd Brigades ran into severe Turkish opposition and became bogged down in front of the Turks' defensive line. By the end of the day the EEF had lost 6,444 men, with 2,870 of these casualties in the 54th Division. The losses fell largely on the two brigades committed to the attack, with some battalions suffering particularly heavily: the 1/4th Norfolks had 478 casualties and the 1/5th Norfolks 662. Major-General Hare estimated that after Second Gaza his rifle strength had been reduced to 6,000 men; very nearly half of the division had been lost in action.[11]

The six months following these two failures were inevitably spent rebuilding 54th Division's strength while entrenched opposite Gaza. This period of attritional warfare came to an end on 31 October when the EEF successfully broke through the Turks' lines at Beersheba, and then seven days later at Gaza. The division led the assault on the town's western defences and became involved in five days of heavy fighting, costing some battalions dearly. A rapid pursuit of the Turks ensued, culminating in the fall of Jerusalem on 9 December 1917. During this advance 54th Division was engaged away from the Judaean hills on the Auja River, north of Jaffa. This fighting, although less damaging in terms of manpower losses, was tactically very difficult and complicated by heavy rains; it was, for one soldier of the 1/6th Essex, 'the most trying ordeal of the campaign'.[12] The EEF's advance again ground to a halt at the end of 1917, and from the infantry's perspective little progress was made for much of 1918, save for occasional adjustments to the line. Much of this stagnation resulted from the loss of most of the EEF's best troops to the Western Front and their replacement with poorly trained and inexperienced Indian units. By September 1918 the EEF was ready to advance again, 54th Division played an important role in the attack at Megiddo, forming the pivot on the right of the line around which Allenby's infantry drive pushed northwards. This allowed the EEF's cavalry to sweep up the coastal plain and inflict a crushing defeat on a heavily demoralized Turkish Army. The division's losses were much smaller than in previous battles, with just over 500 casualties in total.[13] This success ended the East Anglia Division's combat service in Palestine, with the rest of September and October spent marching north to Beirut, before they returned to Egypt in late November.

54th Division had passed through a varied set of military experiences during its campaigns in Sinai and Palestine. It was engaged in operations that alternated between stagnation, attrition and rapid movement. The significant losses faced by the division on a number of occasions, most notably in 1917, did not undermine its fighting abilities. Its morale did not break down at Second Gaza and it was entrusted with a critical role at Megiddo. Therefore it is necessary to examine how the morale of the Territorial infantrymen of this division managed to endure the myriad hardships of campaigning in the Middle East. The citizen soldiers who served with the EEF, much maligned as only part-time warriors, proved that in battle they could match the best of the British Army.

Citizen soldiers

The depiction of soldiers rejoicing at the receipt of Christmas presents on a divisional Christmas card from 1917, hints at the extensive range of influences upon troop morale in the Middle Eastern theatre (see Illustration 4.1). A wide range of factors have been identified as influencing soldiers' endurance on the Western Front, and many of these are also applicable to an analysis of the Middle Eastern theatre; EEF soldiers cannot be seen in isolation from the rest of the First World War. As J. G. Fuller has argued, the British Army 'at least did not experience the war as something totally outside traditional frames of reference'.[14] The horrific nature of the struggle in which they took part meant that many soldiers turned to an image of the pre-war world, which was to a

Illustration 4.1 54th Division Christmas Card, 1917 (IWM, 02/16/1, Hinde Papers).

certain extent imagined, in order to cope. The Christmas presents brought on camels, on the 54th Division's card, fit into this image of soldiers making recourse to their peacetime civilian identity.

Such expressions of civilizing elements were common among Territorial soldiers in 1914-18. Indeed those Territorials who served on the Western Front did not necessarily turn at first to their immediate military primary group in order to help them in times of combat stress, but instead to the civilian world they had left behind. This reflected some of the motives that drove the creation of the TF in 1908. 'The Territorials saw themselves, and were seen by the military authorities, as the essential bridge between the soldier and the civilian.'[15] These part-time soldiers carried their pre-war amateur approach over into their active military service from 1914. The men who made up the Territorial battalions of 54th Division displayed many of these characteristics. Private Albert Surry, for example, made it clear that the members of the 1/7th Essex viewed themselves above all else as 'citizen soldiers'. This civilian association was not confined to the division's infantrymen; it was also evident among its artillery units, who described themselves as 'tinkers, tailors, clerks and sailors'.[16] This focus on a civilian identity could produce strange effects among the battalions serving in the line. 1/5th Bedfordshires' Christmas celebrations in 1916 included a bizarre representation of popular democracy in action; an attempt to turn the military world of hierarchies upside down. Lieutenant New was elected 'Mayor of Oldham Post', part of whose duties included a mock inspection with his own corporation accompanying him, before giving a drunken speech to the battalion from the roof of the officers' mess. Although fuelled by alcohol this event's clear satirical edge demonstrates the ability of the division's Territorial troops to turn to their pre-war, civilian points of reference, as a means of coping with the eccentricities of military service in the Middle East.[17]

The civilian world of the Territorials was used to shape the military arena in which they lived from day to day. Defensive positions were often named after familiar local landmarks relevant to the East Anglia Division, bringing the alien environment of the Middle Eastern battlefield a small step closer to home. This is illustrated by the 1/4th Northamptonshires, who named their post on the Auja River 'Northampton Castle' and worked on trenches outside Gaza that were named Northampton and Suffolk roads. Similarly, the medics from a hospital in Sheffield encountered in September 1917 by Captain E. B. Hinde, of the 1/2nd East Anglian Field Ambulance, had christened their dugouts 'Sheffield Lodge' and 'Sheffield Villa'. This continued a practice that had emerged in the division's battalions at Gallipoli, with the trenches on Hill 60 named Bury, Northampton and Bedford.[18] These local allusions could be very precise, making reference to places that were only of parochial regimental interest, as seen in the 1/7th Essex naming one of the defensive positions outside Gaza 'Warley Redoubt'. Warley was the home of the Essex Regiment's chapel and thus one of the focal points of regimental life.

The role of local identity in determining how Territorials perceived military hardship and combat was at times tenuous. The defensive posts around the Suez Canal, held by 54th Division, were named Oldham, Salford and Manchester by the men of 42nd (East Lancashire) Division. No attempt was made to rename the positions; the men of East Anglia did not feel the need to defend posts entitled Norwich, Hackney or Chelmsford.

Place names with a poignant attachment for a particular regiment were also given to positions that were not necessarily constructed by soldiers who understood these local loyalties. Thus the 1/4th Northamptonshires were responsible for building 'Warley Gap' and 'Chingford Road' in 1918, references with much greater resonance for the men of the Essex Regiment.[19] The prominence of names of English towns was enough of a reminder of home, without the need to resort to specific places of significance. A wider civilian identity was at play, which at times was local, regional and national in character.

The greatest difficulty for soldiers serving in the Middle East was that leave to Britain was almost impossible, only occasionally being given to officers. This made it difficult for the men of 54th Division to gain a clear break from military service, and to express their civilian identities away from the war as well as reaffirming their links with local communities and families. On the rare occasions that home leave was given, the process of selecting individuals proved a tortuous one. Company commanders were required to choose suitable applicants, who would then be interviewed by the battalion's commanding officer. Instead leave in Egypt provided a common form of relaxation and a brief respite from the front line. These intermittent rest periods were often filled with the stereotypical elements of a Cook's Tour, including trips to the pyramids or Cairo's mosques, and donkey rides in the desert. The attractions to be found in Egypt were so varied that many soldiers ended up quickly exhausting all of the funds they had allocated to their trip.[20] For small numbers of men, mainly officers, leave was also granted to Jerusalem in 1918, although the tours of noted religious sites seldom lived up to the visitors' high expectations (as detailed in Chapter 2).

The importance of such breaks from the line can be seen in the diaries of a number of 54th Division soldiers which read very much like travel guides; they realized that the war provided a unique opportunity to sightsee in the Middle East for relatively little cost. The pleasures of leave were often far simpler, with Private Surry eulogizing over the chance to sleep in a bed with sheets and a mattress.[21] Lieutenant-Colonel F. H. Wollaston, commander of the 1/5th Suffolks, expressed similar sentiments while visiting Alexandria:

> Heaven, absolute Heaven, the fact of living in an hotel, and having one's meals off a tablecloth and having food which is not Government rations is bliss, pure and unadulterated. The fact also of seeing people in clothes other than khaki or the French grey and the women in their very short skirts (the writer having at last seen these frocks can now die happy) and being able to order a taxi makes one forget that a war is actually going on at all.[22]

For Captain H. C. Wolton, serving in the 1/5th Suffolks, the sight of green lawns on an island in the Nile provided the simple change that he desired from the sandy monotony of life in Sinai. It was the return to these norms and reminders of their previous lives that made leave such a welcome event for many soldiers, as it offered an opportunity like no other to feel civilized. This return to civilization was not always confined to periods of leave. Rest in brigade or divisional reserve could also act as a significant break from the hardships of front-line life. In late 1917, when the 1/5th Suffolks were billeted in the German colony of Wilhelma in Palestine, Wollaston recorded that 'present life is absolute bliss, houses to live in, beds to sleep in and food to be got'.[23] The conditions were such a contrast to those at the front that he hoped that the next deluge of rain would also find them living in similarly salubrious conditions.

Time spent away from the line allowed troops to shop for local souvenirs. Captain Hinde visited Ludd, in December 1917, in order to acquire local garments to improve his tent, but instead found himself purchasing two Roman gold coins. These provided him with a tangible route into exploring the historic past of the region, even though there was always the chance of them being fakes. Mementoes of the soldiers' experiences were more often than not sent home to friends and family. Souvenirs provided a specific link for the recipients to the theatre in which their loved one was serving. For example, Private R. Overman, of the 1/5th Norfolks, purchased alabaster stones allegedly stolen from a temple at Luxor, as well as a locally produced purse to send to his parents.[24] Such gifts helped to form a bond between the men serving in the Middle East and their relatives, sharing with them some of the exoticism of Egypt and Palestine.

Leave periods in Cairo or Alexandria were dominated by trips to the myriad venues offering entertainment for soldiers, primarily the cities' cinemas and music halls.[25] These acted as reminders of the world they had left behind and for which they were now fighting. They could bring a poignancy and relevance to the war, which the distance of the Middle Eastern front from Britain served to undermine. Concert parties were not confined to the realm of leave in Egypt, as military units frequently put on improvised shows during rest periods, reflecting a common link between British troops, spread across the war's many theatres, from Belgium to Palestine. Many of these shows provided remarkably good performances, often making use of professional actors and entertainers found in units serving in the vicinity. Some divisional shows were so successful, largely due to their use of large numbers of former entertainment professionals, that they were moved to theatres in Egypt. Touring concert parties added to the variety of amusements provided, such as that of Lena Ashwell, a leading actress of the early twentieth century who was also a theatre manager and prominent supporter of the suffrage campaign. The quality of the performances by Ashwell's company was very high, and as a result they found the 54th Division to be a 'very big and appreciative audience'. As with the shows that dominated on the Western Front, those in the Middle East featured content that was largely culled from the music hall. Female impersonators were extremely popular, with many creating impressive feminine façades. It is not, therefore, surprising to find Captain Hinde stating that one such impersonator 'really looked awfully pretty'.[26] The absence of women from the lives of the men at the front meant that these concert party turns were often their only chance for pseudo-feminine contact, or at least engagement with a mythological feminine ideal.

54th Division produced its own concert party in September 1917, entitled 'The Rose of Gaza', which included Major-General Hare's son among the performers. In this case the concert party formula was twisted to fit the peculiarities of the Middle Eastern front, with sketches poking fun both at the military society in which they lived and at the Turks. The lavishly illustrated cover of the programme demonstrates this satire on the British military, as well as touting the sexual appeal of the show's female impersonator (see Illustration 4.2). The performance was a parody of Samson and

Delilah, with Hare's son cast as the villain, an Assistant Provost-Marshal, symbolic of the worst excesses of military discipline. After its mediocre opening night the show improved and later performances proved very popular, with Captain Wolton recalling that he and his men 'shrieked with laughter throughout' the show. Captain Hinde was also impressed, finding the staging, band and songs all of a high quality.[27] The light-hearted entertainment of 'The Rose of Gaza' acted as a useful safety valve for the release of frustrations among the division's troops. 54th Division's battalions also

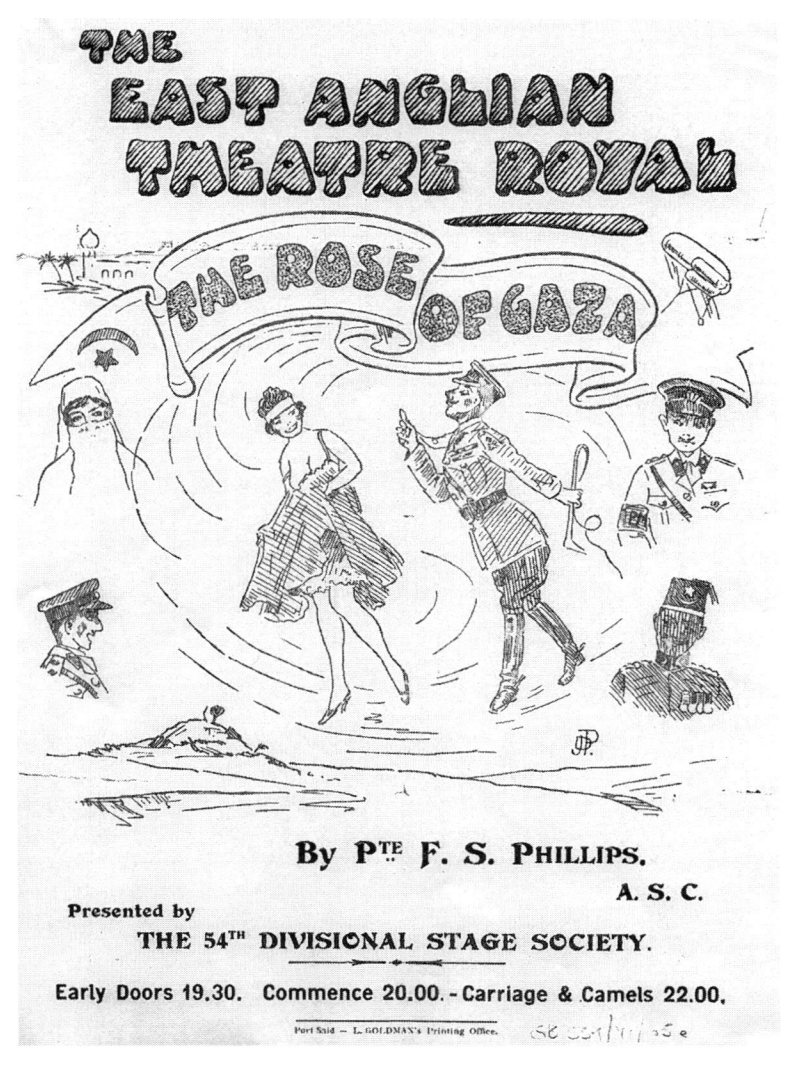

Illustration 4.2 Programme for 54th Division Concert Party, 'The Rose of Gaza', August 1917 (SRO, GB554/Y1/165e, Lee Papers).

produced their own concert parties, which could be better tailored to suit the men's specific local tastes. For example, the 1/10th Londons, originally drawn from Hackney, performed large numbers of sentimental cockney songs. These battalion shows could, however, be much more satirically biting than those at divisional level. That of the 1/6th Essex, performed at Christmas 1916, showed particular disdain for the unit's despised commanding officer, Lieutenant-Colonel Bowker.[28] Concert parties were useful both as a provider of former civilian pleasures and as a means of mocking the everyday life and eccentricities of service within the British Army.

In addition to holding concert parties to counter battle fatigue, 54th Division, as with all others in the Middle East and in Europe, operated an extensive sports programme.[29] Whether these numerous events represented a bizarre manifestation of the sportsmanship ethic among British troops, or simply an attempt to provide healthy recreation is hard to elicit from the often taciturn references made in letters and diaries. It is clear that sport was a common part of divisional life, with football matches frequently taking place, both in the heat of Egypt and close to the line in Palestine. Second Lieutenant G. B. Buxton, of the 1/5th Norfolks, found that these matches were often not a casual affair, and was greatly surprised by the high quality of play. Cross-country races also proved popular over the rugged terrain of Palestine, although inducements such as 10s. prizes may have played a role in boosting participation. While stationed on the Sinai defences, many battalions made use of their proximity to the Suez Canal to organize swimming competitions.

Sport was an officially sanctioned recreation, with meetings frequently arranged at divisional and brigade level, particularly during rest periods. Many units took these competitions very seriously setting up committees to create training programmes for the men, beginning practices months ahead of the actual meetings and even altering the daily work schedules to allow more time for athletics. Aside from the prizes available for competitors, units strove to outperform the other members of their brigade or division. The 1/11th Londons' war diary proudly noted that they had done well enough in 162nd Brigade's competition, in September 1918, to be placed first, for which they received a 'handsome cup'. Such events were not only popular with the men but also with the higher echelons of the EEF. Staff officers frequently attended sports competitions, and at the 163rd Brigade horse and hounds show Allenby, Lieutenant-General Edward Bulfin (XXI Corps commander), and Major-General Hare were all present. The awarding of prizes by the EEF's Commander-in-Chief gave such competitions the endorsement of the military elite, while at the same time replicating the class divisions that had been found at many pre-war, civilian sporting events.[30]

For officers, however, a wider range of recreational activities were available. The sand tennis courts of Egypt attracted many players, including Buxton who chose to relax on his birthday by playing some games with a cavalry officer and the division's Chief of Staff. The traditional pursuits of the British establishment were eagerly followed, although they often seemed incongruous in the climate and terrain of the Middle East. Hare took part in a fox hunt organized by a local Egyptian prince, just after the end of the war. Lieutenant-Colonel T. Gibbons, commander of the 1/5th Essex, enjoyed duck and snipe shooting in the marshes by the Auja River using ancient guns supplied by the local inhabitants. Fishing also proved popular with units stationed on the Auja, not only as a form of relaxation but as a means of supplementing their meagre rations. Gibbons bizarrely chose to combine these pursuits by using rifles for fishing, with the impact of the bullets stunning the fish just long enough for him to catch them.[31]

None of the members of 54th Division could match the sporting enthusiasm of Captain V. H. Bailey, a staff officer with 270th Brigade RFA, who seemed to spend most of his service in the Middle East engaged in horse racing. His enthusiasm was so extensive that he would spend mornings practising his racing starts, and prior to the divisional steeplechase even tried to sweat out water to reduce his weight. The 300-yard victory that he gained at the race led to Major-General Hare asking him to avoid taking part in future events on the same horse. His riding prowess took him as far as the 'Palestine Grand National' against riders from across the whole EEF, although victory eluded him, as his horse fell at the final fence. Bailey's competitive edge was not just expressed via his passion for horse racing. While stationed on the Suez Canal in 1916 he had indulged in duck shooting, on one occasion claiming to have shot 15 of the 26 birds killed by the whole party. The opportunity to indulge in sporting activity dominated his approach to soldiering in the Middle East, to the extent that even when scouting for observation posts in Sinai he took shots at a gazelle that passed within range. Such enthusiasm for sport did, though, have an adverse effect on his staff work. This was seen on an artillery staff ride, where the 'lie of the country as regards fences had more influence on proceedings than the imaginary tactical situation'.[32]

Although sport offered a chance for relaxation within familiar civilian forms of activity, one method of escaping the war was held in higher regard than all others. The ever prevalent dirt of the Middle East meant that bathing allowed men a chance to wipe away the grime that represented their military service. Baths in the Suez Canal were also a welcome interlude from the heat of the Sinai Desert. As Private Surry noted, the effort of marching up to 6 kilometres 'was priceless in its return for the joy of cleanliness'.[33] The men of 1/5th Essex were therefore deeply disappointed at leaving their posts near the Canal for ones further into Sinai as this meant the end of regular bathing parties. Part of the pleasure that was derived from washing stemmed from the infrequency with which it occurred. Surry was not able to clean from 12 March until 27 May 1917, due to the operations around Gaza, and thus when he did eventually bathe in the sea he viewed the experience as a 'red letter day'. Captain Hinde took his first bath for three months in October 1916, and found the experience one that he was reluctant to end. The change that bathing could bring about in the morale of troops was significant. The first bath that the 1/4th Northamptonshire Regiment had after Gallipoli led one participant to state that 'it made us feel like new men'.[34] Some soldiers were not prepared to wait quite so long and set about concocting novel methods of bathing. Behind the front line at Gaza, in summer 1917, Lieutenant J. H. Jewson, of the 1/4th Norfolks, dug a hole in the ground and covered it with a waterproof sheet to form an improvised bath, a practice emulated by Hinde.

The value of bathing, not just for its hygienic benefits, was quickly realized by the military authorities. 1/4th Essex instituted a regular programme of baths in the Canal when stationed at Shallufa in April 1916, with men washing four or five times a week. The instigation of regular bathing could prove unpopular, as the men were marched to the Canal for baths no matter what the time of day or the heat.[35] Once the division had moved closer to Gaza bathing became a dangerous process. In the 1/5th Bedfordshires bathing parties on the coast were limited to only 12 men at a time and had to be covered by a picquet as they were within sight of the Turkish defences. The Mediterranean threw up its own problems with the presence of sharks forcing men to stay close to the shore; the strong currents also made bathing difficult for poor swimmers. These dangers were underlined when Captain Tattersall, of 1/11th Londons, drowned after being carried away by the backwash of a large wave.[36] Despite these significant difficulties, the desire for cleanliness represented one of the many ways that the Territorials of 54th Division tried to remove themselves from the world of war in the Middle East, and instead live all too briefly as civilians.

These various methods of coping, expressly civilian in character, were frequently supplemented by simpler aids to morale. As the 54th Division's 1917 Christmas card demonstrates, the men depicted are rejoicing at receiving gifts of beer, wine, whisky and cigars (see Illustration 4.1). Alcohol-induced narcosis has acted as a powerful addition to the influence of coercion and inducement upon troops throughout history, serving to counteract the natural instinct to run from danger. For those soldiers serving in Palestine and Egypt, drink had just such a prominent role to play in relieving tension. It was felt by Sergeant W. Barron, of the 1/4th Northamptonshires, that 'about the only time a soldier is happy [is] when he is drunk, at other times he is merely contented'.[37] The low price of the locally produced wine in Palestine, such as the 1s. pints of red wine found at Mulebbis, made it easy for soldiers to slip into drink as their chief relaxant. Units took full advantage of these local sources, with Captain Bailey filling up his artillery brigade's water fantasses (storage tanks carried on camels) with white Port, Sauternes and Medoc to provide supplies for their Christmas 1917 festivities. Unit commanders were well aware of the power of alcohol to calm the nerves of soldiers who had been involved in battle. Many of the men in the division were given measures of 'soldier's rum diluted' or beer after combat.[38]

It was not, though, in the best interests of the military authorities to encourage excessive consumption of alcohol, and the amounts provided were usually strictly limited. For those soldiers who were involved in issuing the rum ration there were considerable benefits, as any leftovers resulting from casualties were quickly consumed. Officers as well as other ranks frequently suffered from the over consumption of alcohol. On Christmas Day 1917 Captain Hinde found himself consuming the considerable quantities of Sauternes, Tokay, whisky, and beer, a mixture that had a deleterious effect. Captain Bailey noted in his diary the ill effects that a night of cocktails and liqueurs in the headquarters mess produced. Nevertheless, troops continued to write home asking for alcoholic gifts to sustain them at the front, which in the case of Lieutenant Jewson consisted of the peculiar pairing of whisky and crème de menthe.[39]

Cigarettes excited the imagination of the British soldier as much as alcohol, and some of the perceived hardest times in the line occurred when the 'fag-issue' temporarily broke down. Gifts of food from home, particularly luxuries such as cake or chocolate, fulfilled much the same role as drink or cigarettes.[40] The climate of the Middle East, however, meant that the contents of many eagerly anticipated parcels arrived in a dried out or melted state. Even damaged goods still served the need of soldiers to retain contact with the home front. A rotten Christmas pudding received by Lance-Corporal

William Hickman, of the 1/8th Hampshires, from his mother in February 1916, was consumed with much excitement; he 'appreciated her thoughtfulness just as much as if it had been top hole'.[41] The mailing of rum to Corporal W. M. Town, of the 1/5th Essex, served to lift his spirits after he had been involved in Third Gaza. Similarly, Lieutenant-Colonel Wollaston appreciated the Stilton that one of his battalion officers had brought back from leave in Britain. The palliative effects of alcohol alleviated the strains of active service by inducing temporary narcosis but, as with the gifts of food and other items, also helped cement the link, established by correspondence, to a civilian past and to an awaited civilian future. By drinking what they had consumed before the war, or by eating familiar food, these Territorials could return to a world away from the violence of the First World War in the Middle East.

Expressions of a peacetime identity served a powerful role in maintaining the morale of the troops of 54th Division. The factors highlighted above help to explain how soldiers coped with the wider concerns of being at war, rather than with the specific difficulties of combat in the Middle Eastern theatre. Many of these factors place British soldiers within a universal framework, applicable to the Western Front or elsewhere. Equally, elements such as the use of humour, seen in concert parties, are not culturally specific, but instead 'represent a human response to the situation confronting both sets of belligerents'.[42] British, Turkish, Austrian, French and German soldiers all found laughter a powerful palliative for the stresses induced by death and destruction at the front. The universality of a civilian identity suggests that it may have played its greatest role in alleviating the underlying strains of military service, apparent during the extended periods of static warfare in Sinai and Palestine. It seems to have come to the forefront of the maintenance of morale when the men of 54th Division were stationed in training centres in Egypt or in rest areas behind the front line. It is not, however, evident that civilizing methods helped to sustain the morale of Territorial soldiers during the sporadic periods of intense battle. The motivation for men to fight, rather than simply to remain in the line, was very different.

Territorials as soldiers

Battle, and the experiences of men taking part in it, needs to be at the centre of any consideration of morale.[43] It is not through what armies are that they influence events, but by what they do. As such, a consideration of civilian identity only serves to illuminate the way in which an army operates at war, rather than how its various constituent parts cope with the slaughter of the battlefield. The stresses of military life would have peaked during the spasmodic periods of intense combat on the Middle Eastern Front. It was during the battle of Megiddo, the three battles of Gaza, and the clashes while engaged in trench-based warfare opposite Gaza and in the Plain of Sharon, that the morale of 54th Division's men was put under greatest strain. In these periods soldiers had to cope with the horrors of modern, industrialized combat, framed within the harsh environment and climate of Palestine.

For some men, relief was found by relating closely to their fellow soldiers. This belief in the value of comradeship represents an expression of the basic concepts that lie behind the primary group theory first espoused by S. L. A. Marshall in the late 1940s. Military service could instil a sense of fellowship that was ultimately to the benefit of the individual: 'brotherhood taught us to be good comrades, WE helped one another and by so doing helped ourselves.'[44] The men of the 1/7th Essex demonstrated this unity by rapidly integrating their new drafts, such as Private Surry, teaching them the basics of how to survive and fight in the Sinai Desert. The spirit of comradeship that was seen as integral to military service pervaded many post-war veterans associations, becoming the primary focus for soldiers' recollections. For example, the 54th Division Dinner Club aimed to provide a means of reunion for the officers of the division. Similarly, the 1/4th Norfolks Officers' Club took its duties to its former comrades particularly seriously. Its members were asked to contribute to a fund intended to provide photographs of the graves of men from the battalion, which would then be sent on to their relatives.[45] Such veterans' organizations demonstrate the power that primary group bonds could exercise over the men who had served in the EEF, often extending long into the post-war world.

The identification of soldiers in battle with a small group of fellow servicemen may be too narrow an approach to take. Such close ties were extremely difficult to sustain in the bloody slaughter of battles such as Second Gaza in April 1917. It is at such points, when battle is at its most brutal, that the primary group is of the greatest importance, but is at the same time incapable of surviving the concomitant high casualty rates.[46] Instead, a belief in the abilities of the wider military unit of which the soldier is part could be of critical value. The importance of this loyalty was expressed by the 1/4th Norfolks, who chose to place their battalion flag and colours on the front of the Christmas cards they produced in the Middle East (see Illustration 4.3). For these Norfolk soldiers the expression of their identity was based not in civilian, but military terms. Similarly, it was to the regimental prayer that Private Surry, of the 1/7th Essex, turned after witnessing the horrific losses sustained in March and April 1917. Its expressions of an Essex Regiment family provided him with comfort in a period of intense suffering. This belief in the *esprit de corps* of a battalion or regiment helped men from disparate backgrounds to serve together in the adverse circumstances of the Palestine campaign.[47]

Unit identity was of particular importance after First and Second Gaza, during which the local identities of many of the battalions in 54th Division were destroyed due to the high casualty rates suffered. From mid-1917 conscripts were introduced to replace the losses, fundamentally altering the local composition of eight of the division's battalions. The 161st Brigade, as Surry observed, ceased to be exclusively composed of Essex men after 27 March 1917.[48] Similarly, the 144 drafts that brought the 1/5th Bedfordshires up to strength in December 1917 were not part of the pre-war Territorial battalion family. In summer of 1917, the 1/5th Norfolks, in dire need of men after their mauling at Second Gaza, received drafts from the garrison battalions of both the King's Liverpool Regiment and the Royal Warwicks. The local ties that linked the men of the battalion in civilian and military life had been in decline before the Gaza battles, as replacements composed of volunteers had arrived in late 1915 and early 1916 to alleviate the losses incurred at Gallipoli. Dilution of the local bonds in battalions was to a certain extent limited, as in many cases the initial replacement drafts contained many members of the

Illustration 4.3 1/4th Norfolk Regiment Christmas Card (NRM, Box 11, 1/4th and 1/5th Norfolk Regiment Papers).

regular battalions that had formed the basis of 54th Division's constituent regiments.[49] The majority of these soldiers had served in France and Belgium where they had been wounded, and as a consequence took time to adjust to the fitness standards required for war in the heat of the Sinai Desert. In other cases these early drafts were made up of men from the division's battalions who in 1915 had been left behind in Britain. The breakdown of local ties in a battalion over the course of the war is confirmed by an analysis of the enlistment areas given for soldiers of the 1/4th Norfolks detailed in the War Office publication *Soldiers Died in the Great War 1914–1919* (1920). The proportion of soldiers killed who had enlisted in the battalion from Norfolk declined from 95 per cent in 1915, to 68 per cent in 1917, and then to 58 per cent in 1918. The geographical diversity of these new drafts is illustrated by the battalion's combat deaths for 1917, which featured men who had enlisted in 17 counties other than Norfolk. The destruction of a local attachment within the battalion was therefore greatly accelerated from April 1917 onwards.[50]

For the original members of the battalions in the Middle East the primary concern was not the local backgrounds of these new drafts but their poor level of training. As the 1/10th Londons' war diary lamented in January 1916 on receiving 15 other ranks from Britain, the men were 'of some age; very slow and show little signs of any training'.[51] Major-General Hare became concerned by the decline in the physical fitness of the division after the three battles of Gaza had taken their toll. It was not unusual to find the new drafts incapable of matching the marching speeds of those soldiers who had been in theatre since 1915 and were fully acclimatized. As Lance-Corporal Hickman noted in a letter to his wife, 'the old men are hardened soldiers now'.[52] Aside from the problems of physical stamina many new drafts faced the difficult process of integrating into their new units, in which the surviving soldiers were closely bonded through the hardships of battle. Captain Clarke viewed the last of the Derby volunteers who joined his battalion in late 1916 as 'splendid fellows [. . .] though some were rather old for desert marches, but their hearts were in the right place'.[53] The first conscripts that arrived while they were crossing Sinai were treated very differently, frequently being mocked by the other soldiers as latecomers to the war. Heavy casualties, the failure of local recruiting to sustain the war effort in Britain and the difficulty of integrating new drafts meant that the local nature of 54th Division's battalions was questionable.[54] The absence of a primary group loyalty based on a shared locality meant an alternative means of bonding between these Territorial soldiers had to be in operation to maintain morale.

In such circumstances the regimental ethos of the battalion rose to a prominent place as a universal identity for its members to coalesce around.[55] Regimental *esprit de corps* drew much of its imagery from frequent reminders of historic achievements to which all members of the battalion were heirs. 1/5th Suffolks celebrated 'Minden Day', on 1 August 1916, in the heat of the Sinai Desert, to commemorate the regiment's proud place at the battle in 1759. The Suffolks were one of six regiments within the British Army that remembered Minden as an historic occasion and the foundation point of their military prowess. In preparation for the celebrations Captain Wolton was sent to Alexandria by the commanding officer to purchase 2,000 roses for the men to wear. This drew a direct, and tangible, link back to the regiment's part in the battle, which had seen fighting in a rose garden. The men were also given a bottle of beer and a packet of cigarettes to help commemorate the day; inducements which almost certainly aided the popularity of the occasion. Lieutenant-Colonel Wollaston was deeply disappointed when he was unable to organize similar celebrations in 1917, due to the pressures of being in the front line. In 1918 the battalion was again able to enjoy this regimental festivity, holding a rifle meeting and sports competition during the day. This was followed by entertainments provided by the divisional and brigade concert parties.[56] As in 1916 the emphasis was on allowing the men to enjoy a day away from the hardships of soldiering, but within the framework of the regiment's supposedly historic military ethos.

The links to the past accomplishments of the regiment were also prevalent for Lieutenant-Colonel Gibbons. He hoped that his 'Essex "Terriers" were upholding the traditions of the 44th', who had served in Sir Ralph Abercrombie's 1801 campaign against Napoleon in Egypt. In addition, Gibbons kept in correspondence with the Essex Regiment's Colonel, Field Marshal Sir Evelyn Wood, who had gained fame fighting the Zulus in 1879 and had ultimately risen to the post of Adjutant-General.[57] Wood reminded both Gibbons and the men of their duty to the regiment's place in the history of the British Army. The honorary regimental colonels played a crucial role within the army, helping to liaise between the various battalions of the regiment and presiding over regimental institutions. This historic identity, which the men of the 54th Division were encouraged to preserve, was not just active at a regimental level. The image of the British Army as a whole was often invoked as an exemplar of how Territorial soldiers should behave in battle. Major-General Hare, when writing to

Brigadier-General A. Mudge, commander of 162nd Brigade, after Second Gaza, stated that 'all ranks, those who fell, and those who survived, acted up to the very highest tradition of the British Army'.[58] The men of each battalion therefore had a particular historic regimental identity, which fitted into a wider military background, to live up to while serving in the Middle East.

Regimental identities were not static and immutable. The power of such an association with the past lay very much in the ability of the men of 54th Division to reshape their regimental identities; the ideals of the regiment belonged not just to previous generations but to the present as well, and could be enhanced.[59] This was made evident to members of the 1/6th Essex in 1918 when their commanding officer read them a description of the regiment's battlefield achievements on the Western Front.[60] They were being given a model to strive for; the Essex Regiment men fighting in France and Belgium were acting as an exemplar of how to shape the unit's historic identity. There was also a need to avenge the defeats that the Turks had inflicted upon the British and on the division's regiments. Gallipoli held a pivotal place for 54th Division, representing a wound that could only be healed through the shedding of Turkish blood. Many soldiers noted the anniversaries of the attacks made during the peninsular campaign in their diaries. 1/5th Essex even had a holiday on 14 August 1916 to remember their fallen comrades from the advance at Suvla Bay. The need for revenge helped to motivate 54th Division soldiers who came into contact with the Turks, most of whom had had to wait through 1916 without being able to hit back at the enemy. Private Overman expressed such a sentiment in a letter to his parents, written just prior to Second Gaza, stating that 'we have a few debts to pay back for the Peninsula'.[61] The attack on 19 April did not fulfil his intentions, and he was to die only a month later of the wounds he received trying to avenge Gallipoli. Two defeats at Gaza only added to the sense of grievance that the men of the 54th Division felt over the damage that had been exacted on their military identity. The prominence of Gaza, and the battles fought for it, was evident to the British public in the localities that formed the regional backgrounds to the division's battalions. In July 1917 *The Northampton Independent* launched a scathing attack on the local MP for failing to uncover the truth of the 1/4th Northamptonshires' losses on 19 April. The newspaper saw its role as emulating that of William Russell, the noted Crimean War correspondent, in bringing to the public's attention the full horrors that the town's soldiers had endured.[62] First and Second Gaza thus affected the way in which both 54th Division's soldiers and their relatives back home saw the war with the Ottoman Empire.

As with the defeat at Gallipoli, some battalions chose to commemorate the failures of March and April 1917. 1/6th Essex's band performed a military tattoo on the first anniversary of First Gaza, this was followed by a memorial service for their fallen comrades. Similarly, the men of 1/5th Norfolks held a collection for the 'Palestine Memorial Fund' on 20 April 1918, and amassed a considerable amount of money to remember its dead and wounded members. Eight officers of 1/4th Essex chose to hold a dinner in the Town Commandant's house at Wilhelma, on 26 March 1918, to remember the battalion's part in the action against Gaza the year before.[63] They hoped to create a tradition that would live long after the war, and proposed holding future dinners at the Trocadero Hotel in London. These officers saw themselves as directly shaping the historic identity of the Essex Regiment, by providing it with new points of reference around which to build its military identity.

Success at Third Gaza, the first significant victorious action in which many of 54th Division's Territorials had been involved, came to occupy an important place in the histories of the units that took part. The comments in the diary of Private R. J. France, serving in 1/6th Essex, summed up the opinions of many Essex soldiers who had fought for seven months against the Turks: '"March 26th" avenged.'[64] This victory represented the expurgation of the suffering of March and April 1917. As a consequence it was a battle honour that was proudly displayed at many of the services and reunions held after the war, as well as on one of the Christmas Cards produced by the division (see Illustration 2.6). It also shaped post-war commemoration, with the 54th Division Dinner Club choosing to hold its annual dinner 'on a date as near as possible to that on which the capture of Gaza took place'.[65] Similar attitudes were also integrated into the 'Gaza Day' services held by the Essex and Norfolk Regiments. These occasions served a dual role of remembering the dead and commemorating the regiment's place among the forces that helped defeat the Ottoman Empire. Gaza was displayed as the most prominent battle honour on the 1/4th Essex's Order of Service in March 1941, representing the battle which had done most to shape this Territorial battalion's identity. Essex Regiment 'Gaza Day' services would feature the hymn 'There is a green hill far away', as a point of reference to the 161st Brigade's losses on Green Hill, one of the objectives on 26 March 1917. Regimental services held to remember Second World War battles continued to use the same hymn.[66] The defeat of the Turks at Third Gaza, and the sacrifices in all three battles, were therefore a proud addition to the historic military identities of the battalions in 54th Division.

A regimental ideology, framed through historic allusions and battlefield success, was itself simply an expression of the belief that the soldiers of 54th Division had in their own military identity. This represented a motivational factor wider than the battalion and was created by the tactical and operational achievements resulting from the soldiers' own efforts. These Territorial troops saw themselves as much more than the 'town clerks army' that Lord Kitchener labelled them as in 1914. By June 1918, Private Surry felt that the 'territorials had emerged from Saturday-night soldiers into a force to be reckoned with when it came to getting a job well done'.[67] This expressed very much the same view that Major-General Hare had held since he took command of 54th Division in 1916. Prior to the clash with the Turks in March 1917 the division was involved in a series of tactical exercises, by the end of which Hare had 'come to the conclusion [that] they [54th Division] would be a very tough nut to crack'.[68] Lieutenant-Colonel Wollaston echoed a similar line when his battalion advanced at Second Gaza. In his mind, the discipline of his troops countered any of the negative points relating to these formerly part-time soldiers: 'viewed from my position, the way the battalion went to the attack was an absolute picture and although their peacetime discipline is very much à la Territorial, under fire it was more than excellent.'[69] Hare was again impressed by his men's performance when they seized all of the objectives they had been allotted for the advance on 19 September 1918. As he noted in his diary, 'everyone had said we couldn't possibly do it and we have been well patted on the back'.[70] The general attitude to the Territorials prevalent in the regular army before 1914, and particularly among the officer corps, was that they were incapable of carrying out sophisticated operations and producing effective battlefield results. Hare's comments make it clear that these prejudices continued into the First World War, but 54th Division's battlefield achievements served to counter the critics.

The achievement of the professional military standard of the regular army, as a riposte to attacks on the TF, acted as a powerful motivator for the division's Territorials. Sergeant Barron, involved in operations against the Bedouin in Sinai during mid-1916, expressed considerable pride in the successful completion of the mission. Primarily he was content at having proved wrong those members of the cavalry who claimed the infantry could not handle the Bedouin. Operational achievements were also proudly communicated home to relatives in Britain. 54th Division's 1918 Christmas card depicted an heroic Territorial, rifle at the ready, overlooking the battlefield at Mejdel Yaba, on the Plain of Sharon, which the card states had been captured in March 1918 (see Illustration 4.4). In this case, the visual representation of a proud military identity, based on the division's combat success, was explicitly used to counter civilian prejudices towards these part-time soldiers. The achievements of many Territorial battalions and divisions during the First World War served actually to narrow the gap between them and the regulars. Territorials' military performance has, however, often been overlooked, with the focus instead falling on their more casual disciplinary systems and inter-rank relations.[71] This neglects the fact that although they had been an amateur army up to August 1914, they were still soldiers and had considerably more experience of military life than the men who volunteered or were conscripted after the outbreak of hostilities.

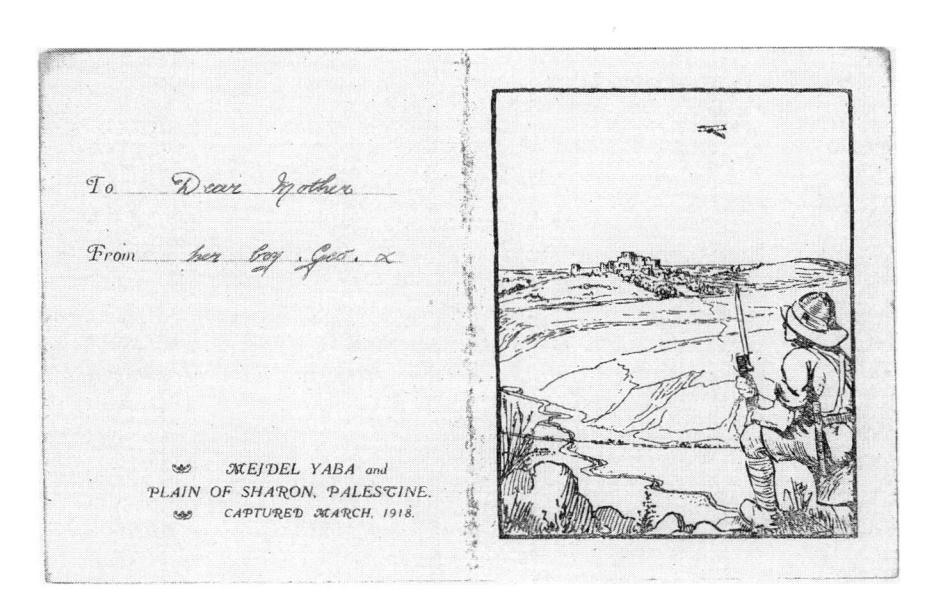

Illustration 4.4 54th Division Christmas Card, 1918 (SRO, GB554/Y1/165k, Lee Papers).

Major-General Hare felt that the men of 54th Division could emulate the model provided by the regular army, observing that the divisional artillery had already reached such a standard by September 1916. Indeed, the division's commander played a critical role in elevating such a professional soldierly ideal for the Territorials to aspire to. Hare believed that men could be moulded through training into disciplined soldiers, who were in his mind vastly superior to even the most hardened 'fighting men'. He was not aiming to create an army of automatons, showing 'unreasoning obedience'. Initiative was of as much value in a soldier as discipline: 'we want to teach a man that as long as he has orders he must carry them out, but if he finds himself without orders he must act for himself and rely on his own judgement, and if our efforts at training him have been successful his judgements will lead him right.'[72] This emphasis on the skills of the individual soldier as an identity to which Territorials should strive was further highlighted to the division after their success at Third Gaza. Hare's 'Order of the Day' on 11 November 1917 closed with a call for his troops to be constantly improving their abilities as soldiers:

> Though we have done well, we must not think that we are perfect and have nothing more to learn. No doubt every officer and man feels that he knows more about soldiering than he did ten days ago, but we must not relax our efforts at self-improvement by training. We must think over all the different events of the battle and find out in what ways we could have done better.[73]

Thus, the Territorials of his division should be continually refining their professional military identity. Hare was a divisional commander who realized the importance of training in preparing men for combat in the Middle East. Many of the great commanders of the twentieth century, most notably Montgomery, were great advocates of the need to develop vigorous and self-reflective training systems. Modern war required generals to realize that citizens could not be thrown into combat without significant preparation, in order to acclimatize them to the shocking sounds, sights and experiences of battle.

As part of developing this process of refinement, 54th Division had engaged in comprehensive training schemes since it arrived in Egypt. The intention was to learn from the mistakes made at Gallipoli in order to avoid similar errors occurring when they next met the Turks in battle.[74] Much of the training in 1916 was designed to improve the physical fitness of the men, crucially making them capable of marching long distances across the difficult terrain of Sinai and Palestine. To this end, 1/10th Londons instigated a weekly march of 15 miles in full marching order, which was to include all members of the battalion, even the cooks and orderlies. In order to instil good water discipline no man was allowed to drink during the march unless he was given permission. This battalion level activity was supplemented by courses at the Imperial School of Instruction at Zeitoun, near Cairo. Each battalion sent a number of its men through the school, with war diaries proudly noting the successes of individual candidates.[75] Lessons at Zeitoun helped to provide a universal training standard for the EEF, which was then disseminated out to units by returning soldiers.

A detailed divisional training programme was devised by Hare and his staff in summer 1917, and was an integral part of the preparations for the assault on the Turkish trenches in November.[76] All the battalions of the division had passed through training camps named Regent's Park and St James' Park, between June and October. These camps focused on company-level training, as 'it is realised that it is in his own Company that the soldier should learn everything that can be required of him in War'.[77] Within these groups soldiers were taught bayonet fighting, use of Lewis guns, sniping, patrolling, musketry, and bombing, as well as further intense courses of physical training. The aim of these camps was made explicit in a memorandum from the 54th Division's GSO1, Lieutenant-Colonel Clive Garsia: 'the work carried out will have for its sole object the training of the Company for active offensive operations. Nothing that is suitable only for trench warfare will be taught during the fortnight's course'.[78] The October round of training developed the skills learnt at company level through battalion and then brigade exercises, involving attacks on full-scale models of the Turkish trenches, by day and night (see Illustration 4.5). Unit cohesion in combat was recognized by the command structure of 54th Division as central to its battlefield performance. The camps prepared men for battle, but allowed them to do so while operating within their company and battalion groups, thus maintaining the regimental ethos of these units. This formal training was supplemented in 1918 by the use of divisional platoon competitions.[79] These meetings allowed the competitive spirit prevalent between the different regiments of the division to be utilized for combat preparation. The multifaceted nature of the extensive training within the division reinforced the concept that its soldiers should be constantly striving to improve their professional military identity.

This focus upon training as a step towards an efficient fighting force filtered down to the ordinary soldier's attitude to what was achieved in combat. Many men took great pride in their victories over the Turkish Army, however large or small. The discipline that the Territorials managed to achieve under fire impressed many of the battalion commanders. One remarked on 1/5th Essex at Second Gaza, that it was only the men's steady advance 'that saved the battalion from complete annihilation'.[80] Captain Clarke was struck by how the Territorials behaved as they attacked the Turks, automatically spreading out into an extended formation when fired upon by machine guns. He felt that 'it was clear that our constant drill in these battle formations was paying a dividend in manoeuvrability and in reducing casualties'.[81] The pride in the troops' professionalism was such that by the time Gaza fell to the British, Captain Hinde could find little elation in the victory. For him, the abilities of 54th Division were self-evident, and as a result he 'never doubted all along but that we should take this place this time'.[82] By the closing stages of the campaign in Palestine the division had been in combat with the Turks for over a year and a half, and had grown in experience as a result. The relatively low loss rates after the battles of March and April 1917 meant that there was a continuation in personnel from mid-1917 through to the battle of Megiddo in autumn 1918. As such, individuals were able to enhance their stock of combat experience, which improved their personal confidence on the battlefield.

Illustration 4.5 Model of the El Arish Redoubt used for training the 54th Division prior to Third Gaza (SRO, GB554/Y1/275c, Wolton Papers).

This continuity of personnel at battalion level meant that junior leadership within the division remained strong and consistent. Battalion and company officers played a crucial role in aiding the endurance of their men and in setting down a clear example of the best aspects of the professional military ethic that they should be striving to achieve. Major-General Hare was well aware of the value of good junior leadership: 'no army could achieve anything in which the men looked upon their officers in the same way which school boys look – or any how mind to look – on their masters, as a sort of natural enemy, the master representing the government and themselves the opposition.'[83] His attitude reflected the regular army's pre-war approach to regimental command: a paternalistic frame of mind should be the paramount concern of officers towards their men.

It was the diffusion of this ethos among the temporary officers of the First World War that played a critical part in maintaining the morale of the British soldier. In the 1/4th Norfolks, Lieutenant Jewson exhibited a concern for his men's needs through the distribution of his food parcels from home within his unit, containing welcome gifts of bully beef and biscuits. Similarly, the commander of the 1/5th Norfolks, Lieutenant-Colonel Darnell, bought 200 loaves of bread and 300 oranges from the locals in November 1917 in order to supplement the battalion's exiguous rations. Such acts were dependent on the munificence of relatives or the personal wealth of individual officers. Some battalion officers instead used their ingenuity to try to alleviate the difficulties of front-line life. Captain Wolton renovated a disused field oven that he discovered at a post near the Suez Canal, and intended to use it to provide the men of 1/5th Suffolks with occasional meals of roast meat.[84] By caring for their men these officers embodied the best elements of the regimental system; they acted as part of a family to help the unit endure the trials of war.

More importantly, junior officers could set an example of the professional military standard that 54th Division was attempting to attain. Captain Hinde felt the best way to encourage the 1/2nd East Anglian Field Ambulance to dig trenches was to join in with the work. By sharing their burden and demonstrating how things should be done, Hinde felt that the work was completed much quicker than would have been the case had he merely supervised the men. Setting a professional military example came to the fore during combat. The loss of a valuable Second Lieutenant in 'C' Company of the 1/4th Norfolks during Third Gaza led the company commander to emphasize how his 'coolness and indifference to fire during the advance' had encouraged the men. Similar sentiments were expressed by rankers who witnessed the deaths of valued officers.[85] Private Surry eulogized his company commander, Captain Jones, who was killed by a Turkish sniper at Third Gaza, as a man who had guided his troops through the difficulties of the campaign, and helped them to develop as soldiers. The few men of the 1/5th Norfolks who managed to reach the Turkish defences along the Gaza-Beersheba road on 19 April were so impressed by the coolness and bravery of the officer with them, Lieutenant Bligh, even though he was severely wounded, that they recommended him for a decoration. Praise for officers was not reserved for leaders who showed kindness to their men, but for those who demonstrated professional competency. Lieutenant Barrat, Surry's platoon commander in Sinai, was thus representative of the regimental officer ethos. He was of weak physique but always persevered with the men of his unit, and for this reason Surry stated that 'his example was much admired by us who were much more hardened sons of the soil'.[86]

The period of trench warfare at Gaza in summer 1917 was instrumental in forming the wider military identity of 54th Division and the pride its Territorials took in their soldiering. Establishing control over no-man's-land through the use of trench raids, served to illustrate the superiority of the division's soldiers. Patrolling was also a frequent activity in the area, beginning in late April 1917. Patrols were, however, only an adjunct to the more aggressive activity seen in raids, which allowed the participants to improve vital combat skills. They were, as Tony Ashworth has elucidated, a clear breach of the 'live and let live' system that could develop during trench warfare.[87] As on the Western Front, these raids were instigated by the higher command as 'it was recognised that, during long periods of stagnation in trench warfare, some enterprises had to be carried out to keep up the fighting spirit of the troops'.[88] In response to these concerns, the 1/8th Hampshires raided the Turkish defences at Beach Post on 14 July 1917, suffering only 23 casualties. The raiders had made use of a model to acquaint themselves with the layout of the position, and as a result 'they were quite at home in Beach Post finding their way about quite as easily as they had at rehearsals'.[89] This action was greatly removed from the amateur activities that Denis Winter caricatured as little better than glorified 'night raids on public school dormitories'.[90] Major-General Hare was concerned by the casualties, but generally felt that it had 'been a great success and will do the whole division a lot of good'.[91]

The value of such a raid was not just in its ability to demoralize the Turks, or for those involved to gain experience, but to set down an example for both the division and the EEF of how aggressive combat activity should be conducted. It also played an integral role in enhancing the prestige of the battalion and the division; Hare's men were now fighting as military professionals. The lessons of this particular raid were considered so valuable that Lieutenant-Colonel Garsia, the division's GSO1, wrote to the commander of the 1/8th Hampshires asking him to construct a model plan for future raids on Beach Post. This was to form part of a pamphlet being prepared by 54th Division's General Staff on how to conduct raids.[92] The 1/8th Hampshires were thus setting the standard to which other battalions would have to aspire.

For 54th Division's troops their military identity was grounded more strongly in the two raids that were carried out on the Turkish Gaza defences at Umbrella Hill. The raids were launched on 20 and 27 July 1917 by the 1/5th Bedfordshires, both proving very successful and resulting in high Turkish casualties. The losses, however, to the battalion in the two actions amounted to 229 men, with the Turks retaliatory shelling of the British line after the first raid causing the greatest damage.[93] Intensive training for the raid lasted nine days, and used a replica of the Turkish defences at Umbrella Hill, which was updated frequently using the latest RFC photographs. The two raids, like that on Beach Post, acted as models of how to plan and carry out such attacks. 1/5th Bedfordshires learnt from the problems of the first raid, where too many troops had entered the Turkish trenches causing confusion among the attackers, and as a result the second raid used a smaller number of soldiers. The Turkish counter-shelling of the 1/5th Bedfordshires' positions also proved instructive. In the second raid a more elastic system for returning the raiders to the British trenches was operated, resulting in far fewer casualties. These lessons were not confined to the 1/5th Bedfordshires as the divisional staff took a keen interest in how the raids worked. After the first had been completed all the commanders involved were instructed to produce reports, which were then forwarded on to Lieutenant-Colonel Garsia.

20 and 27 July 1917 saw the Bedfordshires involved in the two actions that would come to define their war service, and shape their regimental identity. For the home audience, the *Bedfordshire Times and Independent* made the link to the battalion's military identity explicit in its account of the raids. After praising the raid commander, Captain Armstrong, the article stated 'that the County Territorials are keeping up the splendid name and traditions of our Regiment in this part of the globe, and are more than upholding the name they so hardly earned in Gallipoli'.[94] A similar belief in the 1/5th Bedfordshires' ability to maintain their regimental ethos is evident from the battalion's centenary celebrations in March 1964. The order of service contained a short history of the battalion, which was dominated by their exploits on Umbrella Hill. Further proof of the prestige gained from the raids is seen on the Bedfordshire Regiment's war memorial, which lists Umbrella Hill, the actions at which lasted barely a few hours, alongside other battle honours from 1917 most of which were for sustained engagements, such as the battles of Arras and Cambrai. The men of the 1/5th Bedfordshires had thus successfully moulded their historic regimental identity to include their battalion's exploits.[95]

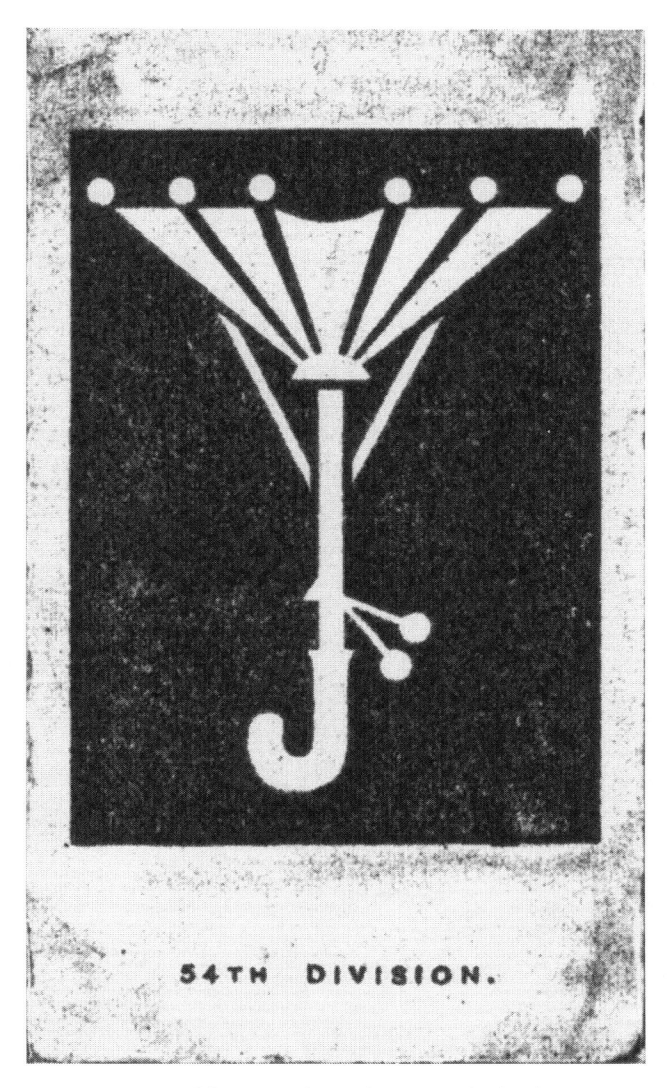

Illustration 4.6 Cigarette card featuring the 54th Division badge (ERM, Surry Papers).

Major-General Hare was considerably impressed by the Bedfordshires' success, stating that 'it was a very fine performance and shows that our men can beat the Turk any time they can get at him'.[96] The resultant boost in the morale of the battalion spread to a wider audience. As Lieutenant-General Philip Chetwode, then commander of Eastern Force, acknowledged in his message of congratulations to the 1/5th Bedfordshires, they had 'certainly set the pace to the rest of the Force by their fine work'.[97] This tactical victory was rapidly subsumed within the military identity that 54th Division was creating for itself. In 1917 a divisional symbol was adopted, the image being of an umbrella that had been blown inside out (see Illustration 4.6). This was allegedly chosen after the suggestion of a March hare had been rejected on the grounds of 'gross insubordination'. The image demonstrates the faith that 54th Division's men placed in their military identity, prominently displaying it for other formations to see. In many respects, this ran counter to other British divisional symbols adopted during the First World War. 55th (West Lancashire) Division, for example, made use of imagery that reflected the local loyalties of its soldiers, choosing the rose of Lancaster as their badge. The association of 54th Division with a single tactical success, as indicative of the Territorials' military prowess, continued into 1918. A rest camp for the use of the division's troops, opened on 14 August, was correspondingly named the 'Umbrella Arms'. In addition, the division hosted a horse race in February known as the 'Umbrella Stakes'.[98] The motivations of these Territorials were therefore developed not just from a strong *esprit de corps*, grounded in historical precedents, but crucially from the specific battlefield achievements of the division. Their experiences in southern Palestine in mid-1917 showed that the flexible military identities of British Army formations could be enhanced and remoulded by Territorial soldiers.

Territorial morale in the Middle Eastern campaign

The Territorial soldiers of the EEF, as seen with the men of 54th Division, drew on points of reference from the norms of the civilian world to cope with the hardships of the Middle Eastern campaign.[99] This demonstrated a shared attitude with the regular, Territorial, volunteer and conscript soldiers of the British Army on the Western Front. The boredom of much of the service in Egypt and Palestine could often only be offset by recourse to the world that the men had known before the war. This is, however, only sufficient to explain how these soldiers were able to cope with their service in the war in general. The brutal experiences of combat could only be assuaged through the strong bonds found between these Territorials. This represented more than the simplicity of the primary group, which was almost certainly torn to pieces in March and April 1917. Instead the unit identity that was turned to stood on the firm foundations of a historic regimental ideology. The enemy could destroy the primary group, but the regimental spirit would always survive. It was this, as on the Western Front, that allowed battalions to sustain crippling losses.

The ancient identities of these regiments were, however, no more than an 'invented tradition'. It is possible to view the creation of new regimental formations in the Cardwell-Childers reforms of the 1870s as part of the wider nineteenth- and early twentieth-century trend throughout Europe of inventing traditions identified in the seminal work of Eric Hobsbawm and Terence Ranger.[100] The fashioning of a robust *esprit de corps*, based on the emulation of historic regimental exploits as a means of sustaining morale, was not confined to the First World War. It also lay at the heart of the, sometimes dubious, combat effectiveness of British Army units during the Second World War. This was seen most prominently in 51st (Highland) Division, which was reconstituted after its surrender in France in 1940. The new divisional commander placed emphasis on the traditional fighting prowess of Highland regiments as a point of focus for his troops, in order to counteract the shame derived from the division's recent combat failure. As a consequence strong unit cohesion was produced among the men of its battalions, which ultimately led to success in battle at El Alamein.[101] This extreme example demonstrates that the malleable nature of regimental *esprit de corps* was crucial in aiding divisions shattered in battle to rebuild their combat effectiveness.

Similarly, it was the ability of the military image of a regiment to be reshaped that allowed it to play such an important role in the endurance of Territorial infantrymen in the Egyptian and Palestinian campaigns of 1916–18.[102] *Esprit de corps* needs to be viewed through the lens of the combat experiences that the infantry went through. It is too simplistic to place the monolithic notion of 'the regiment' at the core of the maintenance of military morale. As the Umbrella Hill raids illustrate, even minor tactical encounters could shape the way in which soldiers saw their professional military identity. The Territorials of 54th Division were members of a force that conspicuously lacked its own historic background. It was the flexibility of regimental identity in the British Army that allowed them to incorporate their own achievements into this wider military group. Through the victories at Third Gaza and Megiddo the men of these Territorial battalions were provided with an entrance ticket into their regiments' glorious histories.

The dominance of loyalty to the regiment as a motivational factor in battle is not so incongruous for a formation made up of amateur soldiers, such as 54th Division, when the wider nature of the Middle Eastern campaign is considered. The explicitly imperial overtones of the defence of the Suez Canal, the advance into Palestine and defeating the strategic aims of the Ottoman Empire placed the men of 54th Division into circumstances that echoed the activities of their regular army colleagues prior to 1914. For the British Army of the nineteenth and early twentieth centuries, fighting imperial wars, particularly in India and Africa, had remained its principal *raison d'être*. In such circumstances, the regiment had provided soldiers with a family they could turn to while they were cut off from the comforts of home. 54th Division, which had left Britain in mid-1915, and was not to return until 1919, fits into this model of a force engaged in an imperial campaign. An imperial military context was one that was evident to many of the formation commanders in the EEF from their pre-war experiences. The generals that commanded 54th Division's brigades drew their military experience largely from imperial campaigns as regimental officers, either in India, South Africa or Egypt. Similarly, Major-General Hare's military expertise was based on imperial operations, such as the Hazara expedition of 1891.[103] He and his brigade commanders thus understood the value of a regimental identity for soldiers serving in 'small' colonial wars. In Egypt and Palestine the civilian world of Britain was very far away, and could only be glimpsed through the lens of the Middle East's peculiar exoticism. In such circumstances belief in the regiment and the military ethos that it espoused, and to which the Territorials could contribute, operated as the prime determinant of morale and combat effectiveness.

5

The Anzac Legend, Mateship and Morale

The romantic image of the Middle Eastern campaign is largely a product of the DMC's sweeping advance northwards from Megiddo in September and October 1918. This operation was 'essentially one of movement' and is frequently held up as a contrast to the laborious battles fought on the Western Front. The nature of the terrain in the Middle East and the distribution of troops over large sections of the front meant that the theatre was suited to the employment of large formations of cavalry.[1] The DMC was principally organized around the mounted troops provided by Australia and New Zealand to aid Britain's imperial war effort. By September 1918 as many as 14 of the 36 mounted regiments in the EEF were formed from Australian Light Horsemen and 3 from New Zealand Mounted Riflemen. Of these regiments those that served in the ANZMD saw the greatest amount of action; they had carried the advance across Sinai in 1916, played a key role in all three battles of Gaza, and in 1918 dominated operations in the Jordan Valley. This division offers the chance to examine a unit that withstood the pressures of combat continuously for three years, in contrast to the British Territorial infantry divisions of the EEF who saw little action in 1916, and often only periodic engagements in 1917–18.

The role of mounted soldiers during the First World War has been the subject of much historiographical controversy, particularly in Britain since hostilities ended in 1918. Events in France and Flanders seemingly suggested that the age of the horse had come to an end. Liddell Hart and J. F. C. Fuller, Britain's two most influential interwar military theorists, developed from this an artificial debate that pitched supposedly reactionary cavalrymen against the advocates of mechanization and motorization.[2] The Middle Eastern theatre, both in Egypt and Palestine and in Mesopotamia, demonstrated lessons that challenged this approach. Here horse-borne formations proved of exceptional value, allowing commanders to exploit fleeting battlefield opportunities for exploitation with their mobility. Furthermore, on these battlefields, cavalry served alongside and integrated fully with the arms of modern, industrialized warfare: tanks, aeroplanes and artillery. The focus of the debate on mounted warfare has been obsessed with tactical and operational concerns; the experiences of the mounted warriors themselves have been too often ignored or subsumed within bitter arguments on technological progress. This study of the ANZMD helps to redress this omission, placing the robust morale of these Antipodean horsemen at the heart of the formation's combat effectiveness in the Middle East.

The Australian Light Horse and New Zealand Mounted Rifles in the Middle East

The mounted troops of Australia and New Zealand made their primary contribution to the war against Turkey in Sinai and Palestine. Both the Light Horse and the Mounted Rifles were the products of the early settler societies in Australia and New Zealand. Cavalry first appeared in the colonial militias formed in Australia from the mid-1850s onwards, and by 1885 all six colonies had mounted units, with the regional headquarters often based in small country towns. Similarly, the first cavalry regiments formed in New Zealand appeared in 1863, with 21 mounted volunteer corps in existence by the 1870s. These mounted troops played an important role in the wars against the Maori, although they often found it hard to deploy shock tactics in battle as their opponents rapidly learnt to avoid flat open ground. Instead they were put to better use as a reconnaissance force for the infantry. The battlefield role of the Mounted Rifleman or the Light Horseman evolved into a distinct one during the later nineteenth century. These men were trained to ride into action and then to fight on foot as infantry, but were also expected to carry out a range of mounted tasks, including reconnaissance operations and providing screens for infantry. In this sense, they were much more versatile than cavalry or mounted infantry. The former were not equipped to fight infantry-style operations and the latter were only trained to ride into battle and then to fight on foot. Mounted infantry offered a commander only tactical benefits, whereas the Light Horse were of value at the operational level of war.[3]

The mounted troops of both countries gained their first experience of modern warfare during the South African War of 1899–1902. New Zealand sent 6,500 men to the conflict, suffering over 230 casualties from combat and disease.[4] Australia also raised Light Horse contingents to serve in the campaign, eventually sending 16,378 men. These volunteers were frequently despatched to the front line with little training. In addition, the administrative arrangements of the units were poor, as they lacked skilled officers and NCOs, creating supply difficulties. Men enlisted for one year of service, after which they returned home, preventing experienced troops from remaining in the theatre to educate new arrivals. Nevertheless, the troops of both nations gained impressive reputations for their versatility, and many British officers felt that the men of the Dominions had a natural affinity for mounted work. They were particularly noted for their ability to fend for themselves while on extended operations far from their bases, a style of campaigning that came to dominate in the latter half of the war. Both nations continued to raise mounted units after the South African War to contribute to the strength of their peacetime militias and these formed a portion of their commitment, from 1909, to provide expeditionary forces to help Britain fight future overseas wars. By 1914 there were as many as 23 Light Horse regiments spread across Australia. These were grouped into seven brigades, formed after federation in 1901. In New Zealand the Liberal government's Defence Act of 1909 made military training compulsory for all males aged 18–25, followed by 5 years of service in the reserve. The militia force contained a provision for 12 Mounted Rifles regiments. The aim was to be able to furnish an expeditionary force of 30,000 men in any future conflict, a component of which would be a Mounted Rifles brigade.

On the outbreak of war in 1914 both countries mobilized their expeditionary forces and began recruiting. Australia initially raised only four Light Horse regiments, forming a single brigade. These were not based on the existing units spread around the country but were recruited on a state basis. Thus the 1st ALH Regiment was drawn from New South Wales, the 2nd ALH from Queensland, the 3rd ALH from Tasmania and South Australia combined, and the 4th ALH from Victoria. Eventually, Australia would provide five ALH brigades spread over two divisions in the EEF, the first two of which served alongside the NZMR in the ANZMD. In New Zealand the existing Mounted Rifles regiments were each used to furnish one of the three squadrons in the four new regiments that were formed for the expeditionary force. These regiments were based on New Zealand's four military districts. Of these the AMR, CMR, and WMR constituted the NZMR Brigade, while the Otago Mounted Rifles acted as divisional cavalry to the New Zealand Division.[5]

Initially both New Zealand's and Australia's regiments were solely comprised of volunteers. New Zealand, however, found it impossible to maintain its forces, which eventually consisted of one infantry division and the NZMR, by voluntary means alone. In August 1916 a military service act set up a conscription system which drew initially on the country's unmarried men and then on its married men in an order derived from the number of their dependents. Australia attempted to introduce conscription twice during the First World War, first in 1916 and then in 1917, as it faced similar manpower difficulties to New Zealand. The two referenda that were held to decide the issue were, however, both rejected by the Australian public; Australia thus retained a volunteer army through to the end of the war. This placed a considerable strain on the units serving in the front line, which was particularly evident in the Australian Corps on the Western Front. The failure to provide sufficient drafts of replacements through conscription meant that the AIF effectively fought itself to destruction in the closing battles of 1918.[6]

The NZMR and 1st ALH Brigade sailed for Egypt in late 1914, and were joined soon after by the 2nd ALH Brigade. Each of the Mounted Rifles and Light Horse regiments only consisted of around 550 men, requiring just over 600 horses. When engaged in combat these regiments could only put about 400 men into the firing line, as 1 in 4 of the troopers would have to be left behind as horse holders.[7] A brigade of three regiments could therefore only muster a rifle strength slightly greater than a single infantry battalion. As a consequence, mounted units were not able to engage in long, drawn-out battles of attrition, but instead had to rely on their mobility to bring their firepower to bear on the weak points of an opponent at a particularly opportune moment.

The first action that they took part in did not allow them to use this mobility. Instead they were confined to the trenches of Gallipoli in an intensive infantry war. The troopers were reluctant to be sent as reinforcements to infantry battalions, and were allowed instead to serve in their own regiments. They arrived on the peninsula in May 1915 and did not leave until the general evacuation in December. The small size of these regiments put them at a disadvantage, as did their lack of training for such operations. In addition, they were not equipped to the same standard as the infantry, and thus suffered hideous casualty rates. Of the 477 men who landed with the 5th ALH only 105 were left at the end of the campaign, of whom only 49 had never been away from the peninsula. Similarly, the 3rd ALH evacuated Gallipoli with only 246 men left serving in the regiment. Most extreme was the case of the CMR, which had arrived with nearly 650 men in its ranks, but returned to Lemnos with only 28. It had lost 118 men killed in action and died of sickness, as well as 45 missing and 443 sent to hospital sick or wounded.[8] The slaughter of the Light Horsemen was characterized by the ill-fated charge of the 10th ALH at the Nek, which later formed the emotive finale to Peter Weir's meditation on the futility of the campaign in *Gallipoli* (1981). Despite the excessive casualties the Light Horse and Mounted Rifles gained considerable military reputations among their contemporaries, exemplified by the WMR's bitter defence of Chunuk Bair in August 1915.

Once the Light Horse and Mounted Rifles had returned from Gallipoli in late 1915 they engaged in an extensive period of rest and recuperation in Egypt. This involved a considerable amount of training and the integration of a large number of new drafts, sent out to replace the casualties suffered during the peninsular campaign. This was followed by a period of patrol work in the Egyptian desert and along the Nile to deal with the rising of the Senussi. Regular patrols were carried out, which in the eyes of one trooper were intended as 'a check against suspected sabotage or revolution, our work was apparently to "show the Flag" and maintain order'.[9] This period of imperial policing soon came to an end, as the Turks decided once again to exert pressure on the British forces defending the Suez Canal. Up to March 1916, the 1st and 2nd ALH Brigades and the NZMR Brigade had operated largely as separate entities. They were now grouped together to form the ANZMD, under the command of Major-General Henry Chauvel.

After the Turkish attack on the British Yeomanry posts at Katia and Oghratina on 23 April 1916, the ANZMD was brought up to Romani to reinforce the northern Canal defences. The Light Horse and NZMR were engaged in a monotonous series of physically wearing patrols across the desert. When the Turks returned to attack the Suez defences in late July, the ANZMD engaged them in running skirmishes as they advanced closer to the Canal. This culminated in the battle of Romani on 4 August, in which 1st and 2nd ALH Brigades fought the Turks to a standstill across the dunes covering the southern flank of the British infantry's defences. The fighting was intense and the outcome far from clear in the early stages. Chauvel commented that the ANZMD 'had a very stiff fight indeed and only just got through by the skins of our teeth at dark as large Turkish re-inforcements were coming up right in my rear'.[10] The division took the initiative and the next day advanced towards the Turks' positions. The losses on 4 August meant, however, that all of the regiments were severely depleted, with 1st ALH going into battle with only 150 men. As a result when they ran into determined Turkish defences at Katia they were unable to make any progress. This was followed by a similarly disappointing battle at Bir el Abd on 8 August, where the Turkish rearguard successfully prevented the ANZMD harassing the retreating force.

An attempt to seize the Turkish defences at Mazar in mid-September also failed, as Chauvel was under strict orders not to hazard his force if the Turks put up significant resistance.[11] The Turks, though, chose to abandon Mazar only a couple of days later. It was not until late December that the ANZMD was next engaged, when it moved on El Arish at the eastern end of Sinai. Again the Turks fled without a fight and the position was captured on 21 December. The Turkish garrison had moved south to Magdhaba, where it was pursued by the ANZMD, and just before Christmas was destroyed in a short battle. This was followed by another minor action against the Turkish border defences at Rafah, in early January 1917. Here the division was required to advance across completely open ground against an entrenched enemy. This was a feat that seemed impossible, until the NZMR were able to work their way slowly forwards and charge a Turkish redoubt, just as Turkish reinforcements were making their way up, causing the position to collapse. These two minor operations brought the division's service in the Sinai Desert to a close. Although the Turks had been pushed back into Palestine they had fought an orderly withdrawal and had dictated the pace of operations.

In late March 1917 the ANZMD spearheaded the EEF's attempt to seize Gaza in a *coup de main*. This bold action was unsuccessful, with the British infantry failing to capture the heights to the south of Gaza. ANZMD's troops, some of whom made it into the outskirts of the town, were forced to fall back despite being close to victory. At the disastrous Second Gaza in April, the division operated with limited results on the right flank of the EEF, against the Turkish defences along the road to Beersheba. ANZMD's casualties in both operations were relatively limited, with only 54 men lost in March and 185 in April, with the number killed minimal in both cases.[12] The EEF's débâcle at Gaza led to the reorganization of its command structure. Chauvel, now promoted to Lieutenant-General, rose to be head of the DMC and Major-General Edward Chaytor, formerly the commander of the NZMR, was given command of the ANZMD. The division settled down to a long period of static warfare along the line opposite Gaza, during which it patrolled the exposed right flank of the British positions, carried out a number of reconnaissance missions and prevented the Turkish cavalry from doing the same.

On 31 October the division led the EEF's return to a war of movement when it took part in the assault on Beersheba. The work of the NZMR in securing the dominating heights at Tel el Saba proved critical to the successful fall of the town. Much greater fame accrued to 4th ALH Brigade for their mounted charge on the Turkish trenches, which culminated in the seizure of Beersheba's vital water supplies. Success at Third Gaza restored movement to the front and the division was able to push northwards towards the coastal plain. This saw it involved in a number of small-scale actions, such as at Tel el Khuweilefe, Ayun Kara, Mulebbis and the crossing of the Auja River. As a result of the continuous fighting between 31 October and 7 December the division lost 149 men killed and 705 wounded, representing the most intense period of combat endured by many of its units since Gallipoli.[13]

1918 saw a move to the Jordan Valley with the division taking part in the capture of Jericho near the end of February. This was followed by two raids across the Jordan into the Mountains of Moab, in late March and late April. Neither operation proved a success, with the men facing extreme physical hardship and heavy fighting. For some regiments these were the most intense operations since Gallipoli; 6th ALH, for example, was engaged in bitter fighting in the attempt to enter Amman in March, which cost it 77 casualties. The ANZMD then settled down for a hard summer of defensive work in the Jordan Valley, with the harsh climate taking its toll on the men. The only major action that occurred was a Turkish attack on 14 July against the 1st ALH Brigade's posts at Musallabeh, which was quickly repelled.

By September 1918 the ANZMD had been joined by troops from the Jewish Legion, the British West Indies Regiment, and a number of Indian cavalry and infantry regiments. The Anzacs remained the most experienced units in the Valley and formed the core of 'Chaytor's Force', which pushed through the Turks' lines a couple of days after Allenby's advance on the Plain of Sharon. These operations saw the ANZMD take the stronghold of Amman and capture over 10,000 Turkish troops, for the loss of only 139 men throughout the whole of Chaytor's Force.[14] The hard fighting and continual service in the malaria-ridden valley now took their toll with large numbers of men evacuated sick to hospital (see Figures 1.7 and 1.8). By the end of September, the NZMR had lost 60 per cent of its strength due to disease. A similar story occurred in the Light Horse, with the 1st ALH Brigade evacuating 591 men sick in the first week of October alone. This had a devastating effect at regimental level with the 3rd ALH being reduced to only 69 men when it left the Jordan Valley.[15] The division was moved to Richon le Zion in order to recover and spent the rest of 1918 convalescing in Palestine.

The combat record of the ANZMD marks it out as one of the most successful of the formations that served in the EEF. It played a key role in the victories that cleared the Turks from Sinai and followed this by impressive mounted operations after Third Gaza. Moreover, it managed to remain in the front line as an effective fighting unit until after the September 1918 offensive when the effects of three years' campaigning finally took their toll. Combat was a constant feature of the ANZMD's wartime experience in the Middle East, as was hardship at the front, with the division only spending one brief period in billets over the course of three years.[16] This raises interesting questions about how a mixed force of Australian and New Zealand amateur soldiers, engaged in an overtly imperial campaign, was able to endure the rigours of combat for so long.

The Anzac legend in Sinai and Palestine

For Henry Gullett, a journalist attached to the Light Horse who was described by one senior British officer as an 'Australian gutter press merchant' and who would later become the official historian of Australia's campaigns in the Middle East, the answer to Anzac endurance lay in the unique characteristics of the Australian fighting man. The Light Horseman was a representative of Australia's rural population and as such had learnt to be an individual, preparing him very well for life on campaign in the Middle East. He was already a skilled horseman, as well as an expert observer and fine judge of country. This was seen as a direct product of growing up on the vast farms that covered much of Australia. The Light Horsemen's individuality could be troublesome, leading to clashes with those who upheld the finer points of military discipline. These characteristics may not have made them good soldiers but their combat abilities on the battlefield made them into outstanding warriors.[17]

Gullett saw the success of the ANZMD as resting on the Anzac spirit, which originated on the beaches of Gallipoli and was first expressed in the despatch of the English reporter Ellis Ashmead-Bartlett. He eulogized the Australian and New Zealand soldiers who landed at Anzac Cove on 25 April 1915, stressing their courage, skill and perseverance. The idea was then explored further by the Australian reporter Charles Bean, who produced his own published account of the Gallipoli landings. He propagated the heroic image in the *Anzac Book* (1916), produced as a souvenir for soldiers to send home to their families. His selective editing of the work constructed a vision of the Anzac soldier as a true bushman, loyal to his comrades, able to endure anything that war could throw at him, and helped along by a strong sense of irony. The work proved very popular, despite the fact that Major-General Chauvel thought that the 'reading matter is very poor and there are some old chestnuts in it'.[18] The official histories of Australia's role in the First World War, some of which were written by Bean while he supervised the production of all the volumes, reinforced the ideas he had put forward during the conflict.

The large number of regimental histories produced in the interwar period elaborated on the parochial elements of the Anzac spirit. The 6th ALH's account reminisced about the 'days of glorious mateship' that the men had enjoyed in the Middle East. Some regimental histories were explicit in their hope that the publishing of such a narrative would help to ensure that the spirit of the AIF, and the spirit of Anzac which was implicit within that, would be instilled in future generations. These works portrayed the war as a common experience for all Australian and New Zealand soldiers, irrespective of whether they were officers or ordinary troopers. This reflected an important element within the mythology of Anzac: the AIF was supposed to be an egalitarian force where anyone had the chance to gain promotion. In particular, this was seen as a direct contrast to the experience of British soldiers, whose advancement prospects were perceived as stultified by the rigidities of the class system.[19]

The Anzac spirit has become the dominant interpretative means by which the experiences of Australian and New Zealand soldiers during the First World War, and subsequent conflicts, have been viewed. Bill Gammage's ground-breaking study on the life of ordinary AIF soldiers falls back on Bean's assertions about the rural nature of the Light Horsemen. They were bushmen used to the harsh life of the outback and thus able to cope easily with the heat and long days in the saddle faced in Sinai and Palestine. For some historians the natural qualities of the Anzac soldier were such that in the Middle East he was able to adapt so well that he came to rival the Bedouin's survival skills in the desert. The image of the jovial digger has been reinforced in the public imagination through numerous literary, cinematic, and televisual incarnations, most notably the characters portrayed by Mel Gibson in *Gallipoli* and Paul Hogan in *Anzacs* (1985).[20] These views of Australian and New Zealand troopers have created a stereotype that has done much to obscure the reality of their military experiences in the First World War.

The reverential status of the Australian combatant has come under considerable attack from historians since the 1970s. The notion that the vast bulk of the AIF's recruits were drawn from rural areas has been effectively demolished by Leslie Lloyd Robson, with an emphasis instead on the nuance needed when examining occupational backgrounds.[21] Similarly, the notion that all AIF officers were drawn from a common pool of talent and that any soldier had an equal chance of promotion has also been undermined. More importantly, the extent to which Australia has monopolized the story of Anzac has become apparent. This rhetoric leaves little room for the experience of New Zealand's soldiers, who are often simply portrayed as nothing more than carbon copies of those from Australia. National differences within the Anzac experience can be striking, and are most notable in the alternative methods of commemoration that have grown up on both sides of the Tasman Sea around Anzac Day.[22]

Nevertheless, much of the mythology of the Anzac spirit remains. The 90th anniversary celebrations of 4th ALH Brigade's charge at Beersheba saw a re-enactment of the event in Israel's Negev Desert that put the Australian's role in the battle centre stage, and reinforced the fallacy that this was 'one of the last successful horse-borne charges in Western warfare'.[23] The 4th ALH Brigade's action at Beersheba was followed by the bloodier, but no less victorious, mounted charge at Huj on 8 November 1917, by the 1/1st Warwickshire and 1/1st Worcester Yeomanry. On 13 November 1917, 6th Mounted Brigade carried out a successful charge at El Mughar which took over 1,100 Turkish prisoners. At Kaukab, on 30 September 1918, the entire Australian Mounted Division deployed to charge a Turkish rearguard, but this exploit, which has a greater claim to being the last successful cavalry charge by British imperial forces, has failed to enter the annals of Australian military history. In the immediate aftermath of the 1914–18 conflict the Russian Civil War and Soviet-Polish War witnessed the massed use of cavalry, which, as in Palestine, could exploit the vast open spaces of Eastern European battlefields. During the Second World War Soviet and German cavalry formations were also deployed in battle; Palestine was not the last hurrah of the *arme blanche*.

Crucially, the NZMR's involvement in the battle for Beersheba was excised from the commemoration in 2007 and local Israeli ceremonies focused on a memorial entitled the 'Park of the Australian Soldier'. To a certain extent this action is the epitome of the Anzac legend, as it displays all those elements that are supposed to define the Australian soldier. The Light Horsemen are portrayed showing undaunted heroism as they pressed on against superior odds, while wielding their bayonets as an improvised *arme blanche*. This is a view propagated in a number of literary works, such as Frank Davison's *The Wells of Beersheba* (1933), or in grand cinematic form in Charles Chauvel's (Major-General Chauvel's nephew) *40,000 Horsemen* (1940) and Simon Wincer's *The Lighthorsemen* (1987). Little mention is made of the role of the NZMR in securing the dominant Turkish defences on Tel el Saba, which allowed the 4th ALH Brigade to cross the battlefield with relative ease. This would only serve to undermine the centrality of the Light Horsemen's role in seizing Beersheba, a moment of the First World War defined in culturally Australian terms. The experiences of troopers in the ANZMD thus remain entombed amidst the clichés of Australian military history.[24]

Some elements of the Anzac myth may have been embellished, either during its creation or subsequent development, but it is still possible to find aspects that have resonance in the experiences of the men who served in the ANZMD. Of crucial importance was the role of Gallipoli in creating the legend of Australian and New Zealand military prowess. Without such a cataclysmic experience it is hard to see how the Anzac legend could have been born. Anzac Day, which came to take on considerable prominence in Australia, and to a lesser extent in New Zealand, was also of relevance to those men serving at the front during the war. For Edwin Brown, a signaller with the ANZMD's 1st Signal Squadron, the first anniversary of the 1915 landing was a day that was 'to be kept sacred' and had similar sacrificial overtones to the events of Easter.[25] All that Trooper J. D. Hobbs, also serving in the signal squadron, wished to remember on the anniversary in 1916 was the loss of his comrades. In some regiments acts of remembrance were formalized. The men of 3rd ALH had to attend a service on 25 April 1918 and were lectured on Anzac by the regimental chaplain. Not all units treated the occasion quite so reverentially, with the AMR choosing to commemorate their losses with a day of sports.

At the level of the ordinary trooper Gallipoli could instil a great deal of hatred, acting as a means to stir up antagonism towards the Turks. The poem of New Zealander H. N. O. Brown, entitled 'Gundagai', encapsulates this attitude:

Yes, they've many scores to settle.
Mostly things from Anzac's shore,
Where there's not a cove amongst 'em,
Didn't leave one pal or more.

But they've sworn that they'll avenge 'em,
And each man's prepared to die,
From the reckoning of his cobbers,
In a go at Gundagai.[26]

For Brown and many other troopers Gallipoli was an open wound that needed to be healed. The instilling of revenge among the men of the ANZMD was not the only role that the peninsular campaign played. It also set a high standard of military accomplishment for the troopers to try to attain in future combat operations. Gallipoli had shown the Anzac soldier at his best, persevering against extreme odds and hardship, and managing to cling on against a determined enemy. Captain Henry Wetherell, of the 5th ALH Regiment, saw the peninsular battles as the pinnacle of success and stated in a letter to his mother that 'I don't think the Regt. will do anything better than it did at Anzac [Cove]'.[27] When units did achieve battlefield victories in Sinai and Palestine they were measured against this standard, as it represented the benchmark for operational brilliance. The 2nd ALH Brigade's report on operations in November and early December 1917 lavished praise on its troopers when it concluded that 'the spirit in which the men accepted various hardships and the great deal of heavy work was wonderful and compared in many respects with the spirit just before the Anzac [Cove] landing'.[28] Their sacrifices at Gallipoli provided the Light Horsemen and Mounted Riflemen with a military standard to which they could aspire.

The importance of the peninsular campaign as a motivational factor was overshadowed by the significant losses suffered by the regiments of the ANZMD. For some, the fact that they were evacuated without achieving a definite victory clouded the whole experience. The deaths of their comrades were seen as futile and the fighting of little value, no matter how much it raised the bar to which they should aspire in future operations. Even the hardened veteran and most noted of all the division's memoirists after the war, Trooper Ion Idriess who had served in the 5th ALH Regiment, could not use Gallipoli as an indicator of military success or endurance. For him it was a mark of incompetence and failure, symbolizing months of static warfare that achieved little. He wrote after First Gaza, while listening to the sounds of British artillery, that he feared that 'this is going to be the Peninsula all over again'.[29]

Gallipoli provided the men of ANZMD with a complex memory. It could be used to herald battlefield achievements, instil a desire for revenge and demonstrate the level of endurance that the Anzacs were capable of achieving. In contrast, it could be a powerful reminder of failure and the loss of war, and, although it rests at the heart of the Anzac legend, it could serve to undermine its value to the combat soldier. Furthermore, it is not evident that Australian or New Zealand soldiers who served at Gallipoli made greater reference to the operations in their letters or diaries than did the British infantry who also took part, as seen with the men of 54th Division. It is hard to see the motivational role of this one campaign as only of value to the development of Anzac battlefield prowess.

The extent to which Gallipoli fostered a flowering of national identity within Australia and New Zealand may have been of some value. Other than the South African War at the start of the century this was the first occasion on which Australian and New Zealand soldiers had served in a major overseas conflict. The assertion, made by Bean and others, that these nations had come into being through the actions and sacrifices of their young men did hold some resonance for the soldiers of the ANZMD. They were constantly reminded that as well as fighting for Britain's empire they were also taking part in a conflict that would win fame for their home countries. The New Zealand Prime Minister, William Ferguson Massey, wrote to Brigadier-General Chaytor in April 1917 to congratulate the NZMR on their achievements at First Gaza, placing the unit's exploits exactly within this framework:

> The capture and bringing in of the guns is another of the many deeds which have thrilled the citizens of the Dominion with pride in the loyalty and fighting capacity of their soldiers. NZ knows that the men from Maoriland will give a good account of themselves every time the opportunity offers.[30]

The pride with which the NZMR was viewed by the home audience was seen by Massey as an important factor that needed to be communicated to the men at the front. It was to reinforce this sense of national success that Arthur Briscoe Moore wrote his account in 1920 of the brigade's campaigns in the Middle East. He wanted to make sure that his readers were given a sense of how the 'Mounted men have done their full share in worthily upholding the name of New Zealand'.[31] For him the NZMR had been so successful that it had matched the high standards of British infantry, placing the nation on a par with the metropolitan centre of the empire.

To have their national abilities recognized by the British was seen as even more significant for some men in the division. Major Ernest Hudson, serving on the staff of 1st ALH Brigade, impressed upon his wife that 'many English officers say they wish they were Australians, men know no fear and it's splendid if they get wounded they smile and tell you nothing'.[32] Pride in one's national achievements could reach the extent to which combat success was seen purely as a consequence of one nation's performance on the field. Thus the battle of Rafah was perceived by one New Zealand machine gunner to have been won solely by the actions of New Zealanders. This national territorialism was also practised by Australians with regard to particular engagements. Trooper Brown saw the battle of Romani as 'absolutely fought and won by Australians with exception of artillery and 1 warship, Jupiter'.[33] In neither case were these Anzacs willing to refer to the involvement of their comrades from across the Tasman Sea in what they saw as nationally specific victories. References to national identity in some units went beyond battlefield exploits, and became a regular part of everyday military life. The 5th ALH Regiment's officers' mess tent was adorned with wattle in order to remind the officers of their national flower. Similarly, the naming of the valley containing wells north of Gererat as 'New Zealand Valley' would have acted to remind individuals of the NZMR's role in the advance across Sinai.[34]

National identity often took second place to references to the local identities expressed in Light Horse or Mounted Rifles units. A prominent local feature near to the 5th ALH Regiment's camp on the Canal was named 'Queensland Ridge'. Similarly, the wells at Bir Parramatta were named after a western suburb of Sydney. An affinity for locally prominent names that would appeal to the men of a specific unit can be seen in the CMR's renaming of the camps it took over from 22nd Mounted Brigade. These were given the names 'Hagley Park' and 'Nelson Camp' in reference to locations in New Zealand; a third camp, though, was given the nebulous and more exotic title of 'Sphinx Post'.[35] Wider regional identities, in both the Light Horse and NZMR could be as important as those of a specific locality. Gullett, in the Light Horse's own version of the *Anzac Book* entitled *Australia in Palestine* (1919), was careful to point out how the gallant defence of Musallabeh post in the Jordan Valley had been conducted by troops from the states of Tasmania, South Australia, Queensland and New South Wales. Australia had only federated in 1901 and state identities remained a prominent and respected aspect of this inchoate nation. 5th ALH Regiment's 1918 Christmas card displays the regimental badge alongside depictions of three symbols of the Australian nation: an emu, a boomerang and wattle (see Illustration 5.1). These are set alongside a large 'Q', denoting the origins of the regiment in Queensland. Similarly, in the NZMR regional identities had to be respected. For example, when the brigade was selected to provide a guard for Lieutenant-General Philip Chetwode's (XXI Corps commander) entry into Jerusalem, the staff were careful to select equal numbers of men from each of the three regiments, drawn from three of New Zealand's military districts.[36] As much as Gallipoli and the Anzac spirit may have heralded the birth of the Australian and New Zealand nations it is clear that specific local and regional identities were still of

Illustration 5.1 5th Australian Light Horse Regiment Christmas Card, 1918 (AWM, 3DRL/3741 Folder 3, Delpratt Papers).

prominence among the men of the ANZMD. The names for prominent battlefield locations did not, however, always reflect these local affiliations, with two of the features at Romani named after temporary brigade commanders, Brigadier-General John 'Galloping Jack' Royston and Lieutenant-Colonel John Meredith.

National identity may have been downplayed within the context of Australian and New Zealand units, but it was to the fore when comparisons were made between them and the British. A chauvinistic attitude was central to the development of the Anzac myth, which vilified British officers in particular, but also the humble Tommy.[37] This denigration of their allies was used to reinforce a sense of Anzac military superiority and exceptionalism. For some Light Horsemen this dislike was fostered while training in Egypt. Corporal Arnold Metcalfe, of 1st ALH Regiment, objected to the British troops in Moascar: 'their ways aren't our ways, and they're trying to make us do as they do, which is something of a contrast I'm thinking.'[38] For most Anzacs it was encounters with British military policemen while on leave that created the greatest difficulties. The lackadaisical attitude of Light Horsemen and Mounted Riflemen towards the finer points of military discipline, most notably their poor dress, was not appreciated by the authorities in Egypt. Trooper Idriess thus found himself falling under the critical gaze of a military policeman in Cairo for wearing a new khaki shirt rather than his standard tunic.[39] The reputation of the military police among Australian and New Zealand troops had been low since they first arrived in Egypt. During the notorious 1915 disturbances in the brothel quarter of Cairo, the Wazza, the appearance of military policemen had served only to inflame the rioting Anzacs. The irritation caused when the military police enforced their powers, as the authorities often insisted they should, only served to have a detrimental effect on the image of the British soldier often out of all proportion to the problems that occurred.[40]

The actions of British officers frequently enraged Australian and New Zealand soldiers. They were seen as removed from the world of the ordinary soldier and unable to understand the difficulties of his life in the army.[41] This attitude rested on the notion of Australian officers displaying a much more egalitarian attitude to their men. The events at Katia oasis in April 1916 demonstrated to the ANZMD all of the classic faults of the British officer corps. When the division carried out a reconnaissance of the post they found vast quantities of equipment and personal belongings that had been abandoned by the Yeomanry. A staff officer of the NZMR, Captain Arthur Rhodes, was appalled by what he found: 'one cannot realise the amount of stuff the officers had consisting of Golf Clubs (they call this war) paintings and all sorts of pictures, carpets, cut glass candlesticks and ---- under their beds. Have never seen such a camp in my life.'[42] In addition he found a list detailing the value of the officers' possessions, including a £15 tea set and £20 knives and forks. When the Yeomanry officers returned to the camp after the ANZMD had secured it, they were appalled to find that the Anzacs had appropriated most of their goods. Brigadier-General Granville Ryrie, the commander of 2nd ALH Brigade, was taken aback at having his men accused of theft, and informed one of the Yeomanry officers that at least his soldiers were not cowards. The experiences of the division at Katia only served to reinforce their view of the stereotypical British officer.

It was only when they were directly affected by British military incompetence that the Anzac relationship to Britain began to break down completely. Of greatest grievance was the failure of the EEF's staff to arrange for the adequate evacuation of the division's wounded after the battle of Magdhaba. The initial intention was to move the wounded to Egypt from the railhead. The plan was then altered to have them evacuated by sea at El Arish. On arrival at the coast the wounded found that they were not to go by boat and had to wait instead for train transport. Most of the wounded took between seven and nine days to reach hospitals in Egypt; their treatment has been described by one Australian historian as 'Crimean in its neglect'. These failures were still sufficient to arouse the indignation of Corporal Roy Dunk, who served in the 3rd ALH Regiment, when he came to write his memoirs over 40 years later:

> Neither the experience of a hundred campaigns, nor the impulsive sympathy of ordinary men towards human suffering, nor, apparently the ease with which simple and effective arrangements could be made, seem able to move a British army staff to give to the wounded in the field – especially if operations are far removed from the influence of public opinion – that treatment which in times of peace is given by civilians to the most despised of dumb animals.[43]

The issue was one which irreparably damaged relations between the ANZMD and the British senior officers of the EEF. Gullett raised it as indicative of the failings of Murray's staff prior to the arrival of Allenby in 1917.[44] The incompetence of British officers alongside the impressive performance of the Anzacs at Gallipoli thus helped to set the lower and upper parameters for the military performance of the division in Sinai and Palestine.

A negative attitude towards the British Army was not a continuous feature of Anzac identity. On occasion the experience of combat could remove any barriers with British troops. The NZMR were very impressed by the fighting abilities of the 5th Mounted Brigade, whom they served alongside in July and August 1916, and noted that 'all ranks are loud in their praises of the way in which the Composite regt. on the 4th August fought with us'.[45] The determination of the Yeomanry to hold the isolated desert post of Oghratina, while their comrades fled from Katia, was also remarked upon. Corporal John Hull, of the AMR, was impressed to find large piles of spent cartridge cases around the dead bodies, with no rounds left in any bandoliers. Of all the British troops they encountered it was the Inverness, Ayr, and Somerset Territorial Batteries, of 18th Brigade Royal Horse Artillery attached to the division, that left the most lasting impression of military excellence. In a letter intended for publication in Australia Lieutenant Maurice Pearce, of the 1st ALH Regiment, was effusive in his praise, stating that the Royal Horse Artillery at Romani 'did admirable work and it was largely due to its excellent shooting that the Turks were so badly beaten'.[46] In its report on Romani the divisional staff went even further, suggesting that 'the gallantry and endurance of the gunners was quite equal to that of their Australasian comrades'.[47] The extent to which members of the ANZMD were prepared to praise as well as criticize British troops suggests that a healthy rivalry existed between the two. Rather than British failures setting a benchmark below which the Anzacs would not wish to fall, a competitive spirit could instead provide a powerful motivational impetus for soldiers in combat.

Competition was also inherent within the Anzac relationship and within the ANZMD itself, particularly between the units of the AIF and the New Zealand Expeditionary Force. The NZMR were considered by many in the division to be its best brigade. Trooper Idriess thought that 'the En Zeds are first-class fighting men and I don't think they grumble as much as we do'.[48] This opinion was shared by Lieutenant Bertram Delpratt, serving in the 5th ALH Regiment, who considered the NZMR to be the best of all the colonial troops in the theatre. He opined that 'you can never get an Australian to say a bad word for them which speaks volumes for them as the average Australian is none too modest about himself'.[49] Much of this respect from the Light Horsemen developed as a result of direct contact with one of the Mounted Rifles regiments. After the WMR had served with the 2nd ALH Brigade in the summer of 1916 they earned the sobriquet of the 'Well-and-Trulies' for their stout performance at Romani. It was not only their fighting prowess that the Australians were envious of. The NZMR possessed a much better organizational and support structure than either of the ALH brigades. Sergeant Tom Crase, of the 3rd ALH Regiment, considered that the NZMR 'reflected everlasting credit upon the business qualities of the New Zealand government during the war', and pointed particularly to its superior rations, canteens and rest facilities.

For Lieutenant-General Chauvel the differences extended as far as the national temperaments of Australian and New Zealand soldiers. He recognized that the Light Horsemen were a lively group, prone to disciplinary problems, and was aware that the NZMR were infinitely better behaved. Chauvel constantly had to explain to other senior EEF officers why the Australians' poor conduct was blackening the Anzac reputation. The New Zealanders often looked down on the Light Horse, seeing them as inferior in combat. One NZMR staff officer, Captain Rhodes, felt that the supporting ALH brigades at Katia had badly let down the NZMR by only attacking in a half-hearted manner. He was particularly shocked by the 3rd ALH Brigade's decision to fall back without informing the New Zealanders, leaving them facing odds which he estimated at six to one. After the fight at Bir el Abd on 9 August he became even more critical as the Mounted Riflemen were again left exposed by the retreat of all the ALH brigades. He stated in his diary that: 'I never want to fight with Australians again they left us again.'[50] He even considered the British Yeomanry who reinforced the division to have shown greater combat abilities. Within the Anzac legend the relationship with the British is often highlighted as setting the minimum standard for battlefield performance. It is clear, however, that Anzac relations within the ANZMD were far from harmonious, with the Light Horse often seen as an amateur military force. The assertion that the ANZMD was 'the finest example of the Anzac connection' is unsupported in much of the archival material.[51] In this case the NZMR set the upper bounds of combat endurance and were the marker against which all others were judged. An internal competitive element within the Anzac spirit of the division was, therefore, of great importance in motivating its soldiers.

Anzac troopers as citizen soldiers

Like their British comrades, the men of the ANZMD coped with the difficulties of military service through frequent reference to their past civilian lives. The Anzac forces were citizen armies, largely made up of volunteers until New Zealand's introduction of conscription in late 1916. In order to establish a link with home many soldiers in the division were prolific letter writers and looked forward eagerly to the days when mail was delivered to their unit. As one Mounted Rifleman emphasized to his brother, 'we all cheer up wonderfully for days after a mail, whereas now, having been without mail for so long, one gets quite irritable.'[52] These letters were an important source of news for troopers overseas who had limited information on military events and knew very little about life back in Australia and New Zealand.

It was, however, easy for soldiers to let the writing of letters become a one-way affair. 'The temptation to use the field service postcard, with its terse, standardised assurances was almost resistless when duty and obligation demanded letter writing, but inclination leaned towards sleep, or gambling or yarning.'[53] Some troopers simply could not understand the ability of their comrades to construct long narratives about their activities in the Middle East. Ernest Pickering, a quartermaster sergeant in 2nd ALH Regiment, was disappointed by his brother's request for a more interesting and lengthy description of the campaign. He informed him that 'those who can write newsy letters from the desert are generally situated in Cairo some hundreds of miles away, and what do really write letters with news in who are out in the Desert are generally damn liars writing all about themselves getting their letters published in the newspapers'.[54] Nevertheless, correspondence with friends or relatives helped to provide a direct link back to the nations and societies that the men of the ANZMD were fighting for in the Middle East.

This association with home was reinforced by the sending of gift parcels to men at the front. These did not have to be of practical value; the arrival of a box of boomerangs for a major of the ANZMD's signal squadron provided much amusement for the officers and men.[55] Of greater value were gifts of food, which were used to supplement the limited rations received in the front line. Trooper D. H. Morrice, of the 2nd ALH Regiment, was very grateful for a cake from his mother, which arrived soon after Romani, and was dutifully shared out among the men of his tent. Most food parcels were seen as the common property of the unit, to be devoured by all those who were present. Gifts that arrived while men were in hospital in Egypt were frequently forwarded on to the men at the front, who were felt to be in greater need of them. Despite the best intentions of friends and family, some of the donations were of little practical value to the recipients. Trooper Robert Chandler, serving in the ANZMD's 1st Signal Squadron, issued clear instructions to his family that he did not want any more socks or handkerchiefs while in Sinai 'as we do not wear boots or socks (light canvas slippers serving during the day when the sand is too hot to go barefooted) and such a thing as a cold is unknown so handkerchiefs are accumulating and we cannot carry much about if we have to move'.[56] The gifts Chandler received demonstrate that the 'imagined front line' among relatives and friends back home in Australia, as well as in Britain, was shaped primarily by perceptions of the war in France and Flanders, rather than the struggle being waged in the Middle East.

Comfort funds back in Australia and New Zealand also sent out gift parcels, providing a link back to home even if they lacked some of the personal relevance of a family donation. Commanders recognized how important it was to maintain this bond. Brigadier-General William Meldrum, commanding the NZMR after Brigadier-General Chaytor, ordered his men to write to those individuals who had sent gift parcels to the brigade to thank them for their help. Not all units received large quantities of donations from home. Brigadier-General Ryrie was very disappointed in the assistance that 2nd ALH Brigade was receiving from the Australian public, and wrote to his wife asking her to investigate how the Australian Comforts Fund was spending its money. In contrast,

New Zealand seemed to provide very well for its men at the front. Most notably, the New Zealand Expeditionary Force in Egypt had its own convalescent home, known as Aotea, near Cairo in which wounded soldiers could recuperate before returning to their regiments. As the official historian of the NZMR stated it 'was a piece of New Zealand, a "home within a home".[57] The direct link it provided to the pre-war lives of the men was reinforced by the fact that it was staffed by New Zealand nurses, who the 'men of the Mounted Brigade hold in the highest honour for their untiring work in bringing sick and wounded men back to health, and giving them a taste of wholesome living after their long spells roughing it in the field'.[58] The illusion of a pre-war civilian world was made complete by providing the men with food products brought from New Zealand, including butter. The Light Horsemen lacked similar facilities which would have allowed them to slip momentarily into a world away from the trials of the First World War.

All Anzac troops could enjoy the delights of the civilian world of the Middle East when they were given the brief opportunity for leave from the front line. Leave to Australia or New Zealand was extremely rare, only being granted in exceptional circumstances and then usually only to officers. For some troopers this was a far from satisfactory state of affairs, one of whom wrote to his sister stating that 'it's about time the people of Australia realised and demanded a home furlough for the 1914 men, we've carried out our duties under trying circumstances for four years, and they expect us to continue until the end of hostilities, and God alone knows when that will be'.[59] The only opportunity for a rest was therefore provided by travelling to towns and cities in Egypt or, as the campaign progressed, in Palestine. When the division was stationed on the western side of Sinai leave could be a fairly regular occurrence. The men of 5th ALH Regiment, for example, were given 48 hours off in Port Said every 3 weeks during summer 1916. Once the ANZMD had crossed Sinai and was entrenched opposite Gaza the situation was somewhat altered. Here the 1st ALH Regiment were informed that they would be given leave to Cairo at the rate of only 1 man in every 30 each month. Trooper Idriess worked out that the whole unit would finally have visited the city after two years of service.[60]

Despite its irregularity, leave was welcomed by the men. As with the Territorial soldiers of the EEF, it offered a chance to break with the norms of military life and return, all too briefly, to some semblance of their previous civilian existence. Even the army rest camp at Kantara could seem like a home from home far removed from the war, with 'comfortable bunks in roomy tents with pin-up pictures on the tent walls, lashings of the kind of ration we sometimes dreamed of, plenty of canteen goods to hand, and even a glimpse of sheets and pyjamas here and there'.[61] For many Anzacs leave offered an opportunity to behave as tourists in a land they would normally have had little chance of visiting. Trooper Chandler, for instance, spent his time at Port Said inspecting Ferdinand de Lesseps' statue and sailing round the harbour taking numerous photographs. For others there was less need to indulge in tourist activities, the break from combat being enough to relax them. The rest periods provided for each brigade in the Jordan Valley were also critical to maintaining the ANZMD's fighting abilities. Corporal Edwin McKay, of the AMR, felt that 'without an occasional chance to breathe sweeter air and eat more varied food, we could not have stuck it'.[62] A chance to express one's civilian identity, through leave or brief breaks from the harsh realities of combat, was an essential element in maintaining the endurance of the EEF's mounted troops.

For some men the experience of leave was not a pleasant one as they found it hard to adjust to their new, non-military surroundings. Life at the front could become so ingrained in them that it was hard to escape it. Trooper Idriess found it difficult to sleep while in Port Said as he kept waking and thinking that he was on duty out in the desert. For most troopers it was their recourse to unruly behaviour while on leave that caused difficulties. Lieutenant Stanley Prince, of the 3rd ALH Regiment, was disappointed in Jerusalem that he was only allowed to look around the city in a large group. He explained to his mother that this was because 'you know what the Australians are when they're "off the chain"'.[63] As a result of difficulties with the behaviour of the ANZMD's men, Jerusalem was eventually placed entirely out of bounds as a leave destination.

The larrikinism of the Anzacs was often fuelled by their recourse to drink as a means to escape the rigours of military life. While the division had served in Sinai and southern Palestine alcohol problems had largely been confined to leave periods, although they had led to many of the worst incidents of Anzac unrest in Cairo.[64] Once a number of Jewish villages had been liberated in Palestine, however, it became much easier for the men to obtain drink on a daily basis. The men of the ANZMD considered the capture of Deiran, in November 1917, with its large winery, to be 'our greatest prize of the war', and a number of days were spent indulging in the delights of its cellars. Attempts to control the Anzacs' access to the local wines proved futile, with ingenious methods found to avoid the restrictions. At Sarona the EEF placed a British infantry guard on the wine press. The men of the NZMR formed a fake guard to relieve them, and by the time senior British commanders had realized that they had been duped, the cellars had been emptied in a carefully choreographed operation. The military authorities were not just concerned with preventing drunkenness; they were also worried about the health of the troops. The WMR's regimental orders contained a prohibition on the purchasing of 'spurious liquor purporting to be whisky and Brandy' from natives in Egypt. Many of these beverages were locally brewed and could easily spread diseases around units. Despite these concerns many Anzacs persisted, choosing to cope with the harsh nature of combat in the Middle East through recourse to the palliative effects of alcohol.

The keenest expression of the men's civilian pasts came when they participated in sport. Sporting activities offered an important bridge between the military and civilian worlds, particularly for volunteer and conscript soldiers not accustomed to army life.[65] Sport was a constant feature of life in the EEF and particularly in the ANZMD. Unsurprisingly for mounted units, horse racing proved very popular. In some instances they did not use their own horses for the races, with the men of the NZMR preferring to use the supply column's donkeys. They even took part in improvised polo matches using walking sticks and a football. Participation in horse races was encouraged by the offer of substantial prizes for those who took part. Often the officers of a unit would donate funds to pay the prize money, and in the case of the 'Anzac Steeplechase' in March 1917, open to the whole division, Major-General Chauvel provided a cup worth over £5. The one sport that animated all members of the division was rugby. It was played at any and every opportunity, proving the Anzacs' equivalent of the British infantry's predilection for football. Rugby competitions were taken very seriously by the men and units taking part. In the 1st ALH Regiment the trials for the divisional team were seen as so important that troopers were even allowed time off from musketry practice to prepare for them. The fascination with rugby was not so great that other sports were squeezed out of the men's lives. Many of the men, however, found that the sandy terrain in Sinai was not suited to playing rugby causing a number of injuries, and that football matches were easier to stage.[66]

Boxing tournaments were always capable of drawing large crowds. The 2nd ALH Brigade competition proved so popular that the crowd was arranged into tiers, with the rear sections made up of men on horses, with men on camels behind them.[67] Some individuals chose to indulge in even more obscure pastimes, with surfing on the beach at Rafah being so favoured that the 6th ALH Regiment had to set up their own beach patrols.[68] Officially organized sports meetings were not always successful. The divisional staff held a negative opinion of 2nd ALH Brigade's efforts in October 1917: 'owing to bad organisation, lack of control over the sale of beer, and dust, they could not be called successful, and it is probable that the C in C who was present with the Divisional Commander, was not favourably impressed.'[69] As a result of this failure, great care was taken over the organization of the divisional sports meeting in January 1918. The staff set down extensive rules for each of the planned 23 events, which even included detailed maps of the various racecourses. Sporting events not only provided a means of relaxation for the men of the ANZMD, but also offered a brief chance for officers and men to socialize on equal terms, indicative of the Anzac spirit. For example, the 5th ALH Regiment staged an officers' rugby match, considered a most amusing spectacle by the men. The commanding officer of 1st ALH Regiment, Lieutenant-Colonel Granville, felt that even he should take part in his regiment's rugby matches. Despite the fact that he had not played for 23 years the men were still impressed by his performance on the pitch. Sport acted as a levelling force within the ANZMD, and represented the best opportunity for these citizen soldiers to cope with military life by returning to a civilian world.

Anzac identity, with its use of Gallipolli as a national rallying point and its reliance on the civilian backgrounds of its citizen soldiers, offers a powerful explanation for the endurance of the ANZMD's troopers during the First World War. This, however, is only sufficient to explain how these men dealt with the concept of taking part in a war. It does little to answer the question of how they coped with the horrors and trials of front-line combat, which lies at the heart of any understanding of morale.[70] The Anzac legend rests on the notion that the skills of Australia and New Zealand's soldiers lay specifically on the battlefield. ANZMD's combat record enhances this belief for the Middle Eastern front. It is therefore necessary to assess the validity of the warrior ethos within the Light Horsemen's and Mounted Riflemen's military identities.

Mateship and the regiment

For British Army units, regimental *esprit de corps* has been identified as lying at the heart of their ability to cope with the rigours of combat.[71] It is a concept rarely used to explain the maintenance of morale in Anzac formations, as it suggests too much similarity to an imposed colonial model. This in many respects ignores the substantial similarities between the British and Dominion military organizations in the first half of the twentieth century. ANZMD's nine regiments acted as the basic tactical and administrative units of the mounted force, and as such were the cornerstone of the men's military experiences. A number of troopers took great pride in their regiment's battlefield abilities. Trooper Idriess felt that 5th ALH was capable of defeating 2,000 Turks in combat in the desert. Another member of the regiment, when offered an external commission in the Australian infantry, turned it down, choosing to remain a Light Horseman. The bonds of individual troopers to their regiment could be very strong, and were reinforced by its success in combat. Lieutenant Delpratt felt proud to have served in 5th ALH, particularly during September 1918 as it was responsible for capturing the largest number of Turks in the 2nd ALH Brigade. The success of individual members of a mounted regiment was often seen as conferring approbation on the whole unit. Corporal Metcalfe noted in a letter to his brother that the 1st ALH had a peculiar attitude to the awarding of medals: the men believed 'that if one man deserves recognition they all do, so when a decoration is given, it generally goes to the Regiment, which means the men don't wear it'.[72] Individual identities were thus subsumed within that of the wider Light Horse or Mounted Rifles regimental community.

Official symbols were used to reinforce loyalty to the wider unit. This is seen clearly in 5th ALH's creation of a new badge in late 1916, designed by the regiment's quartermaster sergeant. It was displayed on a new unit flag, which had the badge superimposed on top of the regimental colours.[73] The unit's 1918 Christmas card chose this badge and the regimental colours for its design (see Illustration 5.1). The identity that these Light Horsemen wished to display to their relatives at home, after three years of campaigning in the Middle East, was that of their regiment, their military family.

The Light Horse and Mounted Rifles regimental references did not rest on the strong, although often invented, historic traditions that were prevalent in the British Army.[74] Both New Zealand and Australia's mounted units were late nineteenth-century creations, and as such could not trace their lines back to units that had showed great fighting characteristics while serving under Marlborough or Wellington. The only significant actions they had been involved in took place during the South African War. 2nd ALH Regiment found that its only battle honours before 1914 were at Kimberley, Paadeberg and Diamond Hill. Most regiments were not fighting to uphold traditions established in South Africa, but those from Gallipoli. It was to this that the eulogizing assessment of the British Empire's war effort, edited by Sir Charles Lucas, a former Colonial Office civil servant and historian of the empire, returned when passing judgement on the NZMR's battlefield exploits. Often the identity of an individual regiment was lost within the wider sphere of the division. From November 1916 all the Light Horsemen of the ANZMD were allowed to wear emu feathers in their hats, a symbol which had previously only been associated with those regiments drawn from Queensland.[75]

Regimental loyalties were often only important to the creation of unit histories in the interwar period. This was a sentiment expressed by C. G. Nicol, the author of the AMR's account, who hoped that it would not just be a chronicle of the unit's battles:

> At the same time an effort has been made to reveal something of the spirit of the Regiment, something of the general attitude of mind of its officers and men, which, at times, may have helped it to engage in operations, forlorn hopes and adventures, with the resolution generally associated with regiments with traditions.[76]

The need to reinforce a regimental identity after the First World War was particularly strong in New Zealand, as the existing Mounted Rifles regiments had only been used to form each of the squadrons in the brigade. It was, therefore, difficult to create a new unit allegiance when the men of the CMR were drawn from the 1st Canterbury Yeomanry Cavalry, 8th South Canterbury and 10th Nelson Mounted Rifles Regiments. A focus on the original regiments was continued in New Zealand's post-war commemorations. The national war memorial in Wellington chose not to honour the AMR, CMR, and WMR on its plaque to the NZMR, but instead displayed the regimental crests of the 12 original Mounted Rifles regiments. The regimental structure of the Light Horse also provided its members with a very confusing picture. Units created in 1914 were raised on a state basis and thus owed little to those that had gone before them in the militia forces. Links to past identities were frequently tenuous due to the numerous reorganizations of the Light Horse in the nineteenth and early twentieth centuries. The regiment known as the 14th ALH in 1919 could trace its roots back to the Seymour, Victoria Troop raised in 1887, which had been converted into the 7th ALH Victorian Mounted Rifles in 1905, then the 15th ALH Victorian Mounted Rifles in 1912.[77] Such tortuous ancestry did little to instil any degree of historic regimental loyalty in the men serving at the front. It would have been unclear for both New Zealand and Australian troopers to know exactly which regiment they owed their allegiance to.

The weakness of a regimental identity suggests that the bonds of loyalty between troopers were formed at a lower level of organization. All Light Horse and Mounted Rifles units were divided into three squadrons, each consisting of four troops. Rather than the regiment it was at the level of the squadron or troop that most men experienced combat in the Middle East. The nature of ANZMD operations meant that often these smaller formations were frequently operating on their own far away from support. This was seen most spectacularly in the AMR's independent action to clear a section of the east bank of the Jordan on 23 March 1918. In this operation the squadrons of the regiment, having crossed the Jordan, each acted independently to destroy Turkish posts and tackle the threat posed by Turkish cavalry. By the end of the day the AMR had scattered the Turkish defenders, enabling the EEF's engineers to establish a bridgehead at Ghoraniyeh, all for the loss of only one officer killed and two men wounded.[78] The strength of the troop rested on the four-man section, which formed the basic tactical unit. These soldiers would live, eat, sleep and fight together. When entering combat the members of the section would take it in turns to be the horse holder for that particular action. Trooper Idriess did not even know all the names of the men in his squadron, instead he concentrated his friendships in his section:

> We growl together, we swear together, we take one another's blasted horses to water, we conspire against the damned troop-sergeant together, we growl against the war and we damn the officers up hill and down dale together; we do everything together – in fact, this whole blasted war is being fought in sections. The fate of all the East at least, depends entirely upon the section.[79]

It was to one's comrades in the section that men turned when they faced difficulties. Sergeant Crase, who had suffered from enteric fever in July 1916, only managed to return to the 3rd ALH Regiment in September. He was still in a weak condition, but his friends in his section provided him with assistance, helping him onto his horse when required and effectively carried his role in the troop for six weeks.

These small groups were also of great value in helping to integrate new recruits into the ways of the squadron and the regiment. The more experienced men would assume a mentoring role for those who had just been drafted in. It was from these veterans that the newcomers 'quickly learnt the necessity of co-operation in all things, and the valuable lesson of always helping others besides themselves'.[80] The ethos of loyalty to one's comrades was thus instilled in reinforcements as soon as they reached their regiment. These new men could also help the veteran soldiers to cope with the difficulties of military life. The drafts that arrived in early 1916 to rebuild the CMR were viewed as invigorating by the few survivors of Gallipoli. They were keen to learn and wished to prove themselves worthy of their more experienced mates in the section. For many troopers it was the bonds with their comrades that helped to motivate them during combat. Captain J. Boyd, serving in the 5th ALH Regiment, wrote to the family of his friend Lieutenant C. R. Morley after he was killed in late 1917, expressing the power these close ties could have. 'This is the sort of life that binds two true Pals together, and never again can I have such a pal, we cemented it time and again on the Battlefield, and shared many dangers.'[81]

The comradeship of the section was a key element of the Anzac legend that endured after the First World War. In this case 'mateship' was seen as a sacred bond that could only truly be forged under the harsh conditions of combat, and formed a central part of Bean's narrative in the official history. This characteristic was held up as a peculiar feature of the Anzacs, seen as critical to their battlefield endurance and success. In many respects this was simply an expression of primary group loyalty, which was later emphasized by S. L. A. Marshall as being of considerable importance in understanding military performance during the Second World War. Primary group loyalty, much maligned in recent historiography, a great deal of which has been influenced by studies of the *Wehrmacht* on the Eastern Front in 1941–5, nevertheless lay at the heart of the ANZMD's experience of combat. For Bean it was a development of the ethos of friendship that was critical to survival in the Australian bush, which he had observed in his pre-war travels.[82] This aspect of the Anzac legend therefore offers a valid route into analysing the reasons for Australian and New Zealand battlefield endurance.

The small group cohesion of the section was enhanced in mounted regiments by the relationship between the troopers and their horses. This was in spite of the fact that Gullett felt many of the ANZMD's men were not initially true military horsemasters, having much to learn about the intricacies of caring for their mounts while on campaign in order to keep them operationally fit. Many men felt a strong affinity with their animals, which was built up over several years of service. By November 1918 Trooper Alec McNeur, of the NZMR Machine Gun Squadron, noted in his diary that 'in the mounteds you always have a partner, a mate, in your horse'.[83] For others the relationship was one of care, with the horses dependent on their riders:

> Right through the whole Middle East Campaign, our horses always came first, no matter how tough a time we had had and no matter how tired and weary we were, we always watered, fed and groomed our horses before we attended to our own needs. This procedure was always strictly adhered to.[84]

The horses, which required constant work to maintain their operational fitness, thus offered a distraction for the men of the ANZMD. Rather than worrying about the capricious nature of combat they could concentrate on the routine of cleaning and feeding their equine comrades.

The bonds between troopers and their horses were often as strong as those between mates in a section. Losses of horses in combat, which could be substantial during periods of sustained artillery fire, enhanced the emotional impact of battle. After being shelled on the Hebron road in early November 1917, Trooper Idriess had to help shoot those horses that were too badly wounded to save, noting that he 'saw men nearly cry to-day – we love our horses'.[85] The greatest sense of loss was felt at the end of the war when the division was required to hand in its horses. The healthiest ones were allotted to the Indian Army, but the older and weaker ones were destroyed. Many men were unhappy with this policy, but it was perceived as preferable to selling the horses to the local population in Egypt and Palestine, as the Arabs were thought to lack even basic skills of animal husbandry. The culling of 3,059 horses in 1919 occasioned a melancholy poetic contribution on the subject by Trooper Bluegum (otherwise known as Major Oliver Hogue) in *Australia in Palestine*. As Jean Bou has argued, this poem has contributed to the mythologization of the Light Horse's wartime experience and the crucial role that the horses played within it.[86] Nevertheless, the horses of the DMC were considered so important that they were given their own memorial in Sydney, which continues as a focal point for commemoration through to the present day.

As powerful a bond as primary group loyalty was, it did not always exist within every troop and squadron of the division. Some units were almost devoid of any bonds of friendship between the men who formed them. As Trooper Jeffrey Holmes found in the 1st Field Squadron of the ANZMD 'there is not any bond of comradeship among the men, and one cannot leave a thing lying about for fear that one of his so-called mates might pinch it'.[87] This is hardly the image of mateship that Bean put forward as central to Anzac identity. In units where there were strong links between men the situation for newly arrived reinforcements could be very difficult. Trooper Chandler found that all the best jobs in his regiment, such as in the signals section, went to the veterans, leaving the new drafts with the more mundane tasks. The bonds of mateship could also produce problems on the battlefield. During the advance on Tel el Saba Sergeant Crase saw his troop leader have the top of his head taken off by a bullet. Two men rushed to the Lieutenant's aid, despite the intense fire and Crase ordering them not to. Both were subsequently killed, and in Crase's opinion they had 'needlessly lost their lives'.[88] Small group loyalties could serve to undermine a section or troop's ability to survive combat by encouraging men to risk their lives to save their mates.

As has been argued in studies of many different theatres of war in the twentieth century, the primary group found it very hard to sustain significant casualties and still function as a motivator to morale. In periods of intense combat a number of sections could be wiped out. At Amman in March 1918, 'B' Squadron of the 6th ALH Regiment attacked a number of Turkish machine guns along a ridge. Earlier battle casualties meant that only 58 men began the assault, but by its conclusion a further 40 had either been killed or wounded. Individual battles thus had an enormous impact on the ability of small groups to remain functioning. The periods of intense combat faced by the ANZMD in August 1916, November 1917, and March and April 1918, took a heavy toll and saw many troops and squadrons severely reduced in size (see Figure 1.5). The effect of sustained combat operations on a regiment over the course of three years of campaigning can be seen clearly by examining the 5th ALH. A census in December 1916 revealed that of the 523 men who had left for the Middle East in 1914 only 169 were still serving with the regiment. A year later this had fallen to 140 men, and by the end of the war there were just 94 original troopers in its ranks.[89] Battlefield attrition ate into the manpower of the regiment and left little opportunity for primary group loyalties to be sustained across the course of the Sinai and Palestine campaigns.

The rural nature of mateship, which is very much integral to the Anzac legend, was also particularly weak within the ANZMD. Bean's official history emphasized the bush credentials of many members of the AIF, which supposedly provided them with the skills to cope with modern warfare.[90] At the heart of the bush experience was the code of mateship that corresponded neatly to the notion of primary group loyalty. For many observers the Light Horse demonstrated the embodiment of the rural origins of the Australian warrior. Lieutenant Delpratt, however, found little evidence of a country ethos in the 5th ALH Regiment, and highlighted instead the fact that 'C' Squadron was composed primarily of bank clerks, earning it the sobriquet of the 'Society Sqdn'. The roll call books for 'A' Squadron of the 5th ALH reinforce the argument that this was not a rural regiment. By the end of 1914 the unit had recruited its necessary complement, but of the 255 men, 160 had occupations related to the countryside. By the end of 1916 the squadron had risen in size to 296 men, but of these only 121 still held rural occupations. Only one man of the initial intake was able to describe himself as a 'bushman', and by 1916 the only truly bush career left in the squadron was the individual who was a 'kangaroo shooter'. A similar story can be observed in 'A' Squadron of the 1st ALH Regiment, whose 256 men in 1918 contained only 101 men who earned their living off the land.[91]

It is clear from these examples that by 1916 around 60 per cent of the ALH was being recruited from urban areas. This counters the assertions of some Light Horse historians that only 20 per cent of the force was drawn from Australia's cities. Nevertheless, the percentage of urban dwellers who became Light Horsemen, although much higher than usually recognized, does highlight the fact that the Light Horse was more rural in its composition than the AIF's infantry units. The fact that in 1916 around 40 per cent of the Light Horse was from rural areas in Australia, a country that was urbanizing rapidly in the early twentieth century, remains striking.[92] Service in a section within the Light Horse and Mounted Rifles regiments and integration into its personal bonds of mateship may have provided some assistance to the morale of the troopers. In most cases, though, the primary group was likely to have been destroyed in at least one major engagement each year. Nor was this small collection of friends in any way the product of the untamed wilderness of the Australian and New Zealand bush.

Training and leadership

Casualties did have a significant effect on the maintenance of a continuous identity within a regiment, squadron, or troop in the ANZMD, but they did not fully destroy it. Those veterans who survived a number of engagements rose up through the ranks of the regiment, to hold positions of authority. In the 5th ALH, of the 94 original men who had served throughout the entire war, 15 were officers and 48 were NCOs. Of the regiment's officers only two had left Australia with commissions, the rest having been promoted while serving in the Middle East. A similar pattern can be observed in other regiments. The 7th ALH received four cadet officers in July 1918, all of whom had been former NCOs and had been promoted as a reward for several years of excellent service. In the 1st ALH the heavy losses suffered in the fighting at Beersheba and Tel el Khuweilefe in late October and early November 1917 provided an opportunity for a number of promotions. A quartermaster sergeant, three sergeants, one corporal, two lance corporals and a trooper were all given commissions. The open promotions system of the AIF and the New Zealand Expeditionary Force, although not unique to those forces and similar in many respects to that operating within the British Army by the later years of the war, allowed the most skilled members of a regiment to gain commissions.[93] The junior leaders within a regiment, serving at troop and squadron level, were thus able to continue the ethos of the unit, despite the impact of battle casualties.

Crucially, the veteran members of a regiment provided a cadre around which the new drafts could be prepared for front-line combat. Many of the reinforcements for the ANZMD were poorly trained and knew little of what to expect in battle. Lieutenant Fred Tomlins, serving in the 1st ALH Regiment, was amazed that of the 12 men drafted to the 1st ALH Machine Gun Squadron none of them knew how to handle their weapons, even after 4 months of training.[94] Nevertheless, the Light Horse and Mounted Rifles depots in Egypt worked hard to make sure that only men who were ready were sent up to the division in the line. As a result, stringent standards were set for riding and shooting tests. Trooper J. Evans was surprised that he was one of only a handful of men out of the 24th Light Horse Reinforcements for the 6th ALH Regiment to pass his musketry test.

Training at base depots, however, could only deal with the basics of military life, and once men reached their unit more intensive training began. Exercises were a common feature of rest periods away from the front. In December 1916 the division organized a large-scale practice assault on a fake Turkish position at Masaid. The scheme involved the ANZMD as well as two infantry divisions, in order for the two arms to practise cooperating with each other. The exercise was designed to find out how long it took troops to march to particular points in Sinai as well as the speed of their deployment into various formations. Training did not always take place on such a grand scale. Regiments regularly put their men through range courses to maintain a high standard of musketry. In order to prevent training becoming a monotonous experience a number of units held musketry competitions between themselves. The CMR tested its Hotchkiss gunners against the Lewis gunners of the Leinsters in January 1918, and held a rematch a few days later to try to even up the score. Attempts were also made to make abstract training exercises, such as range firing, as realistic as possible. The WMR instigated a system whereby men would fire 5 rounds at a target while lying down, then 5 more rapidly in 45 seconds while popping up from behind the cover of sandbags.[95]

These schemes were intended to keep the troopers interested in the process of improving their battlefield skills, and to focus their minds on the task of combat. For this reason the veterans of the division were often used to run training courses and pass on their experience to units and reinforcements. Corporal Metcalfe found himself detailed for three months' service at Moascar teaching new arrivals from Australia how to improve their riding. Similarly Major Hurst, of the CMR, was sent to the divisional school at Jerusalem in the summer of 1918 to lecture on the 'technical handling of Hotchkiss Rifles'. In addition to using men from EEF units, a number of experienced officers from the Western Front were also brought over to Egypt and lectured in the main training centres around Cairo.[96] In this way the major lessons of modern, industrialized war could be disseminated to British imperial forces across all theatres of operations.

The division itself kept tight control over the training regime for its men. While at Abasan el Kebir, in September 1917, the divisional staff issued orders for the conduct of training schemes at brigade level. It stipulated that one brigade scheme would be held each week and that a full divisional scheme would be held every fortnight. In addition, there were to be one or two practice turnouts of the whole division as well as field firing and gas exercises. These proposals were viewed by the divisional staff as a relaxed training schedule that would not put too much strain on the horses.[97] In order to instil the correct ethos towards military operations in its officers the division set up a series of tactical exercises at the same time. These were to be attended by the brigade commanders and staffs of the 2nd ALH and NZMR Brigades, as well as all regimental, machine gun squadron and Royal Horse Artillery battery commanding officers and their seconds in command. They were given various tactical tasks to perform, based around hypothetical Turkish attacks. Additional information was drip fed to the officers as the scheme progressed to mimic the way in which commanders received an ever-changing stream of information during a battle. They were expected to deal with factors such as the loss of 7 per cent of their force, or the expenditure of 30 per cent of their ammunition.[98] The creation of a divisional school in May 1918 at Jerusalem, run by Major H. F. Cadell of the 1st ALH Brigade, helped to formalize and standardize the divisional process of instruction. Brigades were ordered to send small numbers of officers and NCOs from each of their constituent regiments to the school for 14-day periods of training. Each day involved a mounted and dismounted parade as well as lectures and lessons on various topics, including forming rearguards, consolidating positions, organizing picquets and the construction of trenches.

Training remained largely within the control of the division throughout the war. Rarely were regimental or squadron commanders given the opportunity to instigate their own programmes, with schemes often being set out in detail at brigade level. When the Inspector-General of Cavalry in Egypt tried to take control of the ANZMD's training in late 1916, Major-General Chauvel wrote to the commander of Eastern Force, Lieutenant-General Charles Dobell, to ensure that the division kept its own training programmes. This strong emphasis on sophisticated and extensive military training was crucial to the ANZMD's ability to cope with the rigours of combat. Trooper Idriess thought that it was only the men's training that allowed such 'amateur soldiers' to consistently defeat the 'finest soldiers of Turkey' in battle in Sinai and Palestine.[99] The division's training system gave its officers and men confidence in their ability to overcome the enemy in battle.

On the battlefield it was the junior officers who fulfilled the critical role of maintaining morale, as they controlled the squadrons and troops that were involved in the sharp end of combat. Major Hurst, of the CMR, demonstrated at Second Gaza the influence that a squadron commander could have on the local conduct of operations. A Turkish attack on a ridge held by the regiment became very intense and 'things looked pretty ugly at one stage and the Aussies started to make a bolt for it and soon the Yeomanry would have followed but our O.C. ran over and cajoled and entreated them and in the end stopped what promised to be a bad stampede'.[100] In this instance, Hurst was setting the military standard for his men, and those of other units nearby, to live up to. The legitimacy of most junior officers among their men was based on their military competence, demonstrated by their courage and decisiveness in battle. In his letter of condolence to the family of Lieutenant Morley, Captain Boyd stressed the heroic manner in which their son had carried out his duties. 'All through the day he had led his men splendidly, taking all sorts of risks, and exposing himself always first where danger threatened, and in one instance, early in the morning he was one of four that moved forward and remained unwounded.'[101] By setting an example to his men Morley had demonstrated an aggressive military ethic, which if emulated would help his men through battle.

Junior leaders were aware of and understood the importance of their role in combat. Lieutenant Delpratt was conscious that 'an officer has some responsibility on his shoulders in action a mistake may mean the loss of several lives unnecessarily'.[102] Those officers who fulfilled their duty of battlefield leadership effectively won the admiration and respect of their men. Sergeant Crase was deeply upset at the loss of his squadron commander, Major Lewis, at Rafah in January 1917, as he was 'a wonderful leader and soldier'.[103] The staff of the ANZMD were also aware of the essential nature of the junior leader's duties. In a memorandum to Chaytor's Force prior to the operations in

September 1918, the Chief of Staff, Lieutenant-Colonel J. G. Browne, stressed that 'the essence of good leading and command is to bring men into action in the fittest state to fight'.[104] It went on to highlight the need for officers to prepare accurate reports on the situation at the front in order to keep senior commanders informed. Browne suggested that a report should be read to a fellow officer who was not aware of its contents before it was despatched.

The division took great care to make sure that its officers were well trained and skilled in the tasks they were to carry out. A large number of junior officers attended courses at the Imperial School of Instruction at Zeitoun. Here the three-month course taught the various tasks required of a troop leader, including the maintenance of discipline, sanitation, march discipline, the duties of orderly officers and map reading.[105] Within the division officers were constantly tested on their command abilities. In March 1917 Major Claude Easterbrook, serving on the 2nd ALH Brigade's staff, had to write practice reports on operations for an Eastern Force scheme. The marker thought Easterbrook's work the best he had read, although his description of military geography was not perfect. The division's officer corps went through a continuous process of assessment and training in order to maintain its high standards; this was not only applied to junior officers but also to its generals and staff officers. Major-General Chaytor and his GSO1 and GSO2 attended a lecture in October 1917 given by the EEF's Chief of the General Staff, Major-General Louis Bols, on the development of offensive tactics in France. Chaytor was demonstrating an openness towards learning which emphasized the need for all his officers to be constantly refining their military capabilities.

Regimental commanders could have an important impact on the motivation of the troopers under their command. They also provided a critical link between the wishes of the brigade and divisional staffs and the men in the front line. The commander of the 5th ALH Regiment, Lieutenant-Colonel Lachlan Wilson, elicited effusive praise from Lieutenant Morley:

> He is a great old chap and practically lives for the Regt. I think he looks on us all as his family and he takes the keenest interest and pride in everything we do. Everybody thinks the world of him including a lot of other Regiments.[106]

Wilson was fulfilling the paternalistic role expected of regimental officers. It is unsurprising that the loss of their commander, when he was promoted to command 3rd ALH Brigade in late October 1917, left many of the men downcast although they were happy with his replacement by Major Cameron. Lieutenant-Colonel John Findlay, in charge of the CMR, was held in a similarly high regard by his men, who referred to him affectionately as 'Old John'. He used his experiences in the South African War to help inform his command of the regiment. Crucially, he was able to remain as its commander, with a few brief absences, for the entire duration of the regiment's service in the First World War, meaning that the CMR retained a consistent system and style of command. For Major-General Andrew Russell, the commander of the New Zealand Division in France, this was 'an experience on which they may be congratulated and envied'.[107]

Generals at brigade and divisional level, who were able to instil a distinct fighting spirit in the men of the ANZMD, supplemented the effective work of the regimental commanders. Both Major-Generals Chauvel and Chaytor were critical to introducing a professional military ethos into the division. Chauvel's subsequent career as Australia's first corps commander and his successful leadership of the DMC during the Megiddo campaign in 1918 demonstrated his considerable abilities of command. He was not, however, always held in the highest regard by his men, as he was a keen enforcer of military discipline. His frequent inspections of front-line units caused much annoyance among the rank and file of the division. Lieutenant Tomlins noted in his diary that 'these inspections cause a good deal of dissatisfaction among the men as rusty bits stirrup irons etc have to be polished for the occasion, and they are as rusty as ever, a day or so later as they will not keep a polish in the sea air'.[108]

Chauvel's aloof manner was replicated by Chaytor, but the latter's leadership abilities, already demonstrated in the NZMR, set him apart. Of all his brigade commanders, Chaytor, who was also a personal friend, was the only one that Chauvel felt he could entrust the ANZMD to when he was away on leave, and it was to him that it passed permanently in mid-1917. He credited Chaytor's 'dash and initiative' with producing the victory at Rafah in early 1917. Not only did Chaytor's superiors think highly of him, but the troopers of the ANZMD also respected him. This was largely a product of his desire not to sacrifice the lives of his men unnecessarily. At Bir Salmana in 1916 he broke off the engagement when it became clear that little more could be achieved, despite the insistence of a number of his subordinates that the Turks should be charged with the bayonet. Most importantly Chaytor was a military professional. He had served twice in South Africa and was the first New Zealander to attend the Staff College at Camberley, where he excelled. Prior to the First World War he had held a number of staff appointments in New Zealand, including serving as the Adjutant-General and the Director of Military Training and Education. His experience in the latter post led him to take a keen interest in the preparation of men for combat, an ethos that filtered very clearly into the ANZMD's rigorous training programmes. He was relentless in his attempts to improve the efficiency of the division, issuing numerous detailed memoranda on its failings and how they should be improved. In addition, he took a great dislike to any slackness observed among the men, even prohibiting the leave of troop officers in 1918 in order to provoke improvements.[109] The professionalism of Chaytor was critical to the ANZMD's battlefield endurance and success. He instilled in his troopers an ethos of continual improvement, which gave them the ability to learn from their experiences, and allowed them to cope with the unexpected occurrences that mounted operations frequently threw up.

At brigade level Chaytor's professionalism was complemented by an aggressive attitude to battle. His replacement as the head of the NZMR, Brigadier-General Meldrum, held an impressive reputation having conducted a stalwart defence of Chunuk Bair in August 1915, while commanding the WMR. Within this regiment he was known as 'Fix Bayonets Bill' and was considered to be the finest commander in the brigade. Conversely, Brigadier-General Ryrie, an Australian politician and amateur soldier who commanded the 2nd ALH Brigade throughout the Sinai and Palestine campaigns, represented the epitome of the Anzac spirit. Trooper Idriess noted that

Ryrie was liked by nearly everyone in the brigade, and that he was able to 'sling a boomerang better than any white man I know'.[110] Most importantly he often took to the field to see how his men were coping at the front line. During the advance northwards from Beersheba he was proud to note that he had 'stuck to the lads all through the stunt, and was always up where there was anything doing'.[111] This style of command was suited to the mobile operations of a Light Horse regiment, but was pushed to its limit when applied to a brigade.[112] The ANZMD thus possessed a wide range of command styles among its senior generals, which effectively complemented each other when in action. The aggressiveness of Ryrie and Meldrum was tempered by the careful and methodical approach of Chaytor.

A valid legend?

The Anzac legend asserts the independence and unique characteristics of the Australian and New Zealand fighting man. The inherent anti-British chauvinism of this identity clouds the extent to which many of the factors that maintained Anzac morale were similar to those found among British Territorial infantry. Most notable was the regular recourse to a civilian identity, which allowed the troopers to cope with the hardships of military life. Although this demonstrates the citizen-soldier ideal inherent in Anzac mythology, it is difficult to locate the ANZMD in a narrative that sees its members fighting and dying as part of the birth pangs of either Australia or New Zealand.

Through its numerous battlefield successes in the Middle Eastern campaign the division grew to see itself as an elite formation in the EEF. Elitism was often a powerful motivational factor among some British battalions, regiments and divisions on the Western Front. As Brian Bond has illustrated, the Guards Division was able to endure significant losses and integrate new drafts by creating its own elite divisional ethos.[113] In early 1918 Lieutenant-General Chauvel set about creating a badge for the DMC and chose a date palm. When Brigadier-General Richard Howard-Vyse, the DMC's Chief of Staff and affectionately known as 'Wombat', asked the ANZMD to come up with its own crest he received the reply from Lieutenant-Colonel Browne that it would be a date. When questioned as to this peculiar choice he replied, 'because that is what the date palm grew out of'.[114] Browne was emphasizing that the military abilities of the DMC had developed from those of the ANZMD. This belief in the military excellence of the division has continued to the present day. Christopher Pugsley has asserted that although the history of the NZMR is largely forgotten, they remain one of the finest bodies of troops ever raised by New Zealand. A wider emphasis on the superlative combat skills of the DMC has also been made by Stephen Badsey.[115] He argued in his study of British cavalry that the DMC under Chauvel, to a certain extent unintentionally, was one of the leading exponents of a new operational art in Palestine. Its operations at Third Gaza and Megiddo mirrored elements of the 'collapse theory' later advocated as key to the manoeuvrist warfare doctrine that emerged from the Six Day War in 1967, whereby shock action produced institutional paralysis in an opposing army. Although Badsey neglects the Sinai operations of 1916 in his account, it is clear that this approach at corps level drew on the tactical and operational methodology seen in many of the ANZMD's campaigns.

The ANZMD did not, however, possess an unblemished military record. The successes achieved in Sinai and at Beersheba were tempered by the failures at First Gaza and on the two Transjordan Raids. Critically, the operations in Sinai saw the division taking on small, unsupported Turkish forces, most notably at Rafah and Magdhaba. In large-scale operations battlefield success was no longer down to the actions of one division, and the Anzacs were required to play their part in operations controlled by sometimes inadequate corps commanders.[116] The smaller battles fought in Sinai and across the Jordan River in September 1918 closely resembled imperial campaigns, where regiments and divisions operated independently far from support. It was in such circumstances that the benefits of Anzac identity came to the fore. The primary group loyalties engendered by the section and reinforced through the extensive and effective training schemes of the division helped to instil a professional military outlook among its amateur soldiers. This allowed them to act independently away from supporting units. Strong and intelligent leadership by junior officers at squadron and troop level, bolstered by the example of skilled regimental, brigade, and divisional command, helped to maintain the combat endurance of the Light Horse and Mounted Rifles. In an imperial war in the Middle East, the Anzacs proved themselves to be the archetypal professional imperial warriors.

6

The Indian Army Fighting for Empire

By the conclusion of the campaign in Palestine in October 1918 the manpower basis of the EEF had been radically transformed, with the majority of the force composed of units drawn from the Indian Army. Of its eleven divisions, only two, the 54th (East Anglia) and the Australian and New Zealand Mounted Divisions, contained no Indian troops at all. The victory at Megiddo in September which destroyed Ottoman forces in the region was, therefore, largely achieved by the skill and dash of the EEF's newly arrived sepoys and sowars.[1] Between 1914 and 1918 India sent over 1.8 million combatants and non-combatants overseas to serve in a variety of theatres. Of these over 95,000 combatants and 135,000 non-combatants served in Egypt and Palestine.[2] India effectively operated in the First World War as an imperial manpower reserve, providing men to sustain a range of British campaigns. Sepoys saw service in a diverse range of operational contexts, including a bloody period on the Western Front acting as reinforcements for the BEF through to ill-fated attempts to carry the war to Germany's East African territories.

The Indian Army's combat record during the war has been coloured almost entirely by the experiences of Indian Expeditionary Force 'D' sent to Mesopotamia in 1914.[3] The surrender of Major-General Charles Townshend's 6th (Poona) Division at Kut-al-Amara, has become symbolic of the Indian Army's struggles to adapt to the nature of modern warfare in 1914–16. Logistical failures alongside inept command and control arrangements formed the basis of the excoriating verdict pronounced by the Mesopotamia Commission in 1917. This focus on defeat and the incompetence of generals has skewed the historical analysis of the Indian Army's role in the First World War. The 240,000 Indians who served with the EEF and formed the backbone of its first line fighting forces by summer 1918 have been paid little attention by historians.[4] Rather than a narrative based around suffering, incompetence, and defeat, the Indianization of the EEF demonstrates the extent to which the British Empire could function as an integrated military machine. It also reveals the ability of Allenby, his generals and staff officers, and the formations he commanded to adapt to the imperial vicissitudes of the First World War. The Indianized EEF demonstrated in 1918 that it was capable of training and organizing for complex all arms operations.

Moreover, sepoys and sowars, many of them only recently recruited into the Indian Army, proved themselves to be adept at fighting on a modern industrialized battlefield in order to further the British Empire's cause in the Middle East. In many respects Megiddo represents a forgotten victory for the Indian Army, and one which needs to be dissected in order to examine fully the operations of the re-modelled EEF in the latter half of 1918.

The Indian Army that took to the field in the First World War could trace its roots back to the eighteenth century. It was originally created by the East India Company in response to the use of Indian troops by the French to further their imperial aims on the subcontinent.[5] The Company's army, based around the three presidencies of Madras, Bombay, and Bengal, proved very successful, rapidly expanding the Raj's sphere of influence through a series of bold and effective campaigns, notably against the Sikhs in the 1840s. The Bengal Army's achievements in the first half of the nineteenth century, however, came as a result of an increasing reliance on high-caste recruits. This was a product of the army's administration tapping into existing local military labour markets. Such an exclusive attitude to recruiting proved disastrous in 1857 when mutiny among the sepoys combined with agrarian unrest to create a significant threat to British rule in India. Following the bloody suppression of the Mutiny the Company's army was absorbed into the forces of the Crown, beginning a process of an ever-growing formal British commitment to the region. As a result of the chaos seen in the mid-nineteenth century it was decided to increase the ratio of British to Indian troops in the Army in India.[6] Crucially, the financial cost of maintaining the British garrison rested with the Indian taxpayer, a matter that by the late nineteenth and early twentieth centuries was fuelling the growth of the inchoate nationalist movement.

The Army in India was designed to cope with a range of tasks. Its primary role was to serve as a defence force on the North-West Frontier, either repelling what the British perceived as a perpetually imminent threat from Russia, although one which dwindled after 1907, or dealing with the recalcitrant and bellicose trans-Frontier tribes.[7] The needs of defence against these irregular forces meant that much of the training regime was geared towards small-scale, counter-insurgency operations in mountainous terrain. In addition, the army was used to reinforce the Raj's authority in times of civil strife, although the paramilitary police force remained the principal source of internal security. The use of the army could prove disastrous in delicate cases of political or communal unrest, as demonstrated by Brigadier-General Reginald Dyer's bloody overreaction at Amritsar in 1919. Finally, the army was also called upon to act as an imperial 'fire brigade'. This role took on increasing importance between the Mutiny and the First World War, with Indian troops serving in operations from Aden through to China. Offers of military assistance during the Boer War were, however, rejected by the British, reflecting a deep-seated racial fear of using Indian troops to fight white settler communities. The army's three main roles were not compatible and left a number of senior military commanders with reservations about its abilities in the field.

Between 1902 and 1909 the mighty imperial figure of General Lord Kitchener towered over the army as its Commander-in-Chief. He instigated a wide range of reforms, which saw a rationalization of its administrative structures. Ultimately power came to be concentrated – unsurprisingly given Kitchener's megalomaniac tendencies – in the figure of the Commander-in-Chief. At a more prosaic level he carried out a systematic renumbering of Indian infantry and cavalry regiments and brought them on to the same footing. This reorganization was intended to leave enough men to serve on internal security duties while providing a force of nine divisions that could be deployed to fight on the North-West Frontier or to operate as expeditionary forces overseas. These reforms were complemented by the creation of an Indian General Staff in 1910, with Lieutenant-General Douglas Haig as its first chief. This represented a major innovation for British military forces in India. The General Staff effectively acted as the Indian Army's 'brain' devoted to planning for future wars, rather than concentrating on its internal security duties.[8]

Despite Kitchener and Haig's attempts to modernize the Indian Army, when it came to recruiting it was still guided by discourses developed during the nineteenth century.[9] The principal aspect driving recruitment was martial race theory, which had risen to prominence in the 1880s and 1890s as a means of selecting the supposed best recruits for military service. The ascendancy of this conceptual framework was largely a product of Lord Roberts's (Indian Army Commander-in-Chief, 1885–93) interest in constructing an army best adapted to fighting on the North-West Frontier. Consequently, he increasingly focused attention on a small number of martial groups from the north of India and Nepal. Only these communities, most prominently the Sikhs and Gurkhas, were thought to be capable of defending the Raj from external aggressors. Men from these areas were supposedly used to the rugged life of hill communities and could tolerate the inhospitable climate and terrain of the Frontier. These arguments were coloured with a racial dogma that saw the martial skills of these select groups as derived from their Aryan inheritance.

At the same time martial race theory had very practical origins. A number of the martial classes were admitted into the pantheon of military prowess after they had been conquered or subdued by the British, often following bloody and sustained resistance. Those groups who had resisted the British Army with the greatest vigour were felt to have demonstrated sufficient military acumen which could be remobilized in defence of the Raj. More importantly, having a balance of racial and religious groups in the army was intended to prevent a repeat of the Mutiny, as there would be less chance of these soldiers combining together to challenge British authority. Furthermore, the army's preference for illiterate recruits from rural backgrounds prevented the arguments of India's nascent nationalist movement gaining traction among the rank and file. To this extent the theory was highly beneficial, as there were relatively few cases of large-scale indiscipline between 1857 and 1914, and those incidents that did occur rarely saw expressions of nationalist sentiment.[10] Martial race theory was therefore merely a means of rationalizing practical recruiting decisions and integrating them into an overarching and coherent ideological framework. In addition, it is important to note that for many Indians a life in the army was not simply the product of one's martial identity, but a necessity to provide additional income with which to sustain relatives living in marginal agricultural areas. The contemporary fascination with martial race theory and the army's structures has come to dominate much of the historiography on the Indian Army. As Kaushik Roy has elucidated, this has had a myopic effect with the experiences of battle, the task for which the sepoys were trained, slipping from the frame of analysis; by focusing on social factors the sepoys' *raison d'être* has been forgotten.[11]

The desire to recruit only from martial races had a significant impact on the Indian Army's composition by 1914. The policy relied on drawing men from a small range of communities in a select part of India. It was a system that functioned adequately during times of peace or minor operations on the North-West Frontier, but was incapable of expansion to cover the losses that would be incurred in a major interstate war. The army's recruiting base was simply too narrow to sustain its manpower needs. In addition, Indian infantry battalions were smaller in size than their British counterparts, fielding only 764 men, providing a rifle strength of around 500. By comparison, a British infantry battalion could put at least 50 per cent more rifles into the field. Manpower was not the only problem that the army faced. A number of its difficulties stemmed directly from Kitchener's reforms, which resulted in Army Headquarters becoming overwhelmed with administrative concerns. Divisional commanders were similarly overworked, leaving them little time to train their troops for war.[12] There were also serious deficiencies in equipment, with two of the divisions in India having no mountain artillery. None of the divisions had enough Sappers and Miners, with only two companies allocated in each case. The signal service was similarly under-staffed and poorly organized. These difficulties in the technical arms were aggravated by the reluctance to recruit educated, middle-class Indians, for fear that they would spread nationalist ideas among the infantrymen.

Despite these problems the army was better prepared in 1914 for a major conflict than it had ever previously been. The Nicholson Committee of 1912 had begun to consider the Indian Army's role in a possible European war and its ability to maintain an expeditionary force during prolonged operations overseas.[13] Divisional manoeuvres, such as those carried out in 1912 between the 3rd (Lahore) and 7th (Meerut) Divisions, provided an opportunity for commanders and men to test their training and conceptual approaches to combat. General O'Moore Creagh, Indian Army Commander-in-Chief (1909–14), was impressed by the divisions' performance and offered effusive praise in his address to the senior officers involved:

> I am satisfied, gentlemen, that a great advance has been made towards the efficiency of the army for war. The requirements for war are now kept constantly in view, and the training is in consequence more practical, and therefore more interesting and that is reflected in the increased zeal and intelligence shown by all ranks. The conduct and spirit of the troops throughout has been most excellent.[14]

Critically, he emphasized the role of the division as the primary unit for combat operations in any future conflict. The manoeuvres provided an opportunity for all the various constituent arms of a division to learn to work together. The Indian Army may not, therefore, have been fully ready for the scale and intensity of the war that broke out in 1914, but it was beginning to think carefully about operations larger in scope than the counter-insurgency and tribal warfare of the North-West Frontier.

The Indian Army in the First World War

The Committee of Imperial Defence had only begun to consider using Indian troops for a future European war in 1913. By September 1914, however, India was the only viable source for the additional trained military manpower that was desperately needed on the Western Front.[15] In a series of bloody engagements the BEF was drained of a large proportion of its strength, with 75 of its 84 battalions mustering less than 300 men by the end of October. The Indian Corps, consisting of the 3rd and 7th Divisions, provided a useful stopgap to prevent the British contribution dwindling into insignificance. Indian units were thrust into the line in late October in a piecemeal fashion to help stem the German advance around Ypres. These brutal engagements, which saw some battalions lose over half their strength, were followed in 1915 by involvement in the battles of Neuve Chapelle and Loos, before the corps was withdrawn at the end of the year. Ultimately the Indian Army's engagement on the Western Front resulted in over 6,000 sepoys killed and nearly 16,000 wounded.[16]

The losses suffered by the corps put an enormous strain on the army's manpower resources. The difficulties stemmed from the fact that the reserve system had been neglected during the years of peace, and as a result contained many men who were not fit for active service. One survey of 5,250 replacements found that 876 of them were unfit for duty, of whom 50 had never even been on a musketry course. These problems were exacerbated by the need to find reinforcements who could be integrated into the specific racial structures of the army's regiments. Units were organized either as class regiments, where all the men were drawn from a single ethnic group, or as class company regiments, where each company was based on one group. As a result new drafts were often of the wrong class background and could not be properly integrated into the regimental community. If they were introduced they would find the culture and life alien from that which they had experienced in their previous unit. The losses in sepoys were matched by the horrendous toll taken of British officers, of which each battalion had only 13, including their medical officer. For example, the 47th Sikhs lost eight of their British officers in only two days of fighting at Neuve Chapelle in March 1915.[17] In total, the Indian Corps lost over 500 British officers during its service on the Western Front, having arrived in France with an initial complement of 220. These officers were even harder to replace, as there were few available in the reserve and a number of those who had been on leave in Britain at the start of the war had been poached to serve in Kitchener's New Army divisions. It also took a great deal of time to train men to become officers in the Indian Army, as they required a working knowledge of the language spoken by the men in their unit, as well as the army's lingua franca, Urdu.

The role of the Indian Corps on the Western Front has come to dominate much of the discussion of the whole Indian Army's contribution during the First World War. At the heart of this debate is an unyielding critique of its battlefield performance, and in particular the morale problems it suffered in 1914–15. Jeffrey Greenhut has made much of the high levels of self-inflicted wounds among Indian units, nearly all of which exceeded the rates among their British counterparts in the corps. He argues that this was a consequence of the sepoys undergoing a form of 'culture shock' on the Western

Front. These were men used to small-scale warfare on the North-West Frontier, not the mass slaughter of industrialized European conflict.[18] The regimental system in Indian units was constructed in such a way that the British officers came to occupy a prominent position. It was to their officers that the sepoys turned in 1914 to try to understand the war that they had been thrust into. The extensive casualties among the British officers meant that the Indian rank and file lost their cultural interpreters, which had a crippling effect on their morale. In many respects Greenhut's argument reflects that of Lieutenant-General George MacMunn, the great exponent of martial race theory, who emphasized the vital role of British officers in the 1930s, as a means to attack the proposed Indianization of the interwar army's officer corps.[19]

A range of historians have subsequently attempted to rehabilitate the Indian Army's reputation. In some cases this work veers towards panegyric, particularly when written by former officers of Indian units or colonial administrators such as Gordon Corrigan and Philip Mason.[20] In contrast, Alexander Watson's insightful analysis of the BEF's surrender rate in 1914 suggests that it was not just the Indian Corps that experienced morale difficulties on the Western Front. Rather than the loss of British officers creating problems in Indian units, an argument that is related to the specific ethnic character of the Indian Army, it is more likely that the sheer intensity of combat was producing problems across all armies serving in France and Flanders. The 'culture shock' of industrialized mass warfare was not confined to sepoys. Crucially, as George Morton Jack has noted, despite the heavy losses suffered by the corps it managed to fulfil the role for which it was intended. It served as an imperial manpower reserve until the TF and New Army divisions could be mobilized for the Western Front.[21] Once they were available the 3rd and 7th Indian Divisions could be moved to Mesopotamia, where the Indian military base would find it easier to support them.

These previous studies often fail to consider the wide range of combat experiences faced by Indian soldiers during the First World War, overemphasizing the experience of the Indian Corps in 1914–15 at the expense of other formations and theatres. In part this is a product of the limited range of source material relating to how sepoys saw their own military service and the wider war. The focus on recruiting illiterate peasants meant that only a minority of men in the Indian Army were able to produce substantial written accounts of their experiences. In a number of cases soldiers overcame this difficulty by using scribes or their literate comrades to write letters home to their families. Nevertheless, the censor of Indian mails at Boulogne was able to amass an extensive collection of letters, extracts from which were collated into a series of reports. These have allowed a number of innovative studies of the men of the 3rd and 7th Divisions and the Indian cavalry stationed on the Western Front.[22] However, this source base maintains the bias towards the European experiences of the Indian Army and the first two years of the war, rather than examining the other theatres in which it was involved across the whole course of the conflict. In the case of the Indian units in Egypt and Palestine a similar collection of records does not exist, as a centralized censorship scheme was only in operation during 1914 and 1915. After this the Indian forces in the region grew much larger and 'owing to the gradual increase in the bulk of such correspondence, the Indian Field Post Office could not undertake the work any longer'.[23] Censor's stamps were instead issued to units in the field who followed the devolved censorship system in British battalions, where junior officers assessed their men's mail.

Despite the lack of letters and diaries produced directly by sepoys in the EEF it is still possible to reconstruct their experiences in combat, providing a counterpoint to the Eurocentric accounts of the Indian Army's First World War. A similar attempt to tackle the forgotten experiences of the Indian Army has been made by S. D. Pradhan in his examination of the East African campaign. In addition, DeWitt Ellinwood has addressed elements of the Indian military experience in 1914–18 through the analytical lens of national consciousness.[24]

India's commitment to the war effort increased considerably as the war progressed. By 1915 India was burdened with maintaining a force in France, and also had sizeable expeditionary forces in Egypt and most importantly in Mesopotamia. By June of 1915 India had sent 80,000 men overseas.[25] Initially the military authorities tried to persevere with the pre-war system of recruitment. This was organized around 'direct enlistment' in which young men were recruited by individual regiments. It was also a class-based system, with recruiting officers going out to select men from the already heavily tapped martial races. The available manpower resources of particular districts were therefore not being utilized in an efficient manner, as different regiments would frequently compete for the same men. A colonel in the Amritsar district in November 1914 found himself to be one of 42 recruiting parties in the area. As a product of only recruiting from a restricted number of communities within India the number of men available for military service was beginning to dry up by 1916. Enhanced incentives were, therefore, introduced to increase the number of men who came forward. All the troops who served in Europe were given a 25 per cent increase in pay, and had their uniforms issued free. From January 1917 all combatants and some non-combatants received free rations, along with further pay and pension improvements. In addition, a bonus of 50 Rupees was given to new recruits from mid-1917 and a war bonus of 4 Rupees a month was issued from April 1918.

Incentives were not enough to maintain the supply of men required and in some areas bribes and force were integrated into the recruitment process. As the Indian Army's headquarters staff argued in a post-war report, 'a sudden expansion on a large scale was never anticipated, and such a measure under the conditions obtaining necessitated a revolution in the methods of recruitment hitherto in vogue'.[26] The shift in recruiting methods began in the United Provinces and the Punjab, where a territorial system of recruitment was adopted in 1916; a year later it was brought into use across India. Each division was given a recruiting officer aided by district assistants to tap the resources of a particular area. A recruiting board was set up in each province to coordinate the activities of these recruiting officers. In June 1917 a Central Recruiting Board was also created which set quotas for the districts to attain. These alterations to the recruiting structure, which formalized and centralized the system, had begun to produce significant results by the end of 1917.

Most importantly, the recruiting officers were now allowed to draw men from a much wider range of sources. By the end of the war 75 new classes, many of which were previously considered non-martial, were being enlisted. Some of these had been drawn on by the army in the nineteenth century and then dropped, but others were entirely new to soldiering. Groups such as Bengalis, who had provided no men for the army until mid-1916, were the source of 5,586 recruits during the rest of the war. Similarly, Brahmans, who were seen as problematic due to their high-caste requirements, only offered 558 recruits during the year up to 31 July 1915. However, in the year ending 31 July 1918 they contributed 11,884 men. Even Lieutenant-General MacMunn was prepared to accept that some of these new groups, a product of what he termed a 'mass production' method of recruitment, could prove themselves worthy of a place among the Indian Army's martial races. Despite the opening up of the recruitment system it still largely relied on a select number of groups within India. Many of the new classes that had been added were very similar to ones that the army already drew upon. Of the 740,000 recruits drawn in total from all classes during the First World War, over 136,000 were Punjabi Muslims, nearly 89,000 were Sikhs and over 55,500 were Gurkhas. The enlistment of men did not, therefore, fall evenly across all of India's population. By the end of the war the Punjab had been seriously taxed by the recruiters, providing 446,976 recruits, whereas Bengal had contributed just 59,052 men. This disparity is even more striking when it is considered that Bengal's population was over 46.6 million, whereas the Punjab's was only 20.6 million. Some states were drawn on more heavily to provide combatants and others non-combatants. Of Punjab's total only 97,288 were non-combatants, in comparison to the United Provinces' 117,565. By the end of the war the Punjab had provided 60 per cent of the 683,000 combat troops recruited, a staggering proportion considering that it only accounted for 6 per cent of India's population. This continued the pre-war trend towards the Punjabization of the Indian Army, which already drew 63 per cent of its men from the province in 1912.[27]

By 1918 India had developed a sophisticated recruiting machine, which incorporated the local administration and elites into its system, in order to exploit the full manpower resources of the country. A War Conference in Delhi on 27–28 April 1918, which was intended to demonstrate the unity of Indian opinion behind the war effort, set out to refine the process even further. In the year from 1 June 1918 India promised to contribute a further 500,000 men to the war effort. The recruitment reforms produced remarkable results. Prior to the war the army was only drawing in around 15,000 men a year, but in the year up to 31 July 1917 it managed to enlist 128,509 men. Significantly, it was in the following year that India fully exploited her manpower reserves, providing 292,174 recruits. The vast numbers of men provided by India during the war and the numbers promised for the future were even more remarkable as they were the product of a voluntary system. Despite the use of inducements and press gangs in some areas by 1918, the Government of India still remained vehemently opposed to any form of conscription, for fear of the political consequences.[28] Thus by the latter stages of the war India was truly fulfilling its intended role as an imperial manpower reserve.

The policy and practice of Indianization

These Indian troops were to prove critical to the British war effort during 1917–18 and in particular to the campaigns being fought against the Ottoman Empire. By October 1917 it was already clear that there was a severe shortage of British manpower on the Western Front, with General Henry Wilson estimating the deficit at around 25,000 men per month. The Cabinet's Manpower Committee, under Lloyd George, was set up on 6 December 1917 and reported that there was a total shortfall of around 600,000 men in the army.[29] The costly battles of 1916 and 1917, particularly those of the Somme, Arras, and Third Ypres, had taken their toll. As a result the BEF carried out a rationalization process in early 1918, involving the breaking up of 161 infantry battalions. These men then provided drafts for those units remaining in the divisions, which were now reduced to only nine battalions each.

In addition to this reorganization the vast numbers of men being recruited in India were also to be used to offset the British manpower shortage beyond the Western Front. The CIGS, General William Robertson, wrote to the Indian Army Commander-in-Chief, General Charles Monro (1916–20), on 4 December 1917 stressing the need for reinforcements. He stated that 'the question of maintenance of the British forces in the field has become critical and it may be necessary before long to begin reducing British Divisions'.[30] Robertson felt that the best way to prevent this would be to convert the divisions in Palestine into Indian divisions, where each brigade would have one British battalion and three Indian battalions. This would then free up British battalions to act as drafts for the EEF, reducing the numbers which had to be sent directly from Britain. Robertson stressed that it was the British Army's growing level of commitments by the end of 1917 that was creating these problems. In particular he pointed to the defeats suffered by the Italians, which had forced Britain and France to send six divisions each to stem the Central Powers' advance after the disastrous collapse at Caporetto in October–November 1917. Furthermore, he predicted that the Russian peace movement would allow the Germans to transfer 30 to 40 divisions to the Western Front in the near future, raising the prospect of the Allies having to fight a major defensive action. The deciding factor for Robertson was, however, a consideration specific to the imperial campaigns of the Middle East, namely the parlous state of the Turkish military effort:

> Our successes in Mesopotamia and Palestine have rendered this concentration more feasible, and I think we have over-rated Turkish power. Although our successes have upset the German-Turkish plans I doubt if they were ever so formidable as reports indicated, and some reports were probably intended to mislead us. In any case the chances are against any serious attack in Mesopotamia before next cold season. The Turk has, I believe, little desire to do any more fighting anywhere and he is short of men and deficient of other resources.[31]

He noted that the Turkish forces around Jerusalem, comprising a cavalry division and six infantry divisions, were seriously under-resourced only able to muster a total of 15,000 men. Terming the formations as divisions was in his opinion a misnomer. It was suggested that an Indian division should be released from Mesopotamia to travel to Palestine to reinforce the EEF and begin the process of Indianization. As a result, 7th (Meerut) Division was chosen to start transferring to Allenby's command in late December 1917. There were already a number of Indian battalions serving with the EEF, many of whom were on the lines of communication. Within the newly formed 75th Division there were five Indian Army battalions, and these had seen active service since the beginning of autumn 1917. 2/3rd Gurkhas and 58th Rifles, both of which had extensive experience on the North-West Frontier, had proved invaluable in the fighting in the Judaean Hills in November and December.[32]

The initial Indian Army response to Robertson's request for assistance was to offer four infantry battalions per month in March, April, and May 1918, along with a single pioneer battalion in March.[33] The Indian Army Commander-in-Chief, however, immediately offered a number of caveats on the provision of these extra units. Of the eight battalions to be sent in April and May at least two, in his opinion, would only be suitable for work on the lines of communication. In addition, he stressed that the greatest difficulty being faced in India was finding enough suitably qualified British officers to command the regiments and companies. As a short-term solution he asked the CIGS if any could be spared from the Indian Cavalry Corps then serving in France. By 14 December 1917 Monro had re-examined India's ability to contribute to the EEF and now offered a total of 21 battalions of which one would be a pioneer unit. This increase was to be found by using 'immature battalions' in India, in order to free up more experienced ones to serve overseas. The process of conveying these units to Egypt was also to be speeded up, with seven battalions dispatched by the end of January 1918, five by the end of March, three in April and a further five in May. Monro did express some concern at using newly formed regiments for internal security duties, particularly as the vast bulk of the Army in India was now made up of such inexperienced units. By early 1918 only 24 Indian battalions out of 69 then in service in the subcontinent had been in the army in 1914.

In early January 1918 Allenby was informed of the forthcoming changes that were to take place to the EEF. In addition to the 21 infantry and pioneer battalions ordered to Egypt he would also receive four machine gun companies and six Indian Field Ambulances.[34] Importantly, these new Indian battalions were established at a much higher strength than those that had been sent overseas in 1914. The 1/54th Sikhs left India with 1,070 officers and men in its ranks, and the 38th Dogras proceeded from Aden with a complement of 988 soldiers. Indian battalions were now being organized at a strength comparable to British battalions, allowing them to slot into existing formations much more easily. It was suggested by the War Office that these units would be used to convert Allenby's 10th and 75th Divisions into Indian formations, along with the replacement of three British battalions in 74th Division. By 10 March this policy had been extended to 60th and 53rd Divisions as well, in order to free up even more British troops. Those units that were to be replaced would then reinforce the British battalions remaining in the EEF. Thus 2/4th Dorsets were to provide drafts for the 1/4th Wiltshires who they had served alongside in 74th Division. In some cases these units would be broken up to provide drafts for battalions outside their division, as in the case of 2/10th Middlesex who were to go from 53rd Division to the 2/19th Londons of 60th Division. These units were not the end of Monro's response to the EEF's shifting manpower needs. He was confident that by the end of May another 26 battalions would be in the process of forming up in India. Alongside the 14 started in January and February this would provide 40 additional battalions to aid the Empire's war effort by the end of 1918. This reorganization was facilitated in part by the return of 22 battalions from service in East Africa.

Allenby did not just have to accommodate Indian infantry within the EEF. It was also decided to transfer the two Indian Cavalry divisions from the Western Front to Egypt. They had seen relatively little action in France, with the exception of Cambrai in 1917.[35] A total of eleven regiments were to be sent along with a divisional and three brigade headquarters staffs. The CIGS suggested that these Indian regiments be mixed with Yeomanry units to form mounted divisions. In total over 13,000 officers and men were being transferred from France to Egypt. For Allenby, however, it was not made clear as to whether these Indian units were to act as reinforcements or replacements within the EEF. The War Office itself was not sure of the course to be taken and instructed Allenby to be prepared to reduce his Yeomanry regiments and headquarters if necessitated by wider wartime manpower needs.

In order to try to inject some coherency into the campaigns against the Ottoman Empire, Lloyd George dispatched the South African general Jan Smuts to Egypt between 12 and 22 February 1918 to organize a plan to implement Allied strategic policy as set down in Joint Note 12. This had been produced by the Allied Supreme War Council on 21 January and stated that the Allies should launch an offensive to knock Turkey out of the war. Smuts produced his report on 1 March and recommended 'the adoption of a purely defensive role in Mesopotamia and the vigorous prosecution of the campaign in Palestine, and that Mesopotamia should feed Palestine reinforcements from the surplus beyond its reasonable requirements for defence'.[36] The CIGS was convinced that as long as an offensive was launched in Palestine the Turks would not be able to threaten the British gains in Mesopotamia. The Indian Army's Commander-in-Chief was not so content with this plan, as he felt Smuts' policy would impact significantly on India's Persian operations. General Monro opined that an offensive in Palestine could only fully ensure Baghdad's safety if it set Aleppo as its objective in order to sever the rail links that sustained Ottoman forces outside Anatolia.

This was a viewpoint with which Lieutenant-General Philip Chetwode, commander of XX Corps, agreed. In his opinion, Aleppo, which was over 360 miles from the British lines in early 1918, was 'the only really strategical objective, the possession of which would seriously damage the enemy'.[37] Monro was also concerned by Turkish progress on the railway into Mesopotamia. If this was completed he estimated that they would be able to move a division from Aleppo to Mosul in only 14 days. To move reinforcements up from India to Baghdad would take at least 40 days, and even worse if the men had to come from Suez it would take 53 days. As a result he urged the retention of 13th Division, made up entirely of British infantry, in Mesopotamia to act as a nucleus to expand upon with Indian battalions in an emergency situation. In addition, the British troops serving in Mesopotamia were also available as a reserve that could be utilized by the Government of India if serious internal unrest flared up. The removal of British battalions would only make it harder to maintain the correct proportion of British to Indian troops in the subcontinent. Monro's case was not helped by the views of Lieutenant-General William Marshall, commanding the expeditionary force in Mesopotamia. He stated that the removal of a single division or a complete Army Corps would have 'no adverse political effect' in the country.[38] The force was perfectly capable of redistributing its units to ensure the security of its lines of communication. As a result of these discussions the War Cabinet decided to send only one division to

Egypt, and suggested to Marshall that it should be 3rd (Lahore) Division. This would provide Allenby with another 25,000 officers and men, on top of the manpower boost received when 7th Division had been transferred to the EEF.

The long-term policy decisions on how best to employ the Indian Army's manpower in the war's periphery theatres represented an ordered response to the pressures upon the British war effort. The military situation on the Western Front, however, was now about to change dramatically, leading to a significant alteration to these plans for the Indianization of the EEF. On 21 March 1918 the Germans, now reinforced by units that had served on the Eastern Front, launched their first major offensive in France and Flanders for two years. It tore into the British 3rd and 5th Armies causing the abandonment of many positions and leaving several divisions in a state of collapse. British casualties on the first day amounted to 38,500 men, of whom 7,000 were killed and 21,000 captured. As Chetwode noted the 'offensive met with a most disconcerting success', and was followed by a series of further German operations along the Western Front in the spring of 1918 to maintain the pressure on the Allies.[39] The events in France had an immediate impact on the situation in the Middle East. On 27 March the War Office cabled Allenby ordering him to 'adopt a policy of active defence in Palestine as soon as the operations you are now undertaking are completed'.[40] Smuts' policy was rendered unworkable as the EEF was now to become a manpower reserve for the BEF. The War Office asked Allenby to send 52nd (Lowland) Division to France along with 7th Division's artillery as soon as shipping became available. By early April he was also required to send 74th Division to France and to continue with the Indianization of the four divisions selected in early March. This would leave 54th Division as Allenby's only all British division.

The War Office made it clear that the priority for Britain's war effort was now with the BEF: 'in France there is a very serious shortage of Infantry, and we must leave no stone unturned to increase the reinforcements in that theatre.'[41] The process of Indianizing the EEF would have to be accelerated in response. In addition to the 21 Indian battalions under orders at this stage for Egypt a further 13 infantry and 2 pioneer units would be required. The War Office continually put pressure on Allenby to release British units for the Western Front, even before they had been relieved by Indian battalions. It was estimated that the EEF would be able to provide 23,000 reinforcements for the BEF. The War Office was aware of the dangers that this could produce on the Palestine front:

> It is fully realised that this will entail loss of efficiency in your force and temporary reduction in strength, but in view of existing situation and of the fact that the Germans are concentrating every available man in the West this is a risk which should be taken and we are prepared to accept it.[42]

The priority of stabilizing the Western Front thus entailed risks being taken in the wider conduct of the war.

By May Allenby was very concerned by the vast scale of the reorganization that was taking place in the EEF as a result of the acceleration of the Indianization process after late March.[43] In consequence, he was reluctant to release Indian cavalry regiments to serve in India, and was able to persuade the War Office that any further reductions in his strength would have a detrimental effect. Allenby's concerns in early June were such that he called on Wilson to reinforce him with three or four Japanese divisions. Japanese naval forces already provided significant assistance in the Mediterranean guarding Allied shipping convoys, and Allenby's perception was that there were available 'lots of trained Japanese soldiers; spoiling for a fight'.[44] He was insistent that any troops provided must be well trained, in order to offset the deficiencies of some of his existing newly formed and inexperienced units, such as the Jewish Legion.[45] In addition, Japanese troops should provide their own transport so as to be fully mobile, thus allowing them to be integrated into Allenby's offensive plans for September 1918. Ultimately no Japanese soldiers were made available for service in the EEF, but Allenby's protestations make clear his concerns about the quality of the newly recruited sepoys.

These concerns reflected the fact that the drive among senior officers in the War Office and Indian Army was to maintain manpower levels rather than ensure that the troops in the field were as capable as possible. The Indian Army Commander-in-Chief in April 1918 suggested a means of rapidly increasing the size of the Indian force in the Middle East in order to free up more British troops. This involved taking one complete company from most of the Indian battalions allocated to Egypt and Mesopotamia, then combining them to form new units. Any shortages within these battalions would be filled by drafting in partially trained men direct from India. General Monro stated that 'this will weaken the units concerned temporarily but it is the only way of securing promptly the expansion wanted'.[46] The priority was to maintain the strength of the EEF, not the qualitative battlefield superiority it had developed by late 1917. This was a process that had been used in a limited fashion before in the EEF. In February 1917 the 101st Grenadiers was split into two battalions, with the original men and a new draft of nearly 400 troops divided equally between the two. These new units then carried out successful work on the lines of communication, demonstrating that recently formed Indian battalions were of military value.

As a result of Monro's suggestion seven battalions, numbered as Indian Infantry, were formed in the EEF over the course of the summer.[47] For example, the 2/151st Indian Infantry was created from companies drawn from 51st, 53rd, and 54th Sikhs, and the 56th Punjabi Rifles. Some attempt was made to ensure that these new units drew on battalions with reasonably similar class compositions, helping to facilitate the smooth cultural integration of the sepoys. The old battalions also provided the new ones with first- and second-line transport equipment, until they could be equipped with their own. Most importantly, they drew British and Indian officers, who had experience of active service, from the original units. The 38th Dogras provided 3/151st Indian Infantry with a commanding officer, two other British officers, two Subadars, and two Jemadars, alongside the 198 other ranks it transferred across. Some of the sepoys also had considerable military careers behind them. When 2/151st Indian Infantry provided a guard of honour for Allenby at Neby Saleh on 14 September 1918, the war diary was keen to note that on parade were men who had served on five fronts since 1914 and in eight pre-war campaigns. A similar policy was instigated in May among the Indian cavalry then serving in the EEF. Each regiment provided a squadron to fill the ranks of three newly formed units. Thus the 44th Indian Cavalry

Regiment comprised men from the 29th Lancers, 6th Cavalry and 2nd Lancers. Monro harboured deep concerns about this route towards Indianizing the EEF. He pointed to the fact that the class composition of some units, and in particular the difficulties of recruiting certain classes, would make it impossible to use their companies as the basis for creating new battalions.[48]

Despite these reservations the Indianization process continued, and plans were made to expand it even further. On 21 April 1918 the Indian Army was warned that it would be asked later in the year to Indianize four British divisions serving at Salonica, requiring another 36 infantry and 4 pioneer battalions.[49] It was not until early September that a request was placed for these units. Initial requirements were for only 12 battalions, although the War Office wished them to be 'experienced troops as they may have to take part in active operations very shortly after arrival'.[50] The rapid collapse of the Bulgarians in September 1918 intervened to prevent Indians serving on the Macedonian front.

India's manpower contribution to the British Empire's war effort was substantial, not least in its ability to reinforce the EEF when this was called upon to provide men for the Western Front. It took time for the Indian recruiting system to adapt to the needs of a modern war, but by late 1917 it was able to provide enough men to allow India to fulfil the role which had been envisaged for it before the First World War, that of an imperial strategic reserve. Contrary to many existing accounts of the Indian Army in the First World War, the process of Indianizing the EEF was not a direct product of the German spring 1918 offensives.[51] Instead it was a long-term policy that had its origins in the attritional nature of the conflict. The heavy cost of combat on the Western Front in terms of manpower meant that by late 1917 Britain had to increasingly lean on its Indian empire to offset these losses, by taking on the burden of sustaining the extra-European theatres of war. The crisis of March 1918 did not begin this process of Indianization in Palestine, but did alter the rate at which it was enacted.

India's growing share of the war effort demonstrated clearly the all-encompassing and global nature of the 'totalizing logic' of the First World War.[52] This saw an imperial society, although much removed from the bloodshed of the Western Front, experiencing ever increased levels of mobilization. The Indianization of the EEF thus ties those theatres of the conflict often described as 'sideshows' much more closely into the often Eurocentric interpretative framework of 1914–18 as a total war.

The difficulties of Indianization

The introduction of large numbers of Indian soldiers required the EEF's administrative structures to be reworked in order to deal with the requirements of the Indian Army. It was, for example, found necessary in 1918 to rapidly expand the Indian Field Postal Service to meet the needs of the sepoys in Egypt. Two Field Post Offices were attached to each brigade, one British and the other Indian, to serve their respective units. The scheme worked effectively with the Indian Post Service responding well to its vastly increased workload.[53] Organizational alterations did not always progress with such precision and alacrity. The commander of 1/101st Grenadiers, Lieutenant-Colonel

W. B. Roberts, was appalled by the state of the new drafts that reached him in Palestine. He laid the blame on the lack of rest camps designed to cater for the specific needs of Indian soldiers as they moved up to the line. According to Roberts, they should only be allowed to move up from Egypt if they were accompanied by a British officer of the Indian Army, who would be able to deal with the intricate problems of language and food requirements. A more pressing difficulty was the poor or obsolescent state of much of the equipment issued to Indian troops. The 38th Dogras arrived at Tel el Kebir training camp in February 1918 with 1914 pattern rifles, which they had acquired while serving in Aden. Similarly, new drafts for 1/101st Grenadiers often reached the battalion with 'boots that are certainly not Government pattern, but look like the cheap, badly made boots that are sold in all big Indian bazaars'.[54] The rapid increase in the size of the Indian Army had led to a number of compromises being made in the equipping of its soldiers. There were also concerns about the physical quality of the sepoys drafted to the EEF. When the 1/54th Sikhs and 38th Dogras marched from Ludd to Latron in April 1918 the pace had to be slow, as it was the first time that many of the men had carried packs and steel helmets while marching.[55] These administrative, equipment, and stamina concerns could all be solved given time, and were of a parochial nature compared to the main difficulty that exercised the minds of senior British commanders.

The critical problem with Indianization was that it introduced a considerable number of Muslim soldiers into the war against the Ottoman Empire in Palestine. Twenty-nine per cent of Allenby's new infantry was Muslim, raising deep fears that large numbers of men would side with their co-religionists and desert the EEF. Concerns had been raised over this matter since late December 1917, in particular relating to the Pathan members of the Indian cavalry regiments that were to be transferred to Egypt. Lieutenant-General E. Locke Elliot, serving on the BEF's lines of communication, wrote to Lieutenant-General H. V. Cox at the India Office expressing his worries about the employment of Muslim soldiers in Palestine. He pointed to the fact that 19 of the squadrons to be sent contained Muslim sowars, and that some predominantly Muslim units earlier in the war had displayed worrying pan-Islamic tendencies. In closing he noted that 'the men will be nearer the East; but whether they would be rather there killing Turks than further away killing Huns I can't say'.[56] The India Office did not share his concerns, as trans-Frontier recruitment had been stopped earlier in the war. Cox felt that if a squadron contained less than 50 per cent Pathans it would be worth giving it a try out against the Turks. Out of those regiments sent to the EEF the largest proportion of Pathans in any one of them was only 39 per cent. The Army Council, however, left it up to Allenby as to whether these men would be used in combat.

The fears of some officers were to a certain extent justified, as the Turkish Army saw the arrival of thousands of Muslim Indians as a chance to exploit any morale difficulties in the EEF. Turkish front-line patrols began to be accompanied by the regimental imam, who would sing holy greetings and prayers at the British lines. The regimental orders of 77th Turkish Regiment noted that this approach had proved successful, causing at least one desertion. It suggested that 'probably these men [the sepoys] being Moslems, will not fight against us; therefore it is advisable to choose from each Battalion and from each Company, men with good voices to accompany patrols at night'.[57] The war diary of 1/101st Grenadiers noted by June that singing of verses from the Koran was relatively frequent along the front, although the battalion had countered the Turks by carrying out patrols to prevent them operating in no-man's-land. The General Staff of 10th Division was nonetheless concerned by these Turkish attempts to encourage desertions. They suggested to the battalions of the division that they might try laying ambushes to round up Turkish patrols, or alternatively call artillery fire down on them. Even Allenby expressed concern at the activities of the Turkish Army in trying to sow unrest among the sepoys. In June he made clear to Wilson that anti-British propaganda spread by Turkish agents, as well as the activities of Turkish regimental imams, had the potential to harm the morale of Indian units. He argued that the British contingent in the EEF could not be reduced any further without playing into Turkish claims that Indian soldiers were being sacrificed in the Middle East in order to save British lives.[58]

The staff of XX Corps issued a number of memoranda in May 1918 stressing the need to counter Turkish attempts to subvert the loyalties of their Indian troops. They perceived that the greatest threat was likely to come when sepoys were on leave or training courses in Egypt, or when employed as guards over Turkish prisoners of war. Intelligence officers at Suez, Ismailia and Kantara had been instructed to look out for Turkish propaganda. The Government of India despatched an officer of the Criminal Investigation Department to aid the enquiries of the Intelligence Branch of the EEF's General Staff. In order to disabuse any wavering sepoys of ideas of desertion the EEF's military police toured front-line divisions providing them with photographs showing the appalling conditions Indian prisoners of war were being kept in by the Turks. The 10th Division's war diary noted dryly that this was 'the first case of propaganda having been distributed from behind'.[59] XX Corps was, however, equally concerned that too much concentration on the potential for disloyalty among Indian troops could be self-defeating, as it would lower the men's morale. The corps stressed to battalion commanders that care needed to be taken in these matters:

> The utmost discretion should be exercised in pursuing enquiries. Where it is considered advisable to enlist the assistance of selected Indian Officers and Other Ranks in detaching enemy propaganda, it should be made quite clear that prevention of the possible contamination of a few credulous individuals is aimed at, and that the loyalty of our Indian troops themselves is in no doubt whatever. Searching of the mails with a view to interception of seditious literature, where resorted to, should be done quite openly and the reasons stated.[60]

It was clear that if the sepoys became suspicious that a regular system of internal espionage was operating in their midst it could have as disastrous an impact as Turkish entreaties to them to desert.

The Indianization of the EEF was not, however, done in a cultural military vacuum; previous experience of organizing and running imperial armies was of critical importance to ironing out potential problems. Since 1857 the Indian Army had developed a tradition of assiduously caring for its sepoys' spiritual needs, which could be adapted to service in Palestine. In Sikh and Hindu units the military authorities encouraged the development of strong religious identities. Officers and men attended festivals together, which were incorporated into the collective memory of each regiment.[61] During the First World War the British took great pains to respect the religious and caste values of wounded Indian troops recovering in military hospitals in southern England. In addition, an Indian Soldiers' Comfort Fund was set up in October 1914 to provide the men with goods to help them cope with life at the front, such as socks and cigarettes. It sent out thousands of copies of the Koran and the Sikh holy books to units on the Western Front. The religious artefacts that were central to a Sikh's spiritual life, such as the *kora* (bracelet) and *kirpan* (comb), were produced in Sheffield and also shipped out in large quantities to France.[62] Following these examples care was taken to placate Muslim opinion within the Indian battalions in the EEF, by allowing the men to practise openly their faith. Leave parties were thus organized to Jerusalem to allow the sepoys to see its religious sites. In addition, after the end of hostilities small groups were taken from regiments to participate in the pilgrimage to Mecca. Despite these efforts, some officers were concerned that not enough time was given over for leave to allow Muslim troops to visit important religious sites while they had the opportunity to do so. Considerable care was taken throughout the course of the campaign to make sure that mosques, shrines and tombs were not unnecessarily damaged in the fighting. For example, once XX Corps had captured Nablus in September 1918 a strict prohibition was placed on troops entering the town, save for a guard on the Grand Mosque.[63] The intention was to portray the British Empire and the EEF as organizations that cared both for the spiritual needs of their men, but also the wider Islamic heritage of the region in which they were fighting.

The concerns over the loyalties of Muslim soldiers were largely unfounded. Most regimental commanders expected the sepoys to do their duty and were not disappointed. The 1/101st Grenadiers' war diary noted that 'from more or less tentative questions to Indian officers and others it is realized that the men are unlikely to be affected by enemy propaganda'.[64] There were relatively few instances of unrest in the Indian Army during the First World War, although the mutinies of the 5th Light Infantry at Singapore in February 1915 and the 15th Cavalry in Mesopotamia in February 1916 did cause considerable concern. Although both instances contained elements of pan-Islamic rhetoric among the sepoys' grievances, the outbreaks of indiscipline were 'due more to bad management than to religious fanaticism or racial proclivities'.[65] The EEF was fortunate to suffer a total of only 30 Indian desertions in 1918. The worst single occasion of indiscipline among the Indian troops occurred in June when a party of four Trans-frontier Pathans from 19th Lancers deserted. Although a minor incident, Allenby took the precaution of withdrawing the regiment from the front line and asked the War Office if they could be removed from Palestine altogether.[66] When considered in relation to the size of the Indian Army's contribution and the ease with which an individual could slip across to the Turks along the dispersed Palestine front these limited cases of desertion were insignificant. It is clear that the fears surrounding Indianization and the use of Muslim troops against their co-religionists were unfounded; the EEF's sepoys and sowars were prepared to fight for the British imperial cause in Palestine.[67]

Indianization in practice: 10th Division

In order to analyse fully the process of Indianization it is necessary to examine how it operated at lower levels of organization within the EEF, particularly among fighting formations. Historical analyses of Indianization have failed to address this aspect of the process and to question how sepoys were integrated into the army's structures and what the effects of these personnel changes were on the combat effectiveness of units. The best means of engaging with these questions is to consider the experiences of ordinary sepoys and British soldiers in a particular division, in this case 10th (Irish) Division. This was the first Irish division to be formed during the First World War and was part of Kitchener's New Army scheme. Initial recruitment was unsatisfactory with only one of its battalions, the 6th Royal Irish Rifles, gaining a sufficient number of men by the end of August 1914.[68] The division recruited from across the four provinces of Ireland and unlike the subsequent 16th (Irish) and 36th (Ulster) Divisions it did not rely on men from the rival volunteer forces. Its officer corps contained both middle-class Catholics and Anglo-Irishmen. In this sense 10th Division represented the national community of Ireland and bridged the often bitter confessional divide. The division was commanded by Major-General Bryan Mahon, famed for leading the flying column that had relieved Mafeking in the Boer War.

10th Division trained in Ireland and England before heading off to Gallipoli in late June 1915. Here the 29th Brigade served at Anzac, while the 30th and 31st Brigades landed at Suvla Bay to support 11th Division. The troops were engaged in heavy fighting during the division's stay at Suvla, with over 2,000 killed. 6th Royal Dublin Fusiliers alone suffered 69 casualties during the attack on Kiretch Tepe Sirt on 15 August.[69] 10th Division was pulled out of Gallipoli in late September and transferred to Salonica, from where it moved up into Serbia to take positions around Lake Dojran. Bitterly cold winter weather took as great a toll as the fighting, with over 1,600 men evacuated with frostbite and exhaustion. In contrast, the bloodiest battle the men took part in, at Kosturino, only left 300 dead.

By the end of 1915 the division was in need of reorganization and training. Mahon was promoted to command all British forces at Salonica and Major-General John Longley, formerly commander of 82nd Brigade, stepped in to replace him. Much of 1916 was spent building and occupying defences in the malarial Struma Valley, where sickness again became the biggest cause of casualties. In October 1916 the sick rate from malaria reached as high as 6,872 cases, rendering the division largely ineffective. As a result of the cumulative effects of battle and illness, the division was 25 per cent below strength by the end of 1916. Senior commanders stepped in to rectify the situation, transferring three regular Irish battalions (1st Leinsters, 1st Royal Irish Regiment and 2nd Royal Irish Fusiliers) over from 27th Division. These professional army units had been stationed overseas at the outbreak of the war, but had seen some service on the Western Front before moving to Salonica. During its time in Macedonia the division had also absorbed a large number of drafts from English units, notably the Norfolk and Bedfordshire Regiments, and the Oxford and Buckinghamshire Light Infantry. This was partly due to the poor level of recruiting in Ireland, with just over 13,000 men enlisting between January and August 1916 to meet a shortfall of nearly 18,000 across the three Irish divisions.⁷⁰ 10th Division was no longer to be a purely amateur force, nor would it be an all-Irish formation.

In August 1917 the division transferred from Salonica to Egypt, and on its arrival had to place over 3,000 men in hospital with malaria. Allenby inspected 10th Division and decided that it was still capable of taking to the field, and attached it to Lieutenant-General Chetwode's XX Corps for Third Gaza. The division received a further boost of new drafts, this time largely composed of English conscripts.⁷¹ On 5 and 6 November the division successfully assaulted the Turkish Gaza-Beersheba defences at the Wadi esh Sheria and the Hureira Redoubt. The latter action was relatively costly, with the 2nd Royal Irish Fusiliers losing 23 men killed and 99 wounded. The division did not engage in the pursuit of the Turks northwards and was only called back into the line on 1 December to relieve 52nd Division. The next few weeks were devoted to road-building, a task that the men had great experience of from their Macedonian service. In late December the division successfully repelled a Turkish attempt to retake Jerusalem and followed it up with a substantial advance across the rugged terrain of the Judaean Hills.

January and February 1918 were again taken up with the tedious task of road-building, a perennial part of operations in Palestine where the logistical infrastructure required constant maintenance to maintain the army's mobility. In early March the division successfully assaulted the villages of Atara and Ajul, which commanded the Wadi Jib. 1st Royal Irish Regiment became involved in extremely bitter fighting on 9–10 March, with several attacks needed to dislodge the Turkish defenders. Its losses over the two days amounted to 25 men killed and 85 wounded.⁷² By the end of April the cumulative effects of six months of combat had severely depleted 10th Division's rifle strength, with most battalions averaging around 500 officers and men, some being reduced to only two or three companies. 5th Connaught Rangers was in a particularly bad state, with only 329 other ranks left by 29 April. In the 1st Leinsters, 'A' Company was left with only 34 men after sending troops to be trained as Lewis gunners, so it was disbanded at the end of April and its men distributed around the remaining companies. It is clear that combat casualties were responsible for significantly reducing the strength of the division over the course of operations in 1917–18.⁷³ The attritional effects of modern war were beginning to catch up with Longley's soldiers.

It was therefore a logical decision to Indianize 10th Division, as it was unable to maintain its strength without these new units. During May six Indian battalions were introduced, relieving two battalions in each brigade. From 1 May the division officially ceased to be known as an Irish formation.⁷⁴ By the end of the month these new Indian battalions had taken over most of the division's front line, with 2nd Royal Irish Fusiliers being the only British unit left in the defences. In order to prevent the Turks discovering this reorganization, Longley instructed his battalions to maintain an offensive spirit by carrying out forward patrolling. The intention was to ensure pressure on the Turkish troops opposite the division was maintained. The relief of some of the Irish battalions allowed a number to be transferred to the Western Front. Some of these battalions served with the BEF as complete entities, such as 5th Royal Irish Fusiliers, whereas others were used as drafts for their regiment and spread across a number of battalions, as was the case with the 5th Connaught Rangers. Alternatively, the relieved units were used as reinforcements for the three regular army battalions remaining with 10th Division in Palestine. Thus 6th Royal Irish Rifles provided men for 2nd Royal Irish Fusiliers, 1st Leinsters and 1st Royal Irish Regiment. Later in the summer three more Indian battalions were introduced, one for each brigade. Of these only one, the 2/151st Indian Infantry, had been formed in the Middle East. It reflected many of the problems these newly created units experienced in 1918 as they rapidly adapted to service in the EEF. When 29th Brigade's commander inspected it on 11 June he found that it was still short of officers, specialists and a battalion headquarters staff.[75]

Many of the Indian battalions shared 2/151st Infantry's difficulties, having donated companies for the formation of new units and then receiving briefly trained new drafts in return. In order to prevent such problems impacting on the combat effectiveness of the division, the new Indian battalions were slowly integrated into the front line. Thus 74th Punjabis sent two of its companies to serve with the 2nd Royal Irish Fusiliers in late May to gain two days of experience, and were followed by the battalion's remaining companies.[76] Similarly, 1st Leinsters acted as tutors to companies of 1/54th Sikhs and 1/101st Grenadiers. 1/54th Sikhs also sent 1 Indian officer and 12 other ranks each night to join patrols of the 6th Royal Irish Rifles, in order to learn the difficulties of such work in the division's sector. In 30th Brigade the new Indian battalions were used to help construct strong points along the defences. This was in order to give them 'every opportunity to become acquainted with the system of defence, detail of the line, ground in front, routine, trench duties'.[77] The commanding officers of battalions also shared local tactical information, with the 5th Connaught Rangers' commander interviewing the commander of 1/54th Sikhs prior to them taking over the line.

This system of gradually introducing the sepoys to combat in Palestine allowed the division to utilize the experience accrued by the officers and men of its Irish battalions over six months of fighting in the region. This could be passed on to the Indian battalions, allowing them to integrate smoothly into the brigade and the divisional structures. In addition, it provided the three remaining British battalions with a chance to learn how they would operate alongside these new units. This was a managed process of Indianization at the front line, which demonstrated the extent to which middle-ranking and senior EEF officers had got to grips with the problems of training men for battle by 1918.

The Indianization of 10th Division was not always a seamless process. 7th Royal Dublin Fusiliers were alarmed to find that the quartermaster of 1st Kashmir Infantry spoke no English, which did not facilitate the process of handing over the battalion's equipment.[78] Some British soldiers also found it hard to adjust to the peculiarities of the Indian Army division in which they were now serving. Private W. Knott had served as a medical orderly with 10th Division since its inception in 1914. After a brief spell at Kantara he returned to one of the division's new combined field ambulances, and was struck by the contrast in organization. He was informed that the British staff no longer did any manual labour, all of which was left for the Indians to perform. The strictures of the caste system also left him bemused, with washermen, water-carriers, and sweepers all having their own specific tasks, and none being capable of doing anything other than their allotted role.

In the division's signal service the introduction of Indian troops had a significant impact upon its ability to conduct operations. On the arrival of the new battalions each one had been given four British signallers to assist its Indian signallers, who were not considered to be up to the required standard. Major M. E. Webb, commanding the 10th Divisional Signal Company, was particularly dismayed at the inability of Indian signallers to read or write running hand, and as a result all telegrams had to be written in block capitals. He estimated that he would need six to nine months to train the signallers to be proficient, longer if they could not read English. In order to overcome these difficulties he recommended forming a mixed brigade of signallers, with each section containing 28 British and 16 Indian troops. As desirable a policy as this was from Webb's point of view, he was acutely aware that 'there may be serious objections to this mixing of native and British personnel'.[79] Nevertheless, he persevered with his scheme and began mixing Indian and British signallers in May. Some battalion commanders were concerned by the problems over communications and even refused to be responsible for their posts unless a British signaller was present. By the end of July Webb's programme of cross-posting and intensive training had begun to rectify the deficiencies, with some of the Indian signallers being capable of buzzing at a rate of 15 words a minute, matching the basic standards of the signal service.[80] The case of the signal company illustrates the operational problems that could arise from the widespread introduction of insufficiently trained and inexperienced Indian troops into the EEF. Crucially, these difficulties were overcome by a strong emphasis on thorough training which pervaded the EEF from Allenby and the general staff down to the level of the section.

Training for war

10th Division saw itself as a learning institution, constantly adapting to the shifting challenges encountered in war against the Turks. This ethos was propagated through a number of memoranda which analysed recent operations. These set out any problems encountered and which tactics or equipment had proved of particular value. The reports could also be highly scathing of failures in the conduct of operations by particular units. Major J. R. Cartwright, serving on the division's general staff, criticized troops who reported themselves as being 'held up by machine gun fire'. He saw this simply as an excuse used by indolent infantrymen who felt it was the job of the artillery to knock out enemy positions in order to allow the infantry to march in unopposed. His report stated that 'it must be the aim and object of all ranks to carry that attack through with the utmost determination by use of L.[ewis] G[un]'s and most particularly the rifle and bayonet'.[81] The intention was to instil in the division an aggressive combat ethos, in which the infantry would lead the way in combined arms assaults on Turkish positions. These reports served as a means of adapting overall doctrine in the British Army and the EEF to suit the tactical specificities faced by the division and its brigades. In 31st Brigade, the Brigade Major, Captain Hickman, set out a detailed training programme. He insisted on the use of two texts to guide the education of the men: *The Training and Employment of a Platoon, 1918* and *Training and Employment of Divisions, 1918*. 10th

Division was thus imbibing the latest tactical lessons from operations on the Western Front, reflecting the extent to which the whole of Britain's imperial army across all fronts by the last year of the war had adapted to the complexities of a modern, industrialized war. Hickman pointed out that platoon and section commanders were to be taught to prepare for open warfare, and emphasized that 'all training is to be carried out with a view to the offensive'.[82] This perpetuated the aggressive ethos originating at divisional level.

It was through practical field exercises that these doctrinal approaches were passed down to the sepoys. In late August 1918, 30th Brigade carried out a series of field manoeuvres, with 1st Royal Irish Regiment working closely alongside the 1st Kashmir Infantry. These exercises were intended to prepare the men for forthcoming operations, and involved learning how to move across country at night, how to work to a timetable, the use of visual and runner communications and the ability to keep in touch while in extended formations in the dark. There was also a desire to make training as realistic as possible. In order to prepare 'C' and 'D' Companies of the 2/101st Grenadiers for combat an artillery barrage was called down just in front of their sangars. This gave them a taste of what it would be like to work in close proximity to bursting shellfire. Not all of the men's training was quite so harrowing. In August a competition was instituted among the battalions of XX Corps to find the best man at assembling a Lewis Gun while blindfolded.[83] This encouraged a healthy sense of inter-unit rivalry, as well as developing the men's weapon handling skills.

This emphasis on the constant refinement of the soldiers' abilities found a receptive audience in many of the Indian battalions drafted into 10th Division. Prior to moving up to northern Palestine, 1/101st Grenadiers spent five days training at Gaza. Here they practised basic infantry skills, such as musketry, company and battalion drill, and more sophisticated tactics, including artillery formations, and platoon and company assaults under the cover of Lewis Gun fire.[84] This emphasis on the range of infantry skills persisted once battalions had joined the division. 46th Punjabis constructed a detailed training regime during July 1918 to ensure that the men were kept constantly prepared for combat. Each day began with 30 minutes of physical training, followed by three 1-hour classes in the morning and a further 2 classes in the afternoon. The subjects included squad drill, fire control and discipline, rapid loading, throwing of dummy bombs, and the judging of distances. In addition, they were given lectures on the use of bombs, care of arms and on the war in general. The training schemes developed by individual units continued the focus on infantry skills begun at divisional level through an intensive practical military education programme.

In some instances, however, troops were not being prepared for operations that bore much resemblance to the front-line work of the EEF. On 21 March 1918, 2/101st Grenadiers took part in a brigade field day, based around the idea of convoying treasure to a garrison and having to resist attacks by small bands of Arabs.[85] Such training, although rare, was better suited to preparing the sepoys for life on the North-West Frontier rather than combat in the Judaean Hills. In many respects this demonstrates that some officers still saw the need for Indian Army units to develop the techniques that would be of use in post-war operations to protect the Raj. These sepoys were not just training for war in Palestine, but to acquire the multiplicity of skills needed by

Indian soldiers to meet the diverse range of operational scenarios the Indian Army could face.

The arrangements for training were not always satisfactory and difficulties could hamper the development of the men's soldierly abilities. The 1/54th Sikhs found that while at Tel el Kebir camp in Egypt during April 1918, they only had a limited amount of equipment available for exercises. Some of the men had not even been able to fire their new rifles since being issued with them a month earlier. In 1/101st Grenadiers the shortages of training weapons became so severe that the unit's armourer produced dummy Lewis Guns out of tins for use in practice attacks.[86] Of greater concern to Indian battalion commanders was the poor quality of specialist training for sepoys provided at the Zeitoun School of Imperial Instruction, in Cairo. This was supposed to be the EEF's premier instructional centre preparing selected officers and men in the key techniques for achieving battlefield success. Lieutenant-Colonel Roberts, commanding the 1/101st Grenadiers, wrote scathingly of the institution. He believed that its standards were far below those at the regular Indian Army Schools of Instruction in India, where the training was conducted by Indian and British officers who were experts in their field. In contrast, the instructors at Zeitoun were selected by retaining men from front-line units after they had passed a course of instruction. Roberts opined that 'Indian officers, N.C.O.s and men frequently complain that the Indian instructors at Zeitoun although knowing their subject well are quite unable to teach men of their own standing in Rank and Experience – How to Instruct as Instructors'.[87] Major S. G. Beaumont, in temporary command of the battalion in June, followed up on Roberts's complaints by filing a report based on interviews with six NCOs who had recently returned from courses at Zeitoun. These sepoys offered vociferous criticism of the organization and operation of the school. They stated that many of the instructing NCOs were young and frequently made mistakes. They found many of the lectures to be very poor and below the standard of those given by officers of their own regiment. Crucially, they evinced a dislike for the instructors based on the fact that many of them had recently gained temporary promotions and as a corollary their egos had become inflated. For the NCOs of 1/101st Grenadiers, many of whom were senior in rank and service to these instructors, the condescending attitude they experienced from the Zeitoun staff made it hard for them to learn.

The traditional service-based prejudices of the Indian Army thus undermined the value of centralized training schools such as Zeitoun. Moreover, these complaints provide evidence that not every element of the EEF's organization was fully prepared to deal with the process of Indianization. The protestations found in 1/101st Grenadiers' war diary over the problems of training could be perceived as a reflection of difficulties within this battalion rather than the wider EEF. During 1917 it had lost its original commander, Lieutenant-Colonel W. J. H. Hunter, who was considered by his superiors to be a poor leader of men and to have adversely affected the training of his Indian troops.[88] Consequently Roberts and Beaumont may have been trying to shift the blame for training deficiencies from their shoulders on to the instructors at Zeitoun. Nevertheless, the emphasis on military education and development found in 10th Division may have arisen from a need to compensate for failings within the central EEF training system in Egypt. The division, brigades, and individual battalions could better tailor their training to the specific requirements of their men and the combat arena in which they would be operating.

Training through combat

Theoretical exercises were of little use to the men of 10th Division, both Indian and British, unless they could gain combat experience in order to further refine their military skills. One means of achieving this was through regular patrolling of the area in front of the division's line. In a memorandum on the principles of defence, the division's general staff reinforced their belief in the need for an aggressive front policy. It stated that by night the troops should seek to gain mastery of no-man's-land through 'bold and constant patrolling'.[89] This emphasis on challenging the Turks for control of the Judaean Hills on a daily basis was reinforced at brigade level. Captain Hickman, Brigade Major of 31st Brigade, emphasized in a memorandum on patrolling that constant touch should be kept with the enemy. If the Turks attacked then they were to be pushed back and pursued to their lines, in order to keep a watch on them and to gain positions of tactical importance. He noted that 'by means of efficient patrolling it will be impossible for any attack by the enemy by day or night to come as a surprise'.[90] By dominating no-man's-land the battalions would help to secure the brigade's front, but would also learn the tactical skills necessary to defeat the Turks in combat.

The British units of the division took the lead in instigating this aggressive ethos. A patrol of 2 officers and 16 other ranks from 2nd Royal Irish Fusiliers was involved in attacking a Turkish post on the dominant position of the Ghurabeh Ridge on 16 July 1918. The patrol skilfully avoided becoming engaged in a protracted fire fight with the Turkish defenders once they were discovered, and instead called down an artillery barrage on the position.[91] The patrol's shrewd work elicited praise from the brigade commander. This use of overwhelming force would have left the Turks in little doubt as to who controlled this particular stretch of front. Moreover, the operation demonstrated that the division had adapted to the combined arms nature of operations, able to integrate artillery with localized infantry patrols.

The Indian battalions set out to emulate the standard of aggressiveness laid out by the divisional and brigade staffs, and demonstrated by the British units that served alongside them. An observation party of 1/54th Sikhs sent to occupy Khirbet ed Deir in July found that the position was already held by a Turkish post. A short skirmish ensued in which the Lance Naik in command was wounded and the patrol forced back. Rather than allowing the Turks a minor victory a second patrol was sent out, this time consisting of a platoon, which used two sections to work round the Turk's left flank and drive them off the hill.[92] The battalion was thus challenging for the domination of no-man's-land as expected by the doctrinal emphasis of the division. Such encounters had a cumulative psychological effect on the Turks' morale. In August, a 30-man patrol from 1st Kashmir Infantry ran into a force twice its size at Ain Naffa. A short fire fight ensued which culminated in the Kashmiris charging their opponents, who fled precipitately. A month later, when a company of 1/54th Sikhs raided Khirbet Keys, the Turks decamped before the sepoys could even reach them. Over the course of the summer the Indian infantry battalions had absorbed the division's combative ethos and were in clear control of no-man's-land able to carry out patrols at will. Critically, these practical experiences of combat allowed the sepoys to develop a belief in their own professional military abilities. It was clear that they could defeat the Turks in small patrol encounters; all that remained was to refine and test their combat skills and morale in larger operations.

On the night of 12–13 August 1918, 29th Brigade launched a large-scale raid, involving three infantry battalions, on the Turkish defences along the 5,000-yard-long El Burj-Ghurabeh Ridge, which straddled the Jerusalem-Nablus road.[93] The plan was based on a scheme developed by the General Staff of XX Corps, with very little modification added at divisional level. Two columns of troops, each consisting of an Indian battalion, would assault opposite ends of the ridge. Each of these attacks would be followed up by two companies from a British battalion, which would turn inwards and assault into the Turkish defensive works. The defending force was estimated at around 800 rifles and 36 machine guns, drawn from the 33rd Regiment of the Turkish 11th Division, one of the better-trained and more cohesive units in the Ottoman Army in Palestine. Preparations for the operation were meticulous and extensive, with 29th Brigade pulled out of the front line on 20 July to hone its skills. A training ground was built by the 72nd Sappers and Miners before 10th Division had even been allocated the mission, a task which had taken fatigue parties numbering over 400 men 4 days to complete. It consisted of a series of dummy works which were repeatedly assaulted in order 'to get the men fit and handy tactically'.[94] The divisional commander and his staff watched a number of rehearsals, which allowed different tactical approaches to be tested, not all of which proved successful. In order to familiarize the men with the actual ground over which they would be fighting, two cars and a lorry were given to the brigade to take officers and NCOs on reconnaissance visits to the front line. Although the plan for the operation was complex, after three weeks of training the men of 29th Brigade were confident in their abilities to carry it out precisely.

Just before 10 p.m. on 12 August the division's artillery shelled the Turkish defences in a short 15-minute barrage. Prior to this the two assaulting Indian battalions, 1/54th Sikhs and 1/101st Grenadiers, had advanced to their deployment areas. As they moved up a single gun on each flank had fired shells at 15-second intervals in order to muffle the sound of the infantry. To further disguise the noise of the assaulting troops, the men were equipped with felt-soled boots, which were 'invaluable and contributed greatly to the success of the operation'.[95] Further precautions were taken to mask the objective of the raid by having the 2/101st Grenadiers carry out a series of aggressive patrols on 11 August, in order to distract and confuse the Turks. The 1/54th Sikhs and 1/101st Grenadiers moved up close behind the barrage, and then pushed through the Turkish wire, either through gaps cut by the shells or by using double-jointed ladders designed to cross large defensive wire belts. 1/101st Grenadiers found that it took them longer to deploy than in training, which led to criticism being voiced by the commander of the 1st Leinster's left wing attack, who felt that the Indian battalion was 'astonishingly slow'.[96] The Grenadiers' commander, Lieutenant-Colonel Roberts, countered that given the nature of the ground it would have been almost impossible for his men to have advanced any faster. Despite these delays the two Indian battalions broke into the Turkish defences causing mayhem among the defenders. 1st Leinsters followed behind mopping up any posts that had not been silenced before smashing into the flanks of the central defences along the ridge. The Turks put up a stout resistance, but wasted much of their attention on firing to their front, failing to take account of the brigade's tactical dexterity, which had allowed them to attack the defences from the flanks. At midnight the assault was brought to a halt and the British and Indian infantry withdrew from the ridge in an orderly fashion.

The divisional staff estimated that the raid had caused around 450 Turkish casualties, in addition to the 239 prisoners of war captured. 29th Brigade also removed 13 machine guns and 1 automatic rifle from the ridge. The losses to the assaulting battalions had been relatively light given the confused and close quarter nature of much of the fighting in the dark. 1/54th Sikhs and 1st Leinsters lost only 32 and 31 men respectively, the 1/101st Grenadiers suffered much worse with 82 casualties.[97] The troops' success elicited much praise from across the EEF's higher echelons. Brigadier-General E. M. Morris, temporary commander of 10th Division, referred proudly in his report to how 'the operations were carried out with great precision and without confusion in spite of the darkness and difficulties of terrain'.[98] The head of XX Corps, Lieutenant-General Chetwode, was effusive in his praise of the battalions' 'gallantry and determination', as well as the division's excellent training arrangements.[99] It was these detailed preparations that set the raid apart from other operations and proved crucial to its triumph. The division's report noted that:

> The training over the dummy trenches was so valuable that the troops had no difficulty in finding their way about the enemy's positions. The training was carried out by drilling the troops and manoeuvring them over the practice ground at the work which they were intended to carry out. It was impressed upon them that the ground was not exactly similar to the enemy's positions. By this training they were able to become perfect at their tasks and learn to do the work silently and with great speed.[100]

The division's ethos of constant refinement prepared the sepoys and British troops to the highest degree possible for the operation they were to undertake. The intention of XX Corps with this scheme was to foster trust between the newly arrived Indian units and their British counterparts. Not only could they fight alongside the Irishmen of 1st Leinsters, but they could also operate within a larger brigade-controlled operational plan. The El Burj-Ghurabeh raid 'was, in essence, a graduation exercise in a cohesion building programme'.[101] Crucially, it demonstrated that the Indian battalions were now capable of taking part in large-scale assaults.

The night attack on 12–13 August was very similar to the attacks that the division would make just over a month later as part of the battle of Megiddo, which involved brigades operating as independent formations. As Mark Connelly has argued in his study of battalions of the East Kent Regiment on the Western Front, 'in static positional warfare raiding was the only way to test and sharpen infantry skills short of major offensive operations'.[102] The tactical achievement of 29th Brigade was so marked that the raid would later come to be featured in a late Cold War study of night operations by the American Army's Combat Studies Institute at Fort Leavenworth, with it being the only non-American example to be analysed.

In both the patrols and raids carried out by 10th Division it was clear that the Indian officers occupied an important place within their battalions. These men had considerable amounts of military experience behind them, having served in the Indian Army for a number of years. They helped to translate the division's aggressive ethos into small-scale tactical operations that the largely illiterate sepoys could understand. Importantly, they also held a senior position of authority within their regimental community, acting in effect as village elders and intermediaries between the institutional framework of the Indian Army and the rank and file soldiers. It was not only the sepoys who turned to them for advice. The British company commanders of 1/101st Grenadiers were instructed to consult their Indian officers in order to allay any fears that pan-Islamic ideology was filtering through to the ranks.[103]

It was in combat, however, that their personal leadership skills came to the fore. Indian officers frequently demonstrated tremendous reserves of courage, as with the exploits of Subadar Rahim Khan, who single-handedly assaulted a Turkish post while leading a patrol. Often Indian officers continued in their work even though they were badly wounded. Subadar Bhikkam refused medical treatment until his platoon had taken the position it was tasked with assaulting on 20 September, remaining with his men for 4 hours after receiving his first injury.[104]

Acts of personal bravery and endurance under fire may have reflected the strong cultural emphasis within the Indian Army on *izzat* (personal honour). Indian officers would have perceived their duty as encompassing displays of aggressive leadership to their subordinates, and failure to do so would similarly have produced powerful negative psychological motivations of shame. Although many studies, not least the work of David Omissi, emphasize the peculiar role of *izzat* in the motivational culture of the Indian Army and private emotional world of its sepoys, it is, however, misleading to overemphasize this as a unique concept. Most armies throughout history have fostered hyper-masculinized cultures of honour in order to motivate their junior leaders and rank and file soldiers to perform risky acts of valour or extreme violence. Moreover, as Santanu Das has suggested, it is important to stress the multiplicity of interpretations among Indian soldiers of the often complex notion of *izzat*. It was not a static concept and was in a state of flux in 1914–18, being reshaped in response to the experiences of a modern, industrialized war.[105]

In the case of the EEF's Indian officers, personal bravery was frequently combined with demonstrations of professional military skill, revealing an astute grasp of the tactical situation that their men faced. Indian officers were frequently praised for the initiative they demonstrated while under fire and in response to changing situations. On the night of 30–31 May, a patrol of 1/101st Grenadiers heading towards Kurawa ibn Zeid was able to work their way quietly past a Turkish post in order to assault it from the rear. Their stealthy approach allowed them to seize all of the Turkish defenders and their equipment without a shot being fired. The brigade war diary attributed this success to the skill with which the Indian officer commanding the patrol had handled the situation.[106] Indian officers thus demonstrated the technical skills expected of junior commanders, helping to manage the unpredictability of the tactical battlespace for their soldiers.

It was not just in minor operations that Indian leadership was demonstrated. During the division's advance in September 1918 a number of Indian officers were highlighted as having taken on extensive battlefield roles. In the 2/101st Grenadiers' attack on Kefr Haris, Subadar Jiwan Khan played a central part in the success of the operation. He was under constant machine gun fire for 9 hours yet remained at his post with the men. Captain H. M. K. Tracey, commanding 'B' Company, noted that Khan had a 'most excellent grasp of the situation' and organized the stout defence mounted on Sheikh Othman. The report recommending him for the Military Cross stated that 'it is hardly an exaggeration to say that the success of the whole attack was largely due to him'.[107] These examples of the gallantry and leadership abilities of Indian officers at regimental level stand in direct contrast to the vitriolic nature in which Jeffrey Greenhut attacks their conduct on the Western Front. To a certain extent he is simply reworking the skewed racial prejudices of the late nineteenth and early twentieth centuries, which placed the British officer at the heart of the Indian Army's combat effectiveness.[108] In Palestine, however, it was clear that men like Subadar Jiwan Khan were perfectly capable of carrying out to a high standard the command and leadership roles they were given. Lieutenant-General Chetwode, who in the interwar years would become one of the most radical and outspoken of Indian Army Commanders-in-Chief, realized the value of these Indian officers. In early September 1918 he invited the Subadar-Majors from all of the Indian battalions in XX Corps to tea and a tour of Jerusalem. This helped to reinforce the personal leadership bonds between the senior commander and the men he was going to ask to lead his sepoys into battle. The performance of the Indian Officers of XX Corps thus lay at the heart of the formation's combat effectiveness.[109]

The Indianized EEF in battle

The ultimate test of the sepoys came in September 1918 when Allenby decided to launch his climactic attack at Megiddo intended to finally smash the Ottoman Army in Palestine. The initial infantry assault involved four Indian divisions plus the all-British 54th Division of Bulfin's XXI Corps smashing into the Turkish defences on the Plain of Sharon and in the Judaean foothills. After only a few hours of combat, Turkish forces were in full retreat, opening a gap which was then exploited by the DMC. XX Corps, containing 10th and 53rd Divisions, did not begin its attack on the enemy line until late on 19 September. Chetwode's objective was to drive the Turks out of the easily defended Judaean Hills and to reach Nablus, thus maintaining the pressure on the collapsing Turkish position. 10th Division's initial assault was well planned and broke through the first line trenches on the El Burj-Ghurabeh ridge. In many respects this was merely a divisional rerun of 29th Brigade's raid from 12 August. As the division advanced on 20 September it ran into stiffer resistance based around the hills at Ras ed Dar, Iskara and Haris. After heavy fighting the 31st and 29th Brigades were able to outflank the Turks and continue their advance.

It was the endurance of the sepoys that stood out during these operations, with many units marching and fighting continuously for 48 hours, with little additional food and water beyond what the men could carry. Of the division's battalions only 2/42nd Deolis faltered, on 20 September at Ras Aish. Here the Turks mounted a tenacious defence which ground the Deolis' assault to a halt. By midday they were strung out along the hill and were running short of ammunition. A further attack in the early afternoon ran into machine gun and artillery fire and failed to dislodge the Turks. However, the brigade commander, Brigadier-General Morris, was able to utilize his other battalions to assist the Deolis. 74th Punjabis were brought up to reinforce their line and 2nd Royal Irish Fusiliers then attacked to force the Turks out of Ras Aish.[110] This action demonstrated the ability of the Indian and British battalions to cooperate within brigade-level combined arms operations in order to advance towards the overall objective. On 21 September the division pushed ahead as Turkish resistance rapidly began to crumble and eventually reached the Balata gorge north of Nablus, cutting off the Turkish Army's final route of retreat towards the Jordan Valley.

In two days of continuous fighting the division had covered over 20 miles of difficult country. Its casualties had been relatively light, with only 3 officers and 103 other ranks killed, and 17 officers and 683 other ranks wounded.[111] The division's achievements were all the more remarkable considering that for six of its Indian battalions this was essentially their baptism of fire in major operations. Lieutenant-General Chetwode was quick to thank his troops for their efforts. In a message to XX Corps he drew particular attention to the work of 30th Brigade under Brigadier-General F. A. Greer, notably the way in which it had ignored the Turkish forces on its flanks in order to drive further northwards towards Nablus, thus maintaining the momentum of the EEF's assault. He concluded by congratulating the newly formed Indian battalions on their fine work. Acclaim for the sepoys also came from George V, who placed their fighting qualities alongside those of the British infantry, creating a common standard of British imperial military performance.[112] The Indianized 10th Division by the end of September 1918 had fully demonstrated its combat capabilities. It was able to advance rapidly over difficult terrain and engage in a wide range of tactical and operational scenarios, from which it emerged victorious. All of the six Indian divisions of the EEF performed to a similarly high standard at Megiddo, opening up the way for the British, Australian and Indian cavalry of the DMC to complete the rout of the Turkish forces. The campaign in Palestine stands as one of the triumphs of the Indian Army in the First World War, paralleling Lieutenant-General Stanley Maude's success a year earlier against Ottoman forces in Mesopotamia. On the Plain of Sharon and in the Judaean Hills the EEF's Indian units had demonstrated considerable tactical flexibility and military professionalism: the hallmarks of the British imperial army by 1918.

The battlefield abilities of the sepoys were put to best use by the system of Indianization that was introduced in 1917–18. By dropping Indian battalions into existing divisions within the EEF it was possible to retain a large amount of the organizational skills and practical combat experience that had been accrued by these formations over the course of their service in the Middle East. The divisional staffs were able to integrate rapidly the new units into their existing command structures. Within 10th Division a system of conferences at divisional headquarters was in operation by March 1918.

These were used to review recent operations and to learn from mistakes that had been committed.[113] These meetings pooled knowledge and experience within the division, in order to prevent tactical innovations remaining the preserve of individual battalions or brigades. They served to enforce a common standard derived from British Army and EEF doctrine but moulded to the peculiarities of the division's area of operations. This involved a two-way dialogue between the division's general staff and subordinate formations and their commanders. A conference in May, for example, saw considerable disagreement over the defence scheme for the division's sector of the front. In response, each of the brigade commanders was given the opportunity to prepare their own appreciation in writing. The divisional staff was more willing to listen to those with direct experience of the front line than to dictate doctrine to them.

The brigade and divisional generals also took time to meet the officers of the new units that arrived in May–June 1918. Importantly, they spent much time with the Indian officers, a recognition of their central role at regimental level. These engagements were not just bland familiarization exercises. Brigadier-General Morris, for example, took the time to lecture the Indian officers of 74th Punjabis and 2/101st Grenadiers on the details of artillery cooperation.[114] Lieutenant-General Chetwode followed a similar pattern of dropping in on parades to inspect the newly arrived Indian battalions. Lieutenant-Colonel Roberts felt such opportunities to meet the corps commander were invaluable:

> They [the Indian officers] were much impressed by the bearing and quiet manner of the Corps Commander, and as they afterwards remarked the words he spoke were sincere, and for their good. This made them feel more than anything that British and Indian troops were fighting for a common cause, and goes once more to prove that the Indian soldier prefers sound advice to high flown flattering speeches.[115]

In the case of 10th Division the integration of Indian battalions was aided by the command strengths of Major-General Longley and the staff that worked with him. Longley had assumed command of the division in late 1915 and many of the staff officers had also been changed at that stage. By the time the formation was being Indianized they had two and a half years of wartime experience, accumulated in Macedonia and Palestine. Very few of the senior staff officers, though, had previously seen any combat alongside sepoys. The exception was Brigadier-General R. S. Vandeleur, who had served on the North-West Frontier in 1908. He was, however, replaced as commander of 29th Brigade as it was being Indianized. Importantly, Longley was a very able divisional commander; Allenby considered him to be one of the best in the EEF, and felt that he had ensured that 10th Division put up a very finished performance in the operations north of Jerusalem in late 1917. Crucially for Allenby, Longley was 'a Commander who prepares with skill and thoroughness and executes with boldness and determination'.[116] These were attributes that were demonstrated clearly during the summer and early autumn of 1918, most notably in the El Burj – Ghurabeh raid. The established and well-organized command structures of 10th Division were therefore ideally suited to absorbing the Indian troops that they were given in 1918. Most importantly, the division was able to filter down to these new battalions its aggressive ethos based around a strong professional military identity which emphasized skill at arms and tactical astuteness. It was this which allowed the Indianized 10th Division to achieve combat success in the taxing operations of September 1918.

Indianization imposed a considerable burden on the administrative systems of the EEF. It was, however, a structural reorganization that had been extensively and methodically planned, both by the EEF's general staff, the War Office and the high command of the Indian Army. General Robertson's intention in introducing the policy in late 1917 was to maintain and even enhance the strength of Allenby's fighting forces without having to make recourse to fresh drafts from Britain, which was itself facing accumulating manpower problems derived from sustaining forces on the Western Front for over three years. The March 1918 German offensives altered the pace and scale of Indianization but did not determine the logic that lay behind it; this was a response to the attritional grind of modern industrialized warfare. India's recruiting reforms in 1917–18, which put increasing pressure on areas such as the Punjab, nevertheless allowed it to play the role of an imperial strategic reserve, just at the point that it was called upon to do so in earnest.

Within the EEF, Indianization caused a range of organizational difficulties, most notably in training. At the front line, however, the divisional and brigade structures proved perfectly capable of absorbing the newly arrived sepoys. EEF divisions by spring 1918 had developed into sophisticated all arms combat formations, able to adapt rapidly to the exigencies of war in the Middle Eastern theatre. The process of integration was greatly facilitated by the quiescent nature of the Turks by mid-1918. This was a product of the hard-fought battles between October 1917 and January 1918 which saw the Ottoman Army's manpower reserves smashed in repeated offensives as the EEF drove northwards from Gaza to Jerusalem. As a result space and time was created for the Indian infantry to be taught the intricacies of service in Palestine. By September the sepoys had assumed the professional military identity that pervaded the EEF's British and Anzac divisions. The absorption of this ethos was expedited by the regimental structures and traditions of the Indian Army, which closely mirrored those of the British units which they were replacing. This allowed them to strike the fatal blow to the Turkish Army in the region in September. Megiddo thus stands alongside 14th Army's superlative Burma operations, in 1944–5, as evidence that the twentieth-century British-Indian Army was capable of organizing, fighting, and winning a modern military campaign in which all arms operations and manoeuvre warfare were used to dominate their opponent.[117]

Conclusion

The EEF's campaign fought across Sinai and Palestine in 1916–18 ultimately destroyed the Ottoman Empire in the Levant and paved the way for Britain's post-war Middle Eastern empire, obscured behind the façade of the mandatory system. It was a sideshow theatre of the First World War, but one with significant ramifications for interwar European empires and the nascent nation states of the Middle East. However, as David Woodward has elucidated, the men of the EEF who fought on this campaign are very much the 'forgotten soldiers' of the First World War, participants in battles far away from the fulcrum of the conflict on the Western Front. The EEF's campaigns and achievements have made little impact on British popular understanding of the wider dimensions of the war. It remains the romantic exploits of T. E. Lawrence and the Arab Revolt that dominate much of the discourse on the Middle Eastern theatre. This book, in part, has sought to redress this imbalance, relocating the EEF as one of the key elements in Britain's war against the Ottoman Empire; an element of far greater importance in defeating Ottoman forces than the pin-prick strikes of a few desert raiders. Moreover, the EEF's campaign needs to be considered from an imperial dimension, including not only the higher direction of the Middle Eastern war but also the experiences of the men who formed this multinational and multi-ethnic army.

Within the former constituent parts of the British Empire the sideshow theatres of the First World War are treated from a multiplicity of viewpoints. It is possible to suggest that in the case of India a degree of historical amnesia characterizes the approach to the Indian Army's service in Egypt and Palestine. The campaign in Mesopotamia has been much better served by historians over the past 30 years, sitting more firmly within narratives of the hubris of British imperial rule. As Yasmin Khan has suggested in the case of the Second World War, the nationalist aims of the post-1947 Indian state have left little room for the remembrance of campaigns where the Indian Army served largely without complaint and contributed to ultimate British victory, as in Palestine in 1918.[1] Conversely, in Australia the memory of the Anzacs' battlefield heroics from Gallipoli to the Western Front, and inclusive not least of Beersheba and Megiddo, has taken on an almost hagiographical dimension. The Australian Light Horsemen's war is remembered as one of struggle against the terrain, climate, and a tenacious opponent, but this was a struggle from which the Antipodean warriors emerged victorious. They thus contributed a successful element to the birth of the Australian nation narrative that emerged out of the events of 1914–18. Nevertheless, this is still a narrative that pays little attention to how the Anzacs at the front line related their experiences to the war in which they were taking part or to the imperial aims of the mother country.[2] The research presented in this book has brought together these disparate national stories of service in the Egyptian and Palestinian theatres and has placed them within the interlinked framework of the British imperial army's prosecution of a global war.

At the heart of this analysis were questions over the means by which this multinational and multi-ethnic force's morale was sustained over the course of the war and on the battlefield itself. The EEF engaged in a very difficult campaign in the Middle Eastern theatre, contending with a tenacious opponent capable of inflicting major defeats on the British, as seen at First and Second Gaza. It also had to adjust to the myriad difficulties of operations in a region of inhospitable terrain and climate. The environment of the Middle East shaped the operations that the army was able to undertake and pushed the troops to the limits of physical endurance. By October 1918 this limit had been exceeded in the advance northwards from Megiddo to Aleppo. Malaria and influenza caused such high casualty rates that the army ceased to be combat effective; it was thus fortuitous that the Ottoman Empire decided to sue for peace. Although disease placed the greatest strain on the EEF's endurance, it was the brutal reality of combat that made warfare in the region truly horrific. As with the war on the Western Front, artillery, gas, tanks and aircraft all played a significant role. In this sense the campaign in Egypt and Palestine resembled the modern, industrialized battlefields of the Somme or Ypres much more than the sweeping desert vistas encapsulated in David Lean's *Lawrence of Arabia*.

The nature of battle also affected the morale of the EEF. Unlike on the Western Front, combat was not a continuous feature of service in Egypt and Palestine; although it could be as brutal, its intensity was confined to specific periods. As seen with the combat deaths experienced by the NZMR Brigade (see Figure 1.5) across the three years of campaigning, there were only four major periods of combat activity for this formation, only one of which lasted for over a month. For infantrymen there were even fewer instances of intense battle; 163rd Brigade, for example, was only fully engaged at Third and Second Gaza (see Figure 1.4), although both battles took a significant toll. The need for the EEF's soldiers to build up their endurance of battle over a long period was therefore much less than on the Western Front. Nevertheless, the specific combat experiences of individual units could have a considerable impact upon their attitude to battle. As seen with both 54th Division and the ANZMD, those EEF units that had served at Gallipoli were strongly influenced by their experiences on the peninsula. The desire to avenge this defeat proved a powerful motivational force which helped to shape the troops' professional military identity. The defeats at First and Second Gaza only enhanced this desire for revenge. By mid-1917 many EEF soldiers were determined that they would dominate the Turks on the battlefield; the sacrifices of their comrades had to be made worthwhile.

The vast majority of the EEF's soldiers fought unquestioningly for the British Empire's cause in the Middle East. It is striking how few contemporary letters and diaries engaged with a discussion of the imperial war aims of Britain and the Entente. The Ottoman Empire was seen as part of the Central Powers alliance and its defeat would thus contribute to ultimate victory. The campaign until late 1916 was one of imperial defence, intended to protect the Suez Canal, the British Empire's main arterial route which was central to the conduct of a 'total' war, from Turkish attacks. Following the battle of Romani in August 1916 the EEF's war became one of imperial expansion, as the British moved to occupy Sinai and then Palestine.

In part, the absence of a questioning attitude to this imperial aggrandisement in the letters and diaries of combatants is a reflection of the fact that the EEF remained a largely volunteer formation throughout the course of 1916–18. Although suffering heavy casualties at the three battles of Gaza the loss rates of Territorial infantry divisions in the Middle East remained much lower than for comparable formations on the Western Front. The number of conscript replacements entering the EEF's infantry would therefore have been relatively low.[3] By early 1918 the proportion of conscript troops in the EEF would have been at its highest; this was, however, the moment at which large numbers of volunteer Indian soldiers were introduced. Importantly, the ALH regiments, the cutting edge of the EEF's fighting arm, were composed entirely of volunteers throughout the First World War. It is probable that across the course of the Sinai and Palestine campaign at least two-thirds of the EEF was composed of volunteer soldiers who were willing to fight for the British Empire's cause against the Turks.

As with men who served on the Western Front, EEF soldiers displayed a strong recourse to their pre-war civilian identities as part of the process of trying to cope with the rigours of military service in the Middle East. Both TF infantrymen and Anzac mounted troops frequently held concert parties, either to relax after battle, or to fill moments of boredom in rear areas. Sport proved a focal point for the men of the EEF, replicating the working-class cultures of Britain and the Dominions. Even prosaic elements of civilian life could have a powerful mental hold on soldiers, as seen with the eulogizing of bathing in many letters and diaries, a particular element of civilization that countered the squalor of front-line life. These elements suggest that much of J. G. Fuller's analysis of the BEF's war is applicable to the Middle Eastern campaign.[4] As on the Western Front it was these aspects of civilian identity that helped to sustain men during the war; they did not necessarily motivate them to advance and engage in the killing of their opponents in battle. Within the EEF a process of hybridization took place, with this civilian identity combined with a professional military identity in many units. The Territorial infantrymen and Anzac horsemen looked to the combat skills displayed by the pre-war professional British Army in order to set the minimum standard for their performance in battle. This was a measure of military performance continuously emphasized in the speeches and written orders of divisional, brigade and battalion commanders.

In the case of TF battalions this hybridization process was aided through the use of the regimental system. The strong bonds of *esprit de corps* helped bind soldiers together. Although only fully developed in the Cardwell reforms of the 1870s, the British Army's regimental system provided an institution which troops could turn to for psychological sustenance in combat. Crucially, TF units in the EEF were able to contribute to and shape the historic identities of their regiments. The brilliance of the regimental system lay in this flexibility; the historic traditions may have been largely invented but could be added to over time, giving soldiers a feeling of actively belonging to a wider military community, and one which recognized their contribution to it.

In campaigns such as those in Egypt and Palestine, fought a long way from Britain and resembling in their aims the imperial operations of the nineteenth century, the regimental family, espousing a professional military identity, was the primary source of soldiers' morale. The First World War introduced a larger proportion of Britain's population than ever before to the nuances of the British Army's regimental system, and reinforced the institution's emotional significance.[5] After the war veterans could still turn to their former regiments in order to be part of a military community, with regular social events held throughout the interwar period. As a result many memoirs and unit histories written in the 1920s and 1930s chose to emphasize this element of the First World War experience as it remained an ongoing part of veterans' lives.

In contrast, ALH and NZMR units lacked such a well-developed regimental tradition. These Anzac soldiers' loyalties were focused at a much lower level of organization, around the section, consisting of only four men. The organization of ALH and NZMR regiments meant that a primary group identity was effectively forced upon the men of the units. These mounted troops spent their military existence in the four-man section; they lived in it and they fought in it. Although it could not survive the high loss rates of the Transjordan Raids, the section remained a powerful means of integrating men into the unit. As with the TF battalions there was a strong emphasis on both a civilian and a military professional identity among the Australian and New Zealand troopers. This helped to build up the robust morale of the EEF's mounted troops, who were thus able to both endure the wider war and to actively take part in sometimes bloody combat operations.

The key element in this process of reinforcing the EEF's morale was training. An emphasis on a thorough preparation for combat was found across the EEF, from the level of senior staff officers down to platoon and section commanders. Importantly, training helped to rebuild units that had been shattered in battle. During the course of 1916 the EEF had to reconstruct and integrate a large number of battalions, brigades, and divisions which had fought at Gallipoli and in many cases suffered significant losses, both due to combat and disease. In mid-1917 a similar process was followed in order to strengthen those units that had twice experienced bloody defeats at First and Second Gaza. In order to do this the EEF developed a strong formalized training system with large numbers of men sent to the Imperial School of Instruction at Zeitoun, near Cairo. The school's role was to improve the leadership and battlefield skills of junior officers and NCOs. In addition, it provided training courses for specialists within battalions, such as Lewis gunners and rifle grenadiers. Zeitoun's greatest impact was upon the EEF in 1916, while large numbers of men were stationed in Egypt close to its facilities.

Once the EEF moved into Palestine its divisions developed their own training apparatus. After Second Gaza the stabilization of the front allowed divisional schools to be created. As on the Western Front, divisions, both mounted and infantry, were regularly rotated through periods of front-line duty, rest and training. At the divisional schools battalions and companies were tutored in advanced infantry tactics and practised larger brigade-scale operations. As seen with the Umbrella Hill raid in July 1917 small-scale combat actions were also used to develop and test the battlefield skills of units. The experience gained was not, however, restricted to those soldiers who took part, as reports were circulated throughout the army in order to disseminate ideas on the best combat techniques. The EEF thus developed an institutionalized training framework which helped it to inculcate a professional military identity among its soldiers. This reflects the argument made in *Men Against Fire*, where S. L. A. Marshall highlights the primacy of training as the key element in creating strong unit cohesion among US troops during the Second World War.[5]

Moreover, it was this strong emphasis on training that was to prove of critical value in 1918 when the EEF had to integrate large numbers of newly recruited Indian troops into the army. A widespread and sophisticated training apparatus was used to introduce the sepoys to the intricacies and particularities of combat in Palestine. As with the rest of the EEF, Zeitoun remained a key centre for the training of Indian Army NCOs and specialist soldiers. The experiences of the 1/101st Grenadiers, however, make it clear that some sepoys found the central training provided in Egypt to be inadequate and poorly tailored to their needs. At the front there were no such difficulties. The rotation of Indian companies through forward positions allowed the troops to quickly gain an appreciation of the difficulties of combat in the region and allowed experienced British soldiers to pass on valuable and relevant military skills. This process also enabled those British battalions that were remaining with the newly Indianized divisions to gain experience of the Indian Army units they were to serve alongside. Mid-1918 thus saw the EEF undergoing a process of military and cultural adaptation. It was the EEF's institutionalized training ethos that facilitated this, producing the cohesive multinational and multi-ethnic force that destroyed the Turkish Army at Megiddo in September 1918.

For most historians of the EEF's campaigns it was, however, Allenby who was the sole progenitor of the army's strong morale and combat effectiveness. It is evident that there was a shift in the EEF's attitude to warfare in mid-1917, which reflected the increasing professionalization of the campaign. This was a process that Allenby influenced when he took over command, helping to instil attitudes towards all arms cooperation on the battlefield that were derived from the Western Front. Critically, a number of senior EEF corps and divisional commanders, as well as staff officers, were also driving this process. Officers such as Philip Chetwode, Henry Chauvel, Edward Chaytor, Guy Dawnay and Richard Howard-Vyse realized that if the EEF was to become an operationally effective organization it had to adapt to the modern battlefield. No longer could it treat the campaign in Palestine as it had that in Sinai, as a glorified imperial expedition using ad hoc formations. First and Second Gaza demonstrated clearly that Turkish forces and their German advisors had grasped many of the elements that made the modern fire-swept battlefield so deadly. In order to overcome its opponent the EEF had to develop a professional attitude from its Commander-in-Chief down to its soldiers. This meant in part emulating the military skills of the professional British Army, but also adapting the tactical and operational developments occurring on the Western Front to the Middle Eastern theatre.

The ANZMD demonstrated some of these attributes as it spearheaded the Desert Column's advance in 1916, but it was not until Third Gaza that the tactical evolution of the EEF allowed the whole army to achieve significant combat success against the Turks. It was in the series of battles fought between November 1917 and January 1918, which drove the Turkish Army back from the Gaza-Beersheba line to a position north of Jaffa and Jerusalem, that the EEF demonstrated its true operational capabilities. This period of combat effectively broke the back of the Turkish Army in Palestine. The EEF demonstrated that it was capable of defeating Turkish troops in mountainous terrain and appalling winter weather, sustaining complex operations and enduring bloody losses. This was a product of Allenby's organizational reforms and the EEF's robust morale, derived from its institutionalized training ethos. Despite this success the EEF still encountered limits to its battlefield abilities, as demonstrated in the disastrous Transjordan Raids of spring 1918.[7] Here Allenby pushed his troops beyond their logistical and physical capabilities, and underestimated the resilience of Turkish forces. Nevertheless, the collapse of the Ottoman Army in Palestine in September and October 1918 demonstrated that the EEF had fully mastered the all arms battlefield.

Allenby's assumption of command was of critical value for its impact upon the morale of the EEF's corps and divisional commanders as well as its staff officers. Murray's greatest failing by June 1917 was that his inept battlefield management of the EEF, despite his logistical achievements, meant that many of his subordinates lacked confidence in his command. It was among the EEF's general staff that there was a morale crisis in summer 1917, not among the rank and file of the army. As the influential early nineteenth-century military theorist Carl von Clausewitz emphasized in his seminal work, *Vom Kriege*, the morale of commanders was critical to the successful conduct of operations.[8] The psychological consequences of defeat at First and Second Gaza destroyed Murray's ability to lead the EEF's senior officers. Allenby's arrival, his boldness in planning and attack, and in particular his emphasis on creating a modern, all arms force that emulated Western Front armies, invigorated the EEF's staff officers and its subordinate formation commanders. At a tactical level the EEF had been able to defeat the Turks by late 1916, but operationally it was constrained until the summer of 1917. Once Allenby had created an effective command and control system the infantry and mounted troops of the EEF could be put to best use on the battlefield.

The intensive training and emphasis on a professional military identity that pervaded the EEF by late summer 1917 helped to create and reinforce the army's strong morale. It was this robust morale, from senior commanders down to soldiers at the front line, that allowed the EEF to endure the hardships of operations in the deserts and mountains of Sinai and Palestine, and which proved central to its effectiveness on the battlefield. The EEF from October 1917 through to the end of the war was an army that dominated its opponent mentally as well as materially. Psychological endurance, coupled with the ability and willingness to perform in combat, the key elements of morale, lay at the heart of the British imperial army's ability to fight and win its campaigns to defend and expand the empire in the midst of the twentieth century's first 'total' war.

Notes

Introduction

1. J. G. Gray, *The Warriors: Reflections on Men in Battle* (2nd edn, Lincoln, 1970), 24.
2. R. Fuchs, 'Sites of Memory in the Holy Land: The Design of the British War Cemeteries in Mandate Palestine', *Journal of Historical Geography*, XXX (2004), 643–64. For a wider discussion of the commemorative practices of the First World War see J. Winter, *Sites of Memory, Sites of Mourning: The Great War in European Cultural History* (Cambridge, 1995).
3. D. Farr, 'Lamb, Henry Taylor (1883–1960)', *Oxford Dictionary of National Biography*.
4. K. Inglis, *Sacred Places: War Memorials in the Australian Landscape* (3rd edn, Carlton, 2008), 248–9 and 357. A copy of the memorial currently resides on Anzac Parade in Canberra.
5. J. W. Chambers II, 'The New Military History: Myth and Reality', *The Journal of Military History*, LV (1991), 395–406.
6. For an examination of the conflict that relates its European and global elements see H. Strachan, 'The First World War as a Global Conflict', *First World War Studies*, I (2010), 3–14.
7. R. Bowyer, *Dictionary of Military Terms* (3rd edn, London, 2004). Stress can also be placed on the need for individuals to be integrated into goal-oriented groups, although this is very much a reflection of the American Army's post-1945 consideration of morale. See F. J. Manning, 'Morale, Cohesion, and Esprit de Corps', in R. Gal and A. D. Mangesdorff (eds), *Handbook of Military Psychology* (Chichester, 1991), 454–5.
8. S. A. Stouffer, A. A. Lumsdaine, M. H. Lumsdaine, R. M. Williams, M. B. Smith, I. L. Janis, S. A. Star and L. S. Cottrell, *The American Soldier. II: Combat and its Aftermath* (Princeton, 1949), 105; C. Merridale, 'Culture, Ideology and Combat in the Red Army, 1939–45', *Journal of Contemporary History*, XLI (2006), 312.
9. The prominence of fear in battle is discussed in C. H. Hamner, *Enduring Battle: American Soldiers in Three Wars, 1776–1945* (Lawrence, 2011), 66–94.
10. J. Keegan, *The Face of Battle* (London, 1976), 15–77. Keegan's argument is reiterated in a more succinct form in J. A. Lynn, *Battle: A History of Combat and Culture* (Boulder, 2003), xiii–xxv.
11. E. Creasy, *The Fifteen Decisive Battles of the World* (London, 1851).
12. F. M. Richardson, *Fighting Spirit: A Study of Psychological Factors in War* (London, 1978), 2–3; G. L. Cawkwell, 'Introduction', in Xenophon, *The Persian Expedition*, trans. R. Warner (London, 1972), 9–48; R. Holmes, *Acts of War: The Behaviour of Men in Battle* (2nd edn, London, 2004), 293.
13. Keegan, *Face of Battle*, 120; R. H. Vetch and J. Falkner, 'Siborne, William (1797–1849)', *Oxford Dictionary of National Biography*.
14. A. Gat, *A History of Military Thought from the Enlightenment to the Cold War* (Oxford, 2001), 296–310 and 408–9.

15 C.-J.-J.-J. Ardant du Picq, *Battle Studies: Ancient and Modern Battle*, trans. J. N. Greely and R. C. Cotton (New York, 1921), 109; M. Howard, 'Men Against Fire: Expectations of War in 1914', *International Security*, IX (1984), 41–57.
16 C. Bird, 'From Home to the Charge: A Psychological Study of the Soldier', *The American Journal of Psychology*, XXVIII (1917), 315–48; F. C. Bartlett, *Psychology and the Soldier* (Cambridge, 1927), 91–166.
17 Lord Moran, *The Anatomy of Courage* (2nd edn, London, 1966), 97–107 and 155; A. T. A. Browne, 'A Study of the Anatomy of Fear and Courage in War', *The Army Quarterly and Defence Journal*, CVI (1976), 297–303; C. May, 'Lord Moran's Memoir: Shell-Shock and the Pathology of Fear', *Journal of the Royal Society of Medicine*, XCI (1998), 95.
18 S. L. A. Marshall, *Men Against Fire: The Problem of Command in Battle* (2nd edn, Norman, 2000); R. J. Spiller, 'S.L.A. Marshall and the Ratio of Fire', *The Royal United Service Institute Journal*, CXXXIII (1988), 68.
19 E. A. Shils and M. Janowitz, 'Cohesion and Disintegration in the Wehrmacht in World War II', *Public Opinion Quarterly*, XII (1948), 280–315; O. Bartov, *The Eastern Front, 1941–45: German Troops and the Barbarisation of Warfare* (2nd edn, London, 2001), 142–56; O. Bartov, 'Indoctrination and Motivation in the *Wehrmacht*: The Importance of the Unquantifiable', *The Journal of Strategic Studies*, IX (1986), 16–34; O. Bartov, 'Daily Life and Motivation in War: The *Wehrmacht* in the Soviet Union', *The Journal of Strategic Studies*, XII (1989), 200–14. As powerful as Bartov's argument is, it needs to be treated with care as he only focuses on three German divisions, which were among the most politically indoctrinated in the *Wehrmacht*.
20 Stouffer et al., *American Soldier II*, 105–91.
21 R. W. Little, 'Buddy Relations and Combat Performance', in M. Janowitz (ed.), *The New Military: Changing Patterns of Organisation* (New York, 1964), 195–223; W. L. Hauser, 'The Will to Fight', in S. C. Sarkesian (ed.), *Combat Effectiveness: Cohesion, Stress, and the Volunteer Military* (London, 1980), 188; S. W. Gregory, 'Toward a Situated Description of Cohesion and Disintegration in the American Army', *Armed Forces and Society*, III (1977), 465.
22 S. D. Wesbrook, 'The Potential for Military Disintegration', in S. C. Sarkesian (ed.), *Combat Effectiveness: Cohesion, Stress, and the Volunteer Military* (London, 1980), 244–78; Gregory, 'Cohesion and Disintegration', 470; Hauser, 'The Will to Fight', 200–10.
23 Holmes, *Acts*, 11–12. The history of the First World War has spawned a number of such works, see M. Arthur, *Forgotten Voices of the Great War* (London, 2002); R. Van Emden, *Britain's Last Tommies: Final Memories from Soldiers of the 1914–18 War in their Own Words* (Barnsley, 2005). For a more thoughtful approach to the use of the testimony of participants in and witnesses of the conflict see S. Palmer and S. Wallis, *A War in Words* (London, 2003).
24 J. Bourke, *An Intimate History of Killing: Face-to-Face Killing in Twentieth-Century Warfare* (London, 1999).
25 S. Audoin-Rouzeau, *Men at War 1914–1918: National Sentiment and Trench Journalism in France During the First World War* (Oxford, 1992), 46, 155–84 and 186.
26 J. G. Fuller, *Troop Morale and Popular Culture in the British and Dominion Armies 1914–1918* (Oxford, 1990), 81–113 and 172–4. A similar argument on the non-military factors that influenced morale is made in G. Oram, 'Pious Perjury: Discipline and Morale in the British Force in Italy, 1917–1918', *War in History*, IX (2002), 412–30.

27 H. B. McCartney, *Citizen Soldiers: The Liverpool Territorials in the First World War* (Cambridge, 2005), 89–117.
28 B. Ziemann, *War Experiences in Rural Germany, 1914–1923* (Oxford, 2007), 111–54.
29 M. Hanna, *Your Death Would be Mine: Paul and Marie Pireaud in the Great War* (Cambridge, 2006); M. Hanna, 'A Republic of Letters: The Epistolary Tradition in France During World War I', *American Historical Review*, CVIII (2003), 1338–61.
30 M. Roper, *The Secret Battle: Emotional Survival in the Great War* (Manchester, 2009).
31 J. Baynes, *Morale: A Study of Men and Courage. The Second Scottish Rifles at the Battle of Neuve Chapelle 1915* (London, 1967).
32 D. French, *Military Identities: The Regimental System, the British Army, and the British People, c. 1870–2000* (Oxford, 2005), 259–89.
33 G. D. Sheffield, '"A very good type of Londoner and a very good type of colonial": Officer-Man Relations and Discipline in the 22nd Royal Fusiliers, 1914–18', in B. Bond (ed.), *'Look to your front': Studies in the First World War by the British Commission for Military History* (Staplehurst, 1999), 137–46.
34 G. D. Sheffield, *Leadership in the Trenches: Officer-Man Relations, Morale and Discipline in the British Army in the Era of the First World War* (Basingstoke, 2000).
35 A. Watson, *Enduring the Great War: Combat, Morale and Collapse in the German and British Armies, 1914–1918* (Cambridge, 2008), 85–107 and 184–231; A. Watson, 'Junior Officership in the German Army During the Great War, 1914–1918', *War in History*, XIV (2007), 429–53; A. Watson, 'Stabbed at the Front', *History Today*, LVIII (2008), 21–7; A. Watson, 'Self-Deception and Survival: Mental Coping Strategies on the Western Front, 1914–18', *Journal of Contemporary History*, XLI (2006), 247–68.
36 D. R. Woodward, *Forgotten Soldiers of the First World War: Lost Voices from the Middle Eastern Front* (Stroud, 2006). Woodward's attempt to provide a readable and accurate account of the Middle Eastern war addresses the criticisms of the historical profession raised in M. MacMillan, *The Uses and Abuses of History* (London, 2009), 35–6.
37 E. Zürcher, 'Little Mehmet in the Desert: The Ottoman Soldier's Experience', in H. Cecil and P. H. Liddle (eds), *Facing Armageddon: The First World War Experienced* (Barnsley, 1996), 236–7; S. Tamari, 'Rethinking Arab-Turkish Identity After Gallipoli: Diaries of Ottoman Soldiers in World War I', paper at the Middle East Centre seminars, Oxford University, 7 November 2008; G. Lewis, 'An Ottoman Officer in Palestine, 1914–1918', in D. Kushner (ed.), *Palestine in the Late Ottoman Period* (Leiden, 1986), 402–15.
38 The best and most detailed general narrative of the EEF's campaign remains that found in the official histories; see G. MacMunn and C. Falls, *Military Operations Egypt and Palestine. I: From the Outbreak of War with Germany to June 1917* (London, 1928); C. Falls, *Military Operations Egypt and Palestine. II: From June 1917 to the End of the War* (London, 1930).
39 For a discussion of the EEF's 1917 operations and their centrality to the overall Middle Eastern war effort see J. Grainger, *The Battle for Palestine 1917* (Woodbridge, 2006).
40 M. Hughes, *Allenby and British Strategy in the Middle East 1917–1919* (London, 1999), 71–88.
41 The most readable account of Megiddo, although one which appears increasingly dated, remains C. Falls, *Armageddon 1918* (London, 1964).
42 A. J. P. Taylor, *The First World War: An Illustrated History* (London, 1966), 77, 106, 117, 206 and 242; J. Keegan, *The First World War* (London, 1998), 236–8; C. R. M. F. Cruttwell, *A History of the Great War 1914–1918* (Oxford, 1934), 337–58 and 606–23;

H. Strachan, '"The Real War": Liddell Hart, Cruttwell, and Falls', in B. Bond (ed.), *The First World War and British Military History* (Oxford, 1991), 56. Only the first volume of Hew Strachan's impending trilogy on the conflict has attempted to integrate Turkey's role into a detailed narrative of the whole war; see H. Strachan, *The First World War. I: To Arms* (Oxford, 2001), 644–814.

43   W. S. Churchill, *The World Crisis, 1916–1918: Part II* (London, 1927), 336.
44   Jonathan Newell has done much to undermine this argument, highlighting the difficulties of launching amphibious operations in the eastern Mediterranean; see J. C. Q. Newell, 'British Military Policy in Egypt and Palestine, August 1914–June 1917' (University of London, PhD thesis, 1990), 90–7 and 113–32; R. Prior, *Churchill's 'World Crisis'as History* (London, 1983), 272–83.
45   M. Hughes, 'Lloyd George, the Generals and the Palestine Campaign, 1917–1918', *Imperial War Museum Review*, XI (1996), 4–17; Churchill, *World Crisis*, 336–7; D. Lloyd George, *War Memoirs of David Lloyd George* (London, 1936), II, 1910–29; Falls, *Military Operations II*, 633.
46   D. Fromkin, *A Peace to End All Peace: The Fall of the Ottoman Empire and the Creation of the Modern Middle East* (London, 1989); E. Monroe, *Britain's Moment in the Middle East, 1914–1971* (2nd edn, London, 1981), 23–49.
47   B. H. Liddell Hart, *A History of the First World War 1914–1918* (London, 1934), 436; Keegan, *First World War*, 444.
48   Y. Sheffy, 'British Intelligence and the Middle East, 1900–1918: How Much Do We Know?', *Intelligence and National Security*, XVII (2002), 33–52; E. Karsh and I. Karsh, 'Myth in the Desert, or Not the Great Arab Revolt', *Middle Eastern Studies*, XXXIII (1997), 267–312.
49   Cruttwell, *History of the Great War*, 613; B. Holden Reid, 'T.E. Lawrence and his Biographers', in B. Bond (ed.), *The First World War and British Military History* (Oxford, 1991), 227–59.
50   Falls, *Military Operations II*, 120–3 and 274.
51   H. Strachan, 'Back to the Trenches: Why Can't British Historians be Less Insular about the First World War?', *The Times Literary Supplement*, 5 November 2008. This problem has also been identified with regards to the wider study of military history; see M. Moyar, 'The Current State of Military History', *The Historical Journal*, L (2007), 225–40. The problems inherent in comparative historical studies are covered in D. Cohen, 'Comparative History: Buyer Beware', *German Historical Institute, Washington, D.C., Bulletin*, XXIX (2001), 23–33. A comparative approach to the use of imperial troops by Britain and France during the First World War is attempted in C. Koller, 'The Recruitment of Colonial Troops in Africa and Asia and their Deployment in Europe During the First World War', *Immigrants and Minorities*, XXVI (2008), 111–33. For a detailed analysis of the multi-ethnic character of the Indian Army of the Second World War and its impact on combat effectiveness see T. Barkawi, 'Peoples, Homelands, and Wars? Ethnicity, the Military, and Battle Among British Imperial Forces in the War Against Japan', *Comparative Studies in Society and History*, XLVI (2004), 134–63.
52   S. Das, *Touch and Intimacy in First World War Literature* (Cambridge, 2005); J. Bourke, 'The Emotions in War: Fear and the British and American Military, 1914–45', *Historical Research*, LXXIV (2001), 314–30; S. Goebel, 'Beyond Discourse? Bodies and Memories of Two World Wars', *Journal of Contemporary History*, XLII (2007), 377–85.

53 For evidence of this shift see T. Barkawi, 'On the Pedagogy of "Small Wars"', *International Affairs*, LXXX (2004), 19–37; T. Barkawi and M. Laffey, 'The Postcolonial Moment in Security Studies', *Review of International Studies*, XXII (2006), 329–52; P. Porter, *Military Orientalism: Eastern War Through Western Eyes* (London, 2009); P. Porter, 'Good Anthropology, Bad History: The Cultural Turn in Studying War', *Parameters: US Army War College Quarterly*, XXXVII (2007), 45–58; 'Anthropology at War', *BBC Radio 4*, first transmitted 24 April 2009. A wide-ranging critique of Eurocentrism in military history is provided in J. Black, *Rethinking Military History* (Abingdon, 2004), 66–103.

54 The argument for a global and imperial history of the First World War is made forcefully in H. Liebau, K. Bromber, K. Lange, D. Hamzah and R. Ahuja (eds), *The World in World Wars: Experiences, Perceptions and Perspectives from Africa and Asia* (Leiden, 2010), 20.

55 This is equally true of the Ottoman Army which recruited troops from throughout its empire. The impact of the rich range of military cultures and traditions within the Ottoman Empire upon its army's combat effectiveness has yet to be fully appreciated, but a start has been made. See E. J. Erickson, *Ottoman Army Effectiveness in World War I: A Comparative Study* (London, 2007); Y. Yanikdağ, 'Educating the Peasants: The Ottoman Army and Enlisted Men in Uniform', *Middle Eastern Studies*, XL (2004), 92–108.

Chapter 1

1 Falls, *Military Operations II*, 123; Woodward, *Forgotten Soldiers*, 177. Unlike many earlier accounts of the action Woodward takes a balanced view of its overall importance to the EEF's advance northwards.

2 E. Butler, *Autobiography* (2nd edn, Sevenoaks, 1993), 261. Butler's emphasis. This was one of three paintings she produced on the campaigns in Egypt and Palestine, a theatre in which she took great interest as her son served there with the Royal Irish Regiment. In 1917 she depicted the Dorset Yeomanry's charge of the Senussi at Agagia on 26 February 1916, a similarly grandiose battle scene to that of the charge at Huj. A year after the war she produced a prosaic and bleak depiction of a Yeomanry despatch rider being killed by Turkish rifle fire. For further details of Butler's prolific artistic career see P. Usherwood and J. Spencer-Smith, *Lady Butler: Battle Artist, 1846–1933* (Gloucester, 1987); P. Usherwood, 'Butler, Elizabeth Southerden, Lady Butler (1846–1933)', *Oxford Dictionary of National Biography*.

3 M. Ross, 'The Sinai-Palestine Campaign', in C. Lucas (ed.), *Empire at War* (Oxford, 1923), III, 370. A similar emphasis on the difference of the Middle Eastern war in 1942 from operations in the European theatre is found in S. Bungay, *Alamein* (London, 2002), 94. He, however, pushes the argument too far, concluding that 'in a global conflict unprecedented in its comprehensive awfulness, the desert was the nice bit of the war'.

4 The National Archives (TNA), CAB45/78, Comments and Correspondence Relating to the Compilation of the Official Histories – Egypt and Palestine, letter from Lieutenant-General E. S. Bulfin to Major C. Falls, 17 December 1929; TNA, CAB45/78, Comments and Correspondence Relating to the Compilation of the Official Histories – Egypt and Palestine, letter from Colonel J. Anderson to the

Director, Historical Section (Military Branch), Committee of Imperial Defence (CID), 30 May 1928.
5   A. Kramer, *Dynamic of Destruction: Culture and Mass Killing in the First World War* (Oxford, 2007), 34; H. Strachan, *The First World War: A New Illustrated History* (London, 2003), 160; Strachan, *First World War I*, 163–280.
6   For a discussion of the problems of soldiers' correspondence as a source see D. Englander, 'Soldiering and Identity: Reflections on the Great War', *War in History*, I (1994), 300–18; Audoin-Rouzeau, *Men at War*, 67.
7   A. Briscoe Moore, *The Mounted Riflemen in Sinai and Palestine: The Story of New Zealand's Crusaders* (Auckland, 1920), 113.
8   Ziemann, *War Experiences*, 41; J. Bourne, 'The British Working Man in Arms', in H. Cecil and P. H. Liddle (eds), *Facing Armageddon: The First World War Experienced* (Barnsley, 1996), 345. To a certain extent, Fuller's *Troop Morale* also follows this approach; his emphasis is, however, on how men sustained themselves at war rather than in battle.
9   J. Ellis, *Eye-Deep in Hell* (London, 1976), 83–104; D. Winter, *Death's Men: Soldiers of the Great War* (London, 1978), 170–85, quotation on 185.
10 Audoin-Rouzeau, *Men at War*, 67–91; E. Bergerud, *Touched with Fire: The Land War in the South Pacific* (New York, 1996); Bungay, *Alamein*, 67–94; N. Barr, 'The Desert War Experience', in P. Liddle, J. Bourne and I. Whitehead (eds), *The Great World War 1914–1945. I: Lightning Strikes Twice* (London, 2000), 120–35.
11 For a Second World War parallel see Bergerud, *Touched with Fire*, 55–118.
12 TNA, WO95/4639, War Diary of 54th Division Assistant Director of Medical Services, 18 May 1916; Suffolk Record Office (SRO), GB554/Y1/165j, Lee, diary, 31.
13 Imperial War Museum (IWM), 74/149/1, Barron, diary, 9.
14 TNA, WO95/4657, War Diary of 1/5th Norfolk Regiment, July 1916; TNA, WO95/4639, War Diary of 54th Division Assistant Director of Medical Services, May 1916, Appendix C: 'Medical Notes on Operations in Hot Weather', by Assistant Director of Medical Services, 54th Division, 13 May 1916; TNA, WO95/4639, War Diary of 54th Division Assistant Director of Medical Services, August 1916, Appendix A: Letter from the Assistant Director of Medical Services, 54th Division, to the Assistant Adjutant and Quartermaster-General, 54th Division, 14 August 1916.
15 Essex Regiment Museum (ERM), France, diary, 16 and 17 May 1916.
16 T. Gibbons, *With the 1/5th Essex in the East* (Colchester, 1921), 40.
17 IWM, 82/22/1, Surry, diary, 36.
18 Australian War Memorial (AWM), 2DRL/0015, Evans, letter to mother, 1 July 1917.
19 E. Blackwell and E. C. Axe, *Romford to Beirut via France, Egypt and Jericho: An Outline of the War Record of 'B' Battery, 271st Brigade R.F.A. (1/2nd Essex Battery, R.F.A.) with Many Digressions* (Clacton-on-Sea, 1926), 43.
20 TNA, WO95/4650, War Diary of 1/4th Essex Regiment, 3 May 1916.
21 Liddell Hart Centre for Military Archives (LHCMA), Clarke 1/2, Clarke, memoir, 19; SRO, GB554/Y1/426a, Wolton, letter to mother, 30 January 1916.
22 AWM, MSS1071, Crase, memoir, 28.
23 Newell, 'British Military Policy', 126–32 and 177–90; F. L. Petre, *The History of the Norfolk Regiment 1685–1918* (Norwich, 1925), II, 139; SRO, GB554/Y1/165j, Lee, diary, 29; TNA, WO95/4650, War Diary of 1/4th Essex Regiment, 28 May 1916; ERM, Joslin, interview transcript, 5.
24 Bungay, *Alamein*, 69; SRO, GB554/Y1/165j, Lee, diary, 31; AWM, 3DRL/3741 Folder 2, Delpratt, letter to sister, 13 May 1916.

25 H. G. Mansfield, *By Jaffa Way and Other Poems* (London, 1919), 9–10.
26 IWM, Con Shelf, Hinde, diary, 10 May 1917.
27 IWM, 66/85/1, Hare, diary, 19 April 1917.
28 Major W. E. Wilson, 'March 26 and 27 1917', in Gibbons, *With the 1/5th Essex*, 72.
29 TNA, CAB45/78, Comments and Correspondence Relating to the Compilation of the Official Histories – Egypt and Palestine, letter from General P. W. Chetwode to Lieutenant-General G. MacMunn, 17 May 1926.
30 Gibbons, *With the 1/5th Essex*, 123; IWM, 66/85/1, Hare, diary, 18 November 1917.
31 IWM, 06/69/1, Town, memoir, 8.
32 AWM, 2DRL/0817, Chandler, letter to family, 3 January 1918.
33 AWM, AWM4 10/8, War Diary of 3rd Australian Light Horse Regiment, 17 March 1918; Kippenberger Military Archives (KMA), 1993.976, Fabian, diary, 9 December 1917.
34 IWM, 06/69/1, Town, memoir, 8.
35 IWM, 82/22/1, Surry, diary, 97.
36 AWM, 3DRL/7568, Prince, letter to mother, 28 February 1918.
37 TNA, WO95/4653, War Diary of 1/4th Northamptonshire Regiment, 19 September 1918.
38 Mansfield, *By Jaffa Way*, 14.
39 ERM, ER15807.1, Cook, diary.
40 AWM, MSS1071, Crase, memoir, 45.
41 AWM, 2DRL/0337, Dick Papers, 'Beauty Spots' poem; AWM, AWM4 10/12, War Diary of 7th Australian Light Horse Regiment, 6 June 1918; KMA, 1998.31, McKay, memoir, 146; AWM, AWM4 10/10, War Diary of 5th Australian Light Horse Regiment, April 1918, Appendix 4: 'Report on Operations Round Amman and Es Salt from 23 March to 2 April', by Major C. Bolingbroke.
42 R. Holmes, 'Battle: The Experience of Modern Combat', in C. Townshend (ed.), *The Oxford History of Modern War* (2nd edn, Oxford, 2005), 224; Lynn, *Battle*, xiv–xv.
43 IWM, 06/69/1, Town, memoir, 5.
44 IWM, 82/22/1, Surry, diary, 49–50.
45 TNA, WO95/4654, War Diary of 1/10th London Regiment, 27 March 1917; AWM, 2DRL/0211, Macfarlane, diary, 5 August 1916.
46 I. L. Idriess, *The Desert Column: Leaves from the Diary of an Australian Trooper in Gallipoli, Sinai, and Palestine* (Sydney, 1933), 139.
47 IWM, 06/69/1, Town, memoir, 42.
48 TNA, WO95/4659, War Diary of 163rd Machine Gun Company, 15 June 1917 and 14 July 1917.
49 TNA, WO95/4544, War Diary of New Zealand Mounted Rifles Brigade, 10 January 1917.
50 KMA, 1993.1039, Hull, letter to brothers, 16 August 1916.
51 IWM, 82/22/1, Surry, diary, 49.
52 Norfolk Regiment Museum (NRM), Box 11, Emms, 'Account of the Attack on Gaza of 1/5th Norfolks, April 1917', 1 May 1917.
53 Idriess, *Desert Column*, 252.
54 Bourke, *Intimate History*, 51 and 53–5; P. Hodges, '"They don't like it up 'em!": Bayonet Fetishization in the British Army During the First World War', *Journal of War and Culture Studies*, I (2008), 123–38. The declining role of the bayonet and the dominance of firepower were already evident in the mid-eighteenth century; see H. Strachan, *European Armies and the Conduct of War* (Abingdon, 1983), 17;

P. Griffith, *Battle Tactics on the Western Front: The British Army's Art of Attack, 1916-18* (New Haven, 1994), 69-72.
55 TNA, WO95/4653, War Diary of 1/4th Northamptonshire Regiment, November 1917, Appendix: Report on a Turkish attack on 27 November 1917, by Lieutenant-Colonel J. G. Brown, Commanding Officer of 1/4th Northamptonshire Regiment, 30 November 1917; Falls, *Military Operations II*, 221-2.
56 TNA, WO95/4654, War Diary of 1/11th London Regiment, 26 February 1918; G. Gliddon, *VCs of the First World War: The Sideshows* (Stroud, 2005), 177-80 and 202-5.
57 IWM, PP/MCR/218, Thompson, diary, 7 November 1917.
58 TNA, WO95/4657, War Diary of 1/4th Norfolk Regiment, November 1917, Appendix 1: '1/4th Battalion Norfolk Regiment, Narrative of Operations from 1800, 1/11/17 to 1700, 7/11/17'; TNA, WO95/4656, War Diary of 163rd Infantry Brigade Headquarters, November 1917, Appendix: 'Report on (a) Preparations (b) Active Operations of 163rd Infantry Brigade During Period 21 September to Midnight 8/9 November 1917'; Erickson, *Ottoman Army Effectiveness*, 123.
59 Beet Algar interview in N. Boyack and J. Tolerton (eds), *In the Shadow of War: New Zealand Soldiers Talk About World War One and Their Lives* (Auckland, 1990), 119; IWM, 82/22/1, Surry, diary, 84.
60 IWM, 06/69/1, Town, memoir, 9.
61 IWM, 85/4/1, Bailey, diary, 10 August 1917.
62 See Bourke, *Intimate History*; J. Bourke, 'The Experience of Killing', in P. Liddle, J. Bourne and I. Whitehead (eds), *The Great World War 1914-1945. I: Lightning Strikes Twice* (London, 2000), 293-309; N. Ferguson, *The Pity of War* (London, 1998), 357-66.
63 Idriess, *Desert Column*, 74.
64 Beet Algar interview in Boyack and Tolerton, *Shadow of War*, 118. For a detailed discussion of mental coping strategies see Watson, *Enduring the Great War*, 85-107; Watson, 'Self-Deception'.
65 IWM, 84/34/1, Hammond, diary, 7 November 1917.
66 Gibbons, *With the 1/5th Essex*, 83.
67 IWM, 82/22/1, Surry, diary, 46.
68 KMA, 1998.31, McKay, memoir, 152; IWM, 85/4/1, Bailey, diary, 9 November 1917.
69 McCartney, *Citizen Soldiers*, 89-117; Hanna, *Your Death Would be Mine*; Hanna, 'Republic of Letters'; J. Fennell, *Combat and Morale in the North African Campaign: The Eighth Army and the Path to El Alamein* (Cambridge, 2011), 7-8.
70 IWM, 76/74/1, Jewson, letter to mother, 20 June 1917.
71 H. Strachan, 'The Soldier's Experience in Two World Wars: Some Historiographical Comparisons', in P. Addison and A. Calder (eds), *Time to Kill: The Soldier's Experience of War in the West 1939-1945* (London, 1997), 369-78.
72 Falls, *Military Operations II*, 10; TNA, WO95/4653, War Diary of 1/5th Bedfordshire Regiment, 20 June 1917; IWM, 06/33/1, Mortimer, diary, 30; Woodward, *Forgotten Soldiers*, 231.
73 Ellis, *Eye-Deep*, 26-42; Fuller, *Troop Morale*, 58. See T. Ashworth, 'The Sociology of Trench Warfare 1914-18', *The British Journal of Sociology*, XIX (1968), 407-23; T. Ashworth, *Trench Warfare 1914-1918: The Live and Let Live System* (London, 1980).
74 TNA, WO95/4649, War Diary of 161st Infantry Brigade Headquarters, May 1917, Appendix A: 161st Infantry Brigade Order No. 10, 5 May 1917; TNA, WO95/4657, War Diary of 1/5th Norfolk Regiment, 12 June 1917; TNA, WO95/4634, War Diary

of 54th Division General Staff, April 1917, Appendix 13: 54th Division Circular Memorandum No. T.1, 28 April 1917.
75 TNA, WO95/4653, War Diary of 1/4th Northamptonshire Regiment, May 1917; AWM, AWM4 10/6, War Diary of 1st Australian Light Horse Regiment, 1–17 May 1917; Gibbons, *With the 1/5th Essex*, 85.
76 Ellis, *Eye-Deep*, 61; Bourke, *Intimate History*, 51.
77 C. Garsia, *A Key to Victory: A Study in War Planning* (London, 1940), 139–40; TNA, WO95/4634, War Diary of 54th Division General Staff, April 1917, Appendix 10: 'Report on Operations Carried Out by 54th Divisional Artillery Between 16 April and 21 April 1917'.
78 TNA, CAB45/80, Comments and Correspondence Relating to the Compilation of the Official Histories – Egypt and Palestine, letter from Major-General S. C. U. Smith to the Director, Historical Section (Military Branch), CID, 27 November 1925.
79 IWM, 85/4/1, Bailey, preface to diary, v–vi.
80 Erickson, *Ottoman Army Effectiveness*, 135–41. The integral role that artillery would come to play in Allenby's operational decision making, with the EEF becoming a true all arms force, is highlighted in M. Hughes, 'General Allenby and the Palestine Campaign, 1917–18', *The Journal of Strategic Studies*, XIX (1996), 59–88.
81 IWM, 85/4/1, Bailey, diary, 8 July and 11 October 1917.
82 IWM, 66/85/1, Hare Papers, 'Report on Operations, 54th Division, 27.10.17 to 23.12.17. Part I: The Battle of Gaza (27.10.17–8.11.17)', 10 and 30. Falls, *Military Operations II*, 65 erroneously states that 15,000 shells were fired by the artillery of XXI Corps and that of its divisions in the preliminary bombardment.
83 TNA, WO95/4656, War Diary of 163rd Infantry Brigade Headquarters, November 1917, Appendix: 'Report on (a) Preparations (b) Active Operations of 163rd Infantry Brigade During Period 21 September to Midnight 8/9 November 1917'; TNA, WO95/4653, War Diary of 1/5th Bedfordshire Regiment, 2 November 1917; IWM, 06/69/1, Town, memoir, 4.
84 TNA, WO95/4546, War Diary of Canterbury Mounted Rifles Regiment, 5 November 1917; TNA, WO95/4658, War Diary of 1/5th Suffolk Regiment, 18–22 December 1917.
85 IWM, 84/34/1, Hammond, diary, 4 November 1917.
86 SRO, GB554/Y1/426a, Wolton, letter to parents, 27 April 1917.
87 IWM, 85/4/1, Bailey, diary, 27 and 28 July 1917; TNA, WO95/4650, War Diary of 1/4th Essex Regiment, 19–25 April 1917.
88 For a full discussion of the use of gas by the EEF and the policy decisions involved see Y. Sheffy, 'The Introduction of Chemical Weapons to the Middle East', in Y. Sheffy and S. Shai (eds), *The First World War: Middle Eastern Perspective* (2000), 75–84.
89 Alexander Turnbull Library (ATL), MS-Papers-4312/1, Judge, diary, 8 April 1917.
90 TNA, WO95/4634, War Diary of 54th Division General Staff, April 1917, Appendix 10: Memorandum from Brigadier-General G. P. Dawnay, Brigadier-General, General Staff, Eastern Force, regarding the use of gas shells, 17 April 1917; TNA, WO95/4634, War Diary of 54th Division General Staff, April 1917, Appendix 10: 'Report on Operations Carried Out by 54th Divisional Artillery Between 16 April and 21 April 1917'.
91 IWM, 66/85/1, Hare Papers, 'Report on Operations, 54th Division, 27.10.17 to 23.12.17. Part I: The Battle of Gaza (27.10.17–8.11.17)', 10.
92 KMA, 1991.2000, Doherty, diary, 5–14 August 1918; KMA, 2004.131, Currin, diary, 26 September 1917.

93 TNA, WO95/4657, War Diary of 1/5th Norfolk Regiment, 19 April 1917; TNA, WO95/4659, War Diary of 1/8th Hampshire Regiment, 19 April 1917.
94 TNA, WO95/4653, War Diary of 1/5th Bedfordshire Regiment, 2 November 1917; IWM, 66/85/1, Hare Papers, 'Report on Operations, 54th Division, 27.10.17 to 23.12.17. Part I: The Battle of Gaza (27.10.17–8.11.17)', 12.
95 TNA, WO95/4658, War Diary of 1/5th Suffolk Regiment, 17 April 1917; NRM, Box 11, 1/4th and 1/5th Norfolk Regiment Papers, 1/4th Norfolk Regiment operation orders for the Third Battle of Gaza, 29 October 1917.
96 TNA, WO95/4656, War Diary of 163rd Infantry Brigade Headquarters, January 1918, Appendix: Letter from Brigadier-General T. Ward to 54th Division Headquarters, regarding the use of tanks at Gaza, 3 January 1918.
97 For a full account of the role of the RFC and RAF in the Middle East see H. A. Jones, *The War in the Air: Being the Story of the Part Played in the Great War by the Royal Air Force* (Oxford, 1935), V, 160–249; H. A. Jones, *The War in the Air: Being the Story of the Part Played in the Great War by the Royal Air Force* (Oxford, 1937), VI, 175–238; Y. Sheffy, *British Military Intelligence in the Palestine Campaign, 1914–1918* (London, 1998), 184–93, 274–86 and 304–18.
98 W. E. Johns, *Biggles Flies East* (Oxford, 1935). For an analysis of the impact of spy fever on the EEF see Y. Sheffy, 'The Spy Who Never Was: An Intelligence Myth in Palestine, 1914–18', *Intelligence and National Security*, XIV (1999), 123–42.
99 P. Collier and R. Inkpen, 'Mapping Palestine and Mesopotamia in the First World War', *The Cartographic Journal*, XXXVIII (2001), 143–54.
100 NRM, NWHRM 6186, Bland, diary, 15 August 1917.
101 IWM, Con Shelf, Hinde, diary, 29 November 1917.
102 IWM, 03/29/1, Wollaston, diary, 62–3.
103 IWM, 76/74/1, Jewson, letter to mother, 27 June 1917; AWM, 2DRL/0211, Macfarlane, diary, 6 July 1916.
104 ERM, France, diary, 4 May 1918.
105 IWM, PP/MCR/62, Buxton, letter to aunt, 17 January 1917.
106 AWM, AWM4 10/1, War Diary of 1st Australian Light Horse Brigade Headquarters, June 1916, Appendix 22: Report on a Turkish Air Raid, by Lieutenant-Colonel J. B. Meredith, commanding 1st ALH Brigade; AWM, 2DRL/0211, Macfarlane, diary, 1 June 1916.
107 AWM, 1DRL/0364, Hudson, letter to wife, 6 June 1917.
108 ATL, 76–123, Rhodes, diary, 1 June 1916.
109 ATL, 76–123, Rhodes, diary, 11 August 1916.
110 Jones, *War in the Air*, VI, 226; TNA, WO95/4582, War Diary of 30th Infantry Brigade Headquarters, October 1918, Appendix: 'The Operations Round Nablus', by W. T. Massey, General Headquarters (GHQ), 23 September 1918.
111 Jones, *War in the Air*, VI, 225. For the influence of Palestine operations on interwar RAF doctrine on army cooperation see A. D. Harvey, 'The Royal Air Force and Close Support, 1918–1940', *War in History*, XV (2008), 462–86.
112 The aircraft as a psychological weapon reached its apogee with the Stuka dive-bomber; see Bungay, *Alamein*, 79.
113 The emphasis on mounted operations is most clearly expressed in Falls, *Armageddon* and A. P. Wavell, *The Palestine Campaigns* (3rd edn, London, 1931). For a more accurate depiction of the EEF's tactical abilities see Erickson, *Ottoman Army Effectiveness*, 97–154.

114 F. Maurice, *The 16th Foot: A History of the Bedfordshire and Hertfordshire Regiment* (London, 1931), 173; ERM, Joslin, interview transcript, 5.

115 IWM, 66/85/1, Hare, 'Casualties of 54th Division at 1st and 2nd Battles of Gaza'. Hare assumed that the large numbers of missing in both battles had been killed. MacMunn and Falls, *Military Operations I*, 348 lists the EEF's overall losses at Second Gaza as 6,444, with the 54th Division suffering 2,870, the 52nd Division 1,874, the 53rd Division 584, and the Imperial Mounted Division 547; IWM, 66/85/1, Hare, diary, 19 April 1917.

116 IWM, PP/MCR/C1, Chetwode, letter to the EEF Chief of the General Staff, 30 April 1917; TNA, WO95/4634, War Diary of 54th Division General Staff, May 1917, Appendix 10: Strength, casualties and reinforcements during May 1917.

117 TNA, WO95/4649, War Diary of 161st Infantry Brigade Headquarters, August–November 1917 and February–May 1918.

118 TNA, WO95/4656, War Diary of 163rd Infantry Brigade Headquarters, December 1917; TNA, WO95/4657, War Diary of 1/4th Norfolk Regiment, December 1917.

119 AWM, AWM4 10/1, War Diary of 1st Australian Light Horse Brigade Headquarters, 5 August 1916; AWM, AWM4 10/1, War Diary of 1st Australian Light Horse Brigade Headquarters, January 1917, Appendix 67: 'Report on Operations Carried Out by 1st A.L.H. Brigade at Rafa on 9/1/17', by Brigadier-General Cox; TNA, WO95/4386, War Diary of the Egyptian Expeditionary Force Director of Medical Services, 7 August 1916. ANZMD, 42nd Division, and 52nd Division together lost 29 officers and 502 other ranks on 4–7 August 1916, during which the majority of the fighting was done by the ANZMD.

120 This was not the case for 60th Division, which was heavily involved in the fighting at both Amman and Shunet Nimrin in the two operations.

121 AWM, AWM4 1/60, War Diary of Australian and New Zealand Mounted Division General Staff, April 1918, Appendix 207: 'Operations of the A. and N.Z. Mounted Division, East of Jordan, from March 23rd to April 2nd Including Action of Amman', by Lieutenant-Colonel J. G. Browne, 11 April 1918.

122 AWM, AWM4 1/60, War Diary of Australian and New Zealand Mounted Division General Staff, December 1917, Appendix 173: 'Account of the Operations Carried Out by the Australian and New Zealand Mounted Division from October 21st to December 7th 1917', by Lieutenant-Colonel J. G. Browne, 15 January 1918.

123 TNA, WO95/4636, War Diary of 54th Division General Staff, September 1918, Appendix 8: 'Narrative of Operations – 54th Division and D.F.P.S., 18, 19, 20 and 21 September 1918'; AWM, AWM4 1/60, War Diary of Australian and New Zealand Mounted Division General Staff, September 1918, Appendix 38: 'Account of Operations of Chaytor's Force from September 18th to September 30th', 6 October 1918.

124 War Office, *Statistics of the Military Effort of the British Empire During the Great War 1914–1920* (London, 1922), 271 and 283.

125 TNA, WO95/4376, War Diary of Egyptian Expeditionary Force Deputy Adjutant-General, December 1917, Appendix A: 'Statement of Casualties (All Arms), and Infantry and Yeomanry Reinforcements Sent Forward, Remaining Available, En Route from U.K. and Demanded by 3rd Echelon'.

126 TNA, WO95/4649, War Diary of 161st Infantry Brigade Headquarters, 26–28 March 1917.

127 TNA, WO95/4656, War Diary of 163rd Infantry Brigade Headquarters, 19 April 1917. The total losses of the brigade's four battalions amounted to 60 officers and 1,725 other ranks. The additional casualties recorded in the brigade war diary may have occurred in the brigade's headquarters staff and attached units. Alternatively, the difference may reflect the inherent inaccuracies of war diaries, which were often written up several days after the battles they describe. For a discussion of the problems with war diaries see R. R. James, 'Thoughts on Writing Military History', *Royal United Service Institution Journal*, CXI (1966), 104–7.

128 IWM, 66/85/1, Hare, diary, 19 April 1917.

129 TNA, WO95/4657, War Diary of 1/4th Norfolk Regiment, Appendix 3: List of Casualties in November 1917; TNA, WO95/4657, War Diary of 1/5th Norfolk Regiment, 1–7 November 1917; TNA, WO95/4658, War Diary of 1/5th Suffolk Regiment, 4–6 November 1917; TNA, WO95/4659, War Diary of 1/8th Hampshire Regiment, 7 November 1917.

130 Bedfordshire Record Office, X550/6/11, Victoria Cross citation for Private Samuel Needham, 1/5th Bedfordshire Regiment.

131 SRO, GB554/Y1/426b, Wolton, scrapbook, report on the Third Battle of Gaza.

132 IWM, 82/22/1, Surry, diary, 87.

133 LHCMA, Clarke 1/4, Clarke, memoir, 12.

134 R. Prior and T. Wilson, *The Somme* (New Haven, 2005), 80.

135 Fennell, *Combat and Morale*, 252–6.

136 P. Ham, *Kokoda* (Sydney, 2004), 178.

137 O. Bartov, *Hitler's Army: Soldiers, Nazis, and War in the Third Reich* (Oxford, 1991), 42 and 57.

138 H. Strachan, 'Training, Morale and Modern War', *Journal of Contemporary History*, XLI (2006), 212.

139 For detailed studies of medical arrangements in the EEF see E. Dolev, *Allenby's Military Medicine: Life and Death in World War I Palestine* (London, 2007); W. G. Macpherson, *Medical Services General History. III: Medical Services During the Operations on the Western Front in 1916, 1917 and 1918; in Italy; and in Egypt and Palestine* (London, 1924). An examination of the problems caused by disease and the response of the military authorities in Mesopotamia is provided in M. Harrison, 'The Fight Against Disease in the Mesopotamia Campaign', in H. Cecil and P. H. Liddle (eds), *Facing Armageddon: The First World War Experienced* (Barnsley, 1996), 435–89.

140 TNA, WO95/4639, War Diary of 54th Division Assistant Director of Medical Services, 24 April 1917; IWM, PP/MCR/C1, Chetwode Papers, memorandum to General Officers Commanding (GOC) Desert Column and all Divisions, 12 May 1917.

141 IWM, 66/85/1, Hare, diary, 12 May 1917; IWM, PP/MCR/C1, Chetwode Papers, memorandum to GOCs Desert Column and all Divisions, 12 May 1917.

142 TNA, WO95/4386, War Diary of the Egyptian Expeditionary Force Director of Medical Services, May–September 1918.

143 TNA, WO95/4656, War Diary of 163rd Infantry Brigade Headquarters, June 1918, Appendix 7: Brigade casualty and sick rates in June 1918; TNA, WO95/4658, War Diary of 1/5th Suffolk Regiment, 19–23 August 1918.

144 T. J. Mitchell and G. M. Smith, *Medical Services: Casualties and Medical Statistics of the Great War* (London, 1931), 209 and 213.

145 S. M. Miller, *Volunteers on the Veld: Britain's Citizen-Soldiers and the South African War, 1899–1902* (Norman, 2007), 148.
146 TNA, WO95/4653, War Diary of 1/5th Bedfordshire Regiment, May 1917; TNA, WO95/4654, War Diary of 1/10th London Regiment, 25–26 June 1918.
147 Macpherson, *Medical Services General History III*, 434–44.
148 TNA, WO95/4653, War Diary of 1/5th Bedfordshire Regiment, 4 August 1918; TNA, WO95/4654, War Diary of 1/10th London Regiment, August 1918.
149 Macpherson, *Medical Services General History III*, 391–3.
150 The incidence of malaria, although significant by September 1918, never reached the levels which extirpated Australian and American units fighting in New Guinea and the Solomon Islands during the Second World War. See Bergerud, *Touched with Fire*, 90–5.
151 ERM, ER3253, Surry, transcript of reminiscences.
152 TNA, WO95/4650, War Diary of 1/5th Essex Regiment, 26 May–5 June 1918; TNA, WO95/4525, War Diary of Australian and New Zealand Mounted Division Assistant Director of Medical Services, 1 July and 9 September 1918.
153 Macpherson, *Medical Services General History III*, 389.
154 TNA, WO95/4386, War Diary of the Egyptian Expeditionary Force Director of Medical Services, 16 September 1918.
155 TNA, WO95/4653, War Diary of 1/4th Northamptonshire Regiment, September 1918, Appendix: General Instructions, 17 September 1918.
156 The incubation period for malaria meant that many of the men infected in the advances of late September 1918 were only admitted to hospital in October.
157 Falls, *Military Operations II*, 597–8; Dolev, *Allenby's Military Medicine*, 166; TNA, WO95/4377, War Diary of Egyptian Expeditionary Force Deputy Adjutant-General, October 1918.
158 TNA, WO95/4650, War Diary of 1/4th Essex Regiment, 31 October 1918; AWM, AWM4 10/8, War Diary of 3rd Australian Light Horse Regiment, 5 October 1918.
159 Mitchell and Smith, *Medical Services*, 215. For a full study of attempts to control venereal disease rates in Egypt see M. Harrison, 'The British Army and the Problem of Venereal Disease in France and Egypt During the First World War', *Medical History*, XXXIX (1995), 149–56.
160 TNA, WO95/4386, War Diary of the Egyptian Expeditionary Force Director of Medical Services, 10 and 23 July 1918.
161 AWM, AWM4 10/8, War Diary of 3rd Australian Light Horse Regiment, 14 August 1918.
162 TNA, WO95/4386, War Diary of the Egyptian Expeditionary Force Director of Medical Services, 27 January 1918.

Chapter 2

1 S. F. Hatton, *The Yarn of a Yeoman* (London, 1930), 206 and 208.
2 R. Knowles, 'Tale of an "Arabian Knight": The T.E. Lawrence Effigy', *Church Monuments: Journal of the Church Monuments Society*, VI (1991), 67; E. Siberry, *The New Crusaders: Images of the Crusades in the Nineteenth and Twentieth Centuries* (Aldershot, 2000), 95.
3 Falls, *Military Operations II*, 254, 514 and 516.

4   Falls, *Military Operations II*, 47; MacMunn and Falls, *Military Operations I*, 27 and 251.
5   Taylor, *First World War*, 206.
6   Woodward, *Forgotten Soldiers*, 192.
7   Grainger, *Palestine 1917*, 67 and 267–8. Grainger does not list the contemporary accounts that 'repeatedly' invoke this crusading rhetoric and instead seems to be reliant on the official history for this conclusion.
8   Hughes, *Allenby and British Strategy*, 13; M. Snape, *God and the British Soldier: Religion and the British Army in the First and Second World Wars* (London, 2005), 182–3. The other officer was educated at Ampleforth College, a Catholic private school.
9   Siberry, *New Crusaders*, 94–7; E. Siberry, 'Images of the Crusades in the Nineteenth and Twentieth Centuries', in J. Riley-Smith (ed.), *The Oxford History of the Crusades* (Oxford, 1999), 363–84. For a similar interpretation of crusading rhetoric see A. Pendlebury, *Portraying 'the Jew' in First World War Britain* (London, 2006), 70–2.
10 E. Bar-Yosef, *The Holy Land in English Culture 1799–1917: Palestine and the Question of Orientalism* (Oxford, 2005), 247–94.
11 *The Times*, 15 and 18 May, and 28 October 1936.
12 T. Allen, *The Tracks they Trod: Salonika and the Balkans, Gallipoli, Egypt and Palestine Revisited* (London, 1932), 99–100 and 163; D. W. Lloyd, *Battlefield Tourism: Pilgrimage and the Commemoration of the Great War in Britain, Australia and Canada, 1919–1939* (Oxford, 1998), 96.
13 V. Gilbert, *The Last Crusade: With Allenby to Jerusalem* (New York, 1923), 1, 5 and 8. See the analysis of Gilbert by Bar-Yosef, *Holy Land*, 245–56; Siberry, *New Crusaders*, 96; P. Parker, *The Old Lie: The Great War and the Public-School Ethos* (London, 1987), 228–30.
14 D. Maxwell, *The Last Crusade* (London, 1920), 26–7.
15 F. A. M. Webster, *The History of the Fifth Battalion the Bedfordshire and Hertfordshire Regiment (T.A.)* (London, 1930), 138; J. W. Burrows, *The Essex Regiment* (Southend-on-Sea, 1932), V, 136 and 285–6; Blackwell and Axe, *Romford to Beirut*, 59; Gibbons, *With the 1/5th Essex*, 54–60.
16 L. C. Wilson and H. Wetherell, *History of the Fifth Light Horse Regiment (Australian Imperial Force): From 1914 to October, 1917, and from October, 1917 to June, 1919* (Sydney, 1926), 130; C. G. Nicol, *The Story of Two Campaigns: Official War History of the Auckland Mounted Rifles Regiment, 1914–1919* (Auckland, 1921), 97.
17 E. H. H. Allenby, 'Preface', in A. Fair and E. D. Wolton, *The History of the 1/5th Battalion 'The Suffolk Regiment'* (London, 1923), ii; Gibbons, *With the 1/5th Essex*, vii.
18 Briscoe Moore, *Mounted Riflemen*; F. H. Cooper, *Khaki Crusaders: With the South African Artillery in Egypt and Palestine* (Cape Town, 1919); F. S. Brereton, *With Allenby in Palestine: A Story of the Latest Crusade* (London, 1920); J. Bowes, *The Aussie Crusaders with Allenby in Palestine* (London, 1920). For a discussion of fictional accounts of the EEF's campaign see M. Paris, *Warrior Nation: Images of War in British Popular Culture, 1850–2000* (London, 2000), 118–20; J. Shadur, *Young Travelers to Jerusalem: An Annotated Survey of American and English Juvenile Literature on the Holy Land, 1785–1940* (Ramat Gan, 1999), 101–13.
19 Lloyd George, *War Memoirs*, II, 1090; G. A. Smith, *The Historical Geography of the Holy Land: Especially in Relation to the History of Israel and of the Early Church* (20th edn, London, 1919). The work had reached 25 editions by 1931 and had sold 35,237 copies by 1942. For a full analysis of Smith's career and publications see R. Butlin,

'George Adam Smith and the Historical Geography of the Holy Land: Contents, Contexts and Connections', *Journal of Historical Geography*, XIV (1988), 381–404.
20   *The Times*, 17 December 1917.
21   E. Gibbon, *The History of the Decline and Fall of the Roman Empire* (London, 1995), VI, 642; M. Bryant and S. Heneage, *Dictionary of British Cartoonists and Caricaturists, 1730–1980* (Aldershot, 1994), 166.
22   *Hansard*, 5th series, C (20 December 1917), 2211; TNA, CAB23/4, War Cabinet Minutes, 21 November 1917; *Hansard*, 5th series, C (10 December 1917), 875. For a discussion of the fall of Jerusalem and the political machinations surrounding its early British administration see R. Mazza, *Jerusalem: From the Ottomans to the British* (London, 2009), 111–46.
23   L. McKernan, '"The Supreme Moment of the War": *General Allenby's Entry into Jerusalem*', *Historical Journal of Film, Radio and Television*, XIII (1993), 169–80; Hughes, *Allenby and British Strategy*, 41 and 159; R. Low, *The History of the British Film 1914–1918* (London, 1950), 155.
24   *NI*, 21 April 1917.
25   NRM, Order of Service, Memorial Service for Major W. H. Jewson and Captain S. D. Page, both of 1/4th Norfolk, Norwich, 6 May 1917.
26   *The Times*, 22 April 1918.
27   E. W. G. Masterman, *The Deliverance of Jerusalem* (London, 1918), 34.
28   TNA, FO395/152, Foreign Office Correspondence, extract from *The Evening Standard*, 8 November 1917.
29   TNA, FO395/152, Foreign Office Correspondence, Press Bureau notice to the press, No. D.607, 15 November 1917.
30   This fitted into a tradition of imperial governance based on maintaining Britain's prestige in the Muslim world; see D. French, 'The Dardanelles, Mecca and Kut: Prestige as a Factor in British Eastern Strategy, 1914–1916', *War and Society*, V (1987), 45–61.
31   TNA, FO395/152, Foreign Office Correspondence, letter from Edward E. Haig, Wellington House, to C. H. Montgomery, Foreign Office, 27 November 1917; TNA, FO395/152, Foreign Office Correspondence, letter from Stephen Gaslee, Foreign Office, to Oscar S. Ashcroft, Wellington House, 13 December 1917.
32   TNA, FO395/152, Foreign Office Correspondence, telegram from Mark Sykes to Reginald Wingate, 19 December 1917; TNA, FO371/3383, Foreign Office Correspondence, telegram from Reginald Wingate to the Foreign Office, 15 January 1918.
33   TNA, FO371/3383, Foreign Office Correspondence, telegram from Mark Sykes to General Clayton, 16 January 1918; Bar-Yosef, *Holy Land*, 266–7.
34   TNA, WO33/946, War Office Correspondence, telegram from the CIGS to the General Officer Commanding-in-Chief, Egypt, Nos 8582–8584, 21 November 1917; R. Mazza, 'Churches at War: The Impact of the First World War on the Christian Institutions of Jerusalem, 1914–20', *Middle Eastern Studies*, XLV (2009), 212–13.
35   TNA, CAB23/4, War Cabinet Minutes, 26 November 1917; TNA, WO33/946, War Office Correspondence, telegram from the General Officer Commanding-in-Chief, Egypt, to the CIGS, No. 8693, 11 December 1917.
36   IWM, XX02 Special Misc R, proclamation of martial law in Jerusalem issued by Allenby, 11 December 1917; TNA, CAB23/4, War Cabinet Minutes, 19 and 21 November 1917; TNA, FO395/152, Foreign Office Correspondence, telegram from Reginald Wingate to the Foreign Office, India, 13 December 1917; Allenby, letter

to Lady Allenby, 14 December 1917, in M. Hughes (ed.), *Allenby in Palestine: The Middle East Correspondence of Field Marshal Viscount Allenby, June 1917–October 1919* (Stroud, 2004), 112.

37 IWM, PP/MCR/C1, Chetwode Papers, letter from Major-General A. L. Lynden-Bell to Chetwode, 3 May 1917; IWM, PP/MCR/C1, Chetwode, letter to the EEF Chief of the General Staff, 5 May 1917.

38 TNA, WO33/946, War Office Correspondence, telegram from the General Officer Commanding-in-Chief, Egypt, to the Director of Military Intelligence, No. 8884, 15 January 1918; TNA, FO395/152, Foreign Office Correspondence, telegram from the Viceroy of India to the India Office, 27 December 1917; India Office Records (IOR), L/MIL/17/5/2403, Indian Prisoners of War, 'List C: Nominal Roll of Indian Prisoners of War, Suspected of Having Deserted to the Enemy or of Having Given Information to or Otherwise Assisted the Enemy After Capture (Revised to 24 October 1918). Egyptian Expeditionary Force'.

39 A. J. P. Taylor, *English History, 1914–1945* (Oxford, 1965), 168–9. Taylor's sparse two-page coverage of religion in his mammoth study of England between 1914 and 1945 seems very much like a *reductio ad absurdum*. See S. Mews, 'Religion, 1900–1939', in C. Wrigley (ed.), *A Companion to Early Twentieth-Century Britain* (Oxford, 2003), 470; H. McLeod, *Religion and Society in England, 1850–1914* (Basingstoke, 1996), 171–3, 177 and 196–201.

40 S. J. D. Green, *Religion in the Age of Decline: Organisation and Experience in Industrial Yorkshire, 1870–1920* (Cambridge, 1996), 380–90; G. R. Searle, *A New England? Peace and War 1886–1918* (Oxford, 2004), 532–8.

41 A. Gregory, *The Last Great War: British Society and the First World War* (Cambridge, 2008), 159–60 and 178; McLeod, *Religion and Society*, 79–82; J. Harris, *Private Lives, Public Spirit: Britain 1870–1914* (London, 1993), 155; Taylor, *English History*, 169; S. C. Williams, *Religious Belief and Popular Culture in Southwark c. 1880–1939* (Oxford, 1999), 87–104.

42 See C. Moriarty, 'Christian Iconography and First World War Memorials', *Imperial War Museum Review*, VI (1992), 63–75; M. Connelly, *The Great War, Memory and Ritual: Commemoration in the City and East London, 1916–1939* (Woodbridge, 2002), 36–74; J. Davies, 'Reconstructing Enmities; War and War Memorials, the Boundary Markers of the West', *History of European Ideas*, XIX (1994), 47–52.

43 C. G. Brown, *The Death of Christian Britain: Understanding Secularisation 1800–2000* (London, 2001), 1–15. For a criticism of Brown's argument see the defence of the adaptive mechanisms of the Churches in J. Garrett, M. Grimley, A. Harris, W. Whyte and S. Williams (eds), *Redefining Christian Britain: Post-1945 Perspectives* (London, 2006), 289–93.

44 E. S. Talbot and D. S. Cairns (eds), *The Army and Religion: An Enquiry and its Bearing Upon the Religious Life of the Nation* (London, 1919), v–xi, 7, 9 and 33.

45 R. Schweitzer, 'The Cross and the Trenches: Religious Faith and Doubt Among Some British Soldiers on the Western Front', *War and Society*, XVI (1998), 33–57; E. Madigan, *Faith Under Fire: Anglican Army Chaplains and the Great War* (Basingstoke, 2011), 171–202.

46 J. Finley, *A Pilgrim in Palestine Afters its Deliverance: Being an Account of Journeys on Foot by the First American Pilgrim after General Allenby's Recovery of the Holy Land* (London, 1919), 11–12; Allenby, letter to Lady Allenby, 28 November 1917, in Hughes, *Allenby in Palestine*, 100.

47 IWM, 07/8/1, Allenby, letters to mother, 22 and 31 December 1917.

48 Hughes, *Allenby in Palestine*, 1.
49 Museum of Army Chaplaincy Archives (MACA), Jones, diary, 7 January 1917; IWM, 04/9/1, Price, diary, 16 April 1916.
50 IWM, PP/MCR/62, Buxton, letter to mother, 20 November 1916. Hare's diary provides no evidence that he regularly attended church services. KMA, 1998.31, McKay, memoir, 114.
51 R. Schweitzer, *The Cross and the Trenches: Religious Faith and Doubt Among British and American Great War Soldiers* (Westport, 2003), 80; O. Anderson, 'The Growth of Christian Militarism in Mid-Victorian Britain', *The English Historical Review*, LXXXVI (1971), 46–72.
52 IWM, 85/4/1, Bailey, diary, 24 February 1917; AWM, 3DRL/6776, Greatorex, diary, 14 November 1917; IWM, PP/MCR/220, Blagg, letter to father, 16 December 1917; IWM, 94/5/1, Blunt, diary, 12 November 1917.
53 Hampshire Regiment Museum (HRM), M1810, Hickman, letter to wife, 3 January 1916; AWM, PR88/030, Livingstone, memoir, 14; IWM, 05/38/2, MacGregor, letter to mother, 11 July 1918.
54 IWM, 82/22/1, Surry, diary, 24, 38 and 101–2.
55 IWM, PP/MCR/62, Buxton, letters to parents, 15 January, 5 February and 20 March 1916.
56 ATL, MS-Papers-4108/8, McNeur, letters to family, 4 September and 20 October 1917, and 8 February and 10 March 1918.
57 B. Camm, *Pilgrim Paths in Latin Lands* (London, 1923), 254–68. It is surprising to note that the pilgrimage has only been covered in T. Johnstone and J. Hagerty, *The Cross on the Sword: Catholic Chaplains in the Forces* (London, 1996), 151–4. Their analysis is, though, entirely based on Camm's account. It would have been expected that the numerous historians seeking to portray the EEF's campaign as a crusade would have seen this as a critical example. Bar-Yosef also neglects to address this event, which is perhaps a reflection of the fact that the pilgrimage demonstrates the strength of the Catholic Church and does not fit the strong Protestant ethos that he sees as underlining the biblical vernacular tradition evident in soldiers' writings.
58 The Custos, or Custodian, heads the Franciscan order's presence in the Holy Land, a post always held by an Italian. The Franciscan's Custody of the Holy Land was created by Pope Clement VI in the mid-fourteenth century.
59 War Office, *Statistics of the Military Effort*, 64 (vi). The EEF did contain 98,764 Indian and Egyptian troops at this stage of the campaign.
60 TNA, FO882/14, Arab Bureau Papers, letter from Archbishop Randall Thomas Davidson to Bishop Rennie MacInnes, 18 July 1917; TNA, FO882/14, Arab Bureau Papers, letter from General Clayton to Reginald Wingate, 25 October 1917.
61 TNA, FO882/14, Arab Bureau Papers, letter from Rennie MacInnes to Reginald Wingate and note added by Lieutenant-Commander Hogarth, 2 May 1917.
62 TNA, FO882/14, Arab Bureau Papers, letter from G. S. Symes, on behalf of Reginald Wingate, to General Clayton, 12 September 1917.
63 TNA, FO882/14, Arab Bureau Papers, report by Captain R. W. Graves, 2nd Echelon, GHQ, EEF, 15 October 1917.
64 A. F. Winnington-Ingram, *The Potter and the Clay* (London, 1917), 113.
65 IWM, 85/4/1, Bailey Papers, Hare, 'Order of the Day After Third Gaza', 11 November 1917.
66 LHCMA, Clarke 1/4, Clarke, memoir, 21; ATL, MS-Papers-4312/1, Judge, diary, 9 April 1917; IWM, 06/33/1, Mortimer, diary, 48–9; MACA, Jones, diary, 9 December 1917.

67 IWM, 82/22/1, Surry, letter to parents, 26 December 1918. For further discussion of the details of this letter see I. R. Bet-El, 'A Soldier's Pilgrimage: Jerusalem 1918', *Mediterranean Historical Review*, VIII (1993), 218–35.
68 Allenby, letter to Lady Allenby, 21 November 1917, in Hughes, *Allenby in Palestine*, 92.
69 IWM, PP/MCR/220, Blagg, letter to mother, 13 December 1917.
70 See M. Girouard, *The Return to Camelot: Chivalry and the English Gentlemen* (New Haven, 1981), 259–93; A. J. Frantzen, *Bloody Good: Chivalry, Sacrifice and the Great War* (Chicago, 2004); Parker, *Old Lie*, 227–8 and 234. For the role of medieval imagery in post-war memorialization culture see S. Goebel, *The Great War and Medieval Memory: War, Remembrance and Medievalism in Britain and Germany, 1914–1940* (Cambridge, 2007).
71 IWM, 06/33/1, Mortimer, diary, 52; Idriess, *Desert Column*, 289–90; J. P. Wilson, *With the Soldiers in Palestine and Syria* (London, 1920), 6.
72 The role of chaplains in the First World War has been well addressed in a number of studies. See S. H. Louden, *Chaplains in Conflict: The Role of Army Chaplains Since 1904* (London, 1996), 43–68; A. Wilkinson, *The Church of England and the First World War* (London, 1978), 109–35; M. Moynihan, *God on Our Side: The British Padres in World War I* (London, 1983); J. Smyth, *In this Sign Conquer: The Story of the Army Chaplains* (London, 1968), 153–203; D. Crerar, '"Where's the Padre?" Canadian Memory and Great War Chaplains', in D. L. Bergen (ed.), *The Sword of the Lord: Military Chaplains from the First to the Twenty-First Century* (Notre Dame, 2004), 141–63. For a more subtle analysis see P. Porter, 'New Jerusalems: Sacrifice and Redemption in the War Experiences of English and German Chaplains', in P. Purseigle (ed.), *Warfare and Belligerence: Perspectives in First World War Studies* (Leiden, 2005), 101–32; P. Porter, 'Beyond Comfort: German and English Military Chaplains and the Memory of the Great War', *The Journal of Religious History*, XXIX (2005), 258–89; Snape, *God and the British Soldier*, 83–138. A detailed study of the influence of religious rhetoric on the morale of British and German soldiers on the Western Front can be found in P. Porter, 'Slaughter or Sacrifice? The Religious Rhetoric of Blood Sacrifice in the British and German Armies, 1914–1919' (Oxford University, D.Phil. thesis, 2005), 129–69. The impact of chaplains' activities on BEF morale is detailed in Madigan, *Faith*, 89–126.
73 A. V. C. Hordern and E. R. Day, 'The R.A.Ch.D. in the Mediterranean and Egyptian Expeditionary Forces', *Quarterly Journal of the Royal Army Chaplains' Department*, II (1923), 300–3; TNA, WO95/4391, War Diary of the EEF Principal Chaplain, 12 December 1916, 1 and 13 February 1917, 10 March 1917 and 28 February 1918.
74 LHCMA, Shea 6/2a, Shea Papers, 'Some Aspects of Lord Allenby's Palestine Campaign', Staff College lecture by Major-General J. Shea, 25 April 1923; TNA, WO95/4391, War Diary of the EEF Principal Chaplain, 17 May 1917.
75 IWM, 96/48/1, Milsom, memoir, 18; Snape, *God and the British Soldier*, 102–3.
76 IWM, 06/33/1, Mortimer, diary, 44.
77 Hatton, *Yeoman*, 196–7; IWM, 06/33/1, Mortimer, diary, 26.
78 AWM, 2DRL/0817, Chandler, letter to family, 23 November 1916; MACA, Jones, diary, 8 April 1917.
79 Hatton, *Yeoman*, 224; MACA, Jones, diary, 7 January 1917.
80 IWM, 06/33/1, Mortimer, diary, 52; MACA, Jones, diary, 25 May 1917.
81 IWM, 06/33/1, Mortimer, diary, 21. For the difficulties facing the ministry of chaplains in the BEF see Madigan, *Faith*, 127–70.
82 SRO, GB554/Y1/426a, Wolton, letter to mother, 10 February 1916.

83 IWM, Con Shelf, Hinde, diary, 16 June 1916, 9 July 1917 and 5 and 6 September 1917.
84 IWM, 06/33/1, Mortimer, diary, 22.
85 Wilson, *Soldiers in Palestine and Syria*, 33; IWM, 66/85/1, Hare, diary, 14 December 1918; IWM, 06/33/1, Mortimer, diary, 26.
86 J. W. Barrett, *The War Work of the Y.M.C.A. in Egypt* (London, 1919), vii, 86–7, 115 and 126–31; Anonymous, *Anzac Hostel Guide, Cairo* (Cairo, no date), 6–17; AWM, 3DRL/3741 Folder 3, Delpratt, letter to sister, 13 August 1918. For the development of the YMCA's role on the Western Front see Snape, *God and the British Soldier*, 206–36.
87 Barrett, *Y.M.C.A. in Egypt*, 90, 117 and 143; Anonymous, *Anzac Hostel*, 35–44.
88 Barrett, *Y.M.C.A. in Egypt*, 137.
89 IWM, 81/23/1, Shaw, memoir, 1; IWM, 66/85/1, Hare, diary, 27 December 1917; J. G. Lockhart, *Palestine Days and Nights: Sketches of the Campaign in the Holy Land* (London, 1920), 24. This reflected sentiments often expressed in nineteenth-century travel accounts of Palestine; see Bar-Yosef, *Holy Land*, 81.
90 IWM, 05/38/2, MacGregor, letter to sister, 25 August 1918; IWM, 81/23/1, Shaw, memoir, 1.
91 Lockhart, *Days and Nights*, 30 and 34.
92 IWM, Misc 41(726), Gotto, letter to parents, 29 May 1918.
93 ERM, ER15807.1, Cook, diary.
94 AWM, 2DRL/0817, Chandler, letters to family, 28 February and 28 May 1918.
95 SRO, GB554/Y1/426a, Wolton, letter to parents, 7 July 1918. Wolton's underlining.
96 IWM, P386, Dening, diary, 25 June 1918.
97 H. O. Lock, *With the British Army in the Holy Land* (London, 1919), 144–5.
98 IWM, DS/MISC/82, Hampton, memoir, 43.
99 IWM, 98/28/1, Edgerton, memoir, 1.
100 IWM, 96/48/1, Milsom, memoir, 21–2.
101 C. Sommers, *Temporary Crusaders* (London, 1919), v. The idea that the mythology of the First World War shaped how veterans recalled the conflict in public is developed in D. Todman, *The Great War: Myth and Memory* (London, 2005), 187.
102 Hatton, *Yeoman*, 13–14.
103 AWM, 2DRL/0817, Chandler, letter to family, 26 February 1916; IWM, Con Shelf, Hinde, diary, 26 March and 11–21 December 1916; Gibbons, *With the 1/5th Essex*, 47–8; Bar-Yosef, *Holy Land*, 31–5.
104 SRO, GB554/Y1/426a, Wolton, letter to parents, 27 February 1916; SRO, GB554/Y1/165j, Lee, diary, 8.
105 KMA, 1999.2619, McCormack, diary, 6 April 1918.
106 Lockhart, *Days and Nights*, 32.
107 IWM, Misc 41(726), Gotto, letter to parents, 29 May 1918.
108 Briscoe Moore, *Mounted Riflemen*, 136.
109 IWM, 85/4/1, Wink, letter to Mrs Whiffen, 28 December 1917; IWM, Misc 74(1113), Jerusalem Christmas Card, 1917.
110 AWM, 2DRL/0015, Evans, letter to mother, 18 November 1917; HRM, M1810, Hickman, letter to wife, 6 February 1916; IWM, 85/4/1, Bailey, diary, 6–13 January 1919. The tourist experiences of AIF soldiers serving overseas in 1914–18 have been analysed in R. White, 'Sun, Sand and Syphilis: Australian Soldiers and the Orient, Egypt 1914', *Australian Cultural History*, IX (1990), 49–64; B. Ziino, 'A Kind of Round Trip: Australian Soldiers and the Tourist Analogy, 1914–1918', *War*

and Society, XXV (2006), 39–52. For a discussion of the complexities of the tourist experience in the twentieth century see J. Urry, *The Tourist Gaze: Leisure and Travel in Contemporary Societies* (London, 1990).

111 IWM, 05/38/2, MacGregor, letter to family, 6 October 1918.
112 This is an argument raised in relation to the leave trips of AIF soldiers to Paris; see J. Curran, '"Bonjour Paree!" The First AIF in Paris, 1916–1918', *Journal of Australian Studies*, XXIII (1999), 19–26.
113 AWM, PR00740, Holmes, diary, 14 September 1916.
114 Anonymous, *Anzac Hostel*, 18–34.
115 The military's concerns over the public image of the EEF are considered in M. M. Ruiz, 'Manly Spectacles and Imperial Soldiers in Wartime Egypt, 1914–19', *Middle Eastern Studies*, XLV (2009), 351–71.
116 TNA, FO395/240, Foreign Office Correspondence, telegram from Pirie-Gordon to Mark Sykes, 11 February 1918; TNA, FO395/240, Foreign Office Correspondence, telegram from Pirie-Gordon to Colonel Buchan, Foreign Office, 18 March 1918.
117 V. L. Trumper, *Historical Sites in Southern Palestine with a Brief Account of Napoleon's Expedition to Syria 1799* (Cairo, 1917), preface; V. L. Trumper, *Historical Sites in Central Palestine: Part I* (Cairo, 1918), 6–7; V. L. Trumper, *Historical Sites in Central Palestine: Part II* (Cairo, 1918); V. L. Trumper, *Historical Sites in Palestine with a Short Account of Napoleon's Expedition to Syria* (Cairo, 1921), 5–6. Trumper only acknowledged the role of Smith's work in the post-war compendium.
118 E. W. Said, *Orientalism* (3rd edn, London, 2003). For the large corpus of criticism see J. Clifford, review of *Orientalism* by E. W. Said, *History and Theory: Studies in the Philosophy of History*, XIX (1980), 204–23; G. Prakash, 'Orientalism Now', *History and Theory: Studies in the Philosophy of History*, XXXIV (1995), 199–212; J. M. MacKenzie, *Orientalism: History, Theory and the Arts* (Manchester, 1995), 1–19; A. L. Macfie, *Orientalism* (London, 2002), 73–101; R. Irwin, *For Lust of Knowing: The Orientalists and their Enemies* (London, 2006), 277–309. Despite this mighty body of criticism some scholars articulate the bizarre argument that the weight of the attack merely demonstrates Said's continued relevance, rather than the need to reassess his scholarship and the manner in which it has shaped postcolonial studies; see K. Rastegar, 'Revisiting *Orientalism*', *History Today*, LVIII (2008), 49–51. As Mark Bauerlein has noted, this approach reflects key elements of the post-structural or postcolonial turn over the past 30 years in which accuracy of scholarship is sacrificed for the sake of interpretative freedom; see M. Bauerlein, 'Literary Evidence: A Response to Keith Windschuttle', *The Journal of the Historical Society*, II (2002), 77–87.
119 The failure to address mass British attitudes to the Oriental world in the nineteenth century is highlighted in Bar-Yosef, *Holy Land*, 61–104. For a simplistic attempt to apply Said's ideas to a military context see R. Nile, 'Orientalism and the Origins of Anzac', in A. Seymour and R. Nile (eds), *Anzac: Meaning, Memory and Myth* (London, 1991), 32–42. Patrick Porter's boundary-pushing study of military orientalism suggests the extent to which this field has many opportunities for future research; see P. Porter, 'Military Orientalism? British Observers of the Japanese Way of War, 1904–1910', *War and Society*, XXVI (2007), 1–25; Porter, *Military Orientalism*.
120 Nineteenth- and twentieth-century tourism in the Middle East has been addressed in a number of studies. See J. Pemble, *The Mediterranean Passion: Victorians and Edwardians in the South* (Oxford, 1987); L. Withey, *Grand Tours and Cook's Tours:*

A History of Leisure Travel, 1750 to 1915 (London, 1997), 223–62; N. Nasser, 'A Historiography of Tourism in Cairo: A Spatial Perspective', in R. F. Daher (ed.), *Tourism in the Middle East* (Clevedon, 2007), 70–94; P. Brendon, *Thomas Cook: 150 Years of Popular Tourism* (London, 1991), 120–40.

121 R. Fuchs and N. Herbert, 'Representing Mandatory Palestine: Austen St Barbe Harrison and the Representational Buildings of the British Mandate in Palestine, 1922–37', *Architectural History*, XLIII (2000), 281–333. Attempts to utilize a stereotyped Middle Eastern culture as an element of colonial rule had its origins much deeper in the nineteenth century, see T. Mitchell, *Colonising Egypt* (Cambridge, 1988), 161–79.

122 Gregory, *Last Great War*, 184.

Chapter 3

1 W. T. Massey, *How Jerusalem was Won: Being the Record of Allenby's Campaign in Palestine* (London, 1919), 10–11.
2 W. T. Massey, *Allenby's Final Triumph* (London, 1920), 1.
3 T. E. Lawrence, *Seven Pillars of Wisdom: A Triumph* (London, 1935), 392 and 635.
4 Lawrence, *Seven Pillars*, 330.
5 Lawrence, *Seven Pillars*, 61 and 539.
6 Lawrence, *Seven Pillars*, 112 and 329.
7 J. C. Q. Newell, 'Allenby and the Palestine Campaign', in B. Bond (ed.), *The First World War and British Military History* (Oxford, 1991), 211–12.
8 E. Kedourie, 'The Capture of Damascus, 1 October 1918', in E. Kedourie (ed.), *The Chatham House Version and Other Middle-Eastern Studies* (London, 1970), 33–51; M. Hughes, 'Elie Kedourie and the Capture of Damascus, 1 October 1918: A Reassessment', *War and Society*, XXIII (2005), 87–106; M. Hughes, 'What did the Arab Revolt Contribute to the Palestine Campaign? An Assessment', *The Journal of the T.E. Lawrence Society*, XV (2006), 75–87.
9 R. Storrs, *Orientations* (London, 1937), 334–8 and 340–1.
10 G. de S. Barrow, *The Fire of Life* (London, 1942), 43–5 and 193.
11 Barrow had served under Allenby in the Cavalry Division, which later became the Cavalry Corps, sent to France in 1914.
12 R. Savage, *Allenby of Armageddon: A Record of the Career and Campaigns of Field-Marshal Viscount Allenby, G.C.B., G.C.M.G.* (London, 1925), 175 and 177.
13 Falls, *Military Operations II*, 31; Sheffy, *British Military Intelligence*, 273; Y. Sheffy, 'Institutionalized Deception and Perception Reinforcement: Allenby's Campaign in Palestine', in M. I. Handel (ed.), *Intelligence and Military Operations* (London, 1990), 190.
14 R. Meinertzhagen, *Army Diary, 1899–1926* (Edinburgh, 1960), 219–20.
15 Meinertzhagen, *Army Diary*, 219.
16 J. N. Lockman, *Meinertzhagen's Diary Ruse: False Entries on T.E. Lawrence* (Grand Rapids, 1995), 13 and 69; B. Garfield, *The Meinertzhagen Mystery: The Life and Legend of a Colossal Fraud* (Washington, DC, 2007), 14–37.
17 S. Barbara, 'Ornithologists Stunned by Bird Collector's Deceit', *Nature*, CDXXXVII (2005), 302–3; J. Seabrook, 'Ruffled Feathers', *The New Yorker*, LXXXII (2006), 51–61; Julian Putkowski quoted in Garfield, *Meinertzhagen Mystery*, xiii.

18 Allenby's correspondence, collected in disparate archives, was not published until 2004, see Hughes, *Allenby in Palestine*.
19 Newell, 'Allenby and the Palestine Campaign', 213; Newell, 'British Military Policy', 421–2; A. Murray, *Sir Archibald Murray's Despatches (June 1916–June 1917)* (London, 1920), v–vi.
20 MacMunn and Falls, *Military Operations I*, 368–9; Falls, *Military Operations II*, 7 and 634–6.
21 TNA, CAB45/79, Comments and Correspondence Relating to the Compilation of the Official Histories – Egypt and Palestine, letter from Lieutenant-Colonel C. Garsia to the Director, Historical Section (Military Branch), CID, 26 February 1929. The dryness of some of Falls's later historical works has also been noted; see Strachan, 'Liddell Hart, Cruttwell, and Falls', 61–4 and 67.
22 C. Falls, *The First World War* (London, 1960), 217–25, 305–12 and 374–85.
23 Falls, *Armageddon*, 65–86.
24 For accounts of Wavell's EEF career see J. Connell, *Wavell: Scholar and Soldier* (London, 1964), 121–45; V. Schofield, *Wavell: Soldier and Statesman* (London, 2006), 65–80.
25 IWM, 66/85/1, Hare, diary, 15 September 1918.
26 Schofield, *Wavell*, 92; Connell, *Wavell*, 153–4; Wavell, *Palestine Campaigns*, 234–42.
27 B. Bond, 'The Army Between the Two World Wars 1918–1939', in D. G. Chandler and I. F. W. Beckett (eds), *The Oxford History of the British Army* (Oxford, 1994), 256–71; D. French, 'The Mechanization of the British Cavalry Between the World Wars', *War in History*, X (2003), 296–320; Connell, *Wavell*, 154–83; Schofield, *Wavell*, 95–112.
28 A. P. Wavell, 'The Army and the Prophets', *The Journal of the Royal United Service Institution*, LXXV (1930), 665–75; Wavell, *Palestine Campaigns*, 236–8.
29 Schofield, *Wavell*, 110, 281 and 296–7.
30 Hughes, *Allenby in Palestine*, 7.
31 A. P. Wavell, *Allenby: A Study in Greatness. The Biography of Field-Marshal Viscount Allenby of Megiddo and Felixstowe G.C.B. G.C.M.G.* (London, 1940), 294.
32 James, 'Writing Military History', 104; Schofield, *Wavell*, 161.
33 B. H. Liddell Hart, *Reputations* (London, 1928), 251 and 259–60. Liddell Hart rehashed this earlier argument on Allenby in B. H. Liddell Hart, 'Allenby', in B. Parker (ed.), *Famous British Generals* (London, 1951), 119–39.
34 Liddell Hart, *History of the First World War*, 432 and 440.
35 Strachan, 'Liddell Hart, Cruttwell, and Falls', 49–51.
36 See L. James, *Imperial Warrior: The Life and Times of Field-Marshal Viscount Allenby, 1861–1936* (London, 1993), 111–76; A. Farrar-Hockley, 'Field-Marshal the Viscount Allenby', in Lord Carver (ed.), *The War Lords: Military Commanders of the Twentieth Century* (London, 1976), 158–9; B. Gardner, *Allenby* (London, 1965), 116.
37 Grainger, *Palestine 1917*, 81–9.
38 Woodward, *Forgotten Soldiers*, 113 and 256. For a fuller analysis of *Blitzkrieg* as a doctrine see Strachan, *European Armies*, 163–7.
39 Newell, 'British Military Policy', 169–71 and 419–23; Newell, 'Allenby and the Palestine Campaign', 194, 196, 207–8 and 211.
40 Hughes, 'General Allenby and the Palestine Campaign' (1996), 62–3 and 82–3; M. Hughes, 'Command, Strategy and the Battle for Palestine, 1917', in I. F. W. Beckett (ed.), *1917: Beyond the Western Front* (Leiden, 2009), 127; Hughes, *Allenby and British Strategy*, 10, 14–15, 19, 71–88 and 113–57; Hughes, *Allenby in Palestine*, 7.

41 M. Hughes, 'General Allenby and the Palestine Campaign 1917–18', in Y. Sheffy and S. Shai (eds), *The First World War: Middle Eastern Perspective* (Tel Aviv, 2000), 95–7; Hughes, *Allenby in Palestine*, 16; Hughes, 'Battle for Palestine', 128.
42 Jenny Macleod has produced an exemplary analysis of the historiographical problems associated with senior commanders' memoirs in her examination of General Ian Hamilton's reconstruction of his command at Gallipoli; see J. Macleod, *Reconsidering Gallipoli* (Manchester, 2004), 176–208.
43 Barrow, *Fire of Life*, 43; Hughes, 'Battle for Palestine', 127–8; Hughes, *Allenby and British Strategy*, 15; P. Simkins, 'Everyman at War: Recent Interpretations of the Front Line Experience', in B. Bond (ed.), *The First World War and British Military History* (Oxford, 1991), 292. For a thoughtful consideration of oral history sources see A. Thomson, *Anzac Memories: Living with the Legend* (Oxford, 1994); A. Thomson, 'Anzac Memories: Putting Popular Memory Theory into Practice in Australia', in A. Green and K. Troup (eds), *The Houses of History: A Critical Reader in Twentieth-Century History and Theory* (Manchester, 1999), 239–52.
44 IWM, 66/85/1, Hare, diary, April–October 1917.
45 TNA, WO95/4367–4368, War Diary of Egyptian Expeditionary Force General Staff, April–August 1917; TNA, WO95/4450–4451, War Diary of Eastern Force General Staff, April–August 1917; TNA, WO95/4479, War Diary of XX Corps General Staff, August 1917; TNA, WO95/4490, War Diary of XXI Corps General Staff, August 1917.
46 Fennell, *Combat and Morale*, 10 and 27.
47 Neither Newell, Hughes, Woodward, or Grainger, the most scholarly works on the EEF, have made use of this information.
48 Allenby, letter to Lady Allenby, 9 July 1917, in Hughes, *Allenby in Palestine*, 29.
49 Allenby, letter to Robertson, 11 July 1917, in Hughes, *Allenby in Palestine*, 30.
50 L. V. Smith, *Between Mutiny and Obedience: The Case of the French Fifth Infantry Division During World War One* (Princeton, 1994), 175–214; L. V. Smith, 'The French High Command and the Mutinies of Spring 1917', in H. Cecil and P. H. Liddle (eds), *Facing Armageddon: The First World War Experienced* (Barnsley, 1996), 79–92; L. V. Smith, 'Remobilising the Citizen-Soldier Through the French Army Mutinies of 1917', in J. Horne (ed.), *State, Society and Mobilization in Europe During the First World War* (Cambridge, 1997), 144–59.
51 V. Wilcox, 'Discipline in the Italian Army 1915–1918', in P. Purseigle (ed.), *Warfare and Belligerence: Perspectives in First World War Studies* (Leiden, 2005), 73–100; J. Gooch, 'Morale and Discipline in the Italian Army, 1915–1918', in H. Cecil and P. H. Liddle (eds), *Facing Armageddon: The First World War Experienced* (Barnsley, 1996), 434–47; I. Dravidian, 'The Russian Soldier's Morale from the Evidence of Tsarist Military Censorship', in H. Cecil and P. H. Liddle (eds), *Facing Armageddon: The First World War Experienced* (Barnsley, 1996), 425–33; R. C. Hall, '"The Enemy is Behind Us": The Morale Crisis in the Bulgarian Army During the Summer of 1918', *War in History*, XI (2004), 209–19.
52 Watson, 'Junior Officership'; Watson, 'Stabbed at the Front'.
53 Fennell, *Combat and Morale*, 34–49; R. Neillands, 'The Experience of Defeat: Kut (1916) and Singapore (1942)', in P. Liddle, J. Bourne and I. Whitehead (eds), *The Great World War 1914–1945. I: Lightning Strikes Twice* (London, 2000), 278–92.
54 G. D. Sheffield, 'Introduction: Command, Leadership and the Anglo-American Experience', in G. D. Sheffield (ed.), *Leadership and Command: The Anglo-American Military Experience Since 1861* (London, 1997), 1.
55 Ardant du Picq, *Battle Studies*, 119.

56 For the impact of Montgomery on the morale of 8th Army in 1942 see Fennell, *Combat and Morale*, 188–218.
57 TNA, CAB45/78, Comments and Correspondence Relating to the Compilation of the Official Histories – Egypt and Palestine, letter from Major-General E. W. C. Chaytor to the Director, Historical Section (Military Branch), CID, 26 October 1925.
58 TNA, CAB45/78, Comments and Correspondence Relating to the Compilation of the Official Histories – Egypt and Palestine, letter from General P. W. Chetwode to C. Falls, 15 August 1929.
59 AWM, PR00535 Box 2 Series 4/11, Chauvel, letter to Lady Chauvel, 8 December 1917.
60 ERM, France, diary, 19 November 1917; SRO, GB554/Y1/426a, Wolton, letter to parents, 22 November 1917; IWM, 85/4/1, Wink, letter to Mrs Whiffen, 28 December 1917.
61 ATL, MS-Papers-4312/1, Judge, diary, 4 and 8 July 1917.
62 TNA, CAB45/79, Comments and Correspondence Relating to the Compilation of the Official Histories – Egypt and Palestine, letters from Lieutenant-Colonel C. Garsia to the Director, Historical Section (Military Branch), CID, 2 and 7 December 1929; IWM, 66/85/1, Hare Papers, letter from Lieutenant-Colonel C. Garsia to Hare, 8 June 1920.
63 Garsia, *Key to Victory*, 291–3.
64 Lieutenant-General James Aylmer Haldane quoted in Hughes, *Allenby in Palestine*, 4; Woodward, *Forgotten Soldiers*, 113. The 'Bull' part of the signal was a reference to Allenby's sobriquet which he had acquired before 1914.
65 James, *Imperial Warrior*, 84; Wavell, *Allenby*, 188. A kinder view of Allenby's temper is given in Hughes, *Allenby in Palestine*, 4–5; IWM, 66/85/1, Hare, diary, 23 November 1917.
66 C. S. Forester, *The General* (London, 1936); Hughes, *Allenby and British Strategy*, 16–17.
67 AWM, PR84/179 Folder 3, Tomlins, diary, 11 September 1917; ATL, MS-Papers-4312/1, Judge, diary, 16 June 1917; AWM, 3DRL/6595, Horder, diary, 29 August 1916.
68 Grainger, *Palestine 1917*, 87.
69 Similarly, Lieutenant-General Stanley Maude moved his GHQ closer to the front line to better control operations in Mesopotamia. See E. Latter, 'The Indian Army in Mesopotamia 1914–1918', *Journal of the Society for Army Historical Research*, LXXII (1994), 240.
70 TNA, CAB45/78, Comments and Correspondence Relating to the Compilation of the Official Histories – Egypt and Palestine, letter from General P. W. Chetwode to Lieutenant-General G. MacMunn, 12 January 1925; TNA, CAB45/79, Comments and Correspondence Relating to the Compilation of the Official Histories – Egypt and Palestine, letter from Lieutenant-Colonel C. Garsia to the Director, Historical Section (Military Branch), CID, 7 December 1929.
71 TNA, CAB45/79, Comments and Correspondence Relating to the Compilation of the Official Histories – Egypt and Palestine, letter from J. Gammell to Brigadier-General G. Dawnay, 27 October 1925.
72 R. Holmes, *The Little Field Marshal: A Life of Sir John French* (London, 1981), 266–7.
73 Bartov, 'Daily Life and Motivation in War'.
74 Erickson, *Ottoman Army Effectiveness*, 112–14.
75 M. Hughes, 'Edmund Allenby: Third Army, 1915–1917', in I. F. W. Beckett and S. Corvi (eds), *Haig's Generals* (Barnsley, 2006), 21–8.

76 Hughes, 'General Allenby and the Palestine Campaign' (1996) highlights some of the limitations of these reforms at Third Gaza and during the Transjordan Raids.
77 For a full discussion of the Indianization of the EEF see Chapter 6.
78 Erickson, *Ottoman Army Effectiveness*, 151–52. The EEF's operational improvements to a certain extent merely brought it up to the standard of the Turkish Army, although the Turks were hampered by a severe lack of resources and manpower by 1917–18. The Turkish Army on a number of occasions in the first quarter of the twentieth century demonstrated an ability to outperform its opponents, even when they were better equipped; see E. J. Erickson, 'Strength Against Weakness: Ottoman Military Effectiveness at Gallipoli, 1915', *Journal of Military History*, LXV (2001), 981–1011; E. J. Erickson, 'From Kirkilisse to the Great Offensive: Turkish Operational Encirclement Planning, 1912–22', *Middle Eastern Studies*, XL (2004), 45–64.
79 For a discussion of the role of the individual in interpretations of the historical 'juggernaut' of the First World War, see M. Hughes and M. Seligmann, 'People and the Tides of History: Does Personality Matter in the First World War?', in M. Hughes and M. Seligmann (eds), *Leadership in Conflict, 1914–1918* (Barnsley, 2000), 1–9.

Chapter 4

1 Woodward, *Forgotten Soldiers*, 17; Falls, *Military Operations II*, 421.
2 Such parochial concerns can be found in the work of K. W. Mitchinson; see K. W. Mitchinson, *Gentlemen and Officers: The Impact and Experience of War on a Territorial Regiment, 1914–1918* (London, 1995); K. W. Mitchinson, *Amateur Soldiers: A History of Oldham's Volunteers and Territorials, 1850–1938* (Oldham, 1999). The valedictory account of the Territorials' history written by Ian Beckett, produced for the 100th anniversary of their foundation, does little to challenge the stereotypes of the TF in the First World War; see I. F. W. Beckett, *Territorials: A Century of Service* (Plymouth, 2008). A much more nuanced and analytically rigorous approach to the issues of morale, discipline and combat motivation in Territorial battalions is found in McCartney, *Citizen Soldiers*.
3 P. Dennis, *The Territorial Army 1906–1940* (Woodbridge, 1987), 10 and 14; I. F. W. Beckett, *The Amateur Military Tradition 1558–1945* (Manchester, 1991), 204; E. Spiers, 'The Late Victorian Army 1868–1914', in D. G. Chandler and I. F. W. Beckett (eds), *The Oxford History of the British Army* (Oxford, 1994), 187–90; French, *Military Identities*, 10–30. For the complex relationship of British society to its military personnel see Paris, *Warrior Nation*.
4 Dennis, *Territorial Army*, 22–4 and 29; IWM, 66/85/1, Hare, diary, 15 April 1916; IWM, 66/85/1, Hare, draft of a speech to be given to Australian soldiers at Tel el Kebir training camp, contained in his diary, 20 April 1916; French, *Military Identities*, 230.
5 C. C. R. Murphy, *The History of the Suffolk Regiment 1914–1927* (London, 1928), 101–2; Beckett, *Amateur*, 229–30; LHCMA, Clarke 1/2, Clarke, memoir, 14.
6 Petre, *Norfolk Regiment*, II, 126. This was the notorious occasion on which the Sandringham Company suffered heavy casualties, allegedly including the Turks killing some men after they had surrendered. For a full analysis of the 1/5th Norfolks at Gallipoli see T. Travers and B. Celik, '"Not one of them ever came back": What Happened to the 1/5 Norfolk Battalion on 12 August 1915', *The Journal of Military History*, LXVI (2002), 389–406.

Notes

7 Beckett, *Amateur*, 232; Anonymous, *History of the Hampshire Territorial Force Association, 1914–1919* (Southampton, 1921), 175; Petre, *Norfolk Regiment*, II, 135; Murphy, *Suffolk Regiment*, 104 and 110.
8 Maurice, *16th Foot*, 172; Burrows, *Essex Regiment*, V, 101–2; Gibbons, *With the 1/5th Essex*, 39.
9 Burrows, *Essex Regiment*, V, 131–3; I. F. W. Beckett, 'The Territorial Force in the Great War', in P. H. Liddle (ed.), *Home Fires and Foreign Fields: British Social and Military Experience in the First World War* (London, 1985), 25; LHCMA, Clarke 1/1, Clarke, memoir, 7; Falls, *Armageddon*, 71; H. G. Hart, *The New Army List* (London, January 1915), 1006.
10 MacMunn and Falls, *Military Operations I*, 279; Fair and Wolton, *History of the 1/5th*, 49; TNA, WO95/4634, War Diary of 54th Division General Staff, 26–27 March 1917; Burrows, *Essex Regiment*, V, 152.
11 MacMunn and Falls, *Military Operations I*, 348; Petre, *Norfolk Regiment*, II, 147; IWM, 66/85/1, Hare, diary, 19 April 1917.
12 ERM, France, diary, 25 November 1917.
13 TNA, WO95/4636, War Diary of 54th Division General Staff, September 1918, Appendix 8: 'Narrative of Operations – 54th Division and D.F.P.S., 18, 19, 20 and 21 September 1918'.
14 Fuller, *Troop Morale*, 176.
15 French, *Military Identities*, 247; McCartney, *Citizen Soldiers*, 121–88; Dennis, *Territorial Army*, 4–15.
16 IWM, 82/22/1, Surry, diary, 26; Blackwell and Axe, *Romford to Beirut*, 141.
17 Webster, *Fifth Battalion*, 139.
18 McCartney, *Citizen Soldiers*, 78–9; Fair and Wolton, *History of the 1/5th*, 92; TNA, WO95/4653, War Diary of 1/4th Northamptonshire Regiment, May 1917; IWM, Con Shelf, Hinde, diary, 25 September 1917; SRO, GB554/Y1/187b, Oliver Papers, plan of trenches on Hill 60, Gallipoli; TNA, WO95/4651, War Diary of 1/7th Essex Regiment, 18 May 1917.
19 Gibbons, *With the 1/5th Essex*, 42; TNA, WO95/4653, War Diary of 1/4th Northamptonshire Regiment, 14 January 1918.
20 Gibbons, *With the 1/5th Essex*, 131; TNA, WO95/4653, War Diary of 1/5th Bedfordshire Regiment, 11 July 1918; SRO, GB554/Y1/426a, Wolton, letter to mother, 10 February 1916; IWM, 74/149/1, Barron, diary, 14.
21 IWM, 66/85/1, Hare, diary, 27 December 1917; SRO, GB554/Y1/165j, Lee, diary, 13–16; IWM, Con Shelf, Hinde, diary, 3–5 February 1918; IWM, 82/22/1, Surry, diary, 108.
22 IWM, 03/29/1, Wollaston, diary, 35.
23 SRO, GB554/Y1/426a, Wolton, letter to parents, 16 March 1916; IWM, 76/74/1, Jewson, letter to mother, 10 June 1917; IWM, 03/29/1, Wollaston, diary, 73.
24 IWM, Con Shelf, Hinde, diary, 18 December 1917; NRM, Overman, letter to parents, 4 February 1916.
25 Fuller, *Troop Morale*, 94–109; IWM, 74/149/1, Barron, diary, 8 and 14; IWM, Con Shelf, Hinde, diary, 7 November 1916 and 3 April 1918; IWM, 06/33/1, Mortimer, diary, 26; Gibbons, *With the 1/5th Essex*, 49; M. B. Gale, 'Ashwell, Lena (1872–1957)', *Oxford Dictionary of National Biography*.
26 IWM, Con Shelf, Hinde, diary, 19 January 1917 and 1 January 1918; IWM, 66/85/1, Hare, diary, 9 July 1918; Fuller, *Troop Morale*, 106.

27 IWM, Con Shelf, Hinde Papers, Programme for the 54th Division concert party 'The Rose of Gaza', September 1917; LHCMA, Clarke 1/4, Clarke, memoir, 6–7; IWM, 66/85/1, Hare, diary, 17 September 1917; SRO, GB554/Y1/426a, Wolton, letter to parents, 29 October 1917; IWM, Con Shelf, Hinde, diary, 17 September 1917.
28 LHCMA, Clarke 1/4, Clarke, memoir, 7; Burrows, *Essex Regiment*, V, 126–7.
29 IWM, PP/MCR/62, Buxton, letter to father, 29 October 1916; NRM, NWHRM 6186, Bland, diary, 24 January 1917; TNA, WO95/4658, War Diary of 1/5th Suffolk Regiment, 26 April 1916; SRO, GB554/Y1/426a, Wolton, letter to parents, 4 May 1916; TNA, WO95/4649, War Diary of 161st Infantry Brigade Headquarters, 14–30 January 1918; TNA, WO95/4653, War Diary of 1/4th Northamptonshire Regiment, 16 October 1916. For a detailed discussion of the role of sport in the BEF see E. Riedi and T. Mason, '"Leather" and the Fighting Spirit: Sport in the British Army in World War I', *Canadian Journal of History*, XLI (2006), 485–516.
30 TNA, WO95/4654, War Diary of 1/11th London Regiment, 7 September 1918; TNA, WO95/4656, War Diary of 163rd Infantry Brigade Headquarters, 5 August 1918; NRM, NWHRM 6186, Bland, diary, 5 August 1918; Searle, *New England*, 112–14.
31 IWM, 76/74/1, Jewson, letter to father, 31 January 1917; IWM, PP/MCR/62, Buxton, letter to father, 17 October 1916; IWM, 66/85/1, Hare, diary, 26 December 1918; HRM, M653, Nightingale, 'His War Record' pocket book; Gibbons, *With the 1/5th Essex*, 120 and 129–30.
32 IWM, 85/4/1, Bailey, diary, 24 April and 27 September 1916, 10 and 23 December 1916, 22 January 1917, 18 January 1918, and 2, 4 and 28 February 1918.
33 ERM, ER3253, Surry, transcript of reminiscences; ERM, Joslin, memoir, 6; IWM, 82/22/1, Surry, diary, 72; IWM, Con Shelf, Hinde, diary, 26 October 1916.
34 IWM, 74/149/1, Barron, diary, 4; IWM, 76/74/1, Jewson, letter to mother, 3 May 1917; IWM, Con Shelf, Hinde, diary, 4 February 1917.
35 TNA, WO95/4650, War Diary of 1/4th Essex Regiment, 25 April 1916; NRM, Box 11/3978, Littlewood, diary, 26 April 1916.
36 TNA, WO95/4653, War Diary of 1/5th Bedfordshire Regiment, 17 June 1917; TNA, WO95/4658, War Diary of 1/5th Suffolk Regiment, 11 April 1917; TNA, WO95/4654, War Diary of 1/11th London Regiment, 15 June and 28 July 1917.
37 IWM, 74/149/1, Barron, diary, 12; Blackwell and Axe, *Romford to Beirut*, 129; IWM, 85/4/1, Bailey, diary, 25 December 1917; Holmes, *Acts*, 244–54; J. Keegan, 'Towards a Theory of Combat Motivation', in P. Addison and A. Calder (eds), *Time to Kill: The Soldier's Experience of War in the West 1939–1945* (London, 1997), 7.
38 IWM, 82/22/1, Surry, diary, 92; TNA, WO95/4653, War Diary of 1/5th Bedfordshire Regiment, 3 November 1917; Ellis, *Eye-Deep*, 133.
39 National Army Museum, 2004-03-64, Osbourne, diary, 9 November 1917; IWM, Con Shelf, Hinde, diary, 25 December 1917; IWM, 85/4/1, Bailey, diary, 19 May 1918; IWM, 76/74/1, Jewson, letter to mother, 27 June 1917.
40 Blackwell and Axe, *Romford to Beirut*, 113; NRM, Overman, letter to parents, 25 March 1916; R. Duffet, 'A War Unimagined: Food and the Rank and File Soldier of the First World War', in J. Meyer (ed.), *British Popular Culture and the First World War* (Leiden, 2008), 60–1.
41 HRM, M1810, Hickman, letter to wife, 6 February 1916; IWM, 06/69/1, Town, memoir, 5; IWM, 03/29/1, Wollaston, diary, 46.
42 Watson, 'Self-Deception', 255.
43 Keegan, *Face of Battle*, 29–30; Marshall, *Men Against Fire*, 42.

44 IWM, 82/22/1, Surry, diary, 8 and 38. Emphasis in the original. Little, 'Buddy Relations', 199.
45 NRM, Fielding Papers, '54th (East Anglian) Division Dinner Club', letter from R. M. Maurice, Honorary Secretary, to former officers of the division; NRM, Fielding Papers, 'Officers' Dinner Club of 4th Norfolk Regiment', letter to relatives of any member of 1/4th Norfolks killed in Syria or Palestine, 18 February 1922, letter to members, 20 February 1922.
46 Strachan, 'Training', 212.
47 IWM, 82/22/1, Surry, diary, 63; Richardson, *Fighting Spirit*, 20–1.
48 ERM, ER3253, Surry, transcript of reminiscences; Webster, *Fifth Battalion*, 217.
49 TNA, WO95/4657, War Diary of 1/5th Norfolk Regiment, 16 June 1917; Fair and Wolton, *History of the 1/5th*, 41; Webster, *Fifth Battalion*, 123 and 125.
50 TNA, WO95/4652, War Diary of 162nd Infantry Brigade Headquarters, 10 February 1916; TNA, WO95/4653, War Diary of 1/5th Bedfordshire Regiment, 12 February 1916; TNA, WO95/4658, War Diary of 1/5th Suffolk Regiment, March 1916. A similar decline in local social homogeneity within Territorial battalions was also seen on the Western Front; see McCartney, *Citizen Soldiers*, 69–70.
51 TNA, WO95/4654, War Diary of 1/10th London Regiment, 24 January 1916.
52 IWM, 66/85/1, Hare, diary, 19 November 1917; HRM, M1810, Hickman, letter to wife, 22 March 1916.
53 LHCMA, Clarke 1/3, Clarke, memoir, 5.
54 For further analysis of the difficulties of maintaining local identity in battalions during the First World War see French, *Military Identities*, 282; Beckett, 'Territorial Force' (in Liddle), 27; I. F. W. Beckett, 'The Territorial Force', in I. F. W. Beckett and K. Simpson (eds), *A Nation in Arms: A Social Study of the British Army in the First World War* (Manchester, 1985), 137.
55 K. Simpson, 'The British Soldier on the Western Front', in P. H. Liddle (ed.), *Home Fires and Foreign Fields: British Social and Military Experience in the First World War* (London, 1985), 147.
56 R. Holmes, *Tommy: The British Soldier on the Western Front 1914–1918* (London, 2004), 601; SRO, GB554/Y1/426a, Wolton, letter to parents, 3 August 1916; IWM, 03/29/1, Wollaston, diary, 61; TNA, WO95/4658, War Diary of 1/5th Suffolk Regiment, 1 August 1918.
57 Gibbons, *With the 1/5th Essex*, 115; I. F. W. Beckett, 'Wood, Sir (Henry) Evelyn (1838–1919)', *Oxford Dictionary of National Biography*.
58 French, *Military Identities*, 79–80; TNA, WO95/4652, War Diary of 162nd Infantry Brigade Headquarters, 29 April 1917.
59 Holmes, *Acts*, 311.
60 ERM, France, diary, 7 May 1918.
61 NRM, Overman, letter to parents, 12 April 1917; HRM, M1810, Hickman, letter to wife, 22 March 1916; IWM, PP/MCR/218, Thompson, diary, 16 August 1917; NRM, NWHRM 6186, Bland, diary, 12 August 1917; IWM, Con Shelf, Hinde, diary, 21 August 1916; TNA, WO95/4650, War Diary of 1/5th Essex Regiment, 14 August 1916; Gibbons, *With the 1/5th Essex*, 46; NRM, Overman Papers, letter notifying Overman's parents of his death from wounds on 14 May 1917.
62 ERM, France, diary, 14 October 1917; *The Northampton Independent*, 7 July 1917.
63 ERM, France, diary, 26 and 27 March 1918; TNA, WO95/4657, War Diary of 1/5th Norfolk Regiment, 20 April 1918; TNA, WO95/4650, War Diary of 1/4th Essex

Regiment, April 1918, Appendix: Minutes of the Gaza Commemoration Dinner of 1/4th Essex, at Wilhelma, 26 March 1918.
64 ERM, France, diary, 7 November 1917.
65 NRM, Fielding Papers, '54th (East Anglian) Division Dinner Club', rules set down in annual booklet listing the club's members.
66 ERM, ER5304.4, Order of Service and Thanksgiving for 1/4th Battalion the Essex Regiment, Freetown, 23 March 1941; NRM, Order of Service, Memorial Service for Major W. H. Jewson and Captain S. D. Page, both of 1/4th Norfolk, Norwich, 6 May 1917; *Eastern Daily Press*, 12 April 1927 and 20 April 1936; ERM, ER 5315, Order of Service, 2/5th Battalion the Essex Regiment, Service in the Essex Regiment Chapel to Commemorate the 50th Anniversary of the Battle of Deir-el-Shein, Warley, 4 July 1992.
67 IWM, 82/22/1, Surry, diary, 115; Beckett, 'Territorial Force' (in Beckett and Simpson), 130–1.
68 IWM, 66/85/1, Hare, diary, 9 March 1917.
69 IWM, 03/29/1, Wollaston, diary, 56.
70 IWM, 66/85/1, Hare, diary, 19 September 1918; Beckett, *Amateur*, 218–19; Beckett, 'Territorial Force' (in Liddle), 32.
71 IWM, 74/149/1, Barron, diary, 13; French, *Military Identities*, 230; McCartney, *Citizen Soldiers*, 162–88. For an examination of the military as a profession see C. J. Downes, 'To Be or Not To Be a Profession: The Military Case', *Defence Analysis*, I (1985), 147–71.
72 IWM, 66/85/1, Hare, draft of a speech to be given to Australian soldiers at Tel el Kebir training camp, contained in his diary, 20 April 1916; IWM, 66/85/1, Hare, diary, 14 September 1916.
73 IWM, 85/4/1, Bailey Papers, Hare, 'Order of the Day After Third Gaza', 11 November 1917.
74 TNA, WO95/4633, War Diary of 54th Division General Staff, January 1916, Appendix 2: 54th Division Memorandum on Training, 25 January 1916.
75 LHCMA, Clarke 1/2, Clarke, memoir, 26; TNA, WO95/4650, War Diary of 1/6th Essex Regiment, December 1916.
76 Burrows, *Essex Regiment*, V, 198–202; Fair and Wolton, *History of the 1/5th*, 71–2; Petre, *Norfolk Regiment*, II, 149.
77 TNA, WO95/4634, War Diary of 54th Division General Staff, June 1917, Appendix 2: Memorandum on Divisional Training Camp, by Lieutenant-Colonel Garsia, GSO1, 54th Division, 8 June 1917.
78 TNA, WO95/4634, War Diary of 54th Division General Staff, June 1917, Appendix 2: Memorandum on Divisional Training Camp, by Lieutenant-Colonel Garsia, GSO1, 54th Division, 8 June 1917.
79 TNA, WO95/4656, War Diary of 163rd Infantry Brigade Headquarters, 1–13 October 1917; TNA, WO95/4650, War Diary of 1/6th Essex Regiment, 7 March 1918; TNA, WO95/4651, War Diary of 161st Light Trench Mortar Battery, 4 March 1918; Marshall, *Men Against Fire*, 132; Strachan, 'Training', 216.
80 Wilson, 'March 26 and 27 1917', in Gibbons, *With the 1/5th Essex*, 72.
81 LHCMA, Clarke 1/3, Clarke, memoir, 23.
82 War Office, *Statistics of the Military Effort*, 17 November 1917.
83 IWM, 66/85/1, Hare, draft of a speech to be given to Australian soldiers at Tel el Kebir training camp, contained in his diary, 20 April 1916.

84 Sheffield, *Leadership in the Trenches*, 28; IWM, 76/74/1, Jewson, letter to mother, 6 April 1917; NRM, NWHRM 6186, Bland, diary, 22 November 1917; SRO, GB554/Y1/426a, Wolton, letter to parents, 25 June 1916.
85 IWM, Con Shelf, Hinde, diary, 25 August 1916; TNA, WO95/4657, War Diary of 1/4th Norfolk Regiment, November 1917, Appendix 1: 'Report on Operations of C Coy, 4th Norfolk', by Captain T. R. Berrey, 5 November 1917; IWM, 82/22/1, Surry, diary, 88; NRM, Box 11, Emms, 'Account of the Attack on Gaza of 1/5th Norfolks, April 1917', 1 May 1917; Holmes, *Tommy*, 576.
86 IWM, 82/22/1, Surry, diary, 23.
87 Ashworth, *Trench Warfare*, 176–203.
88 TNA, WO95/4634, War Diary of 54th Division General Staff, June 1917, Appendix 18: Notes on Trench Raids.
89 TNA, WO95/4659, War Diary of 1/8th Hampshire Regiment, 14 July 1917; TNA, WO95/4659, War Diary of 1/8th Hampshire Regiment, July 1917, Appendix B: '8th Bn. The Hampshire Regiment, Minor Operations – 14/15 July 1917'.
90 Winter, *Death's Men*, 93.
91 IWM, 66/85/1, Hare, diary, 15 July 1917.
92 TNA, WO95/4656, War Diary of 163rd Infantry Brigade Headquarters, September 1917: Request for a Raid Plan from Lieutenant-Colonel Garsia, GSO1, 54th Division, to Commanding Officer of 8th Hampshire Regiment, 6 September 1917.
93 Webster, *Fifth Battalion*, 163–83; TNA, WO95/4653, War Diary of 1/5th Bedfordshire Regiment, July 1917, Appendix D: 'Casualty Summary for July 1917'; TNA, WO95/4653, War Diary of 1/5th Bedfordshire Regiment, 10–19, 21, 26 and 27 July 1917.
94 *Bedfordshire Times and Independent*, 17 August 1917; Bedfordshire Record Office, X550/6/23, Order of Service for the Centenary Celebrations of 5th Battalion the Bedfordshire Regiment, including a 'Short History of the 5th Battalion the Bedfordshire Regiment (T.A.)', 20 March 1964.
95 Raiding also played an important role in shaping the military identities of the East Kent Regiment's battalions on the Western Front; see M. Connelly, *Steady the Buffs! A Regiment, a Region, and the Great War* (Oxford, 2006), 77–92.
96 IWM, 66/85/1, Hare, diary, 28 July 1917.
97 TNA, WO95/4634, War Diary of 54th Division General Staff, July 1917, Appendix 11: Message of Congratulations to 1/5th Bedfordshire Regiment from GOC Eastern Force.
98 Fair and Wolton, *History of the 1/5th*, 70; McCartney, *Citizen Soldiers*, 81–6; Burrows, *Essex Regiment*, V, 289; IWM, 85/4/1, Bailey, diary, 28 February 1918.
99 Fuller, *Troop Morale*, 175–80; Holmes, *Acts*, 311; Baynes, *Morale*, 169.
100 H. Strachan, 'The British Way in Warfare', in D. G. Chandler and I. F. W. Beckett (eds), *The Oxford History of the British Army* (Oxford, 1994), 412; J. Keegan, 'Inventing Military Traditions', in C. Wrigley (ed.), *Warfare, Diplomacy and Politics: Essays in Honour of A.J.P. Taylor* (London, 1986), 58–79; E. Hobsbawm, 'Introduction: Inventing Traditions', in E. Hobsbawm and T. Ranger (eds), *The Invention of Tradition* (Cambridge, 1983), 1–14; E. Hobsbawm, 'Mass-Producing Traditions: Europe 1870–1914', in E. Hobsbawm and T. Ranger (eds), *The Invention of Tradition* (Cambridge, 1983), 263–307; H. Trevor-Roper, 'The Invention of Tradition: The Highland Tradition of Scotland', in E. Hobsbawm and T. Ranger (eds), *The Invention of Tradition* (Cambridge, 1983), 15–41.

101 C. F. French, 'The Fashioning of *Esprit de Corps* in the 51st Highland Division from St Valery to El Alamein', *Journal of the Society for Army Historical Research*, LXXVII (1999), 275–92.
102 French, *Military Identities*, 259–60 and 282; Baynes, *Morale*, 169.
103 Hughes, *Allenby and British Strategy*, 162; Strachan, 'British Way in Warfare', 414; French, *Military Identities*, 276; Hart, *New Army List* (January 1915), 1006, 1081, 1105 and 1118; L. James, *The Rise and Fall of the British Empire* (London, 1994), 233–4.

Chapter 5

1 Falls, *Military Operations II*, 643; J. Coates, *An Atlas of Australia's Wars* (Oxford, 2001), 96.
2 S. Badsey, 'Cavalry and the Development of Breakthrough Doctrine', in P. Griffith (ed.), *British Fighting Methods in the Great War* (London, 1996), 138–74; G. Phillips, 'The Obsolescence of the *Arme Blanche* and Technological Determinism in British Military History', *War and History*, II (2002), 39–59; G. Phillips, 'Scapegoat Arm: Twentieth-Century Cavalry in Anglophone Historiography', *The Journal of Military History*, LXXI (2007), 37–74; G. Phillips, '"Who Shall Say that the Days of Cavalry are Over?" The Revival of the Mounted Arm in Europe, 1853–1914', *War in History*, XVIII (2011), 5–32.
3 P. Dennis, J. Grey, E. Morris, R. Prior and J. Connor (eds), *The Oxford Companion to Australian Military History* (Oxford, 1995), 349–52; I. McGibbon (ed.), *The Oxford Companion to New Zealand Military History* (Oxford, 2000), 337–8; T. Kinloch, *Echoes of Gallipoli: In the Words of New Zealand's Mounted Riflemen* (Auckland, 2005), 17–18. For a detailed analysis of shifting conceptions of the ALH's tactical role during the First World War see J. Bou, 'Cavalry, Firepower, and Swords: The Australian Light Horse and the Tactical Lessons of Cavalry Operations, 1916–1918', *The Journal of Military History*, LXXI (2007), 99–125.
4 Kinloch, *Echoes of Gallipoli*, 19–22; C. Pugsley, *The Anzac Experience: New Zealand, Australia and Empire in the First World War* (Auckland, 2004), 39–45; R. J. G. Hall, *The Australian Light Horse* (North Blackburn, 1966), 29.
5 Hall, *Australian Light Horse*, 39; McGibbon, *New Zealand Military History*, 337.
6 C. Pugsley, 'New Zealand: "From the Uttermost Ends of the Earth"', in P. Liddle, J. Bourne and I. Whitehead (eds), *The Great World War 1914–1945. II: The People's Experience* (London, 2001), 225; J. Beaumont, 'Australia', in P. Liddle, J. Bourne and I. Whitehead (eds), *The Great World War 1914–1945. II: The People's Experience* (London, 2001), 200; Pugsley, *Anzac Experience*, 69.
7 P. Stanley, '"Our big world": The Social History of the Light Horse Regiment, 1916–1918', *Sabretache: The Journal and Proceedings of the Military Historical Society of Australia*, XXXIX (1998), 4; A. J. Hill, 'General Sir Harry Chauvel: Australia's First Corps Commander', in D. M. Horner (ed.), *The Commanders: Australian Military Leadership in the Twentieth Century* (1984), 61.
8 Dennis et al., *Australian Military History*, 351; N. C. Smith, *The Third Australian Light Horse Regiment 1914–1918: A Short History and Listings of Those Who Served* (Gardenvale, 1993), 29–30; C. G. Powles, *The History of the Canterbury Mounted Rifles 1914–1919* (Auckland, 1926), 65–6.

9 AWM, MSS1022, Billings, memoir, 54; H. S. Gullett, *The Official History of Australia in the War of 1914–1918. VII: The Australian Imperial Force in Sinai and Palestine 1914–1918* (Sydney, 1920), 82.
10 AWM, PR00535 Box 2 Series 4/8, Chauvel, letter to Lady Chauvel, 11 January 1917; AWM, AWM4 10/6, War Diary of 1st Australian Light Horse Regiment, 5 August 1918.
11 Gullett, *Official History VII*, 197–9.
12 AWM, AWM4 1/60, War Diary of Australian and New Zealand Mounted Division General Staff, March 1917, Appendix 54: 'Account of Action by ANZAC Mounted Division from 26 March 1917 to 0830 March 27, and Also Action of Imperial Mounted Division, Imperial Camel Brigade, Nos 11 and 12 L.A.M. Batteries and No 7 Light Car Patrol, while Under the Command of Major-General H.G. Chauvel, K.C.M.G., C.B., During the Battle of Gaza', by Major-General H. G. Chauvel, 4 April 1917; AWM, AWM4 1/60, War Diary of Australian and New Zealand Mounted Division General Staff, April 1917, Appendix 83B: 'A. and N.Z. Mounted Division Casualties in Operations 17/4/17 to 20/4/17'. At First Gaza only 6 other ranks were killed, and at Second Gaza 2 officers and 17 other ranks were killed.
13 AWM, AWM4 1/60, War Diary of Australian and New Zealand Mounted Division General Staff, December 1917, Appendix 173: 'Account of the Operations Carried Out by the Australian and New Zealand Mounted Division from October 21 to December 7 1917', by Lieutenant-Colonel J. G. Browne, 15 January 1918.
14 AWM, AWM4 10/2, War Diary of 2nd Australian Light Horse Brigade Headquarters, March 1918, Appendix 4: Brigade Casualties from 27 March 1918 to 2 April 1918; AWM, AWM4 1/60, War Diary of Australian and New Zealand Mounted Division General Staff, September 1918, Appendix 38: 'Account of Operations of Chaytor's Force from September 18 to September 30 1918', 6 October 1918.
15 Briscoe Moore, *Mounted Riflemen*, 151; AWM, AWM4 10/1, War Diary of 1st Australian Light Horse Brigade Headquarters, October 1918, Appendix 5: List of evacuations sick to hospital during October 1918; AWM, MSS1071, Crase, memoir, 54.
16 P. V. Vernon, *The Royal New South Wales Lancers 1885–1985* (Sydney, 1961), 144.
17 Gullett, *Official History VII*, 29–39; IWM, 04/37/1, Argyle, diary, 14 January 1918; J. Grey, *The Australian Army: A History* (Oxford, 2001), 62.
18 AWM, PR00535 Box 3 Series 4/21, Chauvel, letter to sister, 1 October 1916; K. Fewster, 'Ellis Ashmead Bartlett and the Making of the Anzac Legend', *Journal of Australian Studies*, X (1982), 19; D. Kent, '*The Anzac Book* and the Anzac Legend: C.E.W. Bean as Editor and Image-Maker', *Historical Studies*, XXI (1985), 378–9.
19 G. L. Berrie, *Under Furred Hats (6th A.L.H. Regt.)* (Sydney, 1919), 7; G. H. Bourne, *Nulli Secundus: The History of the 2nd Light Horse Regiment, Australian Imperial Force, August 1914–April 1919* (Tamworth, 1926), 77; D. Blair, '"Those Miserable Tommies": Anti-British Sentiment in the Australian Imperial Force, 1915–1918', *War and Society*, XIX (2001), 73.
20 J. Clancy, 'Images of Australia in World War I: The Film, the Mini-Series and Historical Representation', in J. Smart and T. Wood (eds), *An Anzac Muster: War and Society in Australia and New Zealand 1914–1918 and 1939–1945* (Clayton, 1992), 30–9; B. Gammage, *The Broken Years: Australian Soldiers in the Great War* (Harmondsworth, 1974), 154. Bean's views are also replicated in J. Ross, *The Myth of the Digger: The Australian Soldier in Two World Wars* (Sydney, 1985), 32. I. Jones, *The Australian Light Horse*, (Sydney, 1987), 17. For an analysis of the historiography surrounding the Anzac myth see Macleod, *Reconsidering Gallipoli*, 221–30.

21 L. L. Robson, 'The Origin and Character of the First A.I.F., 1914–1918: Some Statistical Evidence', *Historical Studies*, XV (1973), 737–49; D. Blair, *Dinkum Diggers: An Australian Battalion at War* (Carlton, 2001), 23–9.
22 See J. Bennett, '"Massey's Sunday School Picnic Party": "The Other Anzacs" or Honorary Australians', *War and Society*, XXI (2003), 23–54; P. Stanley, '"Whom at first we did not like . . .": Australians and New Zealanders at Quinn's Post, Gallipoli', in J. Crawford and I. McGibbon (eds), *New Zealand's Great War: New Zealand, the Allies and the First World War* (Auckland, 2007), 182–93; K. Inglis, 'Men, Women, and War Memorials: Anzac Australia', in R. White and P. Russell (eds), *Memories and Dreams: Reflections on Twentieth-Century Australia, Pastiche II* (St Leonards, 1997), 40–59; J. Phillips, 'The Great War and New Zealand Nationalism: The Evidence of War Memorials', in J. Smart and T. Wood (eds), *An Anzac Muster: War and Society in Australia and New Zealand 1914–1918 and 1939–1945* (Clayton, 1992), 14–29; D. B. Waterson, 'Anzac Day in the New Zealand Countryside', in J. Smart and T. Wood (eds), *An Anzac Muster: War and Society in Australia and New Zealand 1914–1918 and 1939–1945* (Clayton, 1992), 143–50.
23 *The Age*, 27 and 30 October 2007.
24 R. Gerster, *Big-Noting: The Heroic Theme in Australian War Writing* (Carlton, 1987), 105–14; S. Ward, '"A War Memorial in Celluloid": The Gallipoli Legend in Australian Cinema, 1940s-1980s', in J. Macleod (ed.), *Gallipoli: Making History* (London, 2004), 61–4; T. Kinloch, *Devils on Horses: In the Words of the Anzacs in the Middle East 1916–19* (Auckland, 2007), 206; I. Jones, 'Beersheba: The Light Horse Charge and the Making of Myths', *Journal of the Australian War Memorial*, III (1983), 26.
25 A similar sentiment was apparent during the first Anzac Day celebrations in Australia due to the late falling of Easter in 1916. See R. Ely, 'The First Anzac Day: Invented or Discovered?', *Journal of Australian Studies*, XVII (1985), 58. AWM, 2DRL/1285, Brown, diary, 25 April 1916; AWM, PR85/289, Hobbs, diary, 25 April 1916; AWM, AWM4 10/8, War Diary of 3rd Australian Light Horse Regiment, 25 April 1918; KMA, 2001.1035, Hull, letter to parents, 21 April 1918.
26 Briscoe Moore, *Mounted Riflemen*, 19–20.
27 AWM, 2DRL/0747, Wetherell, letter to mother, 19 December 1916.
28 AWM, 3DRL/6257, Easterbrook, 'Report on Operations, from the Commencement of Moves Against Beersheba and Gaza on 21 October 1917 and Culminating in the Fall of Jaffa and the Battles of Sheikh Muannis and Khurbit Hadra and of Mulebbis', 16 December 1917.
29 Idriess, *Desert Column*, 265; AWM, 3DRL/3741 Folder 2, Delpratt, letter to sister, 12 January 1916.
30 TNA, WO95/4545, War Diary of Auckland Mounted Rifles Regiment, 13 April 1917.
31 Briscoe Moore, *Mounted Riflemen*, 4.
32 AWM, 1DRL/0364, Hudson, letter to wife, 2 May 1917.
33 AWM, 2DRL/1285, Brown, diary, 9 August 1916; ATL, MS-Papers-4108/6, McNeur, letter to brother, no date (probably July 1917).
34 AWM, 2DRL/0747, Wetherell, letter to mother, 22 July 1917; AWM, AWM4 1/60, War Diary of Australian and New Zealand Mounted Division General Staff, 19 December 1916.
35 AWM, PR01058, Sullivan, diary, 1 February 1916; AWM, AWM4 10/6, War Diary of 1st Australian Light Horse Regiment, 4 December 1916; Powles, *Canterbury Mounted Rifles*, 86.

36 H. S. Gullett, 'Fighting for Palestine: Three Years' Campaigning', in H. S. Gullett and C. Barrett (eds), *Australia in Palestine* (Sydney, 1919), 21; TNA, WO95/4544, War Diary of New Zealand Mounted Rifles Brigade, 10 December 1917.
37 Blair, *Dinkum Diggers*, 4.
38 AWM, 1DRL/0497, Metcalfe, letter to brother, 8 January 1918.
39 Idriess, *Desert Column*, 99–100.
40 K. Fewster, 'The Wazza Riots, 1915', *Journal of the Australian War Memorial*, IV (1984), 51.
41 E. M. Andrews, *The Anzac Illusion: Anglo-Australian Relations During World War I* (Cambridge, 1993), 168.
42 ATL, 76–123, Rhodes, diary, 30 April 1916. Rhodes's underlining. AWM, PR84/240 Folder 1, Truman, diary, 18 May 1916.
43 AWM, 3DRL/7268, Dunk, memoir, Magdhaba section, 7.
44 Coates, *Australia's Wars*, 100; Gullett, *Official History VII*, 227–8.
45 TNA, WO95/4544, War Diary of New Zealand Mounted Rifles Brigade, August 1917, Appendix: 'Report on Operations from 19 July to 13 August 1916', by Brigadier-General E. W. C. Chaytor, GOC, NZMR; KMA, 1993.1039, Hull, letter to brother, 10 June 1916.
46 AWM, PR89/125, Pearce, letter to the editor of the *Western Daily Advocate*, 23 August 1916.
47 AWM, AWM4 1/60, War Diary of Australian and New Zealand Mounted Division General Staff, August 1917, Appendix: 'An Account of the Operations in the Qatia District Against the Turks, July 19 to August 12 1916, Including the Battles of Romani and Bir-el-Abd'.
48 Idriess, *Desert Column*, 162.
49 AWM, 3DRL/3741 Folder 2, Delpratt, letter to sister, 1 March 1917; A. H. Wilkie, *Official History of the Wellington Mounted Rifles Regiment 1914–1919* (Auckland, 1924), 90; AWM, MSS1071, Crase, memoir, 30.
50 ATL, 76–123, Rhodes, diary, 5 and 9 August 1916; AWM, PR00535 Box 2 Series 4/13, Chauvel, letter to Lady Chauvel, 18 September 1918.
51 Pugsley, *Anzac Experience*, 33.
52 B. Harris, letter to mother, 10 March 1917, in G. Harper (ed.), *Letters from the Battlefield: New Zealand Soldiers Write Home, 1914–18* (Auckland, 2001), 79; AWM, 1DRL/0497, Metcalfe, letter to brother, 20 July 1916.
53 KMA, 1998.31, McKay, memoir, 116–17.
54 AWM, PR87/212, Pickering, letter to brother, 6 December 1916.
55 AWM, 2DRL/0817, Chandler, letter to family, 6 June 1916; AWM, 2DRL/0759, Morrice, letter to mother, 20 August 1916; ATL, MS-Papers-4108/8, McNeur, letter to brother, 8 February 1918.
56 AWM, 2DRL/0817, Chandler, letter to family, 30 July 1916. I am grateful to Alisa Miller for highlighting the wider cultural implications revealed by Chandler's troubles with his socks. KMA, 2001.660, Wellington Mounted Rifles Regimental Orders, 26 May 1917; AWM, PR84/193, Ryrie, letter to wife, 22 November 1916.
57 C. G. Powles, *The New Zealanders in Sinai and Palestine* (Auckland, 1922), 275.
58 Briscoe Moore, *Mounted Riflemen*, 144; G. Ranstead, letter to parents, 5 April 1917, in Harper, *Letters*, 87.
59 AWM, PR83/107, Leahy, letter to sister, 12 September 1918.
60 AWM, 3DRL/3741 Folder 2, Delpratt, letter to sister, 12 July 1916; Idriess, *Desert Column*, 300.

61 KMA, 1998.31, McKay, memoir, 122; White, 'Australian Soldiers and the Orient'; R. White, 'The Soldier as Tourist: The Australian Experience of the Great War', *War and Society*, V (1987), 63–77.
62 KMA, 1998.31, McKay, memoir, 152; AWM, 2DRL/0817, Chandler, letter to family, 24 June 1916.
63 AWM, 3DRL/7568, Prince, letter to mother, 28 February 1918; Idriess, *Desert Column*, 99; AWM, AWM4 10/6, War Diary of 1st Australian Light Horse Regiment, 11 October 1918.
64 Fewster, 'Wazza Riots'; AWM, MSS1071, Crase, memoir, 44; Briscoe Moore, *Mounted Riflemen*, 96–7; KMA, 2001.660, Wellington Mounted Rifles Regimental Orders, 3 June 1917.
65 Riedi and Mason, 'Sport in the British Army', 514.
66 Briscoe Moore, *Mounted Riflemen*, 74–5; AWM, PR85/289, Hobbs, diary, 14 April 1916; AWM, PR00535 Box 2 Series 4/8, Chauvel, letter to Lady Chauvel, 13 March 1917; AWM, PR84/179 Folder 2, Tomlins, diary, 23 January 1918; AWM, 2DRL/0817, Chandler, letter to family, 6 June 1916.
67 AWM, PR84/179 Folder 3, Tomlins, diary, 5 September 1917.
68 AWM, PR88/030, Livingstone, memoir, 11.
69 AWM, AWM4 1/60, War Diary of Australian and New Zealand Mounted Division General Staff, 6 October 1917; AWM, AWM4 1/60, War Diary of Australian and New Zealand Mounted Division General Staff, January 1918, Appendix 189: Rules for the Australian and New Zealand Mounted Division sports meeting at Ayun Kara, scheduled for late February 1918; AWM, 2DRL/0747, Wetherell, letter to mother, 5 November 1916; AWM, PR84/179 Folder 2, Tomlins, diary, 2 March 1918.
70 Keegan, *Face of Battle*, 29–30.
71 Baynes, *Morale*, 178; M. Taussig, 'An Australian Hero', *History Workshop Journal*, XXIV (1987), 119; Stanley, 'Our big world', 4.
72 AWM, 1DRL/0497, Metcalfe, letter to brother, 25 March 1917; Idriess, *Desert Column*, 85; AWM, 3DRL/3741 Folders 2 and 3, Delpratt, letters to sister, 24 October 1916 and 5 October 1918.
73 Wilson and Wetherell, *Fifth Light Horse*, 86.
74 Strachan, 'British Way in Warfare', 412.
75 H. G. Chauvel, 'Introduction', in Bourne, *Nulli Secundus*, 5; Ross, 'Sinai-Palestine Campaign', 381; R. A. Butlin, 'Lucas, Sir Charles Prestwood (1853–1931)', *Oxford Dictionary of National Biography*; AWM, 2DRL/0747, Wetherell, letter to mother, 5 November 1916.
76 Nicol, *Two Campaigns*, preface.
77 Powles, *New Zealanders*, 4; Hall, *Australian Light Horse*, 31.
78 Nicol, *Two Campaigns*, 189–94.
79 Idriess, *Desert Column*, 83.
80 Briscoe Moore, *Mounted Riflemen*, 78–9; AWM, MSS1071, Crase, memoir, 35; Powles, *Canterbury Mounted Rifles*, 82.
81 AWM, 2DRL/0081, Morley Papers, condolence letter from Captain J. Boyd to the family of Lieutenant C. R. Morley, 5 December 1917.
82 A. Thomson, '"Steadfast Until Death"? C.E.W. Bean and the Representation of Australian Military Manhood', *Australian Historical Studies*, XXIII (1989), 462–78; A. Thomson, '"The Vilest Libel of the War"? Imperial Politics and the Official Histories of Gallipoli', *Australian Historical Studies*, XXV (1993), 628–36; K. Inglis,

'The Anzac Tradition', *Meanjin Quarterly: A Review of Arts and Letters in Australia*, XXIV (1965), 28; G. Serle, 'The Digger Tradition and Australian Nationalism', *Meanjin Quarterly: A Review of Arts and Letters in Australia*, XXIV (1965), 152.

83 ATL, MS-Papers-4108/8, McNeur, letter to brother, 23 November 1918; Gullett, *Official History VII*, 31–2. Those men most skilled at handling horses were used in the Australian Light Horse remount depot, rather than in combat units. See D. Kent, 'The Australian Remount Unit in Egypt, 1915–19: A Footnote to History', *Journal of the Australian War Memorial*, I (1982), 9–15.

84 AWM, MSS1071, Crase, memoir, 25. Crase's underlining.

85 Idriess, *Desert Column*, 331.

86 Trooper Bluegum, 'The Horses Stay Behind', in H. S. Gullett and C. Barrett (eds), *Australia in Palestine* (Sydney, 1919), 78; J. Bou, 'They shot the horses – didn't they?', *Wartime*, XLIV (2008), 54–7.

87 AWM, PR00740, Holmes, diary, 15 August 1916; AWM, 2DRL/0817, Chandler, letter to family, 31 March 1916.

88 AWM, MSS1071, Crase, memoir, 42.

89 Strachan, 'Training', 212; Berrie, *Furred Hats*, 126–7; AWM, AWM4 10/10, War Diary of 5th Australian Light Horse Regiment, 20 December 1916, December 1917 and October 1918.

90 Gerster, *Big-Noting*, 76; J. Williams, '"Art, War and Agrarian Myths": Australian Reactions to Modernism 1913–1931', in J. Smart and T. Wood (eds), *An Anzac Muster: War and Society in Australia and New Zealand 1914–1918 and 1939–1945* (Clayton, 1992), 40–57.

91 AWM, 3DRL/3741 Folder 3, Delpratt, letter to sister, 13 August 1918; AWM, 3DRL/6501, Lawrance Papers, Roll Call Book for 'A' Squadron, 5th Australian Light Horse Regiment; AWM, PR88/014 Folder 1, Vernon Papers, Roll Call Book for 'A' Squadron, 1st Australian Light Horse Regiment.

92 Jones, *Australian Light Horse*, 19; A. Offer, *The First World War: An Agrarian Interpretation* (Oxford, 1989), 157–8.

93 AWM, AWM4 10/10, War Diary of 5th Australian Light Horse Regiment, October 1918; J. D. Richardson, *The History of the 7th Light Horse Regiment A.I.F.* (Sydney, 1923), 95; Vernon, *Lancers*, 133; Sheffield, *Leadership in the Trenches*, 168.

94 AWM, PR84/179 Folder 3, Tomlins, diary, 1 August 1917; AWM, 2DRL/0015, Evans, letter to mother, 1 July 1917.

95 AWM, AWM4 1/60, War Diary of Australian and New Zealand Mounted Division General Staff, December 1916, Appendix 17: 'General Arrangements for Practising Attack on the Masaid Position on Wednesday, December 13', by Lieutenant-Colonel J. G. Browne, 11 December 1916; KMA, 1991.2000, Doherty, diary, 31 January 1918 and 3 February 1918; TNA, WO95/4547, War Diary of Wellington Mounted Rifles Regiment, 10 October 1917.

96 AWM, 1DRL/0497, Metcalfe, letter to brother, 19 December 1917; TNA, WO95/4546, War Diary of Canterbury Mounted Rifles Regiment, 18 June 1918; AWM, 2DRL/0747, Wetherell, letter to mother, 29 February 1916. This transfer of ideas and training from the Western Front to the DMC has also been emphasized by Stephen Badsey; see S. Badsey, *Doctrine and Reform in the British Cavalry 1880–1914* (Aldershot, 2008), 283.

97 AWM, AWM4 1/60, War Diary of Australian and New Zealand Mounted Division General Staff, September 1917, Appendix 159: Divisional orders for training at Abasan el Kebir, 21 September 1917.

98   AWM, AWM4 1/60, War Diary of Australian and New Zealand Mounted Division General Staff, October 1917, Appendix 165: Divisional notes for tactical exercises; AWM, AWM4 1/60, War Diary of Australian and New Zealand Mounted Division General Staff, May 1918, Appendix 229: Memorandum on Australian and New Zealand Mounted Divisional School, 20 May 1918.
99   AWM, AWM4 10/1, War Diary of 1st Australian Light Horse Brigade Headquarters, January 1916, Appendix 10: Memorandum on 1st Australian Light Horse Brigade training, 23 January 1916; AWM, PR00535 Box 2 Series 4/7, Chauvel, letter to Lady Chauvel, 26 September 1916; Idriess, *Desert Column*, 252.
100 ATL, MS-Papers-4312/1, Judge, diary, 19 April 1917; Ross, *Myth of the Digger*, 92–4.
101 AWM, 2DRL/0081, Morley Papers, condolence letter from Captain J. Boyd to the family of Lieutenant C. R. Morley, 5 December 1917.
102 AWM, 3DRL/3741 Folder 3, Delpratt, letter to sister, 5 October 1918.
103 AWM, MSS1071, Crase, memoir, 39.
104 AWM, AWM4 1/60, War Diary of Australian and New Zealand Mounted Division General Staff, September 1918, Appendix 34: Memorandum to Chaytor's Force, by Lieutenant-Colonel J. G. Browne, 17 September 1918.
105 AWM, 3DRL/3741 Folder 3, Delpratt, letter to sister, 13 January 1918; AWM, 3DRL/6257, Easterbrook Papers, Report Writing Exercise, March 1917; AWM, AWM4 1/60, War Diary of Australian and New Zealand Mounted Division General Staff, 15 October 1917.
106 AWM, 2DRL/0081, Morley, letter to family, 17 October 1917.
107 A. H. Russell, 'Foreword', in Powles, *Canterbury Mounted Rifles*, vii; AWM, 2DRL/0081, Morley, letter to family, 27 October 1917; Idriess, *Desert Column*, 317; Powles, *Canterbury Mounted Rifles*, 84–5; Sheffield, *Leadership in the Trenches*, 82.
108 AWM, PR84/179 Folder 3, Tomlins, diary, 11 September 1917; A. J. Hill, *Chauvel of the Light Horse: A Biography of General Sir Harry Chauvel, G.C.M.G., K.C.B.* (Carlton, 1978); Dennis et al., *Australian Military History*, 142–4.
109 AWM, PR00535 Box 2 Series 4/8, Chauvel, letters to Lady Chauvel, 17 August 1916 and 7 February 1917; KMA, 1991.2000, Doherty, diary, 27 May–3 June 1916; McGibbon, *New Zealand Military History*, 84–5; Kinloch, *Devils on Horses*, 188; KMA, 1991.2000, Doherty, diary, 14 May 1918.
110 Idriess, *Desert Column*, 67; Kinloch, *Devils on Horses*, 32.
111 AWM, PR01288 Folder 2, Beatty, letter from Brigadier-General G. de L. Ryrie to Beatty, 7 January 1918.
112 Dennis et al., *Australian Military History*, 524.
113 B. Bond, *Survivors of a Kind: Memoirs of the Western Front* (London, 2008), 59–73.
114 AWM, PR00535 Box 2 Series 4/12, Chauvel, letters to Lady Chauvel, 11 January 1918 and 10 March 1918.
115 Badsey, *Doctrine and Reform*, 288.
116 Pugsley, *Anzac Experience*, 147; Kinloch, *Devils on Horses*, 350–1.

Chapter 6

1   The term sepoy refers to an Indian infantryman and is derived from the Persian term *sipahi* (soldier); sowar refers to an Indian cavalryman.
2   IOR, L/MIL/17/5/2381, 'Memorandum on India's Contribution to the War in Men, Material, and Money: August 1914 to November 1918', 10.

3 C. C. Trench, *The Indian Army and the King's Enemies 1900–1947* (London, 1988), 81; P. Mason, *A Matter of Honour: An Assessment of the Indian Army its Officers and Men* (London, 1974), 427–39. For recent analyses of the collapse at Kut, which place the blame on morale problems derived from the Indian Army's ethnic peculiarities, see N. Gardner, 'Sepoys and the Siege of Kut-al-Amara, December 1915–April 1916', *War in History*, XI (2004), 307–26; N. Gardner, 'Morale of the Indian Army in the Mesopotamian Campaign: 1914–17', in K. Roy (ed.), *The Indian Army in the Two World Wars* (Leiden, 2012), 393–417. A more insightful analysis of systemic problems in the Indian Army is provided by Andy Syk, see A. Syk, 'Command in the Indian Expeditionary Force D: Mesopotamia, 1915–16', in K. Roy (ed.), *The Indian Army in the Two World Wars* (Leiden, 2012), 63–103.

4 For a good example of the superficial attention paid to Indianization see Woodward, *Forgotten Soldiers*, 227–9. Dennis Showalter's recent work redresses this imbalance slightly, but is far too reliant on published memoirs and unit histories; see D. Showalter, 'The Indianization of the Egyptian Expeditionary Force, 1917–18: An Imperial Turning Point', in K. Roy (ed.), *The Indian Army in the Two World Wars* (Leiden, 2012), 145–63.

5 B. Robson, 'The Organization and Command Structure of the Indian Army from its Origins to 1947', in A. J. Guy and P. B. Boyden (eds), *Soldiers of the Raj: The Indian Army 1600–1947* (Coventry, 1997), 10; T. A. Heathcote, 'The Army of British India', in D. G. Chandler and I. F. W. Beckett (eds), *The Oxford History of the British Army* (Oxford, 1994), 367; D. M. Peers, 'The Martial Races and the Indian Army in the Victorian Era', in D. P. Marston and C. S. Sundaram (eds), *A Military History of India and South Asia: From the East India Company to the Nuclear Era* (London, 2007), 39.

6 'Army in India' refers to all British and Indian forces serving in the subcontinent. Robson, 'Indian Army', 13; K. Jeffery, '"An English Barrack in the Oriental Seas?" India in the Aftermath of the First World War', *Modern Asian Studies*, XV (1981), 379–80; P. Barua, 'Strategies and Doctrines of Imperial Defence: Britain and India, 1919–45', *The Journal of Imperial and Commonwealth History*, XXV (1997), 242.

7 D. Omissi, *The Sepoy and the Raj: The Indian Army, 1860–1940* (Basingstoke, 1994), 194–9 and 218–19; N. Lloyd, 'The Amritsar Massacre and the Minimum Force Debate', *Small Wars and Insurgencies*, XXI (2010), 382–403. For a detailed analysis of the impact of North-West Frontier operations on Indian Army doctrine and combat effectiveness see T. R. Moreman, 'The British and Indian Armies and North-West Frontier Warfare, 1849–1914', *The Journal of Imperial and Commonwealth History*, XX (1992), 35–64; T. R. Moreman, '"Passing it On": The Army in India and Frontier Warfare, 1914–39', in K. Roy (ed.), *War and Society in Colonial India, 1807–1945* (Oxford, 2006), 275–304; T. R. Moreman, '"The Greatest Training Ground in the World": The Army in India and the North-West Frontier, 1901–1947', in D. P. Marston and C. S. Sundaram (eds), *A Military History of India and South Asia: From the East India Company to the Nuclear Era* (London, 2007), 53–73.

8 D. Omissi, 'India: Some Perspectives of Race and Empire', in D. Omissi and A. S. Thompson (eds), *The Impact of the South African War* (Basingstoke, 2002), 215–32; Robson, 'Indian Army', 14–16; T. R. Moreman, 'Lord Kitchener, the General Staff and the Army in India, 1902–14', in D. French and B. Holden Reid (eds), *The British General Staff: Reform and Innovation, c. 1890–1939* (London, 2002), 57–74.

9   See S. L. Menezes, *Fidelity and Honour: The Indian Army from the Seventeenth to the Twenty-first Century* (Oxford, 1993), 286–305; D. Omissi, '"Martial Races": Ethnicity and Security in Colonial India 1858–1939', *War and Society*, IX (1991), 1–27; B. Farwell, *Armies of the Raj: From the Mutiny to Independence, 1858–1947* (London, 1989), 179–90; A. Bopegamage, 'Caste, Class and the Indian Military: A Study of the Social Origins of Indian Army Personnel', in J. van Doorn (ed.), *Military Profession and Military Regimes: Commitments and Conflicts* (1969), 127–54; P. Barua, 'Inventing Race: The British and India's Martial Races', *The Historian*, LVIII (1995), 107–16; L. Caplan, 'Martial Gurkhas: The Persistence of a British Military Discourse on "Race"', in P. Robb (ed.), *The Concept of Race in South Asia* (Oxford, 1995), 260–81; H. Streets, *Martial Races: The Military, Race and Masculinity in British Imperial Culture, 1857–1914* (Manchester, 2004); K. Roy, 'Beyond the Martial Race Theory: A Historiographical Assessment of Recruitment in the British-Indian Army', *The Calcutta Historical Journal*, XXI–XXII (1999–2000), 139–54; K. Roy, 'Recruitment Doctrines of the Colonial Indian Army: 1859–1913', *The Indian Economic and Social History Review*, XXXIV (1997), 321–54. It can be argued that the modern Indian and Pakistani armies are still reliant on martial race theory as a means of selecting their recruits despite the lessons learnt during operations in the twentieth century. See S. P. Cohen, 'The Untouchable Soldier: Caste, Politics, and the Indian Army', *The Journal of Asian Studies*, XXVIII (1969), 453–68; Peers, 'Martial Races', 52; D. Pal, *Traditions of the Indian Army* (Delhi, 1961), 105–47.
10 Omissi, *Sepoy and the Raj*, 113–52.
11 K. Roy, 'Introduction: Armies, Warfare, and Society in Colonial India', in K. Roy (ed.), *War and Society in Colonial India, 1807–1945* (Oxford, 2006), 35; K. Roy, 'The Historiography of the Colonial Indian Army', *Studies in History*, XII (1996), 265–6. Kaushik Roy's recent edited volume, *The Indian Army in the Two World Wars*, goes some way to addressing this imbalance by foregrounding the army's combat experiences in the twentieth century.
12 J. Greenhut, 'The Imperial Reserve: The Indian Corps on the Western Front, 1914–15', *The Journal of Imperial and Commonwealth History*, XII (1983), 54; S. D. Pradhan, 'Organisation of the Indian Army on the Eve of the Outbreak of the First World War', *The Journal of the United Service Institution of India*, CII (1972), 76–7.
13 Menezes, *Fidelity and Honour*, 242–3.
14 IOR, L/MIL/17/5/1814, 'Report on the Inter-Divisional Manoeuvres, Northern Army, 1912', by the General Staff, India.
15 R. McLain, 'The Indian Corps on the Western Front: A Reconsideration', in G. Jensen and A. Wiest (eds), *War in the Age of Technology: Myriad Faces of Armed Conflict* (New York, 2001), 168–9; G. M. Jack, 'The Indian Army on the Western Front, 1914–1915: A Portrait of Collaboration', *War in History*, XIII (2006), 338; G. Corrigan, *Sepoys in the Trenches: The Indian Corps on the Western Front, 1914–1915* (Stroud, 1999), 54.
16 Government of India, *India's Contribution to the Great War* (Calcutta, 1923), 177. These figures are taken from 1918 and include the losses of the two Indian cavalry divisions sent to the Western Front, which remained there until early 1918.
17 McLain, 'Indian Corps', 175; Greenhut, 'Imperial Reserve', 65 and 68.
18 Farwell, *Armies of the Raj*, 100; Greenhut, 'Imperial Reserve', 57; J. Greenhut, 'Sahib and Sepoy: An Inquiry into the Relationship Between the British Officers and Native Soldiers of the British India Army', *Military Affairs: The Journal of Military History, Including Theory and Technology*, XLVIII (1984), 18. Greenhut also suggests that

the racial concepts prevalent within the Indian Army adversely affected morale, see J. Greenhut, 'Race, Sex, and War: The Impact of Race and Sex on Morale and Health Services for the Indian Corps on the Western Front, 1914', *Military Affairs*, XLV (1981), 71–4.

19 G. MacMunn, *The Martial Races of India* (London, 1933), 321. For the Indianization of the Indian Army's officer corps see D. K. Palit, 'Indianisation of the Army's Officer Cadre 1920–47', *Indo-British Review: A Journal of History*, XVI (1989), 55–8; A. Sharpe, 'The Indianisation of the Indian Army', *History Today*, XXXVI (1986), 47–52; T. I. Hashmi, 'Indianisation of the British-Indian Army: 1858–1947', *The Dacca University Studies: Part A*, XXVIII (1978), 30–40.

20 Corrigan, *Sepoys in the Trenches*; D. Omissi, review of *Sepoys in the Trenches: The Indian Corps on the Western Front, 1914–1915* by G. Corrigan, *The Journal of Imperial and Commonwealth History*, XXIX (2001), 178–80; Mason, *Matter of Honour*, 412–43.

21 Watson, *Enduring the Great War*, 143–4; Jack, 'Western Front', 361–2.

22 D. Omissi (ed.), *Indian Voices of the Great War: Soldiers' Letters, 1914–18* (Basingstoke, 1999); S. VanKosi, 'Letters Home, 1915–16: Punjabi Soldiers Reflect on War and Life in Europe and their Meanings for Home and Self', *International Journal of Punjab Studies*, II (1995), 43–63; D. Omissi, 'Europe Through Indian Eyes: Indian Soldiers Encounter England and France, 1914–1918', *English Historical Review*, CXXII (2007), 371–96; R. Visram, 'The First World War and the Indian Soldiers', *Indo-British Review: A Journal of History*, XVI (1989), 17–26.

23 S. C. Sinclair, 'Egypt', in H. A. Sams (ed.), *The Post Office of India in the Great War* (Bombay, 1922), 99.

24 S. D. Pradhan, 'Indians in the East Africa Campaign – A Case Study of Indian Experiences in the First World War', in D. C. Ellinwood and S. D. Pradhan (eds), *India and World War I* (New Delhi, 1978), 69–74; D. C. Ellinwood, 'An Historical Study of the Punjabi Soldier in World War I', in H. Singh and N. G. Barrier (eds), *Punjab Past and Present: Essays in Honour of Dr Ganda Singh* (Patiala, 1976), 337–62; D. C. Ellinwood, 'The Indian Soldier, the Indian Army, and Change, 1914–1918', in D. C. Ellinwood and S. D. Pradhan (eds), *India and World War I* (New Delhi, 1978), 177–211; D. C. Ellinwood, 'Ethnicity and the Colonial Asian Army: British Policy, War, and the Indian Army, 1914–1918', in D. C. Ellinwood and C. H. Enloe (eds), *Ethnicity and the Military in Asia* (New Brunswick, 1981), 89–144; D. C. Ellinwood, 'The Indian Soldier and National Consciousness, 1914–1939', *The Quarterly Review of Historical Studies*, XXVII (1987), 4–24.

25 T. Tai-Yong, 'An Imperial Home-Front: Punjab and the First World War', *The Journal of Military History*, LXIV (2000), 375 and 380; S. D. Pradhan, 'Indian Army and the First World War', in D. C. Ellinwood and S. D. Pradhan (eds), *India and World War I* (New Delhi, 1978), 56–7; Omissi, *Sepoy and the Raj*, 58.

26 IOR, L/MIL/17/5/2398, 'Development of Man Power in India, and its Utilisation for Imperial Purposes', by Army Headquarters, India.

27 IOR, L/MIL/17/5/2381, 'Memorandum on India's Contribution to the War in Men, Material, and Money: August 1914 to November 1918', 11–13; MacMunn, *Martial Races*, 331; Anonymous, *Statistical Abstract for British India with Statistics, where Available, Relating to Certain Indian States, from 1914–15 to 1923–24* (London, 1925), LVIII, 2–5; Tai-Yong, 'Imperial Home-Front', 374; Roy, 'Recruitment Doctrines', 352.

28 IOR, L/MIL/17/5/2381, 'Memorandum on India's Contribution to the War in Men, Material, and Money: August 1914 to November 1918', 11–12; IOR, L/

MIL/17/5/2398, 'Development of Man Power in India, and its Utilisation for Imperial Purposes', by Army Headquarters, India.

29 F. W. Perry, *The Commonwealth Armies: Manpower and Organisation in Two World Wars* (Manchester, 1988), 25–8. For analyses of the political and coalition aspects of the British Army's manpower crisis, but which ignore the imperial dimensions, see D. R. Woodward, 'Did Lloyd George Starve the British Army of Men Prior to the German Spring Offensive of 21 March 1918?', *The Historical Journal*, XXVII (1984), 241–52; E. Greenhalgh, 'David Lloyd George, Georges Clemenceau, and the 1918 Manpower Crisis', *The Historical Journal*, L (2007), 397–421.

30 IOR, L/MIL/5/739, Correspondence on Additional Indian Units, telegram from the War Office to the Commander-in-Chief, India, 4 December 1917.

31 IOR, L/MIL/5/739, Correspondence on Additional Indian Units, telegram from the CIGS to the Commander-in-Chief, India, 3 December 1917.

32 IOR, L/MIL/5/784, Correspondence on 7th (Meerut) Division, telegram from the War Office to the GOC, GHQ Mesopotamia, and the Commander-in-Chief, India, 4 December 1917; F. Younghusband, 'The Near East: Sinai and Palestine', in C. Lucas (ed.), *The Empire at War* (Oxford, 1926), V, 262 and 267.

33 IOR, L/MIL/5/739, Correspondence on Additional Indian Units, telegrams from the Commander-in-Chief, India, to the CIGS, 6 and 14 December 1917 and 5 January 1918.

34 IOR, L/MIL/5/739, Correspondence on Additional Indian Units, telegram from B. B. Cubbitt, War Office, to the Commander-in-Chief, Egypt, 5 January 1918; TNA, WO95/4581, War Diary of 1/54th Sikhs, 18 December 1917; TNA, WO95/4584, War Diary of 38th Dogras, 4 February 1918; IOR, L/MIL/5/739, Correspondence on Additional Indian Units, telegram from the War Office to GHQ, Egypt, 10 March 1918.

35 Trench, *Indian Army*, 44–9; IOR, L/MIL/5/733, Correspondence on Indian Cavalry, telegram from the CIGS to the Commander-in-Chief, India, 4 January 1918; IOR, L/MIL/5/733, Correspondence on Indian Cavalry, minute to the Military Committee on the 'Employment of Pathans in Palestine', by Sir E. G. Barrow, 7 February 1918; IOR, L/MIL/5/733, Correspondence on Indian Cavalry, telegram from the War Office to the Commander-in-Chief, Egypt, 1 February 1918.

36 IOR, L/MIL/5/794, Policy following General Smuts' Recommendations, telegram from the CIGS to the Commander-in-Chief, India, 21 February 1918; Hughes, *Allenby and British Strategy*, 66–8.

37 IWM, PP/MCR/C1, Chetwode, Notes on the Palestine Campaign, 15 February 1918; IOR, L/MIL/5/794, Policy following General Smuts' Recommendations, telegram from the Commander-in-Chief, India, to the CIGS, 23 February 1918.

38 IOR, L/MIL/5/794, Policy following General Smuts' Recommendations, telegram from the Commander-in-Chief, India, to the CIGS, 23 February 1918; IOR, L/MIL/5/794, Policy following General Smuts' Recommendations, telegram from GHQ, Mesopotamia, to the Commander-in-Chief, India, 24 February 1918; IOR, L/MIL/5/794, Policy following General Smuts' Recommendations, telegram from the CIGS, to the Commander-in-Chief, Mesopotamia, 4 March 1918; IOR, L/MIL/5/748, Correspondence on 3rd (Lahore) Division, telegram from the Commander-in-Chief, India, to the GOC, Mesopotamia, 22 March 1918.

39 IWM, PP/MCR/C1, Chetwode Papers, 'Notes on the Palestine Campaign', by Lieutenant-General P. W. Chetwode, 15 February 1918, additional note added 25 May 1918; H. H. Herwig, 'The German Victories, 1917–1918', in H. Strachan (ed.), *The*

Oxford Illustrated History of the First World War (Oxford, 1998), 258–64; P. Simkins, G. Jukes and M. Hickey, *The First World War: The War to End All Wars* (Oxford, 2003), 139–51; Strachan, *New Illustrated History*, 282–92; M. Brown, *The Imperial War Museum Book of 1918: Year of Victory* (London, 1998), 50–1.

40 IOR, L/MIL/5/794, Policy following General Smuts' Recommendations, telegram from the War Office to the Commander-in-Chief, Egypt, 27 March 1918.
41 IOR, L/MIL/5/739, Correspondence on Additional Indian Units, telegrams from the War Office to the Commander-in-Chief, India, 3 and 13 April 1918.
42 IOR, L/MIL/5/739, Correspondence on Additional Indian Units, telegram from the War Office to the Commander-in-Chief, Egypt, 21 April 1918.
43 IOR, L/MIL/5/733, Correspondence on Indian Cavalry, telegram from GHQ, Egypt, to the War Office, 18 May 1918; IOR, L/MIL/5/733, Correspondence on Indian Cavalry, telegram from the War Office to the Commander-in-Chief, India, 22 May 1918.
44 Allenby, letter to Wilson, 5 June 1918, in Hughes, *Allenby in Palestine*, 161.
45 For a full account of the creation and wartime exploits of the Jewish Legion see M. Watts, *The Jewish Legion and the First World War* (Basingstoke, 2004).
46 IOR, L/MIL/5/739, Correspondence on Additional Indian Units, telegram from the Commander-in-Chief, India, to the War Office, 9 April 1918; H. S. Anderson and A. Frankland, *The 101st Grenadiers: Historical Record of the Regiment, 1778–1923* (Aldershot, 1920), 57.
47 IOR, L/MIL/5/739, Correspondence on Additional Indian Units, telegram from the Commander-in-Chief, India, to GHQ, Egypt, 19 April 1918; TNA, WO95/4581, War Diary of 2/151st Indian Infantry, 30 May and 14 September 1918; TNA, WO95/4584, War Diary of 38th Dogras, 8 June 1918.
48 IOR, L/MIL/5/733, Correspondence on Indian Cavalry, telegram from the Commander-in-Chief, India, to GHQ, Egypt, 16 May 1918; IOR, L/MIL/5/739, Correspondence on Additional Indian Units, telegram from the Commander-in-Chief, India, to the War Office, 24 April 1918.
49 IOR, L/MIL/5/739, Correspondence on Additional Indian Units, telegram from the War Office to the Commander-in-Chief, India, 21 April 1918.
50 IOR, L/MIL/5/739, Correspondence on Additional Indian Units, telegram from the War Office to the Commander-in-Chief, Mesopotamia, 2 September 1918.
51 Showalter, 'Indianization', 146; Perry, *Commonwealth Armies*, 96.
52 J. Horne, 'Introduction: Mobilizing for "Total War", 1914–1918', in J. Horne (ed.), *State, Society and Mobilization in Europe During the First World War* (Cambridge, 1997), 3.
53 Sinclair, 'Egypt', 84–5.
54 TNA, WO95/4581, War Diary of 1/101st Grenadiers, 12 and 16 May 1918.
55 TNA, WO95/4581, War Diary of 1/54th Sikhs, 26 April 1918; TNA, WO95/4584, War Diary of 38th Dogras, 11 February and April 1918.
56 IOR, L/MIL/5/733, Correspondence on Indian Cavalry, letter from Lieutenant-General E. Locke Elliot, Headquarters Lines of Communication, BEF, France, to Lieutenant-General H. V. Cox, India Office, 20 January 1918; Hughes, *Allenby and British Strategy*, 69; IOR, L/MIL/5/733, Correspondence on Indian Cavalry, letter from L. D. Holland, Under Secretary of State, India Office, to Unknown, 28 December 1917; IOR, L/MIL/5/733, Correspondence on Indian Cavalry, letter from Lieutenant-General H. V. Cox, India Office, to Lieutenant-General E. Locke Elliot, Headquarters Lines of Communication, BEF, France, 23 January 1918; IOR, L/MIL/5/733, Correspondence on Indian Cavalry, telegram from the War Office to the Under Secretary of State for India, 30 March 1918.

57 TNA, WO95/4581, War Diary of 1/101st Grenadiers, June 1918, Appendix: Memorandum on Turkish Propaganda, by Major C. M. Phillips, Deputy Assistant Adjutant-General, 10th Division, 21 June 1918.
58 TNA, WO95/4581, War Diary of 1/101st Grenadiers, 12 June 1918; TNA, WO95/4581, War Diary of 1/101st Grenadiers, June 1918, Appendix 2: Memorandum by Lieutenant W. A. Strange, General Staff, 10th Division, 11 June 1918; Allenby, letter to Wilson, 22 June 1918, in Hughes, *Allenby in Palestine*, 165.
59 TNA, WO95/4568, War Diary of 10th Division General Staff, 12 July 1918; TNA, WO95/4581, War Diary of 1/101st Grenadiers, June 1918, Appendix 1: Memorandum by Major C. H. McCullum, Deputy Assistant Adjutant-General, XX Corps, 31 May 1918.
60 TNA, WO95/4581, War Diary of 1/101st Grenadiers, June 1918, Appendix 1: Memorandum by Lieutenant-Colonel G. O. Turnbull, Acting Adjutant-General, XX Corps, 2 June 18. Turnbull's underlining.
61 K. Roy, 'The Construction of Regiments in the Indian Army: 1859–1913', *War in History*, VIII (2001), 134–5; S. D. Pradhan, 'The Sikh Soldier in the First World War', in D. C. Ellinwood and S. D. Pradhan (eds), *India and World War I* (New Delhi, 1978), 220.
62 Omissi, 'Indian Eyes', 378–9; M. Harrison, 'Disease, Discipline and Dissent: The Indian Army in France and England, 1914–1915', in R. Carter, M. Harrison and S. Sturdy (eds), *Medicine and Modern Warfare* (Amsterdam, 1999), 191; Omissi, *Indian Voices*, 13–14; Corrigan, *Sepoys in the Trenches*, 198–200.
63 TNA, WO95/4586, War Diary of 2/101st Grenadiers, 12 June and 20 October 1918; TNA, WO95/4581, War Diary of 2/151st Indian Infantry, 9 January 1919; TNA, WO95/4584, War Diary of 1st Kashmir Infantry, 9 January 1919; TNA, WO95/4568, War Diary of 10th Division General Staff, September 1918, Appendix 36: 'Report on Operations by the 10th Division 19–24 September 1918', by Major-General J. R. Longley, GOC 10th Division, 17 October 1918, 9.
64 TNA, WO95/4581, War Diary of 1/101st Grenadiers, 11 June 1918.
65 IOR, L/MIL/5/733, Correspondence on Indian Cavalry, minute to the Military Committee on the 'Employment of Pathans in Palestine', by Sir E. G. Barrow, 7 February 1918; Omissi, *Sepoy and the Raj*, 140 and 148–9.
66 IOR, L/MIL/17/5/2403, Indian Prisoners of War, 'List C: Nominal Roll of Indian Prisoners of War, Suspected of Having Deserted to the Enemy or of Having Given Information to or Otherwise Assisted the Enemy After Capture (Revised to 24 October 1918). Egyptian Expeditionary Force'; Allenby, telegram to War Office, 7 July 1918, in Hughes, *Allenby in Palestine*, 168.
67 The absence of unrest among the EEF's sepoys reflected a wider trend of sustained loyalty to the Raj's military institutions during both the First and Second World Wars; see R. Callahan, 'The Indian Army, Total War, and the Dog that didn't Bark in the Night', in J. Hathaway (ed.), *Repression, Rebellion, Reinvention: Mutiny in Comparative Perspective* (Westport, 2001), 119–28. Gajendra Singh's research suggests that, although extreme forms of unrest were uncommon in the Indian Army during the two world wars, lower levels of disquiet were frequently expressed; see G. Singh, 'The Anatomy of Dissent in the Military of Colonial India During the First and Second World Wars', *Edinburgh Papers in South Asian Studies*, XX (2006), 1–45.
68 T. Denman, *Ireland's Unknown Soldiers: The 16th (Irish) Division in the Great War, 1914–1918* (Dublin, 1992), 23; P. Orr, 'The Road to Belgrade: The Experiences of the 10th (Irish) Division in the Balkans, 1915–17', in A. Gregory and S. Pašeta

(eds), *Ireland and the Great War: 'A war to unite us all'?* (Manchester, 2002), 171–2; T. Johnstone, *Orange, Green and Khaki: The Story of the Irish Regiments in the Great War, 1914–18* (Dublin, 1992), 96–8.

69   M. Dungan, *Irish Voices from the Great War* (Dublin, 1995), 87. For analysis of the particular qualities, both real and imagined, of the Irish soldier in the British Army see P. Karsten, 'Irish Soldiers in the British Army, 1792–1922: Suborned of Subordinated?', in P. Karsten (ed.), *Motivating Soldiers: Morale or Mutiny* (New York, 1998), 47–80; K. Jeffery, 'The Irish Military Tradition and the British Empire', in K. Jeffery (ed.), *'An Irish Empire'? Aspects of Ireland and the British Empire* (Manchester, 1996), 94–122; T. Denman, 'The Catholic Irish Soldier in the First World War: "The Racial Environment"', *Irish Historical Studies*, XXVII (1991), 352–65.

70   C. Falls, *Military Operations Macedonia: From the Outbreak of War to the Spring of 1917* (London, 1933), 65; Johnstone, *Orange, Green and Khaki*, 260 and 265; Denman, *Ireland's Unknown Soldiers*, 138; J. Stanley, *Ireland's Forgotten 10th: A Brief History of the 10th (Irish) Division, 1914–1918. Turkey, Macedonia and Palestine* (Ballycastle, 2003), 56 and 74.

71   Johnstone, *Orange, Green and Khaki*, 322; M. Cunliffe, *The Royal Irish Fusiliers, 1793–1950* (Oxford, 1952), 336.

72   S. Geoghegan, *The Campaigns and History of the Royal Irish Regiment* (London, 1927), II, 97; Johnstone, *Orange, Green and Khaki*, 337; TNA, WO95/4579, War Diary of 5th Connaught Rangers, 29 April 1918; TNA, WO95/4579, War Diary of 1st Leinster Regiment, 25–30 April 1918.

73   This is counter to the argument of Bowman who suggests that it was disease, in particular malaria originally acquired at Salonica, that ultimately led to 10th Division's manpower collapse. He is clearly wrong to suggest that the division was completely broken up; it continued to exist, but it was no longer an expressly Irish division. Nor does he provide any evidence for the assertion that the discipline of its battalions sent to the Western Front improved, as all his examples are drawn from its Macedonian service and not its period with the EEF. See T. Bowman, *The Irish Regiments in the Great War: Discipline and Morale* (Manchester, 2003), 108 and 174–8.

74   TNA, WO95/4567, War Diary of 10th Division General Staff, 2 and 25 May 1918; TNA, WO95/4579, War Diary of 6th Leinster Regiment, 26 April 1918.

75   H. Harris, *The Royal Irish Fusiliers (The 87th and 89th Regiments of Foot)* (London, 1972), 104; S. McCance, *History of the Royal Munster Fusiliers* (Aldershot, 1927), II, 190; TNA, WO95/4580, War Diary of 6th Royal Irish Rifles, 15 May 1918; TNA, WO95/4578, War Diary of 29th Infantry Brigade Headquarters, 11 June 1918.

76   TNA, WO95/4586, War Diary of 74th Punjabis, 28 May 1918; TNA, WO95/4579, War Diary of 1st Leinster Regiment, 6 May 1918; TNA, WO95/4580, War Diary of 6th Royal Irish Rifles, 5 May 1918.

77   TNA, WO95/4582, War Diary of 30th Infantry Brigade Headquarters, May 1918, Appendix: Move order to 1st Kashmir Infantry, by Major R. Bruce, Brigade Major, 30th Infantry Brigade, 3 May 1918; TNA, WO95/4579, War Diary of 5th Connaught Rangers, 29 April 1918.

78   TNA, WO95/4583, War Diary of 7th Royal Dublin Fusiliers, 29 April 1918; IWM, P305, Knott, diary, 16 September 1918.

79   TNA, WO95/4574, War Diary of 10th Divisional Signal Company, April 1918, Appendix: 'Report on Indian Signallers', by Major M. E. Webb, commanding 10th Divisional Signal Company, 23 April 1918; TNA, WO95/4574, War Diary of 10th Divisional Signal Company, 16–21 and 27 April 1918.

80 TNA, WO95/4574, War Diary of 10th Divisional Signal Company, May and July 1918.
81 TNA, WO95/4567, War Diary of 10th Division General Staff, April 1918, Appendix 17a: 'Memorandum on Recent Operations', by Major J. R. Cartwright, General Staff 10th Division, 12 April 1918.
82 TNA, WO95/4585, War Diary of 31st Infantry Brigade Headquarters, July 1918, Appendix 11: Memorandum on training, by Captain Hickman, Brigade Major, 31st Infantry Brigade, 29 July 1918.
83 TNA, WO95/4583, War Diary of 1st Royal Irish Regiment, 27 August 1918; TNA, WO95/4586, War Diary of 2/101st Grenadiers, 7 June 1918; TNA, WO95/4579, War Diary of 1st Leinster Regiment, 26 August 1918.
84 TNA, WO95/4581, War Diary of 1/101st Grenadiers, 1–5 April 1918; TNA, WO95/4584, War Diary of 46th Punjabis, July 1918, Appendix 3: 'Training Programme for Week Ending 20 July 1918'.
85 TNA, WO95/4586, War Diary of 2/101st Grenadiers, 21 March 1918.
86 TNA, WO95/4581, War Diary of 1/54th Sikhs, 1–21 April 1918; TNA, WO95/4581, War Diary of 1/101st Grenadiers, 19 April 1918.
87 TNA, WO95/4581, War Diary of 1/101st Grenadiers, 7 April 1918; TNA, WO95/4581, War Diary of 1/101st Grenadiers, June 1918, Appendix 4: 'Report on the Course of Instruction Held at Imperial School of Instruction Zeitoun, 18 N.C.Os. and Men Returned on 21/6/18', by Major S. G. Beaumont, commanding 1/101st Grenadiers, 22 June 1918.
88 IWM, PP/MCR/C1, Chetwode Papers, 'Report on 101st Grenadiers', by the Brigadier-General commanding 49th Indian Infantry Brigade, 4 May 1917; IWM, PP/MCR/C1, Chetwode Papers, letter from Brigadier-General commanding 49th Indian Infantry Brigade to Major-General E. S. Girdwood, GOC 74th Division, 4 May 1917; IWM, PP/MCR/C1, Chetwode Papers, letter from Lieutenant-Colonel W. J. H. Hunter, commanding 1/101st Grenadiers, to Headquarters, Eastern Force, no date.
89 TNA, WO95/4568, War Diary of 10th Division General Staff, June 1918, Appendix 3: 'Memorandum on General Principles of Defence', by the General Staff, 10th Division, 1 June 1918.
90 TNA, WO95/4585, War Diary of 31st Infantry Brigade Headquarters, June 1918, Appendix 15: Memorandum on patrolling, by Captain Hickman, Brigade Major, 31st Infantry Brigade, 30 June 1918.
91 TNA, WO95/4585, War Diary of 2nd Royal Irish Fusiliers, 16 July 1918.
92 TNA, WO95/4581, War Diary of 1/54th Sikhs, 14 July and 7 September 1918; TNA, WO95/4584, War Diary of 1st Kashmir Infantry, 7 August 1918.
93 Falls, *Military Operations II*, 427; TNA, WO95/4578, War Diary of 29th Infantry Brigade Headquarters, August 1918, Appendix: 'Report on Raid Carried Out by the 29th Infantry Brigade on Night 12/13 August 1918'.
94 TNA, WO95/4568, War Diary of 10th Division General Staff, August 1918, Appendix 19: 'Full Report on the Operation Carried Out by 10th Division on the Night 12/13 August 1918'; TNA, WO95/4578, War Diary of 29th Infantry Brigade Headquarters, 1 August 1918.
95 TNA, WO95/4579, War Diary of 1st Leinster Regiment, August 1918, Appendix: '1st Battalion the Leinster Regiment, Report of Right Wing', by Captain T. D. Murray, commanding the Right Wing, 1st Leinster Regiment, 13 August 1918; TNA, WO95/4586, War Diary of 2/101st Grenadiers, 11 August 1918.

96   TNA, WO95/4579, War Diary of 1st Leinster Regiment, August 1918, Appendix: '1st Battalion the Leinster Regiment, Report of Right Wing', by Captain F. G. Cavendish, commanding the Left Wing, 1st Leinster Regiment, 13 August 1918; TNA, WO95/4581, War Diary of 1/101st Grenadiers, August 1918, Appendix 6: 'Report on the 1/101st Grenadiers Raid on 12.8.1918', by Lieutenant-Colonel Roberts, Commanding Officer of 1/101st Grenadiers, 13 August 1918. This was an argument that the 101st Grenadiers' regimental historian sought to re-ignite in the 1920s.
97   TNA, WO95/4581, War Diary of 1/54th Sikhs, 12 August 1918; TNA, WO95/4579, War Diary of 1st Leinster Regiment, 13 August 1918; TNA, WO95/4581, War Diary of 1/101st Grenadiers, September 1918, Appendix 2: 'Operations Report', by Lieutenant-Colonel W. B. Roberts, Commanding Officer of 1/101st Grenadiers, 22 September 1918.
98   TNA, WO95/4568, War Diary of 10th Division General Staff, August 1918, Appendix 19: 'Full Report on the Operation Carried Out by 10th Division on the Night 12/13 August 1918'.
99   TNA, WO95/4581, War Diary of 1/101st Grenadiers, August 1918, Appendix 7: Message from Lieutenant-General Chetwode to 1/101st Grenadiers, 13 August 1918.
100 TNA, WO95/4568, War Diary of 10th Division General Staff, August 1918, Appendix 19: 'Full Report on the Operation Carried Out by 10th Division on the Night 12/13 August 1918'.
101 A. N. Morris, *Combat Studies Institute Report No. 10: Night Combat Operations* (Fort Leavenworth, 1985), 26.
102 Connelly, *Steady the Buffs!*, 91.
103 TNA, WO95/4581, War Diary of 1/101st Grenadiers, June 1918, Appendix 1: Memorandum from Captain A. E. Murray, Adjutant of 1/101st Grenadiers, to the Battalion's British officers, 11 June 1918.
104 TNA, WO95/4581, War Diary of 1/101st Grenadiers, 30 May 1918; TNA, WO95/4581, War Diary of 1/54th Sikhs, September 1918, Appendix 4: 'Account of Attack by Regiment on Points 1972:2036 on Afternoon of 20 September', by Major O. L. Ruck, commanding 1/54th Sikhs.
105 Omissi, *Sepoy and the Raj*, 77–84; S. Das, 'India and the First World War', in M. Howard (ed.), *A Part of History: Aspects of the British Experience of the First World War* (London, 2008), 67; S. Das, 'Indians at Home, Mesopotamia and France, 1914–1918: Towards an Intimate History', in S. Das (ed.), *Race, Empire and First World War Writing* (Cambridge, 2011), 82–3; R. Ahuja, 'The Corrosiveness of Comparison: Reverberations of Indian Wartime Experiences in German Prisoner of War Camps (1915–1919)', in H. Liebau, K. Bromber, K. Lange, D. Hamzah and R. Ahuja (eds), *The World in World Wars: Experiences, Perceptions and Perspectives from Africa and Asia* (Leiden, 2010), 134–7.
106 TNA, WO95/4578, War Diary of 29th Infantry Brigade Headquarters, August 1918, Appendix: 'Report on Raid Carried Out by the 29th Infantry Brigade on Night 12/13 August 1918'; TNA, WO95/4578, War Diary of 29th Infantry Brigade Headquarters, 31 May 1918.
107 TNA, WO95/4586, War Diary of 2/101st Grenadiers, October 1918, Appendix 2: Recommendations for awards for gallantry and leadership in the field.

108 Greenhut, 'Sahib and Sepoy'; Greenhut, 'Imperial Reserve'; MacMunn, *Martial Races*, 319.
109 TNA, WO95/4581, War Diary of 1/101st Grenadiers, 4 September 1918. For the importance of Indian officers in the Indian Army of the Second World War see T. Barkawi, 'Culture and Combat in the Colonies: The Indian Army in the Second World War', *Journal of Contemporary History*, XLI (2006), 328–44.
110 TNA, WO95/4568, War Diary of 10th Division General Staff, September 1918, Appendix 36: 'Report on Operations by the 10th Division 19–24 September 1918', by Major-General J. R. Longley, GOC 10th Division, 17 October 1918, 6; TNA, WO95/4581, War Diary of 1/101st Grenadiers, 21 September 1918; TNA, WO95/4586, War Diary of 2/42nd Deolis, 20 September 1918.
111 TNA, WO95/4568, War Diary of 10th Division General Staff, September 1918, Appendix 36: 'Report on Operations by the 10th Division 19–24 September 1918', by Major-General J. R. Longley, GOC 10th Division, 17 October 1918, Appendix A: 10th Division Casualties – 20 to 30 September 1918; TNA, WO95/4584, War Diary of 1st Kashmir Infantry, 21 September 1918.
112 TNA, WO95/4568, War Diary of 10th Division General Staff, September 1918, Appendix 41: Message from Lieutenant-General Chetwode to 10th Division, 22 September 1918; IWM, PP/MCR/C1, Chetwode Papers, 'Message of Congratulations to All Ranks of the EEF', GHQ, 28 September 1918. Notably George V did not refer at all to the Anzacs; one can only imagine the colourful responses this omission would have occasioned among the diggers of the EEF. Younghusband, 'Near East', 272.
113 TNA, WO95/4578, War Diary of 29th Infantry Brigade Headquarters, 15 March and 30 May 1918.
114 TNA, WO95/4585, War Diary of 31st Infantry Brigade Headquarters, 13 July 1918.
115 TNA, WO95/4581, War Diary of 1/101st Grenadiers, 5 May 1918.
116 IWM, PP/MCR/C1, Chetwode Papers, letter from Allenby to Chetwode, 2 February 1918; Falls, *Macedonia*, 87; Hart, *New Army List* (January 1915), 1066 and 1207.
117 Roy, 'Construction of Regiments', 128; D. P. Marston, 'A Force Transformed: The Indian Army and the Second World War', in D. P. Marston and C. S. Sundaram (eds), *A Military History of India and South Asia: From the East India Company to the Nuclear Era* (London, 2007), 117–20. The successful training and knowledge transfer systems of the EEF and Indian Army by 1918 were mirrored during the Second World War conflict, see T. R. Moreman, 'From the Desert Sands to the Burmese Jungle: The Indian Army and the Lessons of North Africa, September 1939–November 1942', in K. Roy (ed.), *The Indian Army in the Two World Wars* (Leiden, 2012), 223–54. For a comparative analysis of the morale problems encountered in 14th Army see K. Roy, 'Discipline and Morale of the African, British and Indian Army Units in Burma and India During World War II: July 1943 to August 1945', *Modern Asian Studies*, XLIV (2010), 1255–82. Megiddo also needs to be placed alongside the Indian Army's success in Mesopotamia in 1917–18 to judge fully its performance in the First World War. See Latter, 'Indian Army in Mesopotamia', 232–46; K. Roy, 'The Army in India in Mesopotamia from 1916 to 1918: Tactics, Technology and Logistics Reconsidered', in I. F. W. Beckett (ed.), *1917: Beyond the Western Front* (Leiden, 2009), 131–58.

Conclusion

1 Y. Khan, 'Remembering and Forgetting: South Asia and the Second World War', in M. Geyer and B. Ziino (eds), *The Heritage of War* (Abingdon, 2012), 177–93; K. Roy, 'Introduction: Warfare, Society and the Indian Army During the Two World Wars', in K. Roy (ed.), *The Indian Army in the Two World Wars* (Leiden, 2012), 1–24.
2 F. Bongiorno and G. Mansfield, 'Whose War was it Anyway? Some Australian Historians and the Great War', *History Compass*, VI (2008), 62–90.
3 The same is true for the NZMR, which would also have taken conscript replacements after 1916.
4 Fuller, *Troop Morale*, 175–80.
5 See H. Strachan, *The Politics of the British Army* (Oxford, 1997), 208–9; McCartney, *Citizen Soldiers*, 25–56.
6 Strachan, 'Training', 216–17. For the importance of realistic training in determining British military performance in the Second World War see T. H. Place, 'Lionel Wigram, Battle Drill and the British Army in the Second World War', *War in History*, VII (2000), 442–62.
7 Hughes, *Allenby and British Strategy*, 71–88.
8 H. Strachan, *Carl von Clausewitz's On War: A Biography* (London, 2007), 126.

Bibliography

Unpublished primary sources

Alexander Turnbull Library, National Library of New Zealand, Wellington

H. Judge Papers, MS-Papers-4312/1–3
A. McNeur Papers, MS-Papers-4108/6 and 8
A. E. T. Rhodes Papers, 76–123

Australian War Memorial, Canberra

War Diary of Australian and New Zealand Mounted Division General Staff, AWM4 1/60
War Diary of 1st Australian Light Horse Brigade Headquarters, AWM4 10/1
War Diary of 1st Australian Light Horse Regiment, AWM4 10/6
War Diary of 3rd Australian Light Horse Regiment, AWM4 10/8
War Diary of 2nd Australian Light Horse Brigade Headquarters, AWM4 10/2
War Diary of 5th Australian Light Horse Regiment, AWM4 10/10
War Diary of 7th Australian Light Horse Regiment, AWM4 10/12
R. T. Beatty Papers, PR01288
H. D. Billings Papers, MSS1022
E. A. E. Brown Papers, 2DRL/1285
R. H. Chandler Papers, 2DRL/0817
H. G. Chauvel Papers, PR00535
T. N. Crase Papers, MSS1071
B. B. Delpratt Papers, 3DRL/3741
A. Dick Papers, 2DRL/0337
R. J. Dunk Papers, 3DRL/7268
C. C. Easterbrook Papers, 3DRL/6257
J. Evans Papers, 2DRL/0015
J. J. Greatorex Papers, 3DRL/6776
J. D. Hobbs Papers, PR85/289
J. T. Holmes Papers, PR00740
L. S. Horder Papers, 3DRL/6595
E. A. K. Hudson Papers, 1DRL/0364
E. G. Lawrance Papers, 3DRL/6501
R. Leahy Papers, PR83/107
C. H. Livingstone Papers, PR88/030
S. R. Macfarlane Papers, 2DRL/0211
A. S. Metcalfe Papers, 1DRL/0497
C. R. Morley Papers, 2DRL/0081
D. H. Morrice Papers, 2DRL/0759

M. E. Pearce Papers, PR89/125
E. A. Pickering Papers, PR87/212
S. P. Prince Papers, 3DRL/7568
G. de L. Ryrie Papers, PR84/193
H. E. Sullivan Papers, PR01058
F. H. Tomlins Papers, PR84/179
A. C. Truman Papers, PR84/240
H. V. Vernon Papers, PR88/014
H. Wetherell Papers, 2DRL/0747

Bedfordshire Record Office, Bedford

Order of Service for the Centenary Celebrations of 5th Battalion the Bedfordshire Regiment, 20 March 1964, X550/6/23
Victoria Cross citation for Private Samuel Needham, 1/5th Bedfordshire Regiment, X550/6/11

Essex Regiment Museum, Chelmsford

Order of Service and Thanksgiving for 1/4th Battalion the Essex Regiment, Freetown, 23 March 1941, ER5304.4
Order of Service, 2/5th Battalion the Essex Regiment, Warley, 4 July 1992, ER 5315
W. F. Cook Papers, ER15807.1
R. J. France Papers
F. W. Joslin Papers
A. R. Surry Papers, ER3253

Hampshire Regiment Museum, Winchester

W. Hickman Papers, M1810
S. Nightingale Papers, M653

Imperial War Museum, London

Jerusalem Christmas Card, Misc 74(1113)
Proclamation of Martial Law in Jerusalem, XX02 Special Misc R
E. H. H. Allenby Papers, 07/8/1
E. P. Argyle Papers, 04/37/1
V. H. Bailey Papers, 85/4/1
W. Barron Papers, 74/149/1
S. Blagg Papers, PP/MCR/220
F. V. Blunt Papers, 94/5/1
G. B. Buxton Papers, PP/MCR/62
P. W. Chetwode Papers, PP/MCR/C1
R. Dening Papers, P386
T. G. Edgerton Papers, 98/28/1
G. W. Gotto Papers, Misc 41(726)
F. S. Hammond Papers, 84/34/1

Lord Hampton Papers, DS/MISC/82
S. W. Hare Papers, 66/85/1
E. B. Hinde Papers, Con Shelf
J. H. Jewson Papers, 76/74/1
W. Knott Papers, P305
A. MacGregor Papers, 05/38/2
H. L. Milsom Papers, 96/48/1
E. C. Mortimer Papers, 06/33/1
H. M. E. Price Papers, 04/9/1
C. T. Shaw Papers, 81/23/1
A. R. Surry Papers, 82/22/1
E. C. Thompson Papers, PP/MCR/218
W. M. Town Papers, 06/69/1
C. S. Wink Papers, 85/4/1
F. H. Wollaston Papers, 03/29/1

India Office Records, British Library, London

Correspondence on Indian Cavalry, L/MIL/5/733
Correspondence on Additional Indian Units for Service Overseas: Policy and Employment, L/MIL/5/739
Correspondence on 3rd (Lahore) Division, L/MIL/5/748
Correspondence on 7th (Meerut) Division, L/MIL/5/784
Policy following General Smuts' Recommendations: Egypt and Mesopotamia, L/MIL/5/794
Report on the Inter-Divisional Manoeuvres, Northern Army, 1912, L/MIL/17/5/1814
Memorandum on India's Contribution to the War in Men, Material, and Money: August 1914 to November 1918, L/MIL/17/5/2381
Development of Man Power in India, and its Utilisation for Imperial Purposes, L/MIL/17/5/2398
Nominal Rolls of Indian Prisoners of War Suspected of Having Deserted to the Enemy, L/MIL/17/5/2403

Kippenberger Military Archives, National Army Museum, Waiouru

Wellington Mounted Rifles Regimental Orders, 2001.660
D. Currin Papers, 2004.131
P. G. Doherty Papers, 1991.2000
A. D. Fabian Papers, 1993.976–997
G. B. Hull Papers, 2001.1035
J. K. Hull Papers, 1993.1039
R. D. McCormack Papers, 1999.2619
E. C. M. McKay Papers, 1998.31

Liddell Hart Centre for Military Archives, King's College London

F. S. A. Clarke Papers, Clarke 1/1–4
J. S. M. Shea Papers, Shea 4–6

Museum of Army Chaplaincy Archives, Amport House, Andover

W. A. Jones Papers

The National Archives, Kew

War Cabinet Minutes, CAB23/4
Comments and Correspondence Relating to the Compilation of the Official Histories – Egypt and Palestine, CAB45/78–80
Foreign Office Correspondence, FO371/3383
Foreign Office Correspondence, FO395/152 and 240
Arab Bureau Papers, FO882/14
War Office Correspondence, WO33/946
War Diary of Egyptian Expeditionary Force General Staff, WO95/4367–4368
War Diary of Egyptian Expeditionary Force Deputy Adjutant-General, WO95/4377
War Diary of the Egyptian Expeditionary Force Director of Medical Services, WO95/4386
War Diary of the EEF Principal Chaplain, WO95/4391
War Diary of Eastern Force General Staff, WO95/4450–4451
War Diary of XX Corps General Staff, WO95/4479
War Diary of XXI Corps General Staff, WO95/4490
War Diary of Australian and New Zealand Mounted Division Assistant Director of Medical Services, WO95/4525
War Diary of New Zealand Mounted Rifles Brigade, WO95/4544
War Diary of Auckland Mounted Rifles Regiment, WO95/4545
War Diary of Canterbury Mounted Rifles Regiment, WO95/4546
War Diary of Wellington Mounted Rifles Regiment, WO95/4547
War Diary of 10th Division General Staff, WO95/4567–4568
War Diary of 10th Divisional Signal Company, WO95/4574
War Diary of 29th Infantry Brigade Headquarters, WO95/4578
War Diary of 1st Leinster Regiment, WO95/4579
War Diary of 6th Leinster Regiment, WO95/4579
War Diary of 5th Connaught Rangers, WO95/4579
War Diary of 6th Royal Irish Rifles, WO95/4580
War Diary of 1/54th Sikhs, WO95/4581
War Diary of 1/101st Grenadiers, WO95/4581
War Diary of 2/151st Indian Infantry, WO95/4581
War Diary of 30th Infantry Brigade Headquarters, WO95/4582
War Diary of 1st Royal Irish Regiment, WO95/4583
War Diary of 7th Royal Dublin Fusiliers, WO95/4583
War Diary of 1st Kashmir Infantry, WO95/4584
War Diary of 38th Dogras, WO95/4584
War Diary of 46th Punjabis, WO95/4584
War Diary of 31st Infantry Brigade Headquarters, WO95/4585
War Diary of 2nd Royal Irish Fusiliers, WO95/4585
War Diary of 74th Punjabis, WO95/4586
War Diary of 2/42nd Deolis, WO95/4586
War Diary of 2/101st Grenadiers, WO95/4586
War Diary of 54th Division General Staff, WO95/4633–4637
War Diary of 54th Division Assistant Director of Medical Services, WO95/4639
War Diary of 161st Infantry Brigade Headquarters, WO95/4649

War Diary of 1/4th Essex Regiment, WO95/4650
War Diary of 1/5th Essex Regiment, WO95/4650
War Diary of 1/6th Essex Regiment, WO95/4650
War Diary of 1/7th Essex Regiment, WO95/4651
War Diary of 161st Light Trench Mortar Battery, WO95/4651
War Diary of 162nd Infantry Brigade Headquarters, WO95/4652–4653
War Diary of 1/5th Bedfordshire Regiment, WO95/4653
War Diary of 1/4th Northamptonshire Regiment, WO95/4653
War Diary of 1/10th London Regiment, WO95/4654
War Diary of 1/11th London Regiment, WO95/4654
War Diary of 163rd Infantry Brigade Headquarters, WO95/4656
War Diary of 1/4th Norfolk Regiment, WO95/4657
War Diary of 1/5th Norfolk Regiment, WO95/4657
War Diary of 1/5th Suffolk Regiment, WO95/4658
War Diary of 1/8th Hampshire Regiment, WO95/4659
War Diary of 163rd Machine Gun Company, WO95/4659

National Army Museum, Chelsea

E. Osbourne Papers, 2004-03-64

Norfolk Regiment Museum, Norwich

Order of Service, Memorial Service for Major W. H. Jewson and Captain S. D. Page, Norwich, 6 May 1917
1/4th and 1/5th Norfolk Regiment Papers, Box 11
W. H. Bland Papers, NWHRM 6186
J. Emms Papers, Box 11
K. Fielding Papers
L. Littlewood Papers, Box 11/3978
R. Overman Papers

Suffolk Record Office, Bury St Edmunds

G. E. Lee Papers, GB554/Y1/165j
C. M. Oliver Papers, GB554/Y1/187b
H. C. Wolton Papers, GB554/Y1/426a-b

Published primary sources

Newspapers and periodicals

The Age
Bedfordshire Times and Independent
Eastern Daily Press
The Northampton Independent
Punch
The Times

Official publications

Anonymous, *Statistical Abstract for British India with Statistics, where Available, Relating to Certain Indian States, from 1914–15 to 1923–24* (London, 1925), LVIII.
Government of India, *India's Contribution to the Great War* (Calcutta, 1923).
Hansard, 5th series, C (1917).
Hart, H. G., *The New Army List* (London, January 1915).
War Office, *Soldiers Died in the Great War 1914–1919* (London, 1920).
War Office, *Statistics of the Military Effort of the British Empire During the Great War 1914–1920* (London, 1922).

Memoirs, collections of documents and novels

Allen, T., *The Tracks they Trod: Salonika and the Balkans, Gallipoli, Egypt and Palestine Revisited* (London, 1932).
Barrow, G. de S., *The Fire of Life* (London, 1942).
Bowes, J., *The Aussie Crusaders with Allenby in Palestine* (London, 1920).
Boyack, N. and Tolerton, J. (eds), *In the Shadow of War: New Zealand Soldiers Talk About World War One and Their Lives* (Auckland, 1990).
Brereton, F. S., *With Allenby in Palestine: A Story of the Latest Crusade* (London, 1920).
Butler, E., *Autobiography* (2nd edn, Sevenoaks, 1993).
Camm, B., *Pilgrim Paths in Latin Lands* (London, 1923).
Cooper, F. H., *Khaki Crusaders: With the South African Artillery in Egypt and Palestine* (Cape Town, 1919).
Finley, J., *A Pilgrim in Palestine Afters its Deliverance: Being an Account of Journeys on Foot by the First American Pilgrim after General Allenby's Recovery of the Holy Land* (London, 1919).
Forester, C. S., *The General* (London, 1936).
Gibbons, T., *With the 1/5th Essex in the East* (Colchester, 1921).
Gilbert, V., *The Last Crusade: With Allenby to Jerusalem* (New York, 1923).
Harper, G. (ed.), *Letters from the Battlefield: New Zealand Soldiers Write Home, 1914–18* (Auckland, 2001).
Hatton, S. F., *The Yarn of a Yeoman* (London, 1930).
Hughes, M. (ed.), *Allenby in Palestine: The Middle East Correspondence of Field Marshal Viscount Allenby, June 1917–October 1919* (Stroud, 2004).
Idriess, I. L., *The Desert Column: Leaves from the Diary of an Australian Trooper in Gallipoli, Sinai, and Palestine* (Sydney, 1933).
Johns, W. E., *Biggles Flies East* (Oxford, 1935).
Lawrence, T. E., *Seven Pillars of Wisdom: A Triumph* (London, 1935).
Lloyd George, D., *War Memoirs of David Lloyd George* (London, 1936), II.
Lock, H. O., *With the British Army in the Holy Land* (London, 1919).
Lockhart, J. G., *Palestine Days and Nights: Sketches of the Campaign in the Holy Land* (London, 1920).
Maxwell, D., *The Last Crusade* (London, 1920).
Meinertzhagen, R., *Army Diary, 1899–1926* (Edinburgh, 1960).
Sommers, C., *Temporary Crusaders* (London, 1919).
Storrs, R., *Orientations* (London, 1937).
Wilson, J. P., *With the Soldiers in Palestine and Syria* (London, 1920).
Winnington-Ingram, A. F., *The Potter and the Clay* (London, 1917).

Other contemporary publications

Anonymous, *Anzac Hostel Guide, Cairo* (Cairo, no date).
Barrett, J. W., *The War Work of the Y.M.C.A. in Egypt* (London, 1919).
Garsia, C., *A Key to Victory: A Study in War Planning* (London, 1940).
Gullett, H. S., 'Fighting for Palestine: Three Years' Campaigning', in H. S. Gullett and C. Barrett (eds), *Australia in Palestine* (Sydney, 1919), 1–59.
Hordern, A. V. C. and Day, E. R., 'The R.A.Ch.D. in the Mediterranean and Egyptian Expeditionary Forces', *Quarterly Journal of the Royal Army Chaplains' Department*, II (1923), 300–3.
MacMunn, G., *The Martial Races of India* (London, 1933).
Mansfield, H. G., *By Jaffa Way and Other Poems* (London, 1919).
Massey, W. T., *How Jerusalem was Won: Being the Record of Allenby's Campaign in Palestine* (London, 1919).
—, *Allenby's Final Triumph* (London, 1920).
Masterman, E. W. G., *The Deliverance of Jerusalem* (London, 1918).
Murray, A., *Sir Archibald Murray's Despatches (June 1916–June 1917)* (London, 1920).
Smith, G. A., *The Historical Geography of the Holy Land: Especially in Relation to the History of Israel and of the Early Church* (20th edn, London, 1919).
Talbot, E. S. and Cairns, D. S. (eds), *The Army and Religion: An Enquiry and its Bearing Upon the Religious Life of the Nation* (London, 1919).
Trooper Bluegum, 'The Horses Stay Behind', in H. S. Gullett and C. Barrett (eds), *Australia in Palestine* (Sydney, 1919), 78.
Trumper, V. L., *Historical Sites in Southern Palestine with a Brief Account of Napoleon's Expedition to Syria 1799* (Cairo, 1917).
—, *Historical Sites in Central Palestine: Part I* (Cairo, 1918).
—, *Historical Sites in Central Palestine: Part II* (Cairo, 1918).
—, *Historical Sites in Palestine with a Short Account of Napoleon's Expedition to Syria* (Cairo, 1921).

Published secondary sources

Ahuja, R., 'The Corrosiveness of Comparison: Reverberations of Indian Wartime Experiences in German Prisoner of War Camps (1915–1919)', in H. Liebau, K. Bromber, K. Lange, D. Hamzah and R. Ahuja (eds), *The World in World Wars: Experiences, Perceptions and Perspectives from Africa and Asia* (Leiden, 2010), 131–66.
Anderson, H. S. and Frankland, A., *The 101st Grenadiers: Historical Record of the Regiment, 1778–1923* (Aldershot, 1920).
Anderson, O., 'The Growth of Christian Militarism in Mid-Victorian Britain', *The English Historical Review*, LXXXVI (1971), 46–72.
Andrews, E. M., *The Anzac Illusion: Anglo-Australian Relations During World War I* (Cambridge, 1993).
Anonymous, *History of the Hampshire Territorial Force Association, 1914–1919* (Southampton, 1921).
Ardant du Picq, C.-J.-J.-J., *Battle Studies: Ancient and Modern Battle*, trans. J. N. Greely and R. C. Cotton (New York, 1921).
Arthur, M., *Forgotten Voices of the Great War* (London, 2002).
Ashworth, T., 'The Sociology of Trench Warfare 1914–18', *The British Journal of Sociology*, XIX (1968), 407–23.

—, *Trench Warfare 1914–1918: The Live and Let Live System* (London, 1980).
Audoin-Rouzeau, S., *Men at War 1914–1918: National Sentiment and Trench Journalism in France During the First World War* (Oxford, 1992).
Badsey, S., 'Cavalry and the Development of Breakthrough Doctrine', in P. Griffith (ed.), *British Fighting Methods in the Great War* (London, 1996), 138–74.
—, *Doctrine and Reform in the British Cavalry 1880–1914* (Aldershot, 2008).
Barbara, S., 'Ornithologists Stunned by Bird Collector's Deceit', *Nature*, CDXXXVII (2005), 302–3.
Barkawi, T., 'Peoples, Homelands, and Wars? Ethnicity, the Military, and Battle Among British Imperial Forces in the War Against Japan', *Comparative Studies in Society and History*, XLVI (2004), 134–63.
—, 'On the Pedagogy of "Small Wars"', *International Affairs*, LXXX (2004), 19–37.
—, 'Culture and Combat in the Colonies: The Indian Army in the Second World War', *Journal of Contemporary History*, XLI (2006), 325–55.
Barkawi, T. and Laffey, M., 'The Postcolonial Moment in Security Studies', *Review of International Studies*, XXII (2006), 329–52.
Barr, N., 'The Desert War Experience', in P. Liddle, J. Bourne and I. Whitehead (eds), *The Great World War 1914–1945. I: Lightning Strikes Twice* (London, 2000), 120–35.
Bartlett, F. C., *Psychology and the Soldier* (Cambridge, 1927).
Bartov, O., 'Indoctrination and Motivation in the *Wehrmacht*: The Importance of the Unquantifiable', *The Journal of Strategic Studies*, IX (1986), 16–34.
—, 'Daily Life and Motivation in War: The *Wehrmacht* in the Soviet Union', *The Journal of Strategic Studies*, XII (1989), 200–14.
—, *Hitler's Army: Soldiers, Nazis, and War in the Third Reich* (Oxford, 1991).
—, *The Eastern Front, 1941–45: German Troops and the Barbarisation of Warfare* (2nd edn, London, 2001).
Barua, P., 'Inventing Race: The British and India's Martial Races', *The Historian*, LVIII (1995), 107–16.
—, 'Strategies and Doctrines of Imperial Defence: Britain and India, 1919–45', *The Journal of Imperial and Commonwealth History*, XXV (1997), 240–66.
Bar-Yosef, E., *The Holy Land in English Culture 1799–1917: Palestine and the Question of Orientalism* (Oxford, 2005).
Bauerlein, M., 'Literary Evidence: A Response to Keith Windschuttle', *The Journal of the Historical Society*, II (2002), 77–87.
Baynes, J., *Morale: A Study of Men and Courage. The Second Scottish Rifles at the Battle of Neuve Chapelle* (London, 1967).
Beaumont, J., 'Australia', in P. Liddle, J. Bourne and I. Whitehead (eds), *The Great World War 1914–1945. II: The People's Experience* (London, 2001), 197–210.
Beckett, I. F. W., 'The Territorial Force in the Great War', in P. H. Liddle (ed.), *Home Fires and Foreign Fields: British Social and Military Experience in the First World War* (London, 1985), 21–37.
—, 'The Nation in Arms, 1914–18', in I .F. W. Beckett and K. Simpson (eds), *A Nation in Arms: A Social Study of the British Army in the First World War* (Manchester, 1985), 1–35.
—, 'The Territorial Force', in I. F. W. Beckett and K. Simpson (eds), *A Nation in Arms: A Social Study of the British Army in the First World War* (Manchester, 1985), 127–63.
—, *The Amateur Military Tradition 1558–1945* (Manchester, 1991).
—, *Territorials: A Century of Service* (Plymouth, 2008).
—, 'Wood, Sir (Henry) Evelyn (1838–1919)', *Oxford Dictionary of National Biography*.

Bennett, J., '"Massey's Sunday School Picnic Party": "The Other Anzacs" or Honorary Australians', *War and Society*, XXI (2003), 23–54.
Bergerud, E., *Touched with Fire: The Land War in the South Pacific* (New York, 1996).
Berrie, G. L., *Under Furred Hats (6th A.L.H. Regt.)* (Sydney, 1919).
Bet-El, I. R., 'A Soldier's Pilgrimage: Jerusalem 1918', *Mediterranean Historical Review*, VIII (1993), 218–35.
Bird, C., 'From Home to the Charge: A Psychological Study of the Soldier', *The American Journal of Psychology*, XXVIII (1917), 315–48.
Black, J., *Rethinking Military History* (Abingdon, 2004).
Blackwell, E. and Axe, E. C., *Romford to Beirut via France, Egypt and Jericho: An Outline of the War Record of 'B' Battery, 271st Brigade R.F.A. (1/2nd Essex Battery, R.F.A.) with Many Digressions* (Clacton-on-Sea, 1926).
Blair, D., *Dinkum Diggers: An Australian Battalion at War* (Carlton, 2001).
—, '"Those Miserable Tommies": Anti-British Sentiment in the Australian Imperial Force, 1915–1918', *War and Society*, XIX (2001), 71–91.
Bond, B., 'The Army Between the Two World Wars 1918–1939', in D. G. Chandler and I. F. W. Beckett (eds), *The Oxford History of the British Army* (Oxford, 1994), 256–71.
—, *Survivors of a Kind: Memoirs of the Western Front* (London, 2008).
Bongiorno, F. and Mansfield, G., 'Whose War was it Anyway? Some Australian Historians and the Great War', *History Compass*, VI (2008), 62–90.
Bopegamage, A., 'Caste, Class and the Indian Military: A Study of the Social Origins of Indian Army Personnel', in J. van Doorn (ed.), *Military Profession and Military Regimes: Commitments and Conflicts* (The Hague, 1969), 127–54.
Bou, J., 'Cavalry, Firepower, and Swords: The Australian Light Horse and the Tactical Lessons of Cavalry Operations, 1916–1918', *The Journal of Military History*, LXXI (2007), 99–125.
—, 'They shot the horses – didn't they?', *Wartime*, XLIV (2008), 54–7.
Bourke, J., *An Intimate History of Killing: Face-to-Face Killing in Twentieth-Century Warfare* (London, 1999).
—, 'The Experience of Killing', in P. Liddle, J. Bourne and I. Whitehead (eds), *The Great World War 1914–1945. I: Lightning Strikes Twice* (London, 2000), 293–309.
—, 'The Emotions in War: Fear and the British and American Military, 1914–45', *Historical Research*, LXXIV (2001), 314–30.
Bourne, G. H., *Nulli Secundus: The History of the 2nd Light Horse Regiment, Australian Imperial Force, August 1914–April 1919* (Tamworth, 1926).
Bourne, J., 'The British Working Man in Arms', in H. Cecil and P. H. Liddle (eds), *Facing Armageddon: The First World War Experienced* (Barnsley, 1996), 336–52.
Bowman, T., *The Irish Regiments in the Great War: Discipline and Morale* (Manchester, 2003).
Bowyer, R., *Dictionary of Military Terms* (3rd edn, London, 2004).
Brendon, P., *Thomas Cook: 150 Years of Popular Tourism* (London, 1991).
Briscoe Moore, A., *The Mounted Riflemen in Sinai and Palestine: The Story of New Zealand's Crusaders* (Auckland, 1920).
Brown, C. G., *The Death of Christian Britain: Understanding Secularisation 1800–2000* (London, 2001).
Brown, M., *The Imperial War Museum Book of 1918: Year of Victory* (London, 1998).
Browne, A. T. A., 'A Study of the Anatomy of Fear and Courage in War', *The Army Quarterly and Defence Journal*, CVI (1976), 297–303.

Bryant, M. and Heneage, S., *Dictionary of British Cartoonists and Caricaturists, 1730–1980* (Aldershot, 1994).
Bungay, S., *Alamein* (London, 2002).
Burrows, J. W., *The Essex Regiment* (Southend-on-Sea, 1932), V.
Butlin, R., 'George Adam Smith and the Historical Geography of the Holy Land: Contents, Contexts and Connections', *Journal of Historical Geography*, XIV (1988), 381–404.
Butlin, R. A., 'Lucas, Sir Charles Prestwood (1853–1931)', *Oxford Dictionary of National Biography*.
Callahan, R., 'The Indian Army, Total War, and the Dog that didn't Bark in the Night', in J. Hathaway (ed.), *Repression, Rebellion, Reinvention: Mutiny in Comparative Perspective* (Westport, 2001), 119–28.
Caplan, L., 'Martial Gurkhas: The Persistence of a British Military Discourse on "Race"', in P. Robb (ed.), *The Concept of Race in South Asia* (Oxford, 1995), 260–81.
Cawkwell, G. L., 'Introduction', in Xenophon, *The Persian Expedition*, trans. R. Warner (London, 1972), 9–48.
Chambers II, J. W., 'The New Military History: Myth and Reality', *The Journal of Military History*, LV (1991), 395–406.
Churchill, W. S., *The World Crisis, 1916–1918: Part II* (London, 1927).
Clancy, J., 'Images of Australia in World War I: The Film, the Mini-Series and Historical Representation', in J. Smart and T. Wood (eds), *An Anzac Muster: War and Society in Australia and New Zealand 1914–1918 and 1939–1945* (Clayton, 1992), 30–9.
Clifford, J., review of *Orientalism* by E. W. Said, *History and Theory: Studies in the Philosophy of History*, XIX (1980), 204–23.
Coates, J., *An Atlas of Australia's Wars* (Oxford, 2001).
Cohen, D., 'Comparative History: Buyer Beware', *German Historical Institute, Washington, D.C., Bulletin*, XXIX (2001), 23–33.
Cohen, S. P., 'The Untouchable Soldier: Caste, Politics, and the Indian Army', *The Journal of Asian Studies*, XXVIII (1969), 453–68.
Collier, P. and Inkpen, R., 'Mapping Palestine and Mesopotamia in the First World War', *The Cartographic Journal*, XXXVIII (2001), 143–54.
Connell, J., *Wavell: Scholar and Soldier* (London, 1964).
Connelly, M., *The Great War, Memory and Ritual: Commemoration in the City and East London, 1916–1939* (Woodbridge, 2002).
—, *Steady the Buffs! A Regiment, a Region, and the Great War* (Oxford, 2006).
Corrigan, G., *Sepoys in the Trenches: The Indian Corps on the Western Front, 1914–1915* (Stroud, 1999).
Creasy, E., *The Fifteen Decisive Battles of the World* (London, 1851).
Crerar, D., '"Where's the Padre?" Canadian Memory and Great War Chaplains', in D. L. Bergen (ed.), *The Sword of the Lord: Military Chaplains from the First to the Twenty-First Century* (Notre Dame, 2004), 141–63.
Cruttwell, C. R. M. F., *A History of the Great War 1914–1918* (Oxford, 1934).
Cunliffe, M., *The Royal Irish Fusiliers, 1793–1950* (Oxford, 1952).
Curran, J., '"Bonjour Paree!" The First AIF in Paris, 1916–1918', *Journal of Australian Studies*, XXIII (1999), 19–26.
Das, S., *Touch and Intimacy in First World War Literature* (Cambridge, 2005).
—, 'India and the First World War', in M. Howard (ed.), *A Part of History: Aspects of the British Experience of the First World War* (London, 2008), 63–73.
—, 'Indians at Home, Mesopotamia and France, 1914–1918: Towards an Intimate History', in S. Das (ed.), *Race, Empire and First World War Writing* (Cambridge, 2011), 70–89.

Davies, J., 'Reconstructing Enmities; War and War Memorials, the Boundary Markers of the West', *History of European Ideas*, XIX (1994), 47–52.
Denman, T., 'The Catholic Irish Soldier in the First World War: "The Racial Environment"', *Irish Historical Studies*, XXVII (1991), 352–65.
—, *Ireland's Unknown Soldiers: The 16th (Irish) Division in the Great War, 1914–1918* (Dublin, 1992).
Dennis, P., *The Territorial Army 1906–1940* (Woodbridge, 1987).
Dennis, P., Grey, J., Morris, E., Prior, R. and Connor, J. (eds), *The Oxford Companion to Australian Military History* (Oxford, 1995).
Dolev, E., *Allenby's Military Medicine: Life and Death in World War I Palestine* (London, 2007).
Downes, C. J., 'To Be or Not To Be a Profession: The Military Case', *Defence Analysis*, I (1985), 147–71.
Dravidian, I., 'The Russian Soldier's Morale from the Evidence of Tsarist Military Censorship', in H. Cecil and P. H. Liddle (eds), *Facing Armageddon: The First World War Experienced* (Barnsley, 1996), 425–33.
Duffet, R., 'A War Unimagined: Food and the Rank and File Soldier of the First World War', in J. Meyer (ed.), *British Popular Culture and the First World War* (Leiden, 2008), 47–70.
Dungan, M., *Irish Voices from the Great War* (Dublin, 1995).
Ellinwood, D. C., 'An Historical Study of the Punjabi Soldier in World War I', in H. Singh and N. G. Barrier (eds), *Punjab Past and Present: Essays in Honour of Dr Ganda Singh* (Patiala, 1976), 337–62.
—, 'The Indian Soldier, the Indian Army, and Change, 1914–1918', in D. C. Ellinwood and S. D. Pradhan (eds), *India and World War I* (New Delhi, 1978), 177–211.
—, 'Ethnicity and the Colonial Asian Army: British Policy, War, and the Indian Army, 1914–1918', in D. C. Ellinwood and C. H. Enloe (eds), *Ethnicity and the Military in Asia* (New Brunswick, 1981), 89–144.
—, 'The Indian Soldier and National Consciousness, 1914–1939', *The Quarterly Review of Historical Studies*, XXVII (1987), 4–24.
Ellis, J., *Eye-Deep in Hell* (London, 1976).
Ely, R., 'The First Anzac Day: Invented or Discovered?', *Journal of Australian Studies*, XVII (1985), 41–58.
Englander, D., 'Soldiering and Identity: Reflections on the Great War', *War in History*, I (1994), 300–18.
Erickson, E. J., 'Strength Against Weakness: Ottoman Military Effectiveness at Gallipoli, 1915', *Journal of Military History*, LXV (2001), 981–1011.
—, 'From Kirkilisse to the Great Offensive: Turkish Operational Encirclement Planning, 1912–22', *Middle Eastern Studies*, XL (2004), 45–64.
—, *Ottoman Army Effectiveness in World War I: A Comparative Study* (London, 2007).
Fair, A. and Wolton, E. D., *The History of the 1/5th Battalion 'The Suffolk Regiment'* (London, 1923).
Falls, C., *Military Operations Egypt and Palestine. II: From June 1917 to the End of the War* (London, 1930).
—, *Military Operations Macedonia: From the Outbreak of War to the Spring of 1917* (London, 1933).
—, *The First World War* (London, 1960).
—, *Armageddon 1918* (London, 1964).
Farr, D., 'Lamb, Henry Taylor (1883–1960)', *Oxford Dictionary of National Biography*.

Farrar-Hockley, A., 'Field-Marshal the Viscount Allenby', in Lord Carver (ed.), *The War Lords: Military Commanders of the Twentieth Century* (London, 1976), 144–59.

Farwell, B., *Armies of the Raj: From the Mutiny to Independence, 1858–1947* (London, 1989).

Fennell, J., *Combat and Morale in the North African Campaign: The Eighth Army and the Path to El Alamein* (Cambridge, 2011).

Ferguson, N., *The Pity of War* (London, 1998).

Fewster, K., 'Ellis Ashmead Bartlett and the Making of the Anzac Legend', *Journal of Australian Studies*, X (1982), 17–30.

—, 'The Wazza Riots, 1915', *Journal of the Australian War Memorial*, IV (1984), 47–53.

Frantzen, A. J., *Bloody Good: Chivalry, Sacrifice and the Great War* (Chicago, 2004).

French, C. F., 'The Fashioning of *Esprit de Corps* in the 51st Highland Division from St Valery to El Alamein', *Journal of the Society for Army Historical Research*, LXXVII (1999), 275–92.

French, D., 'The Dardanelles, Mecca and Kut: Prestige as a Factor in British Eastern Strategy, 1914–1916', *War and Society*, V (1987), 45–61.

—, 'The Mechanization of the British Cavalry Between the World Wars', *War in History*, X (2003), 296–320.

—, *Military Identities: The Regimental System, the British Army, and the British People, c. 1870–2000* (Oxford, 2005).

Fromkin, D., *A Peace to End All Peace: The Fall of the Ottoman Empire and the Creation of the Modern Middle East* (London, 1989).

Fuchs, R., 'Sites of Memory in the Holy Land: The Design of the British War Cemeteries in Mandate Palestine', *Journal of Historical Geography*, XXX (2004), 643–64.

Fuchs, R. and Herbert, N., 'Representing Mandatory Palestine: Austen St Barbe Harrison and the Representational Buildings of the British Mandate in Palestine, 1922–37', *Architectural History*, XLIII (2000), 281–333.

Fuller, J. G., *Troop Morale and Popular Culture in the British and Dominion Armies 1914–1918* (Oxford, 1990).

Gale, M. B., 'Ashwell, Lena (1872–1957)', *Oxford Dictionary of National Biography*.

Gammage, B., *The Broken Years: Australian Soldiers in the Great War* (Harmondsworth, 1974).

Gardner, A., *Allenby* (London, 1965).

Gardner, N., 'Sepoys and the Siege of Kut-al-Amara, December 1915–April 1916', *War in History*, XI (2004), 307–26.

—, 'Morale of the Indian Army in the Mesopotamian Campaign: 1914–17', in K. Roy (ed.), *The Indian Army in the Two World Wars* (Leiden, 2012), 393–417.

Garfield, B., *The Meinertzhagen Mystery: The Life and Legend of a Colossal Fraud* (Washington, DC, 2007).

Garrett, J., Grimley, M., Harris, A., Whyte, W. and Williams, S. (eds), *Redefining Christian Britain: Post-1945 Perspectives* (London, 2006).

Gat, A., *A History of Military Thought from the Enlightenment to the Cold War* (Oxford, 2001).

Geoghegan, S., *The Campaigns and History of the Royal Irish Regiment* (London, 1927), II.

Gerster, R., *Big-Noting: The Heroic Theme in Australian War Writing* (Carlton, 1987).

Gibbon, E., *The History of the Decline and Fall of the Roman Empire* (London, 1995), VI.

Girouard, M., *The Return to Camelot: Chivalry and the English Gentlemen* (New Haven, 1981).

Gliddon, G., *VCs of the First World War: The Sideshows* (Stroud, 2005).

Goebel, S., *The Great War and Medieval Memory: War, Remembrance and Medievalism in Britain and Germany, 1914–1940* (Cambridge, 2007).
—, 'Beyond Discourse? Bodies and Memories of Two World Wars', *Journal of Contemporary History*, XLII (2007), 377–85.
Gooch, J., 'Morale and Discipline in the Italian Army, 1915–1918', in H. Cecil and P. H. Liddle (eds), *Facing Armageddon: The First World War Experienced* (Barnsley, 1996), 434–47.
Grainger, J. D., *The Battle for Palestine 1917* (Woodbridge, 2006).
Gray, J. G., *The Warriors: Reflections on Men in Battle* (2nd edn, Lincoln, 1970).
Green, S. J. D., *Religion in the Age of Decline: Organisation and Experience in Industrial Yorkshire, 1870–1920* (Cambridge, 1996).
Greenhalgh, E., 'David Lloyd George, Georges Clemenceau, and the 1918 Manpower Crisis', *The Historical Journal*, L (2007), 397–421.
Greenhut, J., 'Race, Sex, and War: The Impact of Race and Sex on Morale and Health Services for the Indian Corps on the Western Front, 1914', *Military Affairs*, XLV (1981), 71–4.
—, 'The Imperial Reserve: The Indian Corps on the Western Front, 1914–15', *The Journal of Imperial and Commonwealth History*, XII (1983), 54–73.
—, 'Sahib and Sepoy: An Inquiry into the Relationship Between the British Officers and Native Soldiers of the British India Army', *Military Affairs: The Journal of Military History, Including Theory and Technology*, XLVIII (1984), 15–18.
Gregory, A., *The Last Great War: British Society and the First World War* (Cambridge, 2008).
Gregory, S. W., 'Toward a Situated Description of Cohesion and Disintegration in the American Army', *Armed Forces and Society*, III (1977), 463–73.
Grey, J., *The Australian Army: A History* (Oxford, 2001).
Griffith, P., *Battle Tactics on the Western Front: The British Army's Art of Attack, 1916–18* (New Haven, 1994).
Gullett, H. S., *The Official History of Australia in the War of 1914–1918. VII: The Australian Imperial Force in Sinai and Palestine 1914–1918* (Sydney, 1920).
Hall, R. C., '"The Enemy is Behind Us": The Morale Crisis in the Bulgarian Army During the Summer of 1918', *War in History*, XI (2004), 209–19.
Hall, R. J. G., *The Australian Light Horse* (North Blackburn, 1966).
Ham, P., *Kokoda* (Sydney, 2004).
Hamner, C. H., *Enduring Battle: American Soldiers in Three Wars, 1776–1945* (Lawrence, 2011).
Hanna, M., 'A Republic of Letters: The Epistolary Tradition in France During World War I', *American Historical Review*, CVIII (2003), 1338–61.
—, *Your Death Would be Mine: Paul and Marie Pireaud in the Great War* (Cambridge, 2006).
Harris, H., *The Royal Irish Fusiliers (The 87th and 89th Regiments of Foot)* (London, 1972).
Harris, J., *Private Lives, Public Spirit: Britain 1870–1914* (London, 1993).
Harrison, M., 'The British Army and the Problem of Venereal Disease in France and Egypt During the First World War', *Medical History*, XXXIX (1995), 133–58.
—, 'The Fight Against Disease in the Mesopotamia Campaign', in H. Cecil and P. H. Liddle (eds), *Facing Armageddon: The First World War Experienced* (Barnsley, 1996), 435–89.
—, 'Disease, Discipline and Dissent: The Indian Army in France and England, 1914–1915', in R. Carter, M. Harrison and S. Sturdy (eds), *Medicine and Modern Warfare* (Amsterdam, 1999), 185–203.

Harvey, A. D., 'The Royal Air Force and Close Support, 1918–1940', *War in History*, XV (2008), 462–486.
Hashmi, T. I., 'Indianisation of the British-Indian Army: 1858–1947', *The Dacca University Studies: Part A*, XXVIII (1978), 30–40.
Hauser, W. L., 'The Will to Fight', in S. C. Sarkesian (ed.), *Combat Effectiveness: Cohesion, Stress, and the Volunteer Military* (London, 1980), 186–212.
Heathcote, T. A., 'The Army of British India', in D. G. Chandler and I. F. W. Beckett (eds), *The Oxford History of the British Army* (Oxford, 1994), 362–84.
Herwig, H. H., 'The German Victories, 1917–1918', in H. Strachan (ed.), *The Oxford Illustrated History of the First World War* (Oxford, 1998), 253–64.
Hill, A. J., *Chauvel of the Light Horse: A Biography of General Sir Harry Chauvel, G.C.M.G., K.C.B.* (Carlton, 1978).
—, 'General Sir Harry Chauvel: Australia's First Corps Commander', in D. M. Horner (ed.), *The Commanders: Australian Military Leadership in the Twentieth Century* (London, 1984), 60–84.
Hobsbawm, E., 'Introduction: Inventing Traditions', in E. Hobsbawm and T. Ranger (eds), *The Invention of Tradition* (Cambridge, 1983), 1–14.
—, 'Mass-Producing Traditions: Europe 1870–1914', in E. Hobsbawm and T. Ranger (eds), *The Invention of Tradition* (Cambridge, 1983), 263–307.
Hodges, P., '"They don't like it up 'em!": Bayonet Fetishization in the British Army During the First World War', *Journal of War and Culture Studies*, I (2008), 123–38.
Holden Reid, B., 'T.E. Lawrence and his Biographers', in B. Bond (ed.), *The First World War and British Military History* (Oxford, 1991), 227–59.
Holmes, R., *The Little Field Marshal: A Life of Sir John French* (London, 1981).
—, *Acts of War: The Behaviour of Men in Battle* (2nd edn, London, 2004).
—, *Tommy: The British Soldier on the Western Front 1914–1918* (London, 2004).
—, 'Battle: The Experience of Modern Combat', in C. Townshend (ed.), *The Oxford History of Modern War* (2nd edn, Oxford, 2005), 224–44.
Horne, J., 'Introduction: Mobilizing for "Total War", 1914–1918', in J. Horne (ed.), *State, Society and Mobilization in Europe During the First World War* (Cambridge, 1997), 1–17.
Howard, M., 'Men Against Fire: Expectations of War in 1914', *International Security*, IX (1984), 41–57.
Hughes, M., 'Lloyd George, the Generals and the Palestine Campaign, 1917–1918', *Imperial War Museum Review*, XI (1996), 4–17.
—, 'General Allenby and the Palestine Campaign, 1917–18', *The Journal of Strategic Studies*, XIX (1996), 59–88.
—, *Allenby and British Strategy in the Middle East 1917–1919* (London, 1999).
—, 'General Allenby and the Palestine Campaign 1917–18', in Y. Sheffy and S. Shai (eds), *The First World War: Middle Eastern Perspective* (Tel Aviv, 2000), 95–104.
—, 'Elie Kedourie and the Capture of Damascus, 1 October 1918: A Reassessment', *War and Society*, XXIII (2005), 87–106.
—, 'Edmund Allenby: Third Army, 1915–1917', in I. F. W. Beckett and S. Corvi (eds), *Haig's Generals* (Barnsley, 2006), 12–32.
—, 'What did the Arab Revolt Contribute to the Palestine Campaign? An Assessment', *The Journal of the T.E. Lawrence Society*, XV (2006), 75–87.
—, 'Command, Strategy and the Battle for Palestine, 1917', in I. F. W. Beckett (ed.), *1917: Beyond the Western Front* (Leiden, 2009), 113–29.

Hughes, M. and Seligmann, M., 'People and the Tides of History: Does Personality Matter in the First World War?', in M. Hughes and M. Seligmann (eds), *Leadership in Conflict, 1914–1918* (Barnsley, 2000), 1–9.

Inglis, K., 'The Anzac Tradition', *Meanjin Quarterly: A Review of Arts and Letters in Australia*, XXIV (1965), 25–44.

—, 'Men, Women, and War Memorials: Anzac Australia', in R. White and P. Russell (eds), *Memories and Dreams: Reflections on Twentieth-Century Australia, Pastiche II* (St Leonards, 1997), 40–59.

—, *Sacred Places: War Memorials in the Australian Landscape* (3rd edn, Carlton, 2008).

Irwin, R., *For Lust of Knowing: The Orientalists and their Enemies* (London, 2006).

Jack, G. M., 'The Indian Army on the Western Front, 1914–1915: A Portrait of Collaboration', *War in History*, XIII (2006), 329–62.

James, L., *Imperial Warrior: The Life and Times of Field-Marshal Viscount Allenby, 1861–1936* (London, 1993).

—, *The Rise and Fall of the British Empire* (London, 1994).

James, R. R., 'Thoughts on Writing Military History', *The Royal United Services Institute Journal*, CXI (1966), 99–108.

Jeffery, K., '"An English Barrack in the Oriental Seas?" India in the Aftermath of the First World War', *Modern Asian Studies*, XV (1981), 369–86.

—, 'The Irish Military Tradition and the British Empire', in K. Jeffery (ed.), *'An Irish Empire'? Aspects of Ireland and the British Empire* (Manchester, 1996), 94–122.

Johnstone, T., *Orange, Green and Khaki: The Story of the Irish Regiments in the Great War, 1914–18* (Dublin, 1992).

Johnstone, T. and Hagerty, J., *The Cross on the Sword: Catholic Chaplains in the Forces* (London, 1996).

Jones, H. A., *The War in the Air: Being the Story of the Part Played in the Great War by the Royal Air Force* (Oxford, 1935), V.

—, *The War in the Air: Being the Story of the Part Played in the Great War by the Royal Air Force* (Oxford, 1937), VI.

Jones, I., 'Beersheba: The Light Horse Charge and the Making of Myths', *Journal of the Australian War Memorial*, III (1983), 26–37.

—, *The Australian Light Horse* (Sydney, 1987).

Karsh, E. and Karsh, I., 'Myth in the Desert, or Not the Great Arab Revolt', *Middle Eastern Studies*, XXXIII (1997), 267–312.

Karsten, P., 'Irish Soldiers in the British Army, 1792–1922: Suborned of Subordinated?', in P. Karsten (ed.), *Motivating Soldiers: Morale or Mutiny* (New York, 1998), 47–80.

Keegan, J., *The Face of Battle* (London, 1976).

—, 'Inventing Military Traditions', in C. Wrigley (ed.), *Warfare, Diplomacy and Politics: Essays in Honour of A.J.P. Taylor* (London, 1986), 58–79.

—, 'Towards a Theory of Combat Motivation', in P. Addison and A. Calder (eds), *Time to Kill: The Soldier's Experience of War in the West 1939–1945* (London, 1997), 3–11.

—, *The First World War* (London, 1998).

Kent, D., 'The Australian Remount Unit in Egypt, 1915–19: A Footnote to History', *Journal of the Australian War Memorial*, I (1982), 9–15.

—, '*The Anzac Book* and the Anzac Legend: C.E.W. Bean as Editor and Image-Maker', *Historical Studies*, XXI (1985), 376–90.

Khan, Y., 'Remembering and Forgetting: South Asia and the Second World War', in M. Geyer and B. Ziino (eds), *The Heritage of War* (Abingdon, 2012), 177–93.

Kinloch, T., *Echoes of Gallipoli: In the Words of New Zealand's Mounted Riflemen* (Auckland, 2005).
—, *Devils on Horses: In the Words of the Anzacs in the Middle East 1916–19* (Auckland, 2007).
Knowles, R., 'Tale of an "Arabian Knight": The T.E. Lawrence Effigy', *Church Monuments: Journal of the Church Monuments Society*, VI (1991), 67–76.
Koller, C., 'The Recruitment of Colonial Troops in Africa and Asia and their Deployment in Europe During the First World War', *Immigrants and Minorities*, XXVI (2008), 111–33.
Kramer, A., *Dynamic of Destruction: Culture and Mass Killing in the First World War* (Oxford, 2007).
Latter, E., 'The Indian Army in Mesopotamia 1914–1918', *Journal of the Society for Army Historical Research*, LXXII (1994), 232–46.
Lewis, G., 'An Ottoman Officer in Palestine, 1914–1918', in D. Kushner (ed.), *Palestine in the Late Ottoman Period* (Leiden, 1986), 402–15.
Liddell Hart, B. H., *Reputations* (London, 1928).
—, *A History of the First World War 1914–1918* (London, 1934).
—, 'Allenby', in B. Parker (ed.), *Famous British Generals* (London, 1951), 119–39.
Liebau, H., Bromber, K., Lange, K., Hamzah, D. and Ahuja, R. (eds), *The World in World Wars: Experiences, Perceptions and Perspectives from Africa and Asia* (Leiden, 2010).
Little, R. W., 'Buddy Relations and Combat Performance', in M. Janowitz (ed.), *The New Military: Changing Patterns of Organisation* (New York, 1964), 195–223.
Lloyd, D. W., *Battlefield Tourism: Pilgrimage and the Commemoration of the Great War in Britain, Australia and Canada, 1919–1939* (Oxford, 1998).
Lloyd, N., 'The Amritsar Massacre and the Minimum Force Debate', *Small Wars and Insurgencies*, XXI (2010), 382–403.
Lockman, J. N., *Meinertzhagen's Diary Ruse: False Entries on T.E. Lawrence* (Grand Rapids, 1995).
Louden, S. H., *Chaplains in Conflict: The Role of Army Chaplains Since 1904* (London, 1996).
Low, R., *The History of the British Film 1914–1918* (London, 1950).
Lynn, J. A., *Battle: A History of Combat and Culture* (Boulder, 2003).
Macfie, A. L., *Orientalism* (London, 2002).
MacKenzie, J. M., *Orientalism: History, Theory and the Arts* (Manchester, 1995).
Macleod, J., *Reconsidering Gallipoli* (Manchester, 2004).
MacMillan, M., *The Uses and Abuses of History* (London, 2009).
MacMunn, G. and Falls, C., *Military Operations Egypt and Palestine. I: From the Outbreak of War with Germany to June 1917* (London, 1928).
Macpherson, W. G., Horrocks, W. H. and Beveridge, W. W. O. (eds), *Medical Services: Hygiene of the War* (London, 1923), II.
—, *Medical Services General History. III: Medical Services During the Operations on the Western Front in 1916, 1917 and 1918; in Italy; and in Egypt and Palestine* (London, 1924).
Madigan, E., *Faith Under Fire: Anglican Army Chaplains and the Great War* (Basingstoke, 2011).
Manning, F. J., 'Morale, Cohesion, and Esprit de Corps', in R. Gal and A. D. Mangesdorff (eds), *Handbook of Military Psychology* (Chichester, 1991), 453–70.
Marshall, S. L. A., *Men Against Fire: The Problem of Battlefield Command* (2nd edn, Norman, 2000).

Marston, D. P., 'A Force Transformed: The Indian Army and the Second World War', in D. P. Marston and C. S. Sundaram (eds), *A Military History of India and South Asia: From the East India Company to the Nuclear Era* (London, 2007), 102–22.

Mason, P., *A Matter of Honour: An Assessment of the Indian Army its Officers and Men* (London, 1974).

Maurice, F., *The 16th Foot: A History of the Bedfordshire and Hertfordshire Regiment* (London, 1931).

May, C., 'Lord Moran's Memoir: Shell-Shock and the Pathology of Fear', *Journal of the Royal Society of Medicine*, XCI (1998), 95–100.

Mazza, R., 'Churches at War: The Impact of the First World War on the Christian Institutions of Jerusalem, 1914–20', *Middle Eastern Studies*, XLV (2009), 207–27.

—, *Jerusalem: From the Ottomans to the British* (London, 2009).

McCance, S., *History of the Royal Munster Fusiliers* (Aldershot, 1927), II.

McCartney, H. B., *Citizen Soldiers: The Liverpool Territorials in the First World War* (Cambridge, 2005).

McGibbon, I. (ed.), *The Oxford Companion to New Zealand Military History* (Oxford, 2000).

McKernan, L., '"The Supreme Moment of the War": General Allenby's Entry into Jerusalem', *Historical Journal of Film, Radio and Television*, XIII (1993), 169–80.

McLain, R., 'The Indian Corps on the Western Front: A Reconsideration', in G. Jensen and A. Wiest (eds), *War in the Age of Technology: Myriad Faces of Armed Conflict* (New York, 2001), 167–93.

McLeod, H., *Religion and Society in England, 1850–1914* (Basingstoke, 1996).

Menezes, S. L., *Fidelity and Honour: The Indian Army from the Seventeenth to the Twenty-first Century* (Oxford, 1993).

Merridale, C., 'Culture, Ideology and Combat in the Red Army, 1939–45', *Journal of Contemporary History*, XLI (2006), 305–24.

Mews, S., 'Religion, 1900–1939', in C. Wrigley (ed.), *A Companion to Early Twentieth-Century Britain* (Oxford, 2003), 470–84.

Miller, S. M., *Volunteers on the Veld: Britain's Citizen-Soldiers and the South African War, 1899–1902* (Norman, 2007).

Mitchell, T., *Colonising Egypt* (Cambridge, 1988).

Mitchell, T. J. and Smith, G. M., *Medical Services: Casualties and Medical Statistics of the Great War* (London, 1931).

Mitchinson, K. W., *Gentlemen and Officers: The Impact and Experience of War on a Territorial Regiment, 1914–1918* (London, 1995).

—, *Amateur Soldiers: A History of Oldham's Volunteers and Territorials, 1850–1938* (Oldham, 1999).

Monroe, E., *Britain's Moment in the Middle East, 1914–1971* (2nd edn, London, 1981).

Moran, Lord, *The Anatomy of Courage* (2nd edn, London, 1966).

Moreman, T. R., 'The British and Indian Armies and North-West Frontier Warfare, 1849–1914', *The Journal of Imperial and Commonwealth History*, XX (1992), 35–64.

—, 'Lord Kitchener, the General Staff and the Army in India, 1902–14', in D. French and B. Holden Reid (eds), *The British General Staff: Reform and Innovation, c. 1890–1939* (London, 2002), 57–74.

—, '"Passing it On": The Army in India and Frontier Warfare, 1914–39', in K. Roy (ed.), *War and Society in Colonial India, 1807–1945* (Oxford, 2006), 275–304.

—, '"The Greatest Training Ground in the World": The Army in India and the North-West Frontier, 1901–1947', in D. P. Marston and C. S. Sundaram (eds), *A Military History of*

India and South Asia: From the East India Company to the Nuclear Era (London, 2007), 53–73.

—, 'From the Desert Sands to the Burmese Jungle: The Indian Army and the Lessons of North Africa, September 1939–November 1942', in K. Roy (ed.), *The Indian Army in the Two World Wars* (Leiden, 2012), 223–54.

Moriarty, C., 'Christian Iconography and First World War Memorials', *Imperial War Museum Review*, VI (1992), 63–75.

Morris, A. N., *Combat Studies Institute Report No. 10: Night Combat Operations* (Fort Leavenworth, 1985).

Moyar, M., 'The Current State of Military History', *The Historical Journal*, L (2007), 225–40.

Moynihan, M., *God on Our Side: The British Padres in World War I* (London, 1983).

Murphy, C. C. R., *The History of the Suffolk Regiment 1914–1927* (London, 1928).

Nasser, N., 'A Historiography of Tourism in Cairo: A Spatial Perspective', in R. F. Daher (ed.), *Tourism in the Middle East* (Clevedon, 2007), 70–94.

Neillands, R., 'The Experience of Defeat: Kut (1916) and Singapore (1942)', in P. Liddle, J. Bourne and I. Whitehead (eds), *The Great World War 1914–1945. I: Lightning Strikes Twice* (London, 2000), 278–92.

Newell, J. C. Q., 'Allenby and the Palestine Campaign', in B. Bond (ed.), *The First World War and British Military History* (Oxford, 1991), 189–226.

Nicol, C. G., *The Story of Two Campaigns: Official War History of the Auckland Mounted Rifles Regiment, 1914–1919* (Auckland, 1921).

Nile, R., 'Orientalism and the Origins of Anzac', in A. Seymour and R. Nile (eds), *Anzac: Meaning, Memory and Myth* (London, 1991), 32–42.

Offer, A., *The First World War: An Agrarian Interpretation* (Oxford, 1989).

Omissi, D., '"Martial Races": Ethnicity and Security in Colonial India 1858–1939', *War and Society*, IX (1991), 1–27.

—, *The Sepoy and the Raj: The Indian Army, 1860–1940* (Basingstoke, 1994).

Omissi, D. (ed.), *Indian Voices of the Great War: Soldiers' Letters, 1914–18* (Basingstoke, 1999).

Omissi, D., review of *Sepoys in the Trenches: The Indian Corps on the Western Front, 1914–1915* by G. Corrigan, *The Journal of Imperial and Commonwealth History*, XXIX (2001), 178–80.

—, 'India: Some Perspectives of Race and Empire', in D. Omissi and A. S. Thompson (eds), *The Impact of the South African War* (Basingstoke, 2002), 215–32.

—, 'Europe Through Indian Eyes: Indian Soldiers Encounter England and France, 1914–1918', in *English Historical Review*, CXXII (2007), 371–96.

Oram, G., 'Pious Perjury: Discipline and Morale in the British Force in Italy, 1917–1918', *War in History*, IX (2002), 412–30.

Orr, P., 'The Road to Belgrade: The Experiences of the 10th (Irish) Division in the Balkans, 1915–17', in A. Gregory and S. Pašeta (eds), *Ireland and the Great War: 'A war to unite us all'?* (Manchester, 2002), 171–89.

Pal, D., *Traditions of the Indian Army* (Delhi, 1961).

Palit, D. K., 'Indianisation of the Army's Officer Cadre 1920–47', *Indo-British Review: A Journal of History*, XVI (1989), 55–8.

Palmer, S. and Wallis, S., *A War in Words* (London, 2003).

Paris, M., *Warrior Nation: Images of War in British Popular Culture, 1850–2000* (London, 2000).

Parker, P., *The Old Lie: The Great War and the Public-School Ethos* (London, 1987).

Peers, D. M., 'The Martial Races and the Indian Army in the Victorian Era', in D. P. Marston and C. S. Sundaram (eds), *A Military History of India and South Asia: From the East India Company to the Nuclear Era* (London, 2007), 34–52.
Pemble, J., *The Mediterranean Passion: Victorians and Edwardians in the South* (Oxford, 1987).
Pendlebury, A., *Portraying 'the Jew' in First World War Britain* (London, 2006).
Perry, F. W., *The Commonwealth Armies: Manpower and Organisation in Two World Wars* (Manchester, 1988).
Petre, F. L., *The History of the Norfolk Regiment 1685–1918* (Norwich, 1925), II.
Phillips, G., 'The Obsolescence of the *Arme Blanche* and Technological Determinism in British Military History', *War and History*, II (2002), 39–59.
—, 'Scapegoat Arm: Twentieth-Century Cavalry in Anglophone Historiography', *The Journal of Military History*, LXXI (2007), 37–74.
—, '"Who Shall Say that the Days of Cavalry are Over?" The Revival of the Mounted Arm in Europe, 1853–1914', *War in History*, XVIII (2011), 5–32.
Phillips, J., 'The Great War and New Zealand Nationalism: The Evidence of War Memorials', in J. Smart and T. Wood (eds), *An Anzac Muster: War and Society in Australia and New Zealand 1914–1918 and 1939–1945* (Clayton, 1992), 14–29.
Place, T. H., 'Lionel Wigram, Battle Drill and the British Army in the Second World War', *War in History*, VII (2000), 442–62.
Porter, P., 'New Jerusalems: Sacrifice and Redemption in the War Experiences of English and German Chaplains', in P. Purseigle (ed.), *Warfare and Belligerence: Perspectives in First World War Studies* (Leiden, 2005), 101–32.
—, 'Beyond Comfort: German and English Military Chaplains and the Memory of the Great War', *The Journal of Religious History*, XXIX (2005), 258–89.
—, 'Good Anthropology, Bad History: The Cultural Turn in Studying War', *Parameters: US Army War College Quarterly*, XXXVII (2007), 45–58.
—, 'Military Orientalism? British Observers of the Japanese Way of War, 1904–1910', *War and Society*, XXVI (2007), 1–25.
—, *Military Orientalism: Eastern War Through Western Eyes* (London, 2009).
Powles, C. G., *The New Zealanders in Sinai and Palestine* (Auckland, 1922).
—, *The History of the Canterbury Mounted Rifles 1914–1919* (Auckland, 1926).
Pradhan, S. D., 'Organisation of the Indian Army on the Eve of the Outbreak of the First World War', *The Journal of the United Service Institution of India*, CII (1972), 61–78.
—, 'Indian Army and the First World War', in D. C. Ellinwood and S. D. Pradhan (eds), *India and World War I* (New Delhi, 1978), 49–67.
—, 'Indians in the East Africa Campaign – A Case Study of Indian Experiences in the First World War', in D. C. Ellinwood and S. D. Pradhan (eds), *India and World War I* (New Delhi, 1978), 69–74.
—, 'The Sikh Soldier in the First World War', in D. C. Ellinwood and S. D. Pradhan (eds), *India and World War I* (New Delhi, 1978), 213–25.
Prakash, G., 'Orientalism Now', *History and Theory: Studies in the Philosophy of History*, XXXIV (1995), 199–212.
Prior, R., *Churchill's 'World Crisis' as History* (London, 1983).
Prior, R. and Wilson, T., *The Somme* (New Haven, 2005).
Pugsley, C., 'New Zealand: "From the Uttermost Ends of the Earth"', in P. Liddle, J. Bourne and I. Whitehead (eds), *The Great World War 1914–1945. II: The People's Experience* (London, 2001), 211–32.

—, *The Anzac Experience: New Zealand, Australia and Empire in the First World War* (Auckland, 2004).
Rastegar, K., 'Revisiting *Orientalism*', *History Today*, LVIII (2008), 49–51.
Richardson, F. M., *Fighting Spirit: A Study of Psychological Factors in War* (London, 1978).
Richardson, J. D., *The History of the 7th Light Horse Regiment A.I.F.* (Sydney, 1923).
Riedi, E. and Mason, T., '"Leather" and the Fighting Spirit: Sport in the British Army in World War I', *Canadian Journal of History*, XLI (2006), 485–516.
Riley-Smith, J., *The Crusades: A History* (2nd edn, London, 2005).
Robson, B., 'The Organization and Command Structure of the Indian Army from its Origins to 1947', in A. J. Guy and P. B. Boyden (eds), *Soldiers of the Raj: The Indian Army 1600–1947* (Coventry, 1997), 9–19.
Robson, L. L., 'The Origin and Character of the First A.I.F., 1914–1918: Some Statistical Evidence', *Historical Studies*, XV (1973), 737–49.
Roper, M., *The Secret Battle: Emotional Survival in the Great War* (Manchester, 2009).
Ross, J., *The Myth of the Digger: The Australian Soldier in Two World Wars* (Sydney, 1985).
Ross, M., 'The Sinai-Palestine Campaign', in C. Lucas (ed.), *Empire at War* (Oxford, 1923), III, 370–81.
Roy, K., 'The Historiography of the Colonial Indian Army', *Studies in History*, XII (1996), 255–73.
—, 'Recruitment Doctrines of the Colonial Indian Army: 1859–1913', *The Indian Economic and Social History Review*, XXXIV (1997), 321–54.
—, 'Beyond the Martial Race Theory: A Historiographical Assessment of Recruitment in the British-Indian Army', *The Calcutta Historical Journal*, XXI–XXII (1999–2000), 139–54.
—, 'The Construction of Regiments in the Indian Army: 1859–1913', *War in History*, VIII (2001), 127–48.
—, 'Introduction: Armies, Warfare, and Society in Colonial India', in K. Roy (ed.), *War and Society in Colonial India, 1807–1945* (Oxford, 2006), 1–52.
—, 'The Army in India in Mesopotamia from 1916 to 1918: Tactics, Technology and Logistics Reconsidered', in I. F. W. Beckett (ed.), *1917: Beyond the Western Front* (Leiden, 2009), 131–58.
—, 'Discipline and Morale of the African, British and Indian Army Units in Burma and India During World War II: July 1943 to August 1945', *Modern Asian Studies*, XLIV (2010), 1255–82.
—, 'Introduction: Warfare, Society and the Indian Army During the Two World Wars', in K. Roy (ed.), *The Indian Army in the Two World Wars* (Leiden, 2012), 1–24.
Ruiz, M. M., 'Manly Spectacles and Imperial Soldiers in Wartime Egypt, 1914–19', *Middle Eastern Studies*, XLV (2009), 351–71.
Said, E. W., *Orientalism* (3rd edn, London, 2003).
Savage, R., *Allenby of Armageddon: A Record of the Career and Campaigns of Field-Marshal Viscount Allenby, G.C.B., G.C.M.G.* (London, 1925).
Schofield, V., *Wavell: Soldier and Statesman* (London, 2006).
Schweitzer, R., 'The Cross and the Trenches: Religious Faith and Doubt Among Some British Soldiers on the Western Front', *War and Society*, XVI (1998), 33–57.
—, *The Cross and the Trenches: Religious Faith and Doubt Among British and American Great War Soldiers* (Westport, 2003).
Seabrook, J., 'Ruffled Feathers', *The New Yorker*, LXXXII (2006), 51–61.
Searle, G. R., *A New England? Peace and War 1886–1918* (Oxford, 2004).

Serle, G., 'The Digger Tradition and Australian Nationalism', *Meanjin Quarterly: A Review of Arts and Letters in Australia*, XXIV (1965), 149–58.

Shadur, J., *Young Travelers to Jerusalem: An Annotated Survey of American and English Juvenile Literature on the Holy Land, 1785–1940* (Ramat Gan, 1999).

Sharpe, A., 'The Indianisation of the Indian Army', *History Today*, XXXVI (1986), 47–52.

Sheffield, G. D., 'Introduction: Command, Leadership and the Anglo-American Experience', in G. D. Sheffield (ed.), *Leadership and Command: The Anglo-American Military Experience Since 1861* (London, 1997), 1–16.

—, '"A very good type of Londoner and a very good type of colonial": Officer-Man Relations and Discipline in the 22nd Royal Fusiliers, 1914–18', in B. Bond (ed.), *'Look to your front': Studies in the First World War by the British Commission for Military History* (Staplehurst, 1999), 137–46.

—, *Leadership in the Trenches: Officer-Man Relations, Morale and Discipline in the British Army in the Era of the First World War* (Basingstoke, 2000).

Sheffy, Y., 'Institutionalized Deception and Perception Reinforcement: Allenby's Campaign in Palestine', in M. I. Handel (ed.), *Intelligence and Military Operations* (London, 1990), 173–236.

—, *British Military Intelligence in the Palestine Campaign, 1914–1918* (London, 1998).

—, 'The Spy Who Never Was: An Intelligence Myth in Palestine, 1914–18', *Intelligence and National Security*, XIV (1999), 123–42.

—, 'The Introduction of Chemical Weapons to the Middle East', in Y. Sheffy and S. Shai (eds), *The First World War: Middle Eastern Perspective* (2000), 75–84.

—, 'British Intelligence and the Middle East, 1900–1918: How Much Do We Know?', *Intelligence and National Security*, XVII (2002), 33–52.

Shils, E. A. and Janowitz, M., 'Cohesion and Disintegration in the Wehrmacht in World War II', *Public Opinion Quarterly*, XII (1948), 280–315.

Showalter, D., 'The Indianization of the Egyptian Expeditionary Force, 1917–18: An Imperial Turning Point', in K. Roy (ed.), *The Indian Army in the Two World Wars* (Leiden, 2012), 145–63.

Siberry, E., 'Images of the Crusades in the Nineteenth and Twentieth Centuries', in J. Riley-Smith (ed.), *The Oxford History of the Crusades* (Oxford, 1999), 363–84.

—, *The New Crusaders: Images of the Crusades in the Nineteenth and Twentieth Centuries* (Aldershot, 2000).

Simkins, P., 'Everyman at War: Recent Interpretations of the Front Line Experience', in B. Bond (ed.), *The First World War and British Military History* (Oxford, 1991), 289–313.

Simkins, P., Jukes, G. and Hickey, M., *The First World War: The War to End All Wars* (Oxford, 2003).

Simpson, K., 'The British Soldier on the Western Front', in P. H. Liddle (ed.), *Home Fires and Foreign Fields: British Social and Military Experience in the First World War* (London, 1985), 135–58.

Sinclair, S. C., 'Egypt', in H. A. Sams (ed.), *The Post Office of India in the Great War* (Bombay, 1922), 77–102.

Singh, G., 'The Anatomy of Dissent in the Military of Colonial India During the First and Second World Wars', *Edinburgh Papers in South Asian Studies*, XX (2006), 1–45.

Smith, L. V., *Between Mutiny and Obedience: The Case of the French Fifth Infantry Division During World War One* (Princeton, 1994).

—, 'The French High Command and the Mutinies of Spring 1917', in H. Cecil and P. H. Liddle (eds), *Facing Armageddon: The First World War Experienced* (Barnsley, 1996), 79–92.

—, 'Remobilising the Citizen-Soldier Through the French Army Mutinies of 1917', in J. Horne (ed.), *State, Society and Mobilization in Europe During the First World War* (Cambridge, 1997), 144–59.

Smith, N. C., *The Third Australian Light Horse Regiment 1914–1918: A Short History and Listings of Those Who Served* (Gardenvale, 1993).

Smyth, J., *In this Sign Conquer: The Story of the Army Chaplains* (London, 1968).

Snape, M., *God and the British Soldier: Religion and the British Army in the First and Second World Wars* (London, 2005).

Spiers, E., 'The Late Victorian Army 1868–1914', in D. G. Chandler and I. F. W. Beckett (eds), *The Oxford History of the British Army* (Oxford, 1994), 187–210.

Spiller, R. J., 'S.L.A. Marshall and the Ratio of Fire', *The Royal United Services Institute Journal*, CXXXIII (1988), 63–71.

Stanley, J., *Ireland's Forgotten 10th: A Brief History of the 10th (Irish) Division, 1914–1918. Turkey, Macedonia and Palestine* (Ballycastle, 2003).

Stanley, P., '"Our big world": The Social History of the Light Horse Regiment, 1916–1918', *Sabretache: The Journal and Proceedings of the Military Historical Society of Australia*, XXXIX (1998), 3–14.

—, '"Whom at first we did not like ...": Australians and New Zealanders at Quinn's Post, Gallipoli', in J. Crawford and I. McGibbon (eds), *New Zealand's Great War: New Zealand, the Allies and the First World War* (Auckland, 2007), 182–93.

Stouffer, S. A., Lumsdaine, A. A., Lumsdaine, M. H., Williams, R. M., Smith, M. B., Janis, I. L., Star, S. A. and Cottrell, L. S., *The American Soldier. II: Combat and its Aftermath* (Princeton, 1949).

Strachan, H., *European Armies and the Conduct of War* (Abingdon, 1983).

—, '"The Real War": Liddell Hart, Cruttwell, and Falls', in B. Bond (ed.), *The First World War and British Military History* (Oxford, 1991), 41–67.

—, 'The British Way in Warfare', in D. G. Chandler and I. F. W. Beckett (eds), *The Oxford History of the British Army* (Oxford, 1994), 399–415.

—, *The Politics of the British Army* (Oxford, 1997).

—, 'The Soldier's Experience in Two World Wars: Some Historiographical Comparisons', in P. Addison and A. Calder (eds), *Time to Kill: The Soldier's Experience of War in the West 1939–1945* (London, 1997), 369–78.

—, *The First World War. I: To Arms* (Oxford, 2001).

—, *The First World War: A New Illustrated History* (London, 2003).

—, 'Training, Morale and Modern War', *Journal of Contemporary History*, XLI (2006), 211–27.

—, *Carl von Clausewitz's On War: A Biography* (London, 2007).

—, 'Back to the Trenches: Why Can't British Historians Be Less Insular About the First World War?', *The Times Literary Supplement*, 5 November 2008.

—, 'The First World War as a Global Conflict', *First World War Studies*, I (2010), 3–14.

Streets, H., *Martial Races: The Military, Race and Masculinity in British Imperial Culture, 1857–1914* (Manchester, 2004).

Syk, A., 'Command in the Indian Expeditionary Force D: Mesopotamia, 1915–16', in K. Roy (ed.), *The Indian Army in the Two World Wars* (Leiden, 2012), 63–103.

Tai-Yong, T., 'An Imperial Home-Front: Punjab and the First World War', *The Journal of Military History*, LXIV (2000), 371–410.

Taussig, M., 'An Australian Hero', *History Workshop Journal*, XXIV (1987), 111–33.

Taylor, A. J. P., *English History, 1914–1945* (Oxford, 1965).

—, *The First World War: An Illustrated History* (London, 1966).

Bibliography

Thomson, A., '"Steadfast Until Death"? C.E.W. Bean and the Representation of Australian Military Manhood', *Australian Historical Studies*, XXIII (1989), 462–78.

—, '"The Vilest Libel of the War"? Imperial Politics and the Official Histories of Gallipoli', *Australian Historical Studies*, XXV (1993), 628–36.

—, *Anzac Memories: Living with the Legend* (Oxford, 1994).

—, 'Anzac Memories: Putting Popular Memory Theory into Practice in Australia', in A. Green and K. Troup (eds), *The Houses of History: A Critical Reader in Twentieth-Century History and Theory* (Manchester, 1999), 239–52.

Todman, D., *The Great War: Myth and Memory* (London, 2005).

Travers, T. and Celik, B., '"Not one of them ever came back": What Happened to the 1/5 Norfolk Battalion on 12 August 1915', *The Journal of Military History*, LXVI (2002), 389–406.

Trench, C. C., *The Indian Army and the King's Enemies 1900–1947* (London, 1988).

Trevor-Roper, H., 'The Invention of Tradition: The Highland Tradition of Scotland', in E. Hobsbawm and T. Ranger (eds), *The Invention of Tradition* (Cambridge, 1983), 15–41.

Urry, J., *The Tourist Gaze: Leisure and Travel in Contemporary Societies* (London, 1990).

Usherwood, P. and Spencer-Smith, J., *Lady Butler: Battle Artist, 1846–1933* (Gloucester, 1987).

—, 'Butler, Elizabeth Southerden, Lady Butler (1846–1933)', *Oxford Dictionary of National Biography*.

Van Emden, R., *Britain's Last Tommies: Final Memories from Soldiers of the 1914–18 War in their Own Words* (Barnsley, 2005).

VanKosi, S., 'Letters Home, 1915–16: Punjabi Soldiers Reflect on War and Life in Europe and their Meanings for Home and Self', *International Journal of Punjab Studies*, II (1995), 43–63.

Vernon, P. V., *The Royal New South Wales Lancers 1885–1985* (Sydney, 1961).

Vetch, R. H. and Falkner, J., 'Siborne, William (1797–1849)', *Oxford Dictionary of National Biography*.

Visram, R., 'The First World War and the Indian Soldiers', *Indo-British Review: A Journal of History*, XVI (1989), 17–26.

Ward, S., '"A War Memorial in Celluloid": The Gallipoli Legend in Australian Cinema, 1940s-1980s', in J. Macleod (ed.), *Gallipoli: Making History* (London, 2004), 59–72.

Waterson, D. B., 'Anzac Day in the New Zealand Countryside', in J. Smart and T. Wood (eds), *An Anzac Muster: War and Society in Australia and New Zealand 1914–1918 and 1939–1945* (Clayton, 1992), 143–50.

Watson, A., 'Self-Deception and Survival: Mental Coping Strategies on the Western Front, 1914–18', *Journal of Contemporary History*, XLI (2006), 247–68.

—, 'Junior Officership in the German Army During the Great War, 1914–1918', *War in History*, XIV (2007), 429–53.

—, *Enduring the Great War: Combat, Morale and Collapse in the German and British Armies, 1914–1918* (Cambridge, 2008).

—, 'Stabbed at the Front', *History Today*, LVIII (2008), 21–7.

Watts, M., *The Jewish Legion and the First World War* (Basingstoke, 2004).

Wavell, A. P., 'The Army and the Prophets', *The Journal of the Royal United Service Institution*, LXXV (1930), 665–75.

—, *The Palestine Campaigns* (3rd edn, London, 1931).

—, *Allenby: A Study in Greatness. The Biography of Field-Marshal Viscount Allenby of Megiddo and Felixstowe G.C.B. G.C.M.G.* (London, 1940).

Webster, F. A. M., *The History of the Fifth Battalion the Bedfordshire and Hertfordshire Regiment (T.A.)* (London, 1930).
Wesbrook, S. D., 'The Potential for Military Disintegration', in S. C. Sarkesian (ed.), *Combat Effectiveness: Cohesion, Stress, and the Volunteer Military* (London, 1980), 244–78.
White, R., 'The Soldier as Tourist: The Australian Experience of the Great War', *War and Society*, V (1987), 63–77.
—, 'Sun, Sand and Syphilis: Australian Soldiers and the Orient, Egypt 1914', *Australian Cultural History*, IX (1990), 49–64.
Wilcox, V., 'Discipline in the Italian Army 1915–1918', in P. Purseigle (ed.), *Warfare and Belligerence: Perspectives in First World War Studies* (Leiden, 2005), 73–100.
Wilkie, A. H., *Official History of the Wellington Mounted Rifles Regiment 1914–1919* (Auckland, 1924).
Wilkinson, A., *The Church of England and the First World War* (London, 1978).
Williams, J., '"Art, War and Agrarian Myths": Australian Reactions to Modernism 1913–1931', in J. Smart and T. Wood (eds), *An Anzac Muster: War and Society in Australia and New Zealand 1914–1918 and 1939–1945* (Clayton, 1992), 40–57.
Williams, S. C., *Religious Belief and Popular Culture in Southwark c. 1880–1939* (Oxford, 1999).
Wilson, L. C. and Wetherell, H., *History of the Fifth Light Horse Regiment (Australian Imperial Force): From 1914 to October, 1917, and from October, 1917 to June, 1919* (Sydney, 1926).
Winter, D., *Death's Men: Soldiers of the Great War* (London, 1978).
Winter, J., *Sites of Memory, Sites of Mourning: The Great War in European Cultural History* (Cambridge, 1995).
Withey, L., *Grand Tours and Cook's Tours: A History of Leisure Travel, 1750 to 1915* (London, 1997).
Woodward, D. R., 'Did Lloyd George Starve the British Army of Men Prior to the German Spring Offensive of 21 March 1918?', *The Historical Journal*, XXVII (1984), 241–52.
—, *Forgotten Soldiers of the First World War: Lost Voices from the Middle Eastern Front* (Stroud, 2006).
Yanikdağ, Y., 'Educating the Peasants: The Ottoman Army and Enlisted Men in Uniform', *Middle Eastern Studies*, XL (2004), 92–108.
Younghusband, F., 'The Near East: Sinai and Palestine', in C. Lucas (ed.), *The Empire at War* (Oxford, 1926), V, 261–82.
Ziemann, B., *War Experiences in Rural Germany, 1914–1923* (Oxford, 2007).
Ziino, B., 'A Kind of Round Trip: Australian Soldiers and the Tourist Analogy, 1914–1918', *War and Society*, XXV (2006), 39–52.
Zürcher, E., 'Little Mehmet in the Desert: The Ottoman Soldier's Experience', in H. Cecil and P. H. Liddle (eds), *Facing Armageddon: The First World War Experienced* (Barnsley, 1996), 230–41.

Unpublished papers and theses

Newell, J. C. Q., 'British Military Policy in Egypt and Palestine, August 1914–June 1917' (University of London, PhD thesis, 1990).

Porter, P., 'Slaughter or Sacrifice? The Religious Rhetoric of Blood Sacrifice in the British and German Armies, 1914–1919' (Oxford University, D.Phil. thesis, 2005).

Tamari, S., 'Rethinking Arab-Turkish Identity After Gallipoli: Diaries of Ottoman Soldiers in World War I', paper at the Middle East Centre seminars, Oxford University, 7 November 2008.

Films and radio programmes

'Anthropology at War', *BBC Radio 4*, first transmitted 24 April 2009.
Gallipoli (Peter Weir, 1981).
Lawrence of Arabia (David Lean, 1962).
The Lighthorsemen (Simon Wincer, 1987).

Index

Abasan el Kebir 176
Abdullah, Prince 20
Aden 184, 192, 197
aerial reconnaissance 43–4
Afghanistan 22
aircraft 43–6, 86, 106, 109, 216
alcohol 128, 134–5, 168
Aleppo 18, 57, 193, 216
Alexandria 58, 81, 84, 88, 129, 130, 138
Ali Muntar 34–5, 38, 118, 126
All Quiet on the Western Front 91
Allenby, Field Marshal Edmund 17–18, 20–1, 40, 42, 44, 50, 57, 61–71, 72–5, 77–9, 81, 83, 88, 98–9, 101–21, 123, 126, 132, 156, 164, 183, 191–5, 197–9, 201, 203, 210, 212–13, 219–20
Allied Supreme War Council 106, 193
Amman 18, 33, 57, 156, 174
Amritsar 184, 189
Anafarta Plain 125
Anzac Cove 157, 159
Anzac Day 158–9
Anzac legend 156–65, 180
Arab revolt 20, 102–3, 215
Ardant du Picq, Colonel Charles-Jean-Jacques-Joseph 8–9, 114, 120
Armenia 41, 90
Army and Religion Survey, The 76–7
Arras, battle of 108, 119–20, 146, 191
artillery 3, 6, 8, 18, 21, 25–6, 36, 39–41, 42, 44, 46, 59, 66, 74, 79, 86, 89, 91, 101, 106, 117, 119, 128, 133–4, 142, 151, 160–1, 164, 173, 176, 186, 194, 198, 203–4, 206–7, 211–12, 216
Ashmead-Bartlett, Ellis 157
Ashwell, Lena 130
Assouan 95
Auja River 31, 36, 50, 56, 126, 128, 132, 155

Australia 5, 20–1, 66, 74, 151–81, 215, 218
Australian and New Zealand Mounted Division Memorial 2, 4–5
Australian Imperial Force 52, 153, 157–8, 164, 174–5
Australian Military Formations,
  Corps,
    Australian Corps 153
  Divisions,
    Australian and New Zealand Mounted Division 32–4, 42, 49, 50, 56, 66, 86, 94, 97, 114, 118, 151–81, 216, 219
    Australian Mounted Division 66, 158
  Brigades,
    1st Australian Light Horse Brigade 45, 49, 153–4, 156, 161, 177
    2nd Australian Light Horse Brigade 153–4, 159, 163, 165–6, 169–70, 176, 178–9
    3rd Australian Light Horse Brigade 165, 178
    4th Australian Light Horse Brigade 155, 158
  Regiments,
    1st Australian Light Horse Regiment 34, 39, 45, 53–4, 57, 112, 116, 153–4, 163–4, 167, 169, 170, 174–5
    2nd Australian Light Horse Regiment 153, 166, 170
    3rd Australian Light Horse Regiment 29, 32–3, 53, 55, 57–9, 112, 153–4, 156, 159, 164–5, 168, 172
    4th Australian Light Horse Regiment 153
    5th Australian Light Horse Regiment 30, 33–5, 65, 83, 154,

159, 160–2, 164, 167, 169, 170, 172, 174–5, 178
6th Australian Light Horse Regiment 28–9, 79, 156–7, 169, 174–5
10th Australian Light Horse Regiment 154
14th Australian Light Horse Regiment 171
7th Australian Light Horse Victorian Mounted Rifles 171, 175
15th Australian Light Horse Victorian Mounted Rifles 171
Other Units,
Australian and New Zealand Mounted Division 1st Field Squadron 173
Australian and New Zealand Mounted Division 1st Signal Squadron 32, 86, 159, 166
1st Australian Light Horse Machine Gun Squadron 79, 175
2/14th Battalion Australian Imperial Force 52
Austria-Hungary 135
Ayun Kara 155

Baghdad 67, 193
Barrow, Major-General George 103–4, 111
Bartlett, Frederic 9
Bavaria 14, 27
Baynes, Gilbert 2
Bayonets 26, 35, 66, 143, 158, 179, 203
Bean, Charles 157, 160, 172–4
Bedfordshire Times and Independent 146
Beersheba 17, 25, 34, 36, 39, 50, 62, 66, 68, 104, 111, 115, 126, 145, 155, 158, 175, 180–1, 201, 215, 219
Beirut 58, 126
Belgium 130, 137, 139
Bengal 184, 190
Bethlehem 32, 58, 68, 73, 80, 90
Bir el Abd 34, 45, 154, 165
Bir Salem 103
Bird, Charles 9
Blackadder Goes Forth 121
Blomfield, Reginald 2
Bols, Major-General Louis 119, 178
Bombay 184
Bomber Command 9

Briscoe Moore, Arthur 26, 66, 160
British Expeditionary Force 13, 15, 18, 39–40, 52, 59, 77, 84, 108, 118–20, 184, 187–8, 191, 194, 197, 201, 217
British Military Formations,
Armies,
3rd Army 84, 108, 120, 194
4th Army 120
8th Army 27, 52, 64, 112–13, 121
14th Army 1, 213
Corps,
VIII Corps 52
XX Corps 17, 31, 87, 106, 119, 193, 198–9, 201, 204, 207–8, 210–11
XXI Corps 17, 26, 40, 115, 119, 132, 161, 210
Desert Mounted Corps 17–18, 57–8, 106, 114–15, 119, 152, 155, 173, 179–80, 210–11
Divisions,
Guards Division 180
3rd Division 107
4th Cavalry Division 62, 90, 103
5th Cavalry Division 58
10th (Irish) Division 3, 21–2, 81, 192, 198, 200–13
11th Division 200
13th Division 193
16th (Irish) Division 200
27th Division 200
29th Division 126
36th (Ulster) Division 200
42nd (East Lancashire) Division 128
51st (Highland) Division 52, 148
52nd (Lowland) Division 21, 26, 194, 201
53rd (Welsh) Division 21, 50, 79, 84, 118, 126, 192, 210
54th (East Anglia) Division 28, 31, 33, 36–7, 39, 40, 42–3, 45–51, 53, 59, 78–9, 82, 86–7, 93–6, 106, 111, 115, 123–49, 160, 183, 194, 210, 216
55th (West Lancashire) Division 13, 148
60th (London) Division 25, 65, 79, 84, 89, 91, 192
74th Division 86, 192, 194
75th Division 191, 193
Imperial Mounted Division 53

Index

Brigades,
  5th Mounted Brigade 164
  6th Brigade 107
  6th Mounted Brigade 158
  22nd Mounted Brigade 161
  29th Brigade 200, 202, 207–8, 210, 212
  30th Brigade 200, 202, 204, 211
  31st Brigade 200, 203, 206, 210
  82nd Brigade 200
  86th Brigade 126
  161st Brigade 32, 34, 38, 47, 49, 50, 65, 118, 124–6, 136, 140
  162nd Brigade 47–9, 53–4, 57, 85, 87, 112, 124, 126, 132, 139
  163rd Brigade 36, 40, 43, 47–9, 51, 53, 125–6, 132, 216
Infantry Battalions,
  1/5th Bedfordshire Regiment 36, 39, 48, 55, 65, 83, 125, 128, 134, 136, 146–7, 200
  7th Black Watch 52
  5th Connaught Rangers 201–2
  2/4th Dorset Regiment 192
  1/4th Essex Regiment 29, 39, 41, 47, 51, 58, 124, 133, 139–40
  1/5th Essex Regiment 29, 31, 37, 39, 47, 51, 65–6, 92, 124, 132–3, 135, 139, 143
  1/6th Essex Regiment 28, 30, 32, 44, 47, 51, 89, 115, 124, 126, 132, 139–40
  1/7th Essex Regiment 29, 35, 37, 47, 51, 79, 124, 128, 136
  1/8th Hampshire Regiment 36, 43, 48, 51, 79, 125, 135, 145–6
  11th Hampshire Regiment 52
  1/4th King's Own Scottish Borderers 39
  10th King's Shropshire Light Infantry 85
  1st Leinster Regiment 200–2, 207–8
  1/10th London Regiment 34, 48, 51–2, 55, 58, 82, 85, 125, 132, 137, 142
  1/11th London Regiment 36–7, 41, 48, 51, 125, 132, 134
  2/15th London Regiment 93
  2/19th London Regiment 192
  2/10th Middlesex Regiment 192
  1/4th Norfolk Regiment 36, 38, 43, 48–9, 51, 70, 96, 125–6, 133, 136–7, 144–5
  1/5th Norfolk Regiment 35, 39, 43–4, 48, 51, 80, 96, 125–6, 130, 132, 136–7, 139, 144–5
  1/4th Northamptonshire Regiment 28, 32, 36, 38, 48, 51, 70, 86, 125, 128–9, 133–4, 139
  6th Royal Dublin Fusiliers 200
  7th Royal Dublin Fusiliers 202
  22nd Royal Fusiliers 15
  5th Royal Inniskilling Fusiliers 3
  2nd Royal Irish Fusiliers 200–2, 206, 211
  5th Royal Irish Fusiliers 201
  1st Royal Irish Regiment 200–2, 204
  6th Royal Irish Rifles 200, 202
  1/4th Royal Sussex Regiment 83
  24th Royal Welch Fusiliers 78, 83, 85–6
  2/4th Royal West Surrey Regiment 35
  1/5th Somerset Light Infantry 85, 91
  1/4th Suffolk Regiment 125
  1/5th Suffolk Regiment 28, 41, 43, 48, 51, 53, 66, 86, 92, 115, 125, 128–9, 138, 144
  1/4th Wiltshire Regiment 192
Yeomanry Regiments,
  1/1st Middlesex Yeomanry 85–6
  1/1st Warwickshire Yeomanry 25, 158
  1/1st Worcester Yeomanry 25, 91, 158
Other Units,
  1/2nd East Anglian Field Ambulance 31, 86, 128, 145
  163rd Machine Gun Company 34
  53rd Brigade Royal Field Artillery 94
  270th Brigade Royal Field Artillery 37, 133
  271st Brigade Royal Field Artillery 37, 65
  18th Brigade Royal Horse Artillery 164
  10th Divisional Signal Company 203
British West Indies Regiment 158
Brooke, Rupert 83, 103
Buchan, Colonel John 72
Bulfin, Lieutenant-General Edward 17, 26, 119, 132, 210
Bulgaria 18–19, 113, 196

Burnett-Stuart, Major-General Jock 107
Butler, Lady Elizabeth 25, 59

Cairo 58, 83, 88, 92, 95–7, 101, 103, 115, 117–18, 125, 129, 130, 142, 163, 166–8, 176, 205, 218
Callwell, Major-General Charles 107
Cambrai, battle of 146, 193
Cape Helles 126
Caporetto, battle of 113, 191
Cardwell, Edward 124, 148, 217
casualties 46–53
Cemal Pasha 16
censorship 26, 188–9
Chauvel, Lieutenant-General Henry 58, 114, 119–20, 154–5, 157–8, 165, 168, 177, 179, 180, 219
Chaytor, Major-General Edward 114, 155–6, 160, 166, 177–80, 219
Chaytor's Force 156, 177
Chetwode, Lieutenant-General Philip 17, 31, 49, 53, 74, 87, 102, 104, 106, 111, 114, 117–20, 147, 161, 193–4, 201, 208, 210–12, 219
Childers, Hugh 124, 148
China 184
Christianity 72, 75–92
Christmas cards 93–6, 127, 134, 136–7, 140–1, 161–2, 170
Chunuk Bair 154, 179
Church of the Holy Sepulchre 64, 67, 70–1, 73, 81, 83, 89–90
Church of the Nativity 90
Churchill, Winston 18–19
cigarettes 104, 134, 138, 199
Clausewitz, Carl von 220
climate 27–33
Combat Studies Institute, Fort Leavenworth 209
comfort funds 166, 199
commemoration 2, 140, 158, 171, 173
Committee of Imperial Defence 187
concert parties 13, 85, 88, 130–2, 135, 138, 217
conscripts 11, 14–15, 27, 37, 124, 136, 138, 141, 148, 153, 165, 168, 190, 201, 217
Cox, Brigadier-General Charles 59
Cox, Lieutenant-General H. V. 197

Creasy, Edward 7
Crimean War 8, 25, 139, 163
crusades 61–99
Curzon, Lord 74–5, 99

Damascus 18, 57–8, 103
Davidson, Archbishop Randall 81
Dawnay, Brigadier-General Guy 102, 117, 119, 219
Dead Sea 33, 70
Delhi 190
Derby volunteers 138
Desert Column 117–19, 219
desertion 75, 104, 109, 112–13, 197–9
disease 53–9
Dobell, Major-General Charles 49, 117–18, 177
Duff Cooper, Alfred 64
Dyer, Brigadier-General Reginald 184

East Africa 55, 84, 104, 183, 189, 192
East India Company 184
Eastern Force 40, 49, 74, 117–19, 147, 177, 178
Eastern Front 10, 52, 172, 194
Edward VII, King 124
Egyptian Labour Corps 56, 92
El Alamein, battle of 27, 52, 121, 149
El Arish 37, 79, 126, 144, 155, 163
El Burj – Ghurabeh Ridge 206–8, 210, 212
Esprit de corps, 14–15, 21, 136, 138, 148–9, 169, 217
Evening Standard, The 72

Falkenhayn, General Erich von 121
Falls, Cyril 15, 25–6, 62–3, 105–6, 110–11, 114
Feisal, Prince 20, 74
Flanders 19, 21–2, 26, 38–9, 59, 101, 119, 151, 166, 188, 194
flies 30–1
food parcels 14, 134–5, 144, 166
Foreign Office 72–4
Forester, C. S. 116
France 1, 13, 19, 20–2, 26, 38–9, 59, 65, 73–4, 98, 101–2, 106, 118–19, 123, 125, 137, 139, 148, 151, 166, 178, 187–9, 191–4, 199

French Army 8–9, 12–13, 27, 73, 113, 135
Fuller, J. F. C. 108, 151

Gallipoli 16, 18, 30, 33, 53, 66, 83–4, 94, 123, 125–6, 128, 133, 136, 139, 142, 146, 153–7, 159–61, 164, 170, 172, 200, 215–16, 218
Gallipoli (Peter Weir, 1981) 154
Garsia, Lieutenant-Colonel Clive 40, 106, 115–18, 143, 146
gas 41–2, 176, 216
Gaza, First battle of 17, 31, 34–5, 37, 48–50, 53, 70, 110–12, 115–19, 123, 126, 135–7, 139–40, 151, 155, 160, 181, 216–20
Gaza, Second battle of 17, 31, 35, 38–43, 48–9, 51–3, 59, 70, 103, 110–13, 115–17, 119, 123, 126–7, 135–7, 139–40, 143, 145, 151, 155, 177, 216–20
Gaza, Third battle of 17, 26, 31, 34–8, 40–4, 48–52, 82, 91, 101, 104–5, 110–11, 115–16, 120, 126, 135, 140, 142–3, 145, 149, 155, 180, 201, 216–17, 219
George V, King 21, 211
German 1918 Spring Offensives 18, 22, 123, 194, 196
German Air Service 44–5
Gibbon, Edward 67
Gilbert, Web 4–5
Grandmaison, Colonel de 9
Graves, Robert 20
Gray, J. Glenn 1, 5
Green Hill, Gaza 126, 140
Greer, Brigadier-General F. A. 211
Gullett, Henry 156–7, 161, 164, 173
Gurkhas 185, 190

Haifa 18
Haig, Field Marshal Douglas 18, 104, 115, 120–1, 185
Haldane, Richard 124
Halifax, Nova Scotia 70
Hall of Remembrance 2
hand-to-hand combat 35
Hare, Major-General Steuart 31, 40, 45, 49, 51, 78, 82, 87, 89, 106, 112, 115–16, 125–6, 130–3, 137, 140–9

Hejaz 19
Henty, George 66
Hindus 198
Holy Land 2, 61–99
horses 3, 26, 29, 34, 45, 114, 116, 153, 168–9, 172–3, 176
hospital admissions 53–9
Howard-Vyse, Brigadier-General Richard 180, 219
Hughes, William 4
Huj 25–6, 158
Hussein, Sherif of Mecca 20

imperial campaigns 15, 22, 59, 119, 149, 181
Imperial School of Instruction, Zeitoun 142, 178, 205, 218–19
Imperial War Graves Commission 2
Imperial War Museum 2, 63, 65
India 16, 18, 20, 22, 32, 56, 72–5, 79, 88, 89, 108, 120, 124–6, 149, 156, 173, 183–213, 215, 217, 219
Indian Army,
  Corps,
    Indian Corps 187–8
    Indian Cavalry Corps 192
  Divisions,
    3rd (Lahore) Division 94, 186–8, 194
    6th (Poona) Division 183
    7th (Meerut) Division 186–8, 191, 194
  Infantry Battalions,
    1st Kashmir Infantry 202, 204, 206
    2/3rd Gurkhas 192
    5th Light Infantry 199
    38th Dogras 192, 195, 197
    2/42nd Deolis 211
    46th Punjabis 204
    47th Sikhs 187
    51st Sikhs 195
    53rd Sikhs 195
    1/54th Sikhs 192, 197, 202, 205–8
    56th Punjabi Rifles 195
    58th Rifles 192
    74th Punjabis 202, 211–12
    101st Grenadiers 195
    1/101st Grenadiers 196–9, 202, 204–5, 207–9, 219
    2/101st Grenadiers 204, 210, 212
    2/151st Indian Infantry 195, 202
    3/151st Indian Infantry 195

Cavalry Regiments,
  6th Cavalry 196
  15th Cavalry 199
  2nd Lancers 196
  19th Lancers 199
  29th Lancers 196
  44th Indian Cavalry Regiment 195–6
Other Units,
  39th (Reserve) Mountain Battery 79, 95
  72nd Sappers and Miners 207
Indian Expeditionary Force 'D' 183
Indian Mutiny 184–5
Indian recruitment 189–90
Indianization 22, 49, 81, 183–213
influenza 58, 60, 216
Inglefield, Major-General F. S. 124–5
Iraq 20, 22
Islam 21, 72–4, 82, 92–4, 98, 197, 199, 209
Ismailia 198
Isurava, battle of 52
Italian Army 73, 113, 191
Italy 1, 20, 73–4, 113
Izzat 209

Jaffa 17, 31, 36, 67, 70, 73, 80, 86, 115, 126, 220
Janowitz, Morris 5, 10–11
Japan 80, 195
Jericho 155
Jerusalem 2, 17, 25, 33, 36, 58–9, 61–75, 80–4, 87–91, 93–4, 96–9, 101, 103, 120, 126, 129, 161, 168, 176–7, 191, 199, 201, 207, 210, 212–13, 220
Jerusalem (Mount Scopus) Cemetery 2, 64
Jewish Legion 156, 195
Jordan Valley 18, 28, 33, 56, 151, 155–6, 161, 167, 211
Judaean Hills 3, 17, 25–6, 28, 32–3, 36, 46, 50, 77, 126, 192, 201, 204, 206, 210–11
junior officers 10, 125, 145, 177–8, 181, 189, 218

Kantara 112, 167, 198, 202
Karnak 92
Katia Oasis 37, 154–5, 163–5
Kaukab 158
Keegan, John 7, 20

Kennington, Eric 61
Khamsin 29–30
Khan Yunis 101, 117
Kiretch Tepe Sirt 200
Kitchener, General Lord 13, 140, 184–7, 200
Kokoda 52
Koran 198–9
Korean War 11
Kosturino 200
Kressenstein, Colonel Franz von Kress von 64, 115
Kut-al-Amara 183

Lake Dojran 200
Lake Tiberias 18
Lamb, Henry 3
Latron 197
Lawrence of Arabia (David Lean, 1962) 20, 103, 110, 216
Lawrence, T. E. 3, 19–20, 61–2, 98–9, 102–5, 109–11, 114, 215
leadership 5, 8–10, 15, 101–21, 144, 175–81, 209–10, 218
leave 70, 88, 96–7, 113, 129–30, 135, 163, 167–8, 179, 187, 198–9
Leete, Alfred 99
Lemnos 154
letter writing 13–14, 21, 38, 77–8, 80, 83, 95, 165–6, 188–9
Liddell Hart, Basil 19–20, 107–11, 116, 151
Liverpool 13
Lloyd George, David 18–19, 66–9, 73, 99, 105, 191, 193
local identity 13, 70, 124, 128–9, 136–9, 148, 161–2
Locke Elliot, Lieutenant-General E. 197
Longley, Major-General John 200–1, 212
Loos 187
Ludd 82–3, 130, 197
Ludendorff, General Erich 120–1
Luxor 92, 95, 130
Lynden-Bell, Major-General A. L. 119

Macedonia 3, 19, 196, 200–1, 212
MacInnes, Bishop Rennie 81–2
Mackennal, Bertram 4–5
MacMunn, Lieutenant-General George 15, 31, 62, 188, 190

Madras 184
Mafeking 200
Magdhaba, battle of 17, 37, 49, 118, 155, 163, 181
Mahon, Major-General Bryan 200
Malaria 18, 52, 55–8, 60, 156, 200–1, 216
Maori 152
Marshall, Lieutenant-General William 193–4
Marshall, S. L. A. 5, 9–13, 15, 136, 172, 219
Martial Race Theory 185–6, 188–90
Masefield, John 83
Massey, William Ferguson 160
Massey, William Thomas 46, 67, 101–2, 110, 114
Masterman, Ernest 71
Maude, Lieutenant-General Stanley 211
Maxse, Lieutenant-General Ivor 78
Mazar 155
Mecca 74, 199
Medina 74
Megiddo, battle of 18, 22, 32, 35, 42, 44, 48, 50, 53, 56–7, 62, 90, 101–2, 106–7, 109–10, 115, 120–1, 124, 126–7, 135, 143, 149, 151, 179–80, 183–4, 208, 210–13, 215–16, 219
Meinertzhagen, Lieutenant-Colonel Richard 104–5, 111
Mejdel Yaba 33, 141
Meldrum, Brigadier-General William 166, 179–80
Mena Camp 125
Mesopotamia 55, 84, 151, 183, 188–9, 191, 193, 195, 199, 211, 215
Military Traditions 12, 14–15, 21, 138–9, 146, 148, 170–1, 198, 213, 217–18
Minden Day 138
Moascar 163, 176
Monro, General Charles 191–3, 195–6
Montgomery, Field Marshal Bernard 111, 114, 142
Moran, Lord 9
Morris, Brigadier-General E. M. 208, 211–12
Mosque of Omar 73–4, 92–3
Mosul 193
Mountains of Moab 18, 33, 155
mud 22, 25, 32

Mudge, Brigadier-General A. 85, 87, 139
Mudros 94, 125
Mulebbis 134, 155
Murray, General Archibald 16–17, 40–2, 66, 74, 78, 101–6, 110–12, 116–21, 123, 126, 164, 220
Musallabeh 156, 161

Nablus 199, 207, 210–11
Nash, Paul 2
National Service League 124
Nazareth 18, 80
Nepal 185
Neuve Chapelle 187
New Army 14, 187–8, 200
New Guinea 52
New South Wales 153, 161
New Zealand 2, 5, 20, 22, 74, 80, 151–81
New Zealand Expeditionary Force 153, 164, 167, 175
New Zealand Military Formations,
  Divisions,
    Australian and New Zealand Mounted Division see Australian Divisions
    New Zealand Division 153, 178
  Brigades,
    New Zealand Mounted Rifles Brigade 26, 35, 45, 49, 66, 153–6, 158, 160–1, 163–8, 170–1, 173, 176, 179–80, 216, 218
  Regiments,
    Auckland Mounted Rifles 33, 35, 50, 65, 78, 93, 153, 159, 164, 167, 171
    Canterbury Mounted Rifles 41–2, 50, 80, 82, 115, 153–4, 161, 171–2, 176–8
    Wellington Mounted Rifles 37, 50, 153–4, 165, 168, 171, 176, 179
    Otago Mounted Rifles 153
    1st Canterbury Yeomanry 171
    8th South Canterbury Yeomanry 171
    10th Nelson Mounted Rifles Regiment 171
  Other Units,
    New Zealand Mounted Field Ambulance 42
    New Zealand Mounted Rifles Machine Gun Squadron 32, 80, 173

Nicholson Committee 186
Nile 61, 92, 97, 129, 154
North Africa 43, 52, 112, 114, 121
Northampton Independent, The 70–1, 139
North-West Frontier 32, 125, 184–6, 188, 192, 197, 199, 204, 212

official history 15, 19–20, 26, 31, 46, 62, 105–6, 115, 118, 172, 174
Oghratina 154, 164
Oh! What a Lovely War 121
O'Moore Creagh, General Garrett 186
Operation Crusader 113
Orientalism 21, 92–3, 98
Ottoman Army/Empire 2, 7, 16–22, 41, 58, 61, 63, 74, 77, 82, 99, 102–3, 124–5, 139–40, 149, 183, 190, 193, 197, 207, 210–11, 213, 215–16, 220

Pacific 9–10, 20, 27, 52
Palestine Exploration Fund 71, 97
Partridge, Bernard 67–70, 99
Pathans 197, 199
Persia 8, 193
Picot, François George 19, 73
Plain of Sharon 18, 46, 135, 141, 156, 210–11
Poilus 13
Port Said 4, 97, 167–8
Primary Group Theory 10–13, 22, 52–3, 60, 128, 136, 148, 172–5, 181, 218
Prussia 14, 106
Punch 67–9, 99
Punjab 189–90, 213

Queensland 153, 161, 170

Rafah, battle of 17, 35, 37, 49, 118, 155, 161, 169, 177, 179, 181
rain 31–3, 35, 126, 130
Richard I, King 63–7, 71, 83, 91
Richon le Zion 156
Roberts, Lord 124, 185
Robertson, General William 18, 69, 73, 106, 113, 191–2, 213
Roman Army 8
Roman Catholic Soldiers' Congress 80–1
Romani, battle of 17, 33–5, 49, 118, 125–6, 154, 161–2, 164–5, 217

Ross (Terence Rattigan, 1960) 20, 110
Royal Air Force 44–6
Royal Army Chaplaincy Department 84
Royal Flying Corps 43–5, 146
Royal Military Academy Sandhurst 107
Royal Naval Air Service 43
Royal Navy 40, 102, 106
Royston, Brigadier-General John 162
Russell, Andrew 178
Russell, William 139
Russia 16, 19, 22, 52, 74, 94, 113, 184, 191
Russian Civil War 158
Ryrie, Brigadier-General Granville 163, 166, 179–80

Said, Edward 98
Salmond, Major-General Geoffrey 44
Salonica 55, 65, 70, 196, 200–1
sand 28–31, 43, 129, 166, 169
Sandilands, Brigadier-General H. G. 40
sandstorms 28–30
Sarona 168
Savage, Raymond 104, 108–9, 112
Senussi 125, 154
Serbia 56, 200
Seven Pillars of Wisdom 20, 102–3
Shea, Major-General John 25, 84
shell shock 41
Shils, Edward 5, 10–11
Siborne, Captain William 8
sickness rates 53–9, 112–13, 125, 154, 200
Sidi Bishr Camp 30
Sikhs 184–5, 190, 198–9
Singapore 113, 199
Singer Sargent, John 2
Six Day War 180
Slim, Field Marshal William 1, 111
Smith, George Adam 66, 77, 97
Smith, Major-General S. C. U. 40
Smuts, Jan 193–4
Somme, battle of 12, 40, 52, 191, 216
South Africa 66, 149, 179, 193
South African War (1899–1902) 55, 124–5, 152, 160, 170, 178
South Australia 153, 161
South Pacific 27
Soviet-Polish War 158
sport 13, 85, 88, 132–3, 138, 159, 168–9, 217
Storrs, Colonel Ronald 64, 73, 103, 111

Stouffer, Samuel 5–6, 10–12
Struma Valley 200
Sudan 84
Suez Canal 4, 16–17, 28, 30, 44, 47, 53, 112, 118, 124–5, 128, 132–3, 144, 149, 154, 161, 217
sunstroke 28–9
Suvla Bay 125, 139, 200
Sydney 161, 173
Sykes, Mark 19, 73–4, 99

tanks 21, 28, 42–3, 46, 101, 107, 151, 216
Tasmania 153, 161
Tel el Kebir Camp 197, 205
Tel el Khuweilefe 155, 175
Tel el Saba 34, 155, 158, 178
Territorial Force 13–15, 21–2, 37, 65, 84, 123–49, 151, 164, 167, 180, 188, 217–18
Theban Sacred Band 8
Thomas, Lowell 20
Times, The 64, 67, 70
total war 23, 196, 217, 220
tourism 88, 92–9, 167
Townshend, Major-General Charles 183
training 6, 9–12, 15, 17–18, 22, 27–8, 33, 35, 37, 45, 47, 53, 58, 86, 101–2, 107–8, 118, 124–5, 132, 135, 137, 142–4, 146, 152–4, 163, 175–9, 181, 183–4, 186, 197–8, 200, 202–9, 213, 218–20
Transjordan Raids 33, 35, 49, 53, 102, 104, 110, 181, 218, 220
trench press 12–13
trench raids 145–8, 207–10, 212, 218
trenches 12–14, 17, 25, 27, 30, 32, 35–41, 43, 49, 55, 77, 101–2, 107, 113, 116, 123, 126, 128, 135, 143, 145–6, 153, 155, 167, 177, 202, 208, 210
Trumper, Victor 97–8

United Provinces 189–90
US Army 9–12, 22, 209
USA 6, 9–10, 20, 22, 69, 77

Vandeleur, Brigadier-General R. S. 212
venereal disease 58–9, 78

Versailles Conference 19
veterans 1, 8, 11, 33, 35, 53, 59, 64, 111, 120, 136, 160, 172, 174–6, 218
Victoria 153, 171
Victoria Cross 20, 36, 51
Vietnam War 11–12
volunteers 15, 37, 124, 136, 138, 141, 148, 152–3, 165, 168, 190, 200, 217

Wadi Fara 46
War Cabinet 41, 68, 73–4, 103, 105, 110, 191, 193
War Office 66, 74, 84, 104–5, 137, 192–6, 199, 213
War Office Cinematograph Committee 69
Ward, Brigadier-General T. 43
water 17, 28, 31–4, 38, 46, 61, 108, 133–4, 142, 155, 172–3, 202, 211
Waterloo, battle of 7–8
Wavell, Field Marshal Archibald 19, 106–11, 114
Wazza 97, 163
Wehrmacht 10, 52, 118, 172
Wemyss, Admiral Rosslyn 102
Western Front 1, 5, 9, 15, 18–19, 21–2, 25–7, 32, 34, 38–40, 42–3, 45–6, 50, 52, 59, 61, 69, 78, 84–5, 87, 99, 101, 103, 106, 108–9, 115–16, 119–21, 123, 126–8, 130, 135, 139, 145, 148, 151, 153, 176, 180, 183, 187–8, 191, 193–4, 196, 199–201, 204, 208, 210, 213, 215–20
Wildlife 30–1, 78, 103, 133
Wilhelm II, Kaiser 67
Wilhelma 36, 86, 130, 139
Wilson, General Henry 18, 191, 195, 198
Wingate, Reginald 73–4, 81–2
Winnington-Ingram, Bishop Arthur 82, 98
Wood, Field Marshal Evelyn 138

Xenophon 8

Young Men's Christian Association 87–8, 97
Young Turks 16, 19
Ypres, First battle of 187
Ypres, Third battle of 191, 216

Printed in Great Britain
by Amazon